Eurocentric
Polis   shows the fallacies
Aristotles concept of the polis

This study explores how modern scholars came to write Greek history
from a Eurocentric perspective and challenges orthodox readings of
Greek history as part of the history of the West. Since the Greeks
lacked a national state or a unified society, economy or culture, the
polis has helped to create a homogenising national narrative. This
book re-examines old polarities such as those between the Greek
poleis and Eastern monarchies, or between the ancient consumer
and the modern producer city, in order to show the fallacies of
standard approaches. It argues for the relevance of Aristotle's concept
of the polis, which is interpreted in a novel way. Finally, it proposes
an alternative way of looking at Greek history as part of a
Mediterranean world-system. This interdisciplinary study engages
with modern debates on globalisation, nationalism, Orientalism
and history writing, while also debating recent developments in
classical studies.

KOSTAS VLASSOPOULOS is Lecturer in Greek History at the
University of Nottingham.

Mediterrenean — world system
modern debates of , globalisation
                         , nationalism,
                         , Orientalism
                         , debatin recent
                         , development in
                           classical studies

UNTHINKING THE GREEK POLIS

Ancient Greek History beyond Eurocentrism

KOSTAS VLASSOPOULOS

Department of Classics
University of Nottingham

CAMBRIDGE
UNIVERSITY PRESS

CAMBRIDGE UNIVERSITY PRESS
Cambridge, New York, Melbourne, Madrid, Cape Town,
Singapore, São Paulo, Delhi, Tokyo, Mexico City

Cambridge University Press
The Edinburgh Building, Cambridge CB2 8RU, UK

Published in the United States of America by Cambridge University Press, New York

www.cambridge.org
Information on this title: www.cambridge.org/9780521188074

First published 2007   2007
First paperback edition 2011

A catalogue record for this publication is available from the British Library

ISBN 978-0-521-87744-2 Hardback
ISBN 978-0-521-18807-4 Paperback

To the liberty of oppressed peoples Yes

Contents

Contents

Acknowledgements

Writing acknowledgements is of course a pleasure; it is a pleasure to thank people; it is also a pleasure to talk to people through thanking them. But it is also painful; for it requires reconstructing the history of your thought and life within a number of years; and nobody knows better than the historian how difficult and elusive this is. Yet, I will attempt it.

This book comes out of a thesis with the same title; the research for it was undertaken in the Faculty of Classics, University of Cambridge, between 2001 and 2005. I would like to thank my supervisor, Robin Osborne, for his help and his constant availability, before and after the completion of the thesis. His insistence on providing evidence has been a necessary corrective to a thesis that bended overtly towards the theoretical; my work on Aristotle is the result of his encouragement. Paul Cartledge acted as my supervisor for a term, but has always been willing to read and comment. Discussing and, indeed, even disagreeing with Paul has been one of the most stimulating experiences I have had. Dimitris Kyrtatas has been a teacher and a friend for many years; he has been a constant source of support and guidance; and he has been a chief stimulus to my historiographical interests. Anna Missiou has acted as supervisor for the Greek State Scholarship Foundation; my views on Orientalism go back to a seminar she ran many years ago in Crete.

Nicholas Purcell and Paul Millett were the examiners of the thesis, and I would like to express my deep gratitude for their suggestions, comments and tolerance. I hope that the present outcome will fulfil some of their expectations. Oswyn Murray has provided invaluable help with historiographical and more general suggestions, and I have enjoyed our conversations immensely. Marc van de Mieroop has kindly read the whole manuscript, has made very interesting suggestions, and has saved me from a number of embarrassing mistakes. Finally, I would like to thank the anonymous readers of Cambridge University Press for their suggestions and comments. Unfortunately, I have not been able to take into account all the various possibilities of exploration that the people above have suggested. Hopefully, there will be time and space in the future.

Turning the thesis into a book took place while holding a temporary lectureship in Greek history in the Department of Classics, University of Nottingham. Nottingham has provided an excellent environment to pursue this work, and I would like to thank my colleagues for their help and support; a special thanks goes to Steve Hodkinson and Alan Sommerstein for their trust and encouragement at a very difficult point of my life and career.

It is perhaps indicative of the nature of this work that many of my key interlocutors over all these years have been people who are either outsiders to History or Classics, or have started as such. Chiara Ghidini, who works on modern Japanese literature, has been the most Herodotean person I have ever met in my life; she has opened for me horizons I never imagined existed. Giorgos Kyriakou, who is a Chemist, has proved, time and again, that the most stimulating interlocutors are those that do not share the presuppositions of your discipline. We have consumed gallons of wine and whisky, while talking about music, politics and history (and women, of course). Aleka Lianeri has been an invaluable friend and adviser; and she has kept boosting my morale by losing all these bets. Finally, Maro Triantafyllou, the novelist, student of philosophy and historian, has remained a close friend and interlocutor from the days of Crete till now; I owe her much more than she thinks, and I deeply regret I see her so infrequently. All four of them have been sincere and affectionate friends over the years; without them, this work would have been very different.

This work has a political inspiration, in the broad sense of the word, as one can surmise already from its title. But while living in the academic ivory tower, it is often easy to forget the real meaning of words used often in this work, words which have a deadly impact: war, imperialism, nationalism, globalisation, exploitation, domination. In this respect the events of the recent war have kept reminding me of the real meaning of words and things. For myself, I can do no more in the present capacity than making an appropriate dedication to a long-standing cause.

I would like to thank the Cambridge European Trust, the Board of Graduate Studies and King's College for funding my research during the first year; the Greek State Scholarship Foundation for funding the last three; and the Faculty of Classics and King's College for funding fieldwork and travelling expenses. I would also like to thank the Faculty of Classics, Cambridge, for awarding me the Hare Prize for the best dissertation for 2005.

Lastly, I would like to thank the friends and family who have been a constant source of support and joy over all these years. My parents, Makis and Katerina; my brother, Nikos; Vassilis and Spyridoula, who have long been my hosts in Athens; Kyriaki, who has been a wonderful housemate and trusted friend in Nottingham; Sofia; Michalis; Olga; Evi; Alkis; Ailiana; Aptin; Manpreet; Nandini; Ioanna; Kelli; Anastasia; Haris, Artemis; Elton; Eytyxia.

The last word goes to Olga. Not only due to her love, care and tenderness, but especially for managing to convince me that, once I would finish this book, I would be able to lie uf dä fuulä huut.

Abbreviations

AE	*Archaiologikê Ephêmeris*
AHR	*American Historical Review*
AJA	*American Journal of Archaeology*
AJPh	*American Journal of Philology*
AmAnt	*American Antiquity*
ASNP	*Annali della Scuola Normale Superiore di Pisa*
BCH	*Bulletin de Correspondance Hellénique*
BSA	*Annual of the British School at Athens*
CA	*Cultural Anthropology*
CH	*Cahiers d'histoire*
CPh	*Classical Philology*
CQ	*Classical Quarterly*
CSSH	*Comparative Studies in Society and History*
EMC	*Echos du Monde Classique/Classical Views*
G&R	*Greece and Rome*
GRBS	*Greek, Roman and Byzantine Studies*
H&T	*History and Theory*
JESHO	*Journal of the Economic and Social History of the Orient*
JFA	*Journal of Field Archaeology*
JHI	*Journal of the History of Ideas*
JMA	*Journal of Mediterranean Archaeology*
JS	*Journal des Savants*
Magna Grecia	*Magna Grecia e Oriente mediterraneo prima dell'età ellenistica: atti del trentanovesimo convegno di studi sulla Magna Grecia.* Taranto, 2000.
MAS	*Modern Asian Studies*
OJA	*Oxford Journal of Archaeology*
PCPhS	*Proceedings of the Cambridge Philological Society*
P&P	*Past and Present*
Problemi	*Problemi della chora coloniale dall'Occidente al Mar Nero: atti del quarantesimo convegno di studi sulla Magna Grecia.* Taranto, 2001.

Abbreviations

REA	*Revue des Etudes Anciennes*
REG	*Revue des Etudes Grecques*
Review	*Review, a Journal of the Fernand Braudel Center*
SS	*Studi Storici*
TAPhA	*Transactions of the American Philological Association*
WA	*World Archaeology*
ZPE	*Zeitschrift für Papyrologie und Epigraphik*

Exasperating contradictions

Occidentalism

Introduction

This work is a study of history, and 'all of history is contemporary history'.[1] Which, then, are the contemporary issues that influence the perception and articulation of this study? Our era is characterised by the exasperating contradictions of the ideology that one could call 'Occidentalism'. Occidentalism is the ideology that there exist clearly bounded entities in world history, such as the West, the Orient and the primitives, and that these metaphysical entities have a genealogy (or rather only the Occident has a true genealogy);[2] that there is a pattern in human history, which leads to the evolution of the modern West, which is the natural path of history, while the history of the Rest of the world is a story of aberrations that have to be explained; that the whole world is actually following the lead of the West and one day it will manage to assimilate; that the conceptual tools and the disciplines created by the West are in some way the natural way to organise experience and analyse reality, and that the reality of the past, and the present outside the West, ought to be explicable in these Western terms.[3]

These are not simply academic arguments; they have a real, deadly impact in the world around us. German Christian democrats and French conservatives oppose the entry of Turkey into the EU, because Europe is a Christian culture;[4] the French Front National argues for the expulsion of African immigrants, because they partake of an alien culture;[5] non-Western countries are invaded to impose liberty and democracy, because they are presumed to be unable to achieve them by their own means;[6] anger and despair among the oppressed of the Middle East are denigrated as religious fanaticism, in contrast to Western liberal secularism.[7]

[1] Croce 1921: 11–26.   [2] For this metageography, see Lewis and Wigen 1997.
[3] For these issues, see Chakrabarty 2000: 3–23.
[4] See e.g. *Guardian*, 27 November 2002; also 17 September 2002.   [5] *Guardian*, 25 April 2002.
[6] Ali 2002.   [7] See a characteristic example: Huntington 1998.

I

At the same time, the bastions of Occidentalism, evolutionism and the idea of progress seem less and less plausible.[8] Colonialism, once thought of as part of a left-behind past, is again on the agenda. The growing progress of secularism is a mirage; it is not only in the Orient that 'religious fanatics' gain control; for the first time since more than a century ago, leaders of Western powers argue that they owe an account of their actions only in front of the Supreme Being.[9] In an age of globalisation and borders surpassed, nationalism is a more potent force than ever. The growing advancement of civil rights is reversed; habeas corpus is a dead letter even in the country of its inception.[10] The triumph of the modern rational state is reversed; in whole regions of the globe state power has collapsed and 'feudal' groups and interests fight each other and run countries;[11] areas that were safely visited a hundred years ago are as impenetrable now as they were three centuries ago.[12]

Few I hope would dispute that Greek history has played an important part in fostering Occidentalist/Eurocentric agendas in the past;[13] it is equally true that it continues to do so in the present.[14] But this book will not focus on the ways that Greek history has been used to support these agendas in the larger political, cultural and social environment. My subject is to study this process the other way round. The central argument of this work is that the modern study of Greek history has been fundamentally shaped by the perspectives of Occidentalism/Eurocentrism. We can easily point to a number of key aspects. To start with, Greek history is always treated as part of Western or European history.[15] It is not treated as part of the continuous history of an area of the Mediterranean through the ages; it becomes part of a chain of historical evolution that starts in the Near East, moves to Greece, passes to Rome, before moving on to the Middle Ages and the modern Western world. Greece, as part of the Mediterranean, is nothing more than a temporary setting for this chain of evolution. Ancient Greek history is not written from the perspective of the continuous history of this geographical area; rather, the history of this area becomes irrelevant, once the torch has passed to the next bearer of Western civilisation.

As a consequence, the history of the ancient Greeks has been separated from the history of the wider Mediterranean and the Near East; it has

---

[8] See Albrow 1996.   [9] *Guardian*, 4 May 2003.   [10] *Guardian*, 26 November 2001.
[11] See Mbembe 2001 on Africa.   [12] Hobsbawm 1997.
[13] Turner 1981; Bernal 1987; Canfora 1989.
[14] Hanson and Heath 1998; Berlinerbau 1999; Hanson 2004.
[15] See the two different, but equally characteristic, Occidentalist perspectives on Greek history in Hanson 2002; Meier 2005.

become a segregated and apparently autonomous entity.[16] The story of the opposition between Oriental despotism and Western freedom, which originated with the Greeks, is too well known to be rehearsed here.[17]

Even more, this Eurocentric perspective has created an implicit mentality whereby Europe, in its medieval, early modern and modern forms, has become the sole standard of comparison for ancient Greek history (as a matter of fact, for all areas and periods of history). To give just one example, the economic history of antiquity is still written from a perspective that tries to assess to what extent ancient economies approximated medieval/modern European economies.[18] The implicit assumption is that the path that medieval, early modern and modern European economies followed is the normal path that every economy should have followed; therefore, the issue becomes whether ancient economies did follow that path, and, if not, why not. The idea that there is no reason to take the (northern) European economies as the standard of comparison; the idea that there can exist other, non-European, standards of comparison; or the idea that economies are parts of wider world-systems and conjunctures, which we cannot randomly abstract, seem unimaginable from the viewpoint of the current dominant perspective.[19]

Finally, one of the effects of the appropriation of ancient Greek history for the history of Europe has been the imposition of a quasi-national framework on Greek history. The Greeks had no centre or institution around which their history could be organised; Greek-speaking communities were scattered all over the Mediterranean and they never achieved political, economic or social unity; while their cultural unity was not centred on a dominant institution, such as a church or a temple. Therefore, Greek history could not be written in the way that Roman or Jewish history could, centred on the Roman state or the Jewish temple. The emergence of nationalism and racialism in nineteenth-century Europe, and the construction of national narratives for all European nations, influenced deeply the way modern historians attempted to narrate Greek history; the homogenising fictional entity of the nation was ready at hand. But equally important were the needs of the Eurocentric account of historical evolution. The story of the evolution of the West, passing from one stage to the next and from one locale to another, necessitated a clear story of beginning,

---

[16] Bernal 1987: 281–336. [17] Koebner 1951; Venturi 1963; Vidal-Naquet 1964; Hall 1989.
[18] Finley 1973b: 123–49. See the comments of Nafissi 2005: 237–43.
[19] For such an approach, see Pomeranz 2000, 3–27.

Finley 1973 b:123-49

the concept of the polis & the Greek city state

acme and fall. A homogenising national narrative could serve such a function, and was thus easily adopted.

The concept that came to encompass and serve all these needs of Eurocentric history is the concept of the polis, the Greek city-state. It has served to differentiate the Greeks, originators of liberty and democracy, from Oriental monarchies and despotisms. Moreover, since the Greeks lacked a national state, the city-state served as the equivalent: the various Greek poleis were so many replicas of the common national form of state and society, the city-state. It could thus serve as a handy means of homogenisation.[20] It could also serve ideally the Eurocentric scheme of historical evolution: the polis could be portrayed as a historical form that emerged, prospered and finally declined, passing the sceptre to new forms, such as the Hellenistic monarchies and the Roman empire. Finally, it could be used to pursue all sorts of Eurocentric comparisons. To give an example, the Greek polis, perceived as a consumer city, has been compared to medieval and modern producer cities, in order to explain why ancient economies did not develop the way modern European economies did.[21]

As it is clear already from the title, this work is polemical to a large extent; but the reader is entitled to ask: has it been the case that all study of ancient Greek history so far has been Eurocentric and dominated by the currents of thought and methodologies that you criticise? Am I not constructing straw men, given the variety of views expressed by different scholars? Am I not conspiratorial, when arguing that alternative traditions to the current orthodoxy have been silenced or marginalised?

I am using the term *silencing* to describe the process of the formation of the modern orthodoxy and the exclusion of alternatives in two different ways. On the one hand, it refers to the process by which certain approaches and the people who foster them are put aside and marginalised; but this is the least important for my discussion here, and in the absence of a history of scholarship for the twentieth century it would be impossible to substantiate.[22] But I do not intend this work to be conspiratorial;[23] I hope it is relatively easy for the reader to see that many scholars have supported a variety of alternative views and that there is no concentrated or conscious effort to silence certain views. The problem is indeed deeper and much more difficult to handle: silence is created by the very act of historical writing.

---

[20] Gawantka 1985.   [21] Finley 1977.

[22] The lonely efforts of Karl Christ are not enough: Christ 1972, 1999.

[23] And in this way I differ profoundly from Bernal 1987, as much as I agree with his general theme.

Silences enter the process of historical production at four crucial moments: the moment of fact creation (the making of *sources*); the moment of fact assembly (the making of *archives*); the moment of fact retrieval (the making of *narratives*); and the moment of retrospective significance (the making of *history* in the first instance).[24]

The silence at the moment of fact creation means that evidence for a subject or an event might exist, and yet not be utilised as a historical fact (e.g. archaeological evidence is underutilised by historians); the silence at the moment of fact assembly implies that there is uneven power in the production of sources (e.g. our literary archives represent the voice of elite Greeks, while subaltern Greeks are generally voiceless); the silence in the making of narratives implies that certain ways of writing a narrative eliminate certain kinds of evidence and certain subjects (e.g. writing Greek history as a story of the rise, acme and decline of the polis silences the history of the Greek communities in the Black Sea, where such a narrative cannot be constructed); finally, the silence at the moment of retrospective significance forces certain questions, while making others impossible (e.g. if Greek history is important, because it is the beginning of European history, then it is worth asking why the Greek polis did not develop economically like the medieval European city, but it becomes pointless to compare the Greek poleis with Indian cities).

There are therefore multiple silences; this is the reason that alternative views and approaches can exist, but without challenging the overall framework. A new fact can be added (e.g. numismatic evidence) without challenging the way of constructing a narrative or the wider metanarrative; a new assembly of facts can be created, which gives voice and opens a window to people and subjects previously underrepresented (e.g. the intensive surveys opening a window to the silent countryside and the lower classes that inhabited it), and still be situated within the same narrative. The varieties of alternative views that are endorsed in this study, along with the variety of views that are criticised, accept and deny different kinds of silences. What has not been done so far is an examination of all these silences and, even more, of the narratives and metanarratives that form the necessary background of writing Greek history.

The purpose of this book therefore is to examine and make explicit the forms of silences employed in writing Greek history. The making of sources and archives is more extensively discussed in the final chapter, suggesting how we can utilise the variety of sources at our disposal, in order

[24] Trouillot 1995: 26.

to overcome the usual Athenocentric and Hellenocentric accounts. The main part of this book though is more concerned with the making of narratives and the metanarratives on which these narratives depend. But it should be clear from the discussion above that the creation of silences is inherent in any kind of historical production. It would be a self-delusion to pretend that one can substitute the bad silences for the light of truth. But it is possible, legitimate and necessary to question certain kinds of silences and offer different criteria, different questions and different forms of silences.

The current study therefore has two aims: to challenge the implicit assumptions and the larger discursive framework behind the study of Greek history; and to offer an alternative analytical and conceptual framework. I argue that the current dominance of the polis as the single organising tool of the study of Greek history is responsible for the problems underlined above. I will examine the various ways in which the polis has been used as the key analytical tool to study the political, economic and social history of the ancient Greeks and show the insurmountable problems that are created. I therefore attempt to supplement an 'unthinking' of the concept of the polis with other analytical levels and conceptual tools.

To achieve the above aims, this study follows developments in the wider historical discipline. Comparative history and the history of historiography are two fundamental aspects of my work. There is a strong tendency among many ancient historians to consider both as optional and rather irrelevant to the day-to-day practice of the historian. In this understanding, comparative history resorts to nothing more than trying to find arguments or evidence in other periods or societies, when we lack them for the period or society that we study; and the history of historiography resorts to the study of first-rate minds from second-rate minds, or otherwise little more than a combination of intellectual curiosity and antiquarianism.[25] In my perspective, they both are an indispensable part of historical thinking. They function as the anthropological conscience of historiography: they remind us that the past is a foreign country, since people do things in a different way there. They challenge and help to rethink (or, indeed, unthink[26]) all that is taken for granted.

---

[25] The general absence of undergraduate courses in both comparative history and the history of historiography of antiquity speaks volumes about general attitudes. There are of course exceptions; but as always, this reinforces rather than undermines the rule.

[26] The concept of 'unthinking' refers to Wallerstein 1991. My attempt to unthink the foundations of my discipline has been fundamentally shaped by Wallerstein's attempt to unthink the foundations of the social sciences. This does not imply identification with all of his theses; Wallerstein has justly

The history of historiography shows that there is no inevitability in the way we have come to study history; that there have been alternative approaches, which have been silenced, and may be still worth pursuing; and that there are certain metahistorical reasons for which some approaches have been endorsed instead of others. Comparative history helps to illustrate issues and aspects that have not been clearly visible; it allows us to view our subjects from alternative perspectives; and it provides us with controlled and explicit historical assumptions, in order to approach our sources. A fundamental difference between my use of comparative history and that of many ancient historians is the starting point: many ancient historians start from problems encountered in the field of ancient history and turn to comparative study, in order to illuminate these points; their comparative quest is driven from the particular problems of their field, and is seen only from the entrenched perspective of their discipline.[27] Thus, they end up finding what they are already geared to find.

On the contrary, I start from the perception that our colleagues in other fields of history have been devising new approaches, methods, perspectives and issues, which have not found resonance in the world of historians of antiquity.[28] A key issue of this work is to look at the study of ancient Greek history from the perspective of what has been accomplished in other fields of history and to attempt to introduce such concerns to the study of ancient history.[29] There is of course a growing number of other ancient historians who pursue a comparative agenda; but there are differences about which comparative agendas should be adopted and this study makes an argument in favour of certain agendas, instead of others.

Post-colonialism and the critique of Orientalism have by now a long history;[30] yet, until now they had a very limited influence on the study of ancient history. To a certain extent, this is because even the few scholars that have attempted to converse with this current of thought have mainly turned their attention to works dealing with literary criticism, such as the work of Said; very little attention has been paid to the *historical* studies

been criticised as partly remaining within a Eurocentric perspective; see e.g. Washbrook 1990. I also find his economistic outlook often reductive and unsatisfactory. Yet, I find his challenge to the foundations of the modern social sciences both fully justified and highly stimulating. I have attempted to develop some of his many challenges and insights, without necessarily accepting all of his conclusions.

[27] See the remarks of Detienne 2000.
[28] The chief influences on this work are the historiographical traditions of the *Annales*, the *Past and Present* and the *Subaltern Studies*. See Kaye 1984; Dosse 1994; Chaturvedi 2000; Ludden 2002.
[29] To give an example, I attempt to introduce the insights of Braudel's *Civilisation matérielle* (Braudel 1982, 1984) to the study of Greek economic history.
[30] See the pioneering Said 1978.

emanating from post-colonialism, which are far more challenging and relevant. My work attempts to take this historical production into account; in particular, I have found the historiographical production of India extremely stimulating.[31] The other shortcoming is the general indifference towards the work of those scholars studying the ancient societies of the Near East. Many misconceptions are due to the neglect of scholarly achievements in this field in the last fifty years.[32] I present some very important insights coming out of this work, and I hope this will act as a catalyst towards further constructive interaction.

The study and critique of nationalism and ethnocentrism has been an equally strong influence.[33] Since the Historicist revolution of the nineteenth century, the national state has become the unchallenged unit of analysis for historical narrative and analysis.[34] The emergence of social history, gender history and ethnohistory has done much to undermine the coherence of national narratives and present the multiple histories of the lower classes, women and outcasts.[35] There has been a large discussion, in particular among American historians, on the need for new units of analysis and new forms of historical narrative, which will enable us to study and portray the multiple histories of various groups of peoples, instead of the homogenising and subjugating national narrative.[36] I have followed these insights by arguing that the domination of the concept of the polis on the study of Greek history serves to homogenise and submerge these various histories. And I attempt to offer an alternative analytical framework by studying Aristotle's conceptualisation of the polis and its constituent *koinôniai*.

Globalisation is probably the key word of the early twenty-first century.[37] The challenge to the national state as the unit of analysis has not come only from those arguing for levels below the national level; it is equally important to pay attention to those arguing for new conceptual tools in order to study diasporas,[38] international systems of moving goods, peoples and ideas,[39] and the interlinked history of various groups of peoples and states.[40] This study uses the work of scholars on globalisation,[41] world-systems theory[42] and world history[43] in order to argue that Greek history has to be liberated from the Eurocentric narrative of a

[31] Prakash 1990; Chakrabarty 2000; Chaturvedi 2000.
[32] The best reflection of this work is van de Mieroop 1997b.   [33] Anderson 1991; Duara 1995.
[34] Iggers 1968.   [35] Bender 1986.   [36] Bender 2002a.   [37] Robertson 1992, 2003.
[38] Gilroy 1993; Clifford 1994.   [39] Curtin 1984.
[40] See the innovating Linebaugh and Rediker 2000.   [41] Appadurai 2001.
[42] Wallerstein 1974; Abu-Lughod 1989.   [43] Wolf 1982; Stuchtey and Fuchs 2003.

segregated and autonomous Greek history. We need to insert Greek
history into the interlinking history of the wider Mediterranean and
Near Eastern world;[44] but in order to do this, while avoiding the old
billiard approach of interaction between autonomous and separate entities,
we need new concepts and analytical tools; I attempt to provide a beginning for such a framework. Eric Wolf many years ago asked some questions
that I still find relevant:

> If there are connections everywhere, why do we persist in turning dynamic,
> interconnected phenomena into static, disconnected things? Some of this is
> owing, perhaps, to the way we have learned our own history. We have been
> taught, inside the classroom and outside of it, that there exists an entity called
> the West, and that one can think of this West as a society and civilization
> independent of and in opposition to other societies and civilizations. Many of
> us even grew up believing that this West has a genealogy, according to which
> ancient Greece begat Rome, Rome begat Christian Europe ... If history is but a
> tale of unfolding moral purpose, then each link in the genealogy, each runner in
> the race, is only a precursor of the final apotheosis and not a manifold of social and
> cultural processes at work in their own place and time. Yet, what would we learn of
> ancient Greece, for example, if we interpreted it only as a prehistoric Miss Liberty,
> holding aloft the torch of moral purpose in the barbarian night? We would gain
> little sense of the class conflicts racking the Greek cities, or of the relations between
> freemen and their slaves. We would have no reason to ask why there were more
> Greeks fighting in the ranks of the Persian kings than in the ranks of the Hellenic
> Alliance against the Persians. It would be of no interest to us to know that more
> Greeks lived in southern Italy and Sicily, then called Magna Graecia, than in
> Greece proper. Nor would we have any reason to ask why there were soon more
> Greek mercenaries in foreign armies than in the military bodies of their home
> cities. Greek settlers outside of Greece, Greek mercenaries in foreign armies and
> slaves from Thrace, Phrygia or Paphlagonia in Greek households, all imply
> Hellenic relations with Greeks and non-Greeks outside of Greece. Yet, our
> guiding scheme would not invite us to ask questions about these relationships.[45]

I have used this introduction to present the greater framework within
which I situate my study. My debts and reactions to developments in the
particular field of ancient history are discussed in much more detail in the
historiographical part of this work, and in many other cases in all other
parts of the book, of course. I also regret that cultural and religious history
have received little place in this study. This should not be taken to imply
that they are derivative on the 'deep' economic, social and political structures. But apart from problems of personal competence and familiarity,

---

[44] A move in this direction is of course Horden and Purcell 2000; see also Gras 1995b.
[45] Wolf 1982: 4–5.

and pressure of time and space, the reader will hopefully agree that the kind of approach, which is espoused here for social, economic and political history, is readily applicable to cultural and religious history as well.[46]

From the perspective defended in this work, it is possible to move beyond national histories into histories of how the interaction and interdependence between various communities and groups has shaped the past; to move beyond teleological and Eurocentric Grand Narratives into an understanding of the multiple, yet co-existing, and co-dependent courses of history; to save the peripheries, the subalterns and the marginal from 'the enormous condescension of posterity',[47] without therefore fragmenting the past into a 'histoire en miettes'. Greek history is an ideal field to apply all these concepts. The Greeks never had a centre around which one could organise their history; their communities were scattered over a wide space; their interactions with other communities and polities played a paramount role in their history; the varying temporal and spatial settings and configurations of their communities makes it feasible *and* necessary to apply the historical concepts that we have described. The Greek *poleis* are fascinating because they defy the obligatory logic of all the great explanatory schemes of Occidentalism. They are the decisive proof that history matters; what greater pleasure for the historian?

[46] See for example the similar approach of Antonaccio 2003.
[47] Thompson 1980: 12.

PART I

Defining the contexts of thinking about the polis

CHAPTER I

An archaeology of discourses

I have chosen the title of this book, *Unthinking the Greek polis*, to indicate that it is an attempt to look back, question and deconstruct the various discourses that underlie the modern study of the Greek polis. Today the polis is certainly the organising principle of the study of ancient Greek history. Every study of the political, economic, social, cultural and religious life of the ancient Greek world has to engage seriously with this concept. It has come to look as if it is perfectly natural to analyse Greek history within such a framework. But in fact, instead of being the natural, or the most plausible, way of studying Greek history, the polis approach is a relatively recent one, being the product of specific decisions and methodologies within larger discursive arguments.

The Greek word polis has a very ancient pedigree. It is thought to be an Indo-European word denoting the sense of 'stronghold'.[1] But it is its widespread and all-encompassing use by the ancient Greeks of the first millennium BCE that has given it an importance transcending its linguistic meaning. Nevertheless, it is only since the middle of the nineteenth century with the publication of works such as those of Burckhardt and Fustel[2] that the word polis has started to attract the attention of modern scholars, and has become part of Western European discourses and literature.[3] It is therefore important to pay much attention to the following question: how had these wider discourses formulated the study of ancient Greek history, and the content of that history, *before* the polis became the organising principle of the study of ancient history?

Let me clarify my question somewhat. It is obvious that the polis was a concept (indeed a constellation of meanings) of fundamental importance

---

[1] For references, see Hansen 2000b: 145.
[2] Fustel de Coulanges, *La cité antique: Etude sur le culte, le droit, les institutions de la Grèce et de Rome*, Paris, 1864; Jacob Burckhardt, *Griechische Kulturgeschichte, I–II*, Berlin, 1898.
[3] See Gawantka 1985. I think it is much more than a coincidence that the term city-state was coined first for Rome and not for any Greek polis; see Hansen 1998: 15–16.

for the political, economic, social and cultural world of the ancient Greeks. Therefore, the discovery of this importance by modern scholarship was clearly a great advantage. But the utilisation of this discovery was predetermined by the nature and limits that the history of Greece had already acquired by then; and in fact, its utilisation was severely limited by the progressive hardening of these limits.

We need, then, to study the historiography of Greek history in a non-teleological way;[4] this does not mean that the historiographical excursion, which will follow, will cover all the aspects and approaches to the study of Greek history. My historiographical survey is limited to the creation of a framework for the critique of the current approaches to the polis. But I believe it is important to show that there have been many alternative ways of approaching Greek history, which have been sidestepped and forgotten.[5] This is crucial for two reasons: on the one hand, in order to understand that the polis approach emerged as an alternative to these other ways of studying Greek history, and that the features of this approach have been determined by this opposition; on the other hand, since my aim is to offer not just a critique, but an alternative approach to the study of Greek history, the historiographical excursion will provide us with glimpses of previous attempts to provide such a framework, which can be still adopted and utilised.

Moreover, despite having a specific aim in mind, it is necessary to broaden our field of enquiry. The polis approach depends on a number of larger metahistorical premises: the placement of Greek history within European history; an evolutionist and/or progressivist philosophy of history; a mechanistic and/or functionalist historical methodology; specific decisions about the subject and the extent of Greek history and its unit of analysis; decisions about the narrative genres within which Greek history is pursued; and so on. We need to study the polis-centred approach within these larger discursive contexts. And, given that my argument will be that we have to pay more respect to the ancient Greek perceptions of their history, we need to start the historiographical enquiry with their own approaches.

Therefore, the study of the historiography of the Greek polis needs to be placed within a study of the historiography of Greek history. In what follows, I define six periods in the study of the history of ancient Greek

---

[4] For a similar approach, see Collini *et al.* 1983, 3–21; Heilbron 1995: 1–15.
[5] To give an example, one can cite the attempt of Eduard Meyer to bring together the history of Greece with the history of the Near East. His attempt e.g. to study the parallel development of Greek and Jewish history under the common influence and pressure of the Persian empire, remains still unsurpassed. See Ampolo 1997: 90–3.

communities: (a) ancient Greek accounts of their own history (b) from the Renaissance to the French Revolution (c) from the French Revolution to the 1860s (d) from the 1860s to the Second World War (e) the formation of modern orthodoxy in the post-war period and (f) alternative approaches since the 1980s.[6]

THE GREEKS AND THEIR HISTORY GENRES

It is always bewildering to find out how recent the history of Greece is. In antiquity, there existed a history of the Jews (e.g. the *Jewish Antiquities* of Josephus); a history of the Romans (e.g. the *Roman Antiquities* of Dionysius of Halicarnassus or Livy); and since the revolutionary feat of Eusebius, there even existed a history of the Christians, or more precisely of *the* Christian Church.[7] But until the eighteenth century, nobody had ever written either a history of the Greeks, or a history of Greece.[8]

There is a very elementary difference between Roman and Greek history to which perhaps not enough attention has been paid. Roman history, to the ordinary educated man, has definite limits in space and time: it has a beginning, it has an end; and it is obvious, if you speak of Roman history, that you mean the history of a well-defined territory ... With the Greeks it was the opposite. There were no obvious limits of time and space, no proper beginning, no agreed end and no geographical boundaries.[9]

The Greeks had no centre or institution around which their history could be organised; Greek-speaking communities were scattered all over the Mediterranean, and they never achieved political, economic or social unity; while their cultural unity was not centred on a dominant institution, such as a church, or a temple.

When Greeks wrote history, they wrote under five categories.[10] We will not be much interested in a late classical category, which centred on the careers and feats of illustrious individuals (e.g. the *Histories of Alexander*). Instead, we will pay much more attention to the other four categories: the

---

[6] I owe much to Ampolo 1997. Since it is a little book meant to be more an introduction than a comprehensive account, I have avoided citing it for every single assertion in the following pages. Yet, my debt is no less for that.

[7] Momigliano 1990: 80–108, 132–52.

[8] See the comments of Adolph Holm: 'the conception of a history of Greece belongs only to recent times. The Greeks themselves might have conceived the idea, since they contrasted Hellenism with barbarism; but we find no Greek history written by a Greek; even Ephorus wrote chronicles of the Hellenes and the barbarians. In modern times Englishmen were the first to write histories of Greece': *The History of Greece from its Commencement to the Close of the Independence of the Greek Nation*, London and New York, 1894, 7.

[9] Momigliano 1984a: 133–4, 1990.   [10] For what follows, see the account in Fornara 1983: 29–46.

first and most ancient, tracing its origin to the Homeric epics, was the narration of a single war or military engagement: although it would be a great mistake to think of the work of Herodotus in these terms, since as a pioneering work it did contain many more avenues and agendas than this,[11] nevertheless, both Herodotus, and much more Thucydides, ultimately attempted to narrate a single great war. Many other authors continued throughout antiquity to write narratives of single wars.

Since Xenophon decided in his *Hellênika*, instead of restricting himself to completing the unfinished Thucydidean narrative of the Peloponnesian war, to continue his narrative of the political and military history down to his own time,[12] a third genre developed under that name: it was contemporary history, which each historian brought down to his own time (*Zeitgeschichte*). It is important to recognise that despite the name *Hellênika*, this was no history of the Greeks, or of Greece, in the modern sense: those accounts dealt only with the history of a limited number of Greek communities, and even for these, only to the extent that their history was at some points connected with the political and military affairs and concerns of the 'great powers', which, strictly speaking, formed the subject of the *Hellênika*. The writers of *Hellênika* felt no need to be comprehensive, and reasonably so. Therefore, the history of each individual community, or of whole regions (such as the *Sikelika*), which remained outside the scope of the *Hellênika*, was narrated under the category of local history; here it is important to emphasise that, with very few exceptions, all this vast literature on local history was already lost when ancient texts were transmitted to the West in the Renaissance.[13]

Finally, when the Greeks extended their vision to the past and the beginnings of history, they wrote, starting with Ephorus, universal history, narrations of 'all the deeds of Greeks and barbarians'.[14] It is again important to emphasise that, with the partial exception of Polybius, whose work is limited to a short period of time, but nevertheless has an important particular agenda surpassing the aims of universal history, the only work of universal history that survived in the Renaissance was that of Diodorus (and this with very serious gaps).

It is important not to ignore that a whole part of Greek discourses on their past was not conducted under the name of history.[15] To give one

---

[11] See Momigliano 1958; Payen 1997.   [12] Dillery 1995.
[13] On the lost works of Greek historiography, see Strasburger 1990.
[14] On the origins of universal history, see Momigliano 1982a.
[15] Von Fritz 1956; Weil 1964; Huxley 1972, 1973.

example, the Aristotelian tradition of social, political and historical studies (and his approach to the polis in particular) was not thought of as part of history-writing in antiquity; yet its value for our assessment of Greek perceptions of their past is definitely high. But we are not going to deal with this issue here, since the whole next chapter is devoted to it.

RENAISSANCE TO THE FRENCH REVOLUTION

Since the Renaissance, therefore, and the rediscovery of an extremely limited quantity of the historiographical production of antiquity (limited both in amount and in scope), there existed no Greek history *tout court* until the eighteenth century. What was the reason?

The European neoclassical tradition,[16] which was decisively influenced by classical historiography,[17] perceived history largely as a narrative of military and political deeds performed by great persons.[18] The counterpart to this definition of the historical field was the perception of *historia magistra vitae*, whereby the past served as a rich field of exempla for modern use.[19] This had a double effect. On the one hand, it meant that early modern scholars did not attempt to write narrative histories of ancient Greece.[20] It was the ancient historians who had narrated the political and military events of ancient Greece in an exemplary manner. If the task of the historian was to bear witness of the events in an exemplary narrative, whether personally, or through the living witnesses he has examined, little remained for moderns to do; accordingly, they concentrated their efforts either to periods of ancient history for which no ancient account survived,[21] or, from the eighteenth century onwards, to compilations that would bring together into a single account all the stories related by ancient historians.[22]

On the other hand, what we now term social, economic and cultural history remained outside the field of neoclassical history writing. Instead, the evidence for these aspects of past life was concentrated in systematic accounts, called *Antiquitates*, organised around subject matter and not

[16] Hicks 1996: 7–14.   [17] Momigliano 1980a.   [18] Burke 1969: 105–30; Levine 1991: 267–90.
[19] Grell 1993: 125–64.   [20] Momigliano 1950: 6–8, 1977b: 254–6.
[21] As for example the Hellenistic period: see J. Foy-Vaillant, *Imperium Seleucidarum, Sive Historia Regum Syriae*, Paris, 1681; *idem*, *Historia Ptolemæorum Ægypti Regum, ad Fidem Numismatum Accommodata*, Amsterdam, 1701.
[22] Such is the first Greek history ever written by T. Stanyan, *The Grecian History: From the Original of Greece, to the End of the Peloponnesian War, I–II*, London, 1707–39; and the first ancient history by C. Rollin, *Histoire ancienne des Egyptiens, des Carthaginois, des Assyriens, des Babyloniens, des Mèdes et des Perses, des Macédoniens, des Grecs*, Amsterdam, 1736.

according to time.[23] Partly, the reason was that *Antiquitates* emerged as textual commentaries, enabling the reader and the scholar to emend classical texts and comprehend their true meaning. But more important was the fact that early modern scholars lacked a conceptual apparatus in order to narrativise these aspects and to insert them into a temporal framework.[24] Political and military history had great men as actors and narrated events; but social, economic and cultural history could not function simply with great men as subjects of action,[25] and could not be organised only around events. It needed collective subjects and concepts of time that did not exist either in the classical tradition that had survived, or in the *outillage mental* of early modern thinkers.

This is the reason that a central contradiction in the humanist study of antiquity from Renaissance onwards remained unresolved.[26] While the purpose of the humanist agenda was to imitate antiquity, thus positing no fundamental historical difference between antiquity and modernity, the attempt to resurrect antiquity from its vestiges, in order to imitate it, revealed exactly how different antiquity was.[27] The efforts of philologists and antiquaries to reconstruct texts, coins and monuments were based on an understanding of the peculiarities of ancient institutions, practices and beliefs. To give just one example, the revival of Roman law was based on the belief that there existed no fundamental difference between Roman society and early modern Europe. But the application of Roman law necessitated the reconstruction of the texts and its exegesis; and this in turn necessitated the study of the Latin language and the Roman institutions and practices, in order to emend texts and understand their meaning. This study revealed in fact how different Roman society was from those of early modern Europe; some lawyers and humanists in sixteenth-century France (François Hotman, Andrea Alciato) came to accept this, and to argue that Roman law was inapplicable to their society.[28] The contradiction between relevance and *altérité* within humanist scholarship remained unresolved, precisely because there was no conceptual apparatus that could

---

[23] Momigliano 1950.

[24] See Klempt 1960: 69–75; Bravo 1968: 29–40. Stanyan's history is a good example. He is interested in cultural history; but he has no way of narrating it, apart from introducing little notes about the eminent artists and thinkers who flourished in each period he deals with.

[25] Unless, of course, one was writing about great inventors of things, customs and institutions in the ancient tradition. This is probably why it was easier to write a history of learning, artists and scholars than any other kind of social, economic or cultural history; and why this form of cultural history was the first to enter into narratives of ancient history.

[26] Muhlack 1988: 165–70.   [27] See Grafton 1987; Levine 1991.

[28] Kelley 1970: 53–148; Monheit 1997.

narrativise these issues, and no discourse that could explain what constituted the basis of these differences and the source of historical change.[29]

But if the ancient authors of history provided examples of noble conduct, ingenious stratagems and despicable actions, the political, social and economic life of Greek communities was also directly available and relevant to early modern Europeans through the discourse of civic Humanism. This discourse can be traced back to the ancient Greeks, and in particular to Aristotle, and was still evolving up to the eighteenth century.[30] It viewed the polis or *civitas* as a community of citizens, who are heads of households. The *civitas* could be governed in a variety of ways, depending on whether the governing element was an individual (monarchy), a few (oligarchy), many (democracy) or a mixed constitution,[31] and whether the governing element governed for the public benefit, or for its own sake (corrupted constitutions). The participation in the political community was dependent on political virtue, and the preservation of the community was equally dependent on the virtue of its members. But the political community was perennially threatened by the substitution of virtue for the particular interest of the citizens, or of the governing element alone. This was the phenomenon of corruption, and each form of *civitas* was always susceptible to be transformed into its corrupt form, or to a different form.

Therefore, the central concern of this paradigm was how to attain and retain civic virtue: the totality of relationships between humans, and between humans and things, were viewed through this looking glass. What we would call economic aspects were of interest only to the extent that they guaranteed, or satisfied, the political virtue of the citizens and the community. Political economy was still viewed until the end of the eighteenth century as the administration of the public household, in a way that could make the political community and its members as efficient as possible.[32] In the same way the multitude of *koinôniai* that form the political community were of interest only to the extent that they serve the autarky and the good life of the community; the same holds true for the study of relations between polities.

---

[29] This is not to deny that there were efforts to construct such an apparatus. The French scholars and humanists of the sixteenth century are perhaps the best example; see Huppert 1970. But whatever explanation one is to give, their efforts did not manage to create a long-term historical paradigm.

[30] Pocock 1975c. But see now Nelson 2004.

[31] See Nippel 1980.

[32] Adam Smith, still in 1776, argued that 'Political oeconomy, considered as a branch of the science of a statesman or a legislator, proposes two distinct objects; first, to provide a plentiful revenue or subsistence for the people, or more properly to enable them to provide such a revenue or subsistence for themselves; and secondly, to supply the state or commonwealth with a revenue sufficient for the publick services'; Smith 1976: Book IV, 138, 1.

The paradigm was formed by selecting and focusing only on those aspects that can be administered, or geared, to the benefit of the political community. The processes that go beyond, or defy, this administration by the political community were beyond the analysis of the paradigm.[33]

Thus, the discourse of civic Humanism blended what from the nineteenth century onwards would be seen as the three distinct fields of society, economy and the state into the single whole of the polis or *civitas*. In so doing, and in presenting the *civitas* as a voluntary association of citizens, it gave politics the pre-eminent role: the image of the lawgiver, who constructs or reshapes the polity, was of crucial value. Therefore, the political history and experience of the ancients was readily available to early modern Europeans: their solutions to constructing a successful and virtuous polity, and in reforming a corrupted community, could be studied and potentially applied to modern problems. Furthermore, in analysing the forms of polities on the basis of their governing element, this discourse allowed direct comparisons between ancient and modern democracies, oligarchies and monarchies. The history of ancient communities was used as a comparative standard for modern polities, even as arguments in contemporary political debates. Machiavelli's *Discourses on Livy* was an early example of the use of the historical experience of the Greek and Roman polities, in order to draw conclusions about similar phenomena in the contemporary world. Sparta and Athens provided a context for discussing the current issues and affairs of European societies, in issues such as the mixed constitution, the use of luxury, corruption or the role of education in society.[34]

The only genre in which Greek history was presented as a continuous narrative was universal history. The Christian version of universal history had evolved since late antiquity; it amalgamated the universal history of the ancients, and in particular the idea of the succession of empires,[35] and the tradition of sacred history that was initiated by Eusebius.[36] But Greek history had a very limited role to play in this genre. Universal history in our period was mainly organised in two schemes: the one was the succession of the four empires; Greek history was treated as part of the history of the

---

[33] Ste Croix has described this phenomenon in Thucydides, in relation to international relations. Relations between polities cannot be administered by a higher authority, since there is no authority overarching the polis. Therefore, the rules applying to the relations of individuals within the political community cannot apply to the relationships between polities; Ste Croix 1972: 5–34. On the early modern conception of the issue, see Tuck 1999.

[34] See Rawson 1969 on Sparta; Roberts 1994 on Athens.

[35] Fabbrini 1983.   [36] Momigliano 1990: 132–52.

second empire (the Persian) and played a role in the history of the third one (the Macedonian); the other was the scheme of the three *aetates* (from Creation to Abraham, from Abraham to Jesus, from Jesus until the present).[37] In both cases, Greek history played a subordinate role, in the one to Rome, in the other to sacred history.

Lastly, it is important to clarify how Greek communities were conceived in this period. What is remarkable about the treatment of Greek history is the absence of a homogeneous national identification of the Greeks, and the inclusion of a large number of Greek communities in early modern accounts. Accounts of the Greek polities were seldom amalgamated under a unified national label: for the authors of this period, every 'polity' could easily approximate a 'nation'. Thus Montesquieu could speak about the 'esprit d'une nation', while putting Athenians and Spartans on the same level with the Chinese, the Japanese and the French; Greeks, Italians and Germans, nations which were divided into a great number of polities, were simply represented by some of their polities, and not as a unified whole.[38] Moreover, the nature of those contexts of discussion permitted the inclusion of a fairly large number of Greek polities. Universal history had of course ideological aims to serve that directed its narrative; but its universal character enabled it to be all-inclusive; each human community was part of humanity and could claim a place in the narrative of universal history. To give an example, the English *Universal History* covered a huge number of Greek polities and their history.[39] The *Antiquitates* were by definition inclusive: a large number of Greek (and in fact non-Greek, as in the Aristotelian manner) polities were always represented in works such as that of Ubbo Emmius.[40]

We can also see this attitude persisting in some places until the end of the Enlightenment. The manual of universal history of A. H. L. Heeren, one of the most popular historical works of the period is a good example.[41] There, the motif of the succession of empires plays its clear role in the main narrative of Greek history from the Persian wars to Chaironeia, which leads from the Persians to the Macedonians and Romans. But the account of Greek history before the Persian wars is dedicated to tracing the various regions of Greek communities and narrating their history up to the end of

---

[37] Meyer-Zwiffelhoffer 1995: 256–67; Klempt 1960.   [38] See Gawantka 1985: 83–8.
[39] The *Universal History, Ancient and Modern from the Earliest Account of to the Present Time*, London, 1736–44. See Ampolo 1997: 118–27.
[40] *Vetus Graecia, I–III*, Leiden, 1626.
[41] *Handbuch der Geschichte der Staaten des Alterthums, mit besonderer Rücksicht auf ihre Verfassungen, ihren Handel und ihre Colonien*, Göttingen, 1799. Though slightly after the Revolution, it is absolutely within the Enlightenment tradition.

the classical period: they can have their history narrated, but the main account has to serve a different function. This characteristic difference between the unifocal character of Roman history and the multifocal character of Greek history is nicely illustrated by two French histories of the 1780s with the same title: *Histoire générale et particulière de la Grèce*.[42]

COUNTER-TENDENCIES

But during the eighteenth century, the picture we have presented showed a variety of changes. The transformation of the wider European discourses, which were associated with the main current of the Enlightenment, and the diverse parallel or counter-currents, changed profoundly the context of thinking about Greek history. If it was not until after the French Revolution that Greek history emerged as an independent field, it is still the case that the changes during the eighteenth century shaped to a large extent what was to follow.

Some people came to argue that antiquity was fundamentally different from modernity, and defined it on the grounds of how it differed from modernity. This created a whole discourse on how antiquity was different, why it was so and why it had not developed in the same way as modern Europe had. At the same time, others came to see antiquity as particularly relevant: its history could provide examples of how to reform society during the great crisis of the late eighteenth century;[43] equally, Greek history came now to be written as a narrative, in order to foster arguments in contemporary political debates. Others came to value Greek history for different reasons: precisely because it was different from contemporary society, and allowed the discovery of alternative forms of expression and feeling. From this perspective, they came to discover how the field of history could be expanded in order to encompass social, cultural and economic history. They discovered the collective subject of the *Volk* and the temporal concept of the *Zeitgeist*. Finally, others came to discover new, 'secular' temporalities, within which history could be narrated: they discovered that history could be seen as moving through distinct stages, and they discovered new metahistories. The emergence of Greek history as an independent field during the *Sattelzeit* was shaped by all these different developments.[44]

---

[42] By L. Cousin-Despréaux (1780–6) and Delisle de Sales (1783). See Grell 1993: 165–8.
[43] For this crisis, see Venturi 1989, 1991.
[44] For the concept of the *Sattelzeit*, see Koselleck 1972.

During this period emerged a completely new way of approaching antiquity. This was the idea that there was a complete and insuperable gap between antiquity and modernity. This attitude had diverse sources. One was the famous *Querelle des anciens et des modernes*, which had taken place from the end of the seventeenth till the first two decades of the eighteenth century.[45] In this debate, the *modernes* had come to argue against the essence of Humanism, that modernity had come to surpass antiquity in many, if not all, fields of learning and technology. The debate had no clear winners, but a consensus was more or less reached, in which it was recognised that modernity had surpassed antiquity in the sciences and technology, but was still behind in the creative arts. The importance of the *Querelle* lay in that it was the first construction of a notion of modernity in opposition to antiquity.

But the gap was soon to grow wider. During the eighteenth century, many thinkers came to believe that their age was experiencing developments that were unique and differentiated it from all past history. The cessation of bloody civil and religious wars, commercial expansion and the advances of science were seen as symptoms and causes of a larger process. There emerged what has been described as 'the Enlightened narrative': a narrative and metahistory of how the spread of commerce since the end of the Middle Ages had destroyed the feudal relations of dependence, diffused property, created a stable system of states and introduced order and good government, and thus liberty and the security of individuals.[46]

Seen in this perspective, the ancient republics ceased to be valuable *exempla*. They were based on agriculture and slavery; their *raison d'être* was war and conquest; the community had absolute right over its subjects, without recognising individual rights; thus, their political quarrels took the form of bloody civil wars and political stability was impossible.[47] The old paradigm of civic Humanism seemed to many now as redundant: the changes in property and manners, the role of commerce and civility, created a new form of society, economy and state, in which the virtue of the citizen was irrelevant.[48]

The debate on the populousness of ancient nations is a good illustration of wider trends.[49] The issue was long treated by antiquarians; but it was also of direct interest in contemporary debates about the desired density of population and the measures needed to achieve it. David Hume's contribution to the debate illustrates nicely the new perspective of the *modernes*. He showed that the debate on ancient populations was not simply a matter

---

[45] By far the best account is Levine 1991.   [46] See Pocock 1999: 1–6.
[47] See Guerci 1979; Avlami 2001.   [48] Pocock 1975a, 1985.   [49] See Cambiano 1984b.

of numbers; instead it involved the whole social structure of ancient and modern societies.[50] He argued that slavery, constant warfare, brutal civil wars and the low volume of trade, which were essential characteristics of ancient Greek polities, were unfavourable to high populations; therefore, free labour, political stability and the expansion of trade, which characterised modernity, proved that modern societies had larger populations.

Thus, for the first time some thinkers attempted to reflect in a systematic way about the differences between antiquity and modernity. They also tried to discover and show the structural interconnections between the various features of ancient societies, and their modern counterparts. Finally, some of them, belonging to the Scottish school of moral philosophy and conjectural history (Adam Smith, John Millar), tried to discover a scheme of historical development that would explain how the world had passed from antiquity to modernity: ancient societies were incorporated in these schemes as part of a less developed, agricultural stage, before the commencement of the modern commercial one.[51] Thus emerged a new way of thinking about antiquity: a new temporal framework and a new, Eurocentric, standard of comparison.

But others felt that antiquity was still directly relevant for contemporaries and refused to accept this fundamental gap. It would be superfluous to refer here extensively to the works of thinkers like Rousseau[52] or Mably.[53] What is important to note is that the politicisation of Greek history in the decades before the French Revolution had ultimately important repercussions. The use of the models of ancient republics by the French revolutionaries created heightened reactions; as we shall see in the next period, the liberal and conservative reaction to the Revolution forced the universal acceptance of the axiom that there existed a clear gap between antiquity and modernity. More relevant here is that, paralleling the politicisation of Greek history by Rousseau and Mably, some English scholars, with whom we will deal shortly, started writing narrative histories of Greece for the first time as arguments in the contemporary political debates.

---

[50] 'Of the populousness of ancient nations', in *Political Discourses*, London, 1752.

[51] Schneider 1988.

[52] J. J. Rousseau, *Discours sur si le rétablissement des sciences et des arts a contribué à épurer les mœurs*, Paris, 1751; see Yack 1986: 35–85.

[53] Abbé de Mably, *Observations sur l'histoire de la Grèce*, Geneva, 1766. See Grell 1995: 449–553; Wright 1997.

Meanwhile, there emerged a new evaluation of Greek history, mainly in Germany, along with a new historical language.[54] The currents that contributed to this were diverse, but they all shared an opposition to the main thrust of the Enlightenment:[55] a stress on the field of the experience and feeling, instead of rationality (Hamann);[56] a stress on national character, instead of the universalising principles of the Enlightenment (Herder);[57] on simplicity and originality, instead of subtlety and artificiality (Winckelmann);[58] and a resistance to the secularising tendencies of the Enlightenment.

The feelings and traditions, which bound a people together, and which were expressed in their culture, were not rationally grounded, nor to be rationally justified. Such feelings and traditions sprung from a common language, a common heritage of customs, a common facing of the exigencies of life in a particular locale.[59]

The concept of the *Volksgeist*, the living psychic unity of a nation, was their discovery: it allowed the construction of a new historical subject, a new actor in historical narrative.

At the same time, other people discovered the concept of *Zeitgeist*, the most renowned among them being Giambattista Vico.[60] Vico tried to save sacred history from the attacks of sceptics, who used the historical traditions of the Babylonians, the Egyptians and the Chinese, narrating histories much older than allowed by the Bible, in order to challenge it.[61] They were mistaken, argued Vico, because they imputed their own assumptions and ideas to periods that were very different. Instead of the wise lawgivers and statesmen, which pagan annals credited with the beginnings of their history, in reality the early stages of nations were characterised by savagery and ignorance. Only gradually did the nations manage to move towards civilisation; each particular phase of their history was autonomous and different, having its own institutions, practices and values. In this way Vico discovered the historicity of each society and each different historical period.

A new language was now created that allowed scholars to write about culture in its totality, in its historical development, and with a historical actor at its centre.[62] These developments coincided and interacted with the contemporary re-evaluation of Greek culture and history in Germany:[63] the discovery of the history of Greek art;[64] the discovery of the Homeric

[54] Trevelyan 1934. [55] Berlin 1979. [56] Manuel 1959: 283–309. [57] Berlin 1977.
[58] Fuhrmann 1979. [59] Mandelbaum 1971: 56. [60] Grafton 1999. [61] See Rossi 1984: 168–87.
[62] Schaumkell 1905. [63] Butler 1935; Rehm 1936; Marchand 1996: 3–35.
[64] J. J. Winckelmann, *Geschichte der Kunst des Alterthums*, Dresden, 1764. See the remarks of Bravo 1968: 51–63; Potts 1994.

and the archaic as distinct historical periods;[65] the new evaluation of mythology, religion and social institutions.[66] This combination would bear fruits in the coming period.

Before moving on, it is important to look at an approach that did not survive the French Revolution. Between Christian universal history and the emergence of nineteenth-century Eurocentric philosophies of history, the Enlightenment saw the emergence and demise of alternative ways of looking at world history; if they did not survive, this does not minimise their value.

The eighteenth century saw the emancipation of Greek history from the theological scheme of universal history, which predominated until then. The reaction to the Christian apologetics of such a universal history took two forms: the one was an investigation of alternative, non-theological approaches to universal history; the other was the study of national and regional histories in their own merit.[67] Greek history was treated until then as part of a universal history within a Near Eastern background, due to the fundamental importance of the Old Testament for Christian conceptions of universal history. The break-up of this theological presumption left it open, which background would be adopted for the study of Greek history, and whether Greek history would form an independent field. We know that in the end Greek history became a (peculiar) form of national history, severed from this Near Eastern background.[68] But there were alternative approaches and I will now focus on them.

One alternative approach was mainly employed in Enlightenment Germany;[69] and indeed Germany retained a tradition of writing universal history long into the nineteenth century, when it had been practically abandoned by everybody else.[70] A group of German historians, mainly associated with the pioneering University of Göttingen, attempted to rethink and rewrite a universal history, which would not follow the premises of Christian theology and its scheme of the four monarchies.[71] Johann

---

[65] See the works of Vico, Herder and Wood, among others, culminating in F. A. Wolf, *Prolegomena ad Homerum*, Halle, 1795; see Simonsuuri 1979; Grafton 1981.

[66] E.g. C. G. Heyne, *Opuscula academica collecta, I–VI*, Göttingen, 1785–1812; see Wohlleben 1992; see also Levine 1991.

[67] For the development of these processes, see Muhlack 1991: 97–150.

[68] See the pioneering account of Bernal 1987: 189–399.

[69] For German Enlightenment historiography, see Reill 1975; Bödeker *et al.* 1986.

[70] See C. F. Schlosser, *Universalhistorische Übersicht der Geschichte der alten Welt und ihrer Cultur, I–VIII*, Frankfurt, 1826; M. Duncker, *Geschichte des Altertums, I–IV*, Leipzig, 1852–7. See Heuss 1989.

[71] On Göttingen, see Butterfield 1955: 32–61. For the contribution of these German historians to the study of Greek history, see Gawantka 1985: 146–61.

Christoph Gatterer introduced a scheme of *Völkersystemen*.[72] He wanted to study how the history of the various peoples and polities interlinked, and, in order to do this, he argued that we should study how a group of peoples was brought together under a dominant people or polity; he distinguished eight such systems in world history: the Assyrians, the Persians, the Macedonians, the Parthians, the Germans and Slavs, the Arabs, the Mongols and the Tartars. In his system, Greek history was not an independent history, but formed part of the wider concurrence of political power and cultural development in the Eastern Mediterranean.

A. H. L. Heeren, whom we have already encountered, offered an alternative path.[73] He argued that peoples and states, although each having individual characteristics, are brought together into systems (*Vereine*), due to their political, economic, social and cultural interaction; and that these systems have their own existence and history, beyond that of every individual member of the system.[74] Heeren was the author of an influential study of the interactions between the various peoples of the ancient Mediterranean.

The epochs of the Roman and Macedonian empires are far from being the most important or the most instructive, either as respects the polity or the trade of the Ancients. The variety, which distinguished the Ancient forms of government, was necessarily overwhelmed by an universal dominion, and Commerce herself was apt to be fettered with the same bondage in which every other civil relation was necessarily confined. We must ascend to a more distant age, if we would contemplate the constitutions of the Ancients in all their diversity, and their commerce in its most tranquil and flourishing condition. The period immediately preceding the establishment, and during the continuance of the Persian monarchy, appears to offer the historian the most satisfactory survey and the richest field of inquiry . . . In like manner, by ascending to the age referred to, we behold, as it were, everything in its proper place, before the success of one nation had deprived the rest of their independence.[75]

---

[72] *Einleitung in die synchronistische Universalhistorie zur Erläuterung seiner synchronistischen Tabellen*, Göttingen, 1771.

[73] On Heeren, see Blanke 1983; Becker-Schaum 1993.

[74] *Handbuch der Geschichte des Europäischen Staatensystems und seiner Colonien*, Göttingen, 1809. There he argues that such systems had existed before the modern European one, in ancient Greece (i.e. in the classical period and after the partition of Alexander's kingdom the various Hellenistic states) and in medieval Italy.

[75] *Historical Researches into the Politics, Intercourse and Trade of the Carthaginians, Ethiopians and Egyptians*, Oxford, 1832, xxxvi. This is the English translation of a part of *Ideen über die Geschichte, die Verkehr und den Handel der vornehmsten Völker der alten Welt*, Göttingen, 1793–6.

He presented a survey of the communities of the whole Mediterranean basin and their interrelationships in a period before the domination of a single power over the whole world, roughly between 600 and 300 BCE. Two hundred years later, and a modern study in these lines is still a desideratum.

It is an important question why this approach was so totally abandoned that even the names of Heeren or Gatterer are unknown to most ancient historians nowadays; I am afraid I have no clear-cut answer to offer. Part of the answer is the enormous success of philology and source criticism: in the post-Wolf, post-Niebuhr age, the works of the German Enlightenment historians were found inadequate and were ridiculed.[76] Moreover, sources for Near Eastern history, before the decipherment of the cuneiform scripts in the 1860s, could not bear the kind of treatment that philologists and historians gave to classical sources.[77] Therefore, while Greek history became an autonomous field based on a critical examination of its sources, Near Eastern history was relegated to a quasi-mythic prehistory. It was not until the end of the nineteenth century, with the pioneering work of E. Meyer, that its history could be written in the same way as ancient Greek and Roman history. But this is only a partial answer. In order to understand the total abandonment of this approach, we have to turn our attention to the fundamental readjustment of European realities and discourses in the aftermath of the French Revolution.

FROM THE FRENCH REVOLUTION TO THE 1860S

These seventy years saw the revolutionary readjustment of European discourses and the formation of Greek history as an independent field. One cannot differentiate the one from the other, and this is the approach adopted here. The so-called 'twin revolutions', the French Revolution and the Industrial Revolution readjusted the European political, economic and social discourses.[78] The French Revolution put inescapably on the agenda the issue of the nature of the political community and the rights of its members.[79] For the first time in many centuries people felt that they could rebuild society from scratch; the Jacobin attempt to reshape French society, and its demise, fuelled a huge debate on the nature of society and

---

[76] In particular Niebuhr offered a severe criticism on philological grounds of Heeren's work in his *Kleine historische und philologische Schriften*, II, Berlin, 1843, 107–58.

[77] See Meyer-Zwiffelhoffer 1995.   [78] For the 'twin revolutions', see Hobsbawm 1962: 1–4.

[79] See e.g. Livesey 2001.

its institutions, the form and nature of social change, the relevance of the past for the present and the attainable future of humanity.[80] Moreover, the Revolution saw the development of nationalism as a potent political force and it helped to reshape perceptions of identity and belonging and collective destinies.[81]

The Industrial Revolution had equally important consequences. The West was now in a position to bid for unchallenged world supremacy due to the great advancement of its technology, productivity and power;[82] these monumental changes impressed so much the (European) people of the time that they tried to explain this successful Western bid for world supremacy. All the great nineteenth-century thinkers strove to explain 'the rise of the West'.[83] Many different answers have been attempted. What they all shared was a belief that a comparison of the successive stages of the West (antiquity – Middle Ages – modernity) would enable scholars to understand its rise.[84] At the same time, the rise of the West was accompanied by the fall of the East. The East was now finally relegated to a position of eternal stagnation, outside history proper; the West owed nothing to the East, but had advanced by its own internal dynamic.[85] Racial theories, such as the discourse on the Indo-Europeans, served to intensify this gap.[86]

These historical changes affected the study of ancient Greek history in three ways. The first was the construction of temporalities. Greek history became now an independent field of study. What were the temporal frameworks that historians used in order to narrate Greek history? We have already seen some created; but in this period they were further articulated, others were added and, in a sense, the temporalities within which Greek history is still studied were ultimately settled. The second issue was constructing the subject of Greek history: Was it a geographical area? A people? A concept? And what were the frameworks within which historians could conceive and analyse such a subject? Finally, the last issue was historical narrative. What were the sources used to construct such a narrative? What was included and what was excluded? Or, in other words, how were temporalities and conceptions of the historical subject applied to the writing of Greek history?

---

[80] Koselleck 1985: 3–54. See also Vidal-Naquet 1979; Avlami 2000b.
[81] Thom 1995; Thiesse 1999. [82] Wolf 1982.
[83] For the eighteenth-century background, which explains much about the nineteenth as well, see now Pocock 2005.
[84] Blaut 1993. [85] See the classic Said 1978; also Inden 1990.
[86] Poliakov 1974; Olender 1992. Concerning Greek history, Bernal 1987: 317–99.

TEMPORALITIES

We have already seen how during the eighteenth century diverse groups of thinkers came to argue in favour of a radical discontinuity between antiquity and modernity. Now, the Jacobin use of antiquity to reshape contemporary society gave added importance and urgency to the issue.[87] A group of French liberals, the so-called *Idéologues*, tried to argue that the invocation of ancient models by the Jacobins was fatally wrong, because it misinterpreted both antiquity and modernity.[88] Antiquity could not be imitated by the moderns, because social, economic and political structures had fundamentally changed. The liberty of the ancients, centred on citizen participation and based on agriculture, slavery and small polities, could not be imitated in the world of the moderns, based on commerce, free labour and large states; therefore, only the liberty of the moderns was relevant, centred on the individual enjoyment of property, freedom of conscience and the rights of the private sphere.[89] Antiquity was therefore totally different from modernity and the only way to understand it was by its own means. Antiquity was a wholly different structure from the structure of modernity and one had to show how every aspect of antiquity fitted together to form this different structure.

Because the *Idéologues* argued forcefully that antiquity had no relevance for modernity, French historians focused their interest on what seemed to matter: the Revolution, the Middle Ages and the national history of France, in an attempt to understand what should be retained and what should be dismissed from the past and how that past threw light on the present.[90] Consequently, there was very little work concerning ancient history and almost nothing concerning Greek history.[91] But the great contribution of the *Idéologues* to the study of ancient history bore fruit in the next period, through the work and influence of a fellow soul, namely Fustel de Coulanges. I will examine his contribution in the next part. What needs to be stressed for the time being is that, since the *Idéologues*, French ancient historians have shown a particular interest in a structural study of antiquity that shows the interdependence between its various aspects and

---

[87] Vidal-Naquet 1990a; Hartog 2000.

[88] See Vidal-Naquet 1979; Hartog 2000; Avlami 2000b, 2001.

[89] C. F. Volney, *Leçons d'histoire*, Paris, 1795; P.-C. Levesque, *Etudes de l'histoire ancienne et de celle de la Grèce*, Paris, 1811; B. Constant, *De la liberté des anciens comparée à celle des modernes*, Paris, 1819. See Vidal-Naquet 1979.

[90] For French historians in the first half of the nineteenth century, see Crossley 1993.

[91] It was not before 1851, when V. Duruy published his *Histoire grecque* that the first work on Greek history appeared. See Avlami 2000b.

its difference from modernity; an approach that we can describe as **distant-iation**. Their main interest has not been how actual people have shaped and changed their history, but how structures have shaped the behaviour and attitudes of ancient people.[92]

But not everybody was convinced about this radical discontinuity. German historians were equally adamant that the misapplication of ancient models was fatal. In fact, the ancestor of German ancient histor-ians, B. G. Niebuhr, wrote with the explicit aim in mind of refuting the demand of the French revolutionaries for an agrarian law that would limit and redistribute property; a demand that revolutionaries legitimated by appeal to the reforms of the Gracchi. Niebuhr showed that the Gracchan reforms pertained to the public property of *ager publicus*, and not to the sacrosanct private property.[93] But in the attempt to do so, he discovered the importance of source criticism: given that the origins and nature of the *ager publicus* was so confused in ancient sources, one could not trust the accounts of ancient historians as such, and source criticism was necessary to show which reading of the ancient historians was correct. A further step was the realisation that one could actually write an account of ancient history which did not depend on the priorities and aims of the ancient sources.[94] The crucial question was then, in Momigliano's words, 'how are we going to proceed, where we cannot be guided by the ancient histor-ians?'[95] The aim was to give life to antiquity, to present an account of how ancient people shaped and changed their lives. This approach can be described as **actualisation**.[96] In the exemplary words of Mommsen, the task of the historian was 'To take down the Ancients from the imaginary high heels, from which they appear to the mass of the public, and to shift them into the real world of the reader, where there was hate and love, sawing and hammering, imagination and lies – and therefore the consul had to become a mayor.'[97]

These thinkers came to argue that the categorical distinction between antiquity and modernity was rather misleading. There had been important changes during the long span of antiquity. Moreover, these changes were coherent enough to divide ancient history into distinct periods. Finally, these periods were not unique to antiquity; rather, they were recurrent

[92] On the tradition stemming from the French approach, see Di Donato 1990 in respect of Glotz, Gernet and Vernant.
[93] See Momigliano 1982b: 225–36.   [94] Muhlack 1988.
[95] Momigliano 1980a: 33. For the debates and questions emanating from the challenges put to classical models of historiography, and the attempts to create new models, see Hicks 1996; Phillips 2000.
[96] Walther 2001.   [97] Cited in Schneider 1990: 427.

stages in the history of every nation, civilisation and society. This was an elaboration of the Viconian theory of historical cycles and was followed by many German historians and their followers in other countries.[98] Thomas Arnold called for 'a more sensible division of history than that which is commonly adopted of ancient and modern':

The largest portion of that history, which is commonly called ancient is practically modern, as it describes society in a state analogous to that in which it is now, while on the other hand much of what is called modern history [he means the Middle Ages] is practically ancient, as it relates to a state of things which has passed away.[99]

Thus, although accepting that there is a larger, universal frame of development, they argued that every nation and every society passed through successive stages of birth, adulthood and maturity.[100] Antiquity was not homogeneous: it had passed through successive stages, each with its own characteristics. One could still see similarities between antiquity and modernity: but they were similarities between equivalent stages of antiquity and modernity.[101] Thus, the Homeric age was seen as the Greek Middle Ages, the archaic period as similar to early modern Europe, the classical resembled the nineteenth century and the Hellenistic period would be seen as the equivalent of late nineteenth- to early twentieth-century imperialist Europe.

Interestingly enough, though many thinkers fostered the approach on theoretical grounds, and it was applied to Roman history by Niebuhr and Mommsen, it was not applied to Greek history until the last decades of the nineteenth century, with the work of Beloch and Meyer.[102] Indeed, from Niebuhr onwards the majority of German historians turned their attention to Roman history for two generations.[103] We have learnt in the last few decades how misleading their modernist assumptions for the nature of the ancient economy and society have been.[104] What has seldom been grasped is that their attempt to actualise their narratives of ancient history was revolutionary and valid, despite the fallacy of their modernist assumptions. The overthrow of modernism, followed by the dominance of an approach

---

[98] For the theory, and its English adherents, see Forbes 1952: 12–65.

[99] *Thucydides, I*, Appendix 1, Oxford, 1830, 636.

[100] A somewhat similar idea, the biological metaphor of phases of birth, acme and decline, is more general and could in fact easily be accommodated with all three different approaches. The Viconian approach is quite different, though not necessarily contrary.

[101] Turner 1981: 25–30.

[102] Characteristically, Arnold wrote a Roman history, but no history of Greece.

[103] Yavetz 1976; see also Turner 1989 for the opposite development in Britain.

[104] Demolished effectively in Finley 1973b.

influenced by the French structuralist distantiation, should accordingly b[e] viewed with mixed feelings.

The last approach can be described as evolutionist or developmenta[l]. There were indeed many different sources of this approach.[105] One wa[s] Scottish conjectural history;[106] another, related to the first one, were th[e] evolutionary schemes deriving from the sociology of Saint-Simon an[d] Comte;[107] and, finally, there were the various philosophies of history tha[t] followed in the wake of Herder.[108] Probably the best indication of why al[l] these currents should be seen together is that Marxism, another develop-mental approach,[109] was equally influenced by all three of them.[110] I wil[l] focus here on the philosophies of history, simply because they present my point more clearly. They had strong philosophical overtones. Yet, the fact that few scholars subscribe to these nowadays should not obstruct from our view the real influence of this approach.

In every philosophy of history, each society or civilisation is viewed from the perspective of how, or what, it has contributed to the larger process at hand (whether the development of the Spirit, Civilisation, the West, the State, Capitalism, etc.), and only to the extent that it has done so.[111] Combining a Christian perception of a linear history moving towards redemption, and the argument of the *modernes* that the world was actually advancing, the new philosophies of history were showing not Greeks borrowing from Orientals, or any other primeval source of wisdom and civilisation, but each society and civilisation building upon the foundations of their predecessors and thus leaving them behind for ever: thus, the Greeks built upon the Orientals and superseded them, the Romans upon the Greeks, etc.[112] This perspective had a double effect. It meant that Greek history was inserted as part of a process that was clearly Eurocentric. Greek history existed as an independent field only as a stage in the larger Eurocentric development: otherwise, later periods of Greek history were subsumed under the Roman empire; the history of Greek communities

---

[105] Mandelbaum 1971: 41–138 argues, convincingly in my view, that they should be treated together.
[106] Meek 1976.
[107] Here one has to include nineteenth-century evolutionist anthropology; see Burrow 1967; Stocking 1987. For the approaches to Greek history of Condorcet and Comte, see Garlan 2000b and Fedi 2000 respectively.
[108] J. G. Herder, *Ideen zur Philosophie der Geschichte der Menschheit*, Riga and Leipzig, 1784–91; F. von Schlegel, *Philosophie der Geschichte*, Vienna, 1805–6; G. W. F. Hegel, *Vorlesungen über die Philosophie der Geschichte*, Berlin, 1837. See Bravo 1968: 140–68; Krieger 1989.
[109] It has of course to be said that not all forms of Marxism are developmental. For a defence of an alternative form of Marxism, see Thompson 1978.
[110] On Marxism, temporalities and ancient history, see, with caution, Lekas 1988.
[111] See in general Sampson 1956.   [112] Bernal 1987: 196–201.

after the classical period had no interest in itself and was not studied from a Greek perspective.[113] When later Droysen, under the heavy influence of Hegel's philosophy of history, came to invent the concept of *Hellenismus*, as a new stage in the development of world history, the history of Greek communities in the last three centuries BCE was subsumed within this new stage.[114] It also meant that Greek history was seen to have a unity, only to the extent that it was such a stage in the Eurocentric progression; no other conception of Greek history was admissible.

The new philosophies of history created, therefore, a radical distinction between an ancient Orient which had remained static, and a Greece which came now to be totally separated and inserted, under certain terms, in the Eurocentric narrative. In a sense, the belief in the existence of two different entities, the East and the West, can be traced back to the ancient Greeks.[115] The discourse, to use Foucault's terminology, started thousands of years ago; but until the nineteenth century, the Orient could still be seen as superior to the West in a number of respects, or even as a model to be followed by the West. The Industrial Revolution and the imperialist run of the long nineteenth century created a fundamentally new perception of the differences between the East and the West. All the great thinkers of the nineteenth century strove to explain what separated the East and the West and explained their allegedly divergent paths. Greece then was critical, in being the original and primeval West. It had nothing to do anymore with the East. Antiquity came to be restricted to the Greeks and the Romans: the Near Eastern societies and cultures were to be excluded from the *Altertumswissenschaft*.[116] The invention of the Indo-European racial discourse helped further to severe the links with the East; the Eastern contributions and connections were systematically minimised and denigrated.[117] Greek history then was withdrawn from accounts of universal history; it acquired its own beginning and end.

Thus, we can see how three temporalities of antiquity and Greek history emerged. The one posed an unbridgeable gap between antiquity and modernity; it constructed antiquity as a homogeneous and unified entity, on the basis of how it differed from modernity, and it largely saw no

---

[113] For the effects created on the study of the ancient Near East by this passing the torch approach, see Larsen 1989.

[114] See Bravo 1968; Canfora 1987; Wagner 1991.

[115] See Hall 1989; see also the alternative reactions described in Springborg 1992.

[116] For F.A. Wolf's exclusion of the Near East from his conception of antiquity, see Meyer-Zwiffelhoffer 1995: 249–50.

[117] Bernal 1987: 189–399.

developmental link between antiquity and modernity. On the contrary, the emergence of modernity was usually attributed to some fundamental discontinuity that took place in Europe in the late Middle Ages.[118]

The second approach was more positive to the idea that antiquity was not a homogeneous entity; it distinguished between different periods within antiquity, and argued that every ancient society had seen phases of development and change; it argued that the best way to understand them was by comparing different periods of antiquity with their counterparts in modern times. This approach was more historically sensitive; but what marred it ultimately, was again its Eurocentric and modernist angle. Historical change and development could be seen only on the terms posed by change and development in modern European history: the expansion of trade, the emergence of the bourgeoisie, the decline of superstition, etc. The German modernist approach, as we will see in later pages, followed this approach and fell with the demise of its theoretical foundation.

The third approach (evolutionism and philosophy of history) created the long-term narrative into which Greek history was inserted, and helped to set the terms on which Greek history would become an independent field. It ensured that Greek history existed as an independent field only to the extent that it formed a stage in the larger Eurocentric process. In the archaic and classical periods, when it existed as an independent field, it was abstracted from the larger Mediterranean and Near Eastern background that it formed part; in the later Hellenistic and Roman periods, it was subsumed under the stages of *Hellenismus* and Rome. The effects that this had on the study of Greek history will be analysed later on.

The three different approaches were not always mutually exclusive. Herder discovered both national individuality *and* a philosophy of history which saw nations from the perspective of how they contributed to the process of universal history.[119] Fustel was adamant on the unbridgeable gap between antiquity and modernity, and engaged in a structural analysis of ancient society, and yet saw the modern world emerging out of antiquity as a result of a series of revolutions.[120] The liberal Anglican followers of Vico and Niebuhr could see both recurring stages of national development in all periods of history *and* a universal progression of history.[121] There was, and still is, plenty of space for ambiguities and contradictions here.

---

[118] E.g. Smith 1976: Book III, iii. The work of Moses Finley is probably the best example of the continuation of this approach until the present. In Finley's case, the influence of Hume is clearly strong. See Finley 1973b: 21–2, 137.

[119] See Meinecke 1972: 322–61.   [120] Momigliano 1970: 333–7.   [121] Forbes 1952: 55–86.

CONSTRUCTING THE SUBJECT

French revolutionaries attempted to change society by decree. In this respect they were following the glorious ancient tradition of the wise lawgiver; and they were within the limits of a civic humanist discourse. The response of liberals and conservatives to the Jacobin experiment led to the final demise of this discourse. What they both tried to argue was that society could not be reformed by will, because it was not a voluntary association of individuals; instead, society was a machine, with clear and well-regulated laws of function.[122] Revolutionary attempts to remake society at will would end up in anarchy, terror and, ultimately, despotism. One should pay respect to the laws of social function, in order to effect any change. Moreover, every society had a distinct past: it had evolved according to its own inherent pattern and the attempt to disregard this past and employ in one society recipes that have been invented by another would be catastrophic. Naturally enough, liberals tended to put the stress on the laws of social function, conservatives on the determining importance of the past.

The results were radical. Before the nineteenth century, society (the Greek *koinônia*) was thought of as a limitless aggregate of voluntaristic associations and partnerships;[123] now this notion was superseded by a perception of society as a well-defined and clearly limited mechanism, bringing together individuals and groups with invisible and necessary bonds.[124] In the same way, economy (the Greek *oikonomia*) was thought of as the administration of the household and writ large (in the form of *politikê oikonomia*) the administration of the public realm; now it came to be conceived of as an independent field, a mechanism bringing together individuals and groups, with its own limits, laws and rules.[125] Finally, the ancient conception of government or order (the ancient *politeia*) evolved into the state, a field independent of 'civil society', with its own boundaries and rules and its own internal mechanism.[126]

German intellectuals reacted to the French revolutionary occupation and cultural domination by stressing the particular path of German national history, thus arguing for the importance of national particularity, instead of Enlightenment universality. Surely, one must here clearly differentiate between the combination of universal history, cultural interaction

---

[122] The debate had already started in England in the eighteenth century; see Pocock 1975a, 1985; see also Goldsmith 1987. For the liberal argument, in particular in connection with antiquity, see Avlami 2000b.
[123] On the evidence about pre-revolutionary France, see Baker 2001.
[124] See Wokler 1987.   [125] Tribe 1978.   [126] Skinner 2002.

and national individuality in early thinkers such as Herder, and the exclusionist, internalist and racialist conceptions of nationalism that developed later in the nineteenth century.[127] But it is the later conception that had the lasting effects and with which we are here primarily concerned. The voluntaristic conception of society in the civic humanist discourse was substituted by the objectivist conception of nationalism. Nationalist discourse argued for an isomorphism between language, society, culture and state: all these were co-extending boundaries that distinguished one *Volk* from the other.[128] Therefore, the Greeks had their own national identity that distinguished them from other contemporary peoples. The aim of historical study, as we will see propounded in a while, was to recover this national identity.

These developments shaped the conception of the subject of Greek history. Greeks were now credited with a distinct form of society, a distinct form of economy and a distinct form of state: there might be differences between them, which could easily be explained within the evolutionary scheme (e.g. the *ethnê* as tribal survivals), but overall they shared enough for there to be a distinctive form of Greek society, economy and state. This can be easily observed by tracing the changing vocabulary of the works written in the first half of the nineteenth century, as Wilfried Gawantka has done.[129] The references to the 'civitates et populi Graecorum' or the 'Griechische Staat*en*kunde', implying the multiformity of Greek communities and polities, are gradually replaced by references to *the* Greek conception of the state and ultimately to *the* Greek form of the state; the idea that each people ought to have its own distinct form of state was established.

These influences became evident only gradually; it was not before the next period that they transformed radically the nature and genres of Greek history. During this period, the *Antiquitates* continued on a larger than ever scale and with the same antiquarian aims.[130] But there emerged a significant difference: instead of recording the variety of institutions and customs of the multiplicity of ancient Greek communities, priorities now diverged. The *Antiquitates* were now restricted, almost without exception,

---

[127] On this distinction, and in particular concerning Herder, see Berlin 1977: 145–216. The issue has particular relevance for the evaluation of the work of K. O. Müller.

[128] See Thom 1995.   [129] See Gawantka 1985: 79–110.

[130] See F. W. Tittmann, *Darstellung der griechischen Staatsverfassungen*, Leipzig, 1822; K. F. Hermann, *Lehrbuch der griechischen Staatsalterthümer*, Göttingen, 1831; G. F. Schoemann, *Griechische Alterthümer*, Berlin, 1855; G. Gilbert, *Handbuch der Griechischen Staatsaltertümer*, Leipzig, 1881. The masterpiece of the *Antiquitates* is of course A. Böckh, *Die Staatshaushaltung der Athener*, Berlin, 1817.

to three Greek polities: the Spartan, the Athenian and the Cretan.[131] On the
one hand this reflected the focus on contemporary political issues that lay
behind the creation of Greek history by British scholars; on the other hand,
these three forms of polities were taken to be representative of the two
variants of the Greek nation, the Dorian and the Ionian race. The nationalist and racialist aspirations and discourses of the period created the
powerful image of the *Volk*: the belief that there exist collective entities
called nations, with their own distinct personalities, characteristics and
features. In direct contrast to the preoccupation of previous works, the
message of the new works that appeared in this period was clear:

The real subject area of Greek antiquities is the direct expressions of the national
character . . . Before people saw the Greek antiquities as such as the premonition of
their own, all-pervading *Volksgeist*, the understanding of what were called Greek
Antiquitates was restricted to a large extent to learned, but dull, compilations . . .
The gigantic progress in the last twenty or thirty years has found its completion in
the efforts of nowadays, which centre all particularities of the rich Greek life in
historical conception under the focal point of the national spirit and the idea of
the state.[132]

We see then for the first time an attempt to delineate what was *the*
particular Greek form for every aspect of political, economic, social and
cultural life. Not any more the different characteristics of each particular
Greek community, but the particular ones of Greeks in general, as a
collective, but unified, entity. Finally, it is interesting to note the structure
of those *Altertumskunde*: in many cases, the books are divided into two
parts, under the titles of 'Geschichte' and 'Antiquitates': the historical part
narrates the political and military history, while the antiquarian part
describes those aspects of economic, social and cultural life that have not
yet made their entrance to the narrative part. The attempts to overcome
this dichotomy will be one of the most marked characteristics of the next
period, when the reshaping of the subject matter of the *Antiquitates*
changed the nature of ancient Greek history for good.[133]

HISTORICAL NARRATIVE

It is time to see how the new temporalities and new constructions of subject
were applied to the study of the new field that Greek history constituted.
But here we have to complicate our account by introducing a further factor.

[131] Gawantka 1985: 146–8.   [132] Hermann, *Lehrbuch der griechischen Staatsalterhümer* §§ 1–2.
[133] On the *Antiquitates* in the nineteenth century, see Gawantka 1990.

The first narratives of ancient Greek history had a distinct origin. They were the results of the politicisation of Greek history in the age of the American and French Revolutions; and they were to a great extent a native product of Britain.[134] The creation of a history of ancient Greece in the late eighteenth and early nineteenth centuries served clear and important political aims.[135] The first histories of Greece by Gillies[136] and Mitford[137] were conservative reactions to the anti-royal, republican and democratic messages of the American and French Revolutions; the study of ancient Greek history revealed the follies and crimes of popular rule and the merits of the mixed constitution. Thirlwall's[138] and Grote's[139] histories were a powerful defence of the liberal ideas of political representation and freedom.[140] The British reaction was, in terms of its theoretical foundations, the most conservative, in comparison to the French and German scholars we have dealt with. No important questions about the particular and different nature of Greek society from that of modernity were asked; nor was there any attempt to move beyond the accounts of ancient historians, into those aspects of the economic, social and political activities that were not covered by the ancient historians.[141] The English approach found in Grote its culmination and ultimate intellectual death. Almost no other major and innovative work on ancient Greek history appeared in the English-speaking world in the next hundred years,[142] until the revolutionary work of Moses Finley and G. E. M. de Ste Croix in the post-Second World War period.[143] Nevertheless, the English approach has been crucial, since it provided the model for any subsequent narrative of Greek history.

---

[134] See Turner 1981: 187–234.
[135] 'The early conservative historians of Athens had determined the manner in which its democracy would be considered and examined, and in doing so, they largely established which problems of democratic government would be considered through discussions of Athens. This situation meant that the debate over the Athenian constitution was primarily a debate over the conservative image of democracy, and not over democracy itself'; Turner 1981: 263.
[136] *The History of Ancient Greece, its Colonies and Conquests, I–II*, London, 1786.
[137] *The History of Greece, I–VIII*, London, 1784–1806.
[138] *A History of Greece, I–VIII*, London, 1835–44.
[139] *A History of Greece, I–XII*, London, 1846–56.   [140] Momigliano 1952.
[141] Grote was a banker, yet he introduced no economic factors into his Greek history. The contrast with the contemporary approach of Mommsen could not be more evident: see his *Römische Geschichte*, *I–III*, Leipzig and Berlin, 1854–6.
[142] Partial exceptions are the works of J. P. Mahaffy, *Social Life in Greece from Homer to Menander*, London, 1874; and A. E. Zimmern, *The Greek Commonwealth: Politics and Economics in Fifth-Century Athens*, Oxford, 1911. On Mahaffy, see Stanford and McDowell 1971; on Zimmern Millett n.d. Thanks to Paul Millett for comments and permission to cite his unpublished article.
[143] Both, by the way, outsiders: Finley was American, and both of them were trained as lawyers and not as historians, or classicists.

When modern scholars of the eighteenth and nineteenth century created the history of ancient Greece, they did not follow the Greeks very closely. They put aside almost completely the Greek attempts at universal history. Instead they focused on another tradition of historiography that, although initiated in antiquity, had nothing to do with the Greeks: national history. This is the reason that Arnaldo Momigliano termed one of his chapters in *The Classical Foundations of Modern Historiography* as 'Fabius Pictor and the origins of national history',[144] giving credence for the invention of national history to a Roman, and not to a Greek historian. Therefore, the Diodoran approach, presenting developments synchronously in mainland Greece, Magna Graecia and the Near East was utterly discarded. Diodorus was marginalised into a source to be mined for events that were not covered by the *Hellênika*, chiefly developments in Magna Graecia and the Near East (the different, but equally wide-ranging approach of Herodotus suffered the same fate).

Modern scholars took as their basis the narratives of the *Hellênika*, in order to create a history of a potential nation that was called Greece. It naturally follows that this history of Greece was severely limited: the loss of the vast majority of local histories, the discarding of universal history and the narrative limits and aims of the *Hellênika*, which we have already stressed, created a history of Greece from which seven-tenths of the Greeks were more or less permanently excluded. As finally formulated by Grote in the mid-nineteenth century, the history of ancient Greece came to mean essentially 'Central Greece and the Peloponnese from Solon (or Homer) to Aristotle'. The Greek communities of Magna Graecia, Asia Minor and the Black Sea were not an organic part of the history of Greece; they usually received a treatment in the narrative of the archaic colonisations, and then they were usually forgotten, until they entered the political-military affairs of the great powers of the mainland. And of course, the same holds true for the vast majority of the communities of the mainland, apart from Athens, Sparta, Corinth, Argos and Thebes.

It is fascinating to find this problem raised in the very first *History of Greece* ever to be written in 1707:

But as the affairs of Greece and Rome were very different, so they could not be related altogether after the same manner. Rome you see at one view, as well in its progress, as its rise ... Which makes their affairs admit of a more clear and even thread than the Grecians; who, besides that they had to do with most parts of the then known world, were among themselves so many distinct republicks, almost

---

[144] Momigliano 1990: 80–108.

wholly independent one of another, differing in laws and customs ... To (relate their matters in a more united manner) with the less confusion, I have observ'd a rule of referring the chief transactions to Athens as the head, and mentioning the other states only as they had dependence on it.[145]

This exclusion was not simply the result of the loss of ancient information. One reason was the presentism dominating the British approach, whose practitioners were the inventors of Greek history as an independent field. The political relevance of Greek history necessitated a focus on those communities whose political and military history could be written using the fragments of ancient historiography that had survived. Therefore, accounts of Greek history concentrated on Athens and Sparta (and of course later Macedonia).

But there were more lasting causes at work. Once the history of the Greek polities was constructed as a history of a national entity called Greece, its character necessarily changed. The history of Greece was some- thing more than the aggregate of the individual histories of the Greek polities: in fact, the history of the individual polities was important only to the extent that it was relevant for this quasi-national history of Greece. The Greeks were now identified as a *Volk*, with a distinct identity and destiny that surpassed those of its individual members. The history of Greece was therefore a history of an imagined entity and not a history of the Greek communities: this is the reason that the history of Greece could end with Chaironeia, although the history of the Greek communities obviously continued beyond this point. Again, this is the reason that the history of the Greek communities in Asia Minor or the Black Sea has no organic connection with the history of Greece: their history cannot follow the pattern of a national history with a clear progression and destiny – an account with rise, acme, decline and fall.

This becomes most clear if one considers the fate of those communities that form the nucleus of the history of Greece (e.g. Athens or Sparta) in the post-Chaironeia accounts. Try to find an account of mainland Greece as such in the Hellenistic period and you will utterly fail: the history of these communities is now amalgamated into an account of the relations between Hellenistic monarchies. There has never been a history of Hellenistic Greece or of Greece in the Hellenistic period; the history of Greece has no independent existence any more. This is obviously not simply because the fate of those Greek communities was fundamentally linked with those larger monarchies. The history of fourth-century Greek communities was

---

[145] Stanyan, *The Grecian History*, unnumbered pages of the preface of vol. 1.

equally enmeshed in relations with Persia (Persian funding of Greek wars, Greek communities sending their citizens as allies to fight Persian wars, Greek mercenaries in Persian armies, Greeks high in the service of Persians, Persians fighting Greeks); yet you will never find an account of fourth-century Greek communities under the heading 'Persia and Greece', while it seems perfectly legitimate to title the same account of the third century as 'Macedonia and Greece'.[146]

The history of the Greek communities was amalgamated under an entity called ancient Greece, which along with Rome formed the ancestors of the West. The incommensurability between the two linked entities (on the one hand a huge number of communities scattered in space and without political, economic or social unity, and on the other hand a city-state and a city-empire with clear beginning and end) created little problem, since it played perfectly the role it was assigned within this Eurocentric discourse. If ancient Greece was to be an ancestor of the West, before passing the sceptre to Rome, it had to have a beginning and an end (just as the Orient, in most Western handbooks, has no history after it has passed the torch of progress to the Greeks). Thence arose the great debate about the origins of ancient Greece and the end of Greek history.

Before finishing this part, it is useful again to draw attention to an exceptional case: the reference is to Karl Otfried Müller, the only important German historian of this period who dealt with Greek history.[147] As we shall see, the work of Müller embodies most of the characteristics of the formative period of Greek history between the French Revolution and the 1860s; at the same time he spans the gulf between the two different currents that will crystallise in the next period (the one represented by Fustel and Burckhardt, the other by Meyer, Beloch and Rostovtzeff). Müller was one of the key figures in the separation of Greek history from that of the Near East, and in its independent treatment;[148] moreover, the new concepts of nationalism and racialism played a key role in his perception of Greek history.[149]

He conceived a Greek history that was the amalgam of the interactions and conflicts between the various Greek *Stämme* and *Städte*. His project

---

[146] This note is even more strengthened when one is reminded that the accounts of the third century were constructed by modern scholars *ex nihilo*. The loss of any ancient continuous narrative of this period could have enabled a variety of narrative constructions; yet, the almost total unanimity shows the strong ideological bias under work.

[147] For Müller see the volume dedicated to him in *ASNP* 14, 1984; the conference in Calder and Schlesier 1998; and Momigliano 1985.

[148] For his role, see Bernal 1987: 308–16; but see a necessary, if pedantic, corrective in Blok 1996.

[149] See the comments of Losemann 1998.

then had a two-fold character: on the one hand, the writing of Greek history should be based on the inclusion of the variety of Greek *Stämme* and cities; therefore a variety of regional histories was necessary, before one could embark on the writing of a synthetic Greek history.[150] Müller planned to cover the totality of Greek communities and was the first to give great importance to the geographical setting for the history of every Greek community.[151] On the other hand, he attempted to study the economic, social, political and cultural aspects of each city or *Stamm* as an organic and coherent unity. And, in fact, here was the tendency to construct ideal types and representations, as when he took Sparta as the ideal personification of the imaginary Dorian state.[152]

Müller stands one step before the invention of the polis as the organising principle of Greek history. But what is fascinating in his work is the way his racial analysis creates a middle path between the static and a-chronic structural analysis of the Fustel – Burckhardt current, and the dynamic and interactive narrative of Meyer, Beloch and Rostovtzeff. He anticipated Fustel and Burckhardt by creating a holistic image of the 'Dorian polis' (to which an 'Ionian polis' would be the equivalent); but recognising that Greece included a variety of different *Stämme*, with different character-istics, opened the way for a multiform picture and a dynamic analysis of the interactions between the different *Stämme* and cities and the variety of interlinking factors that created the differences between the various *Stämme* and cities.[153] Müller did not live to write his synthetic narrative of Greek history; we can only regret the loss and simply speculate about the way he would have constructed a synthesis of the history of his various *Stämme*.[154]

---

[150] These regional studies started with his monograph on Aegina in 1817, the first monograph on a Greek city ever to be written; followed by the three volumes of the series *Geschichten Hellenischer Stämme und Städte*: *Orchomenos und die Minyer*, Breslau, 1820; and the two-volume *Die Dorier*, Breslau, 1824.

[151] His eagerness in this respect caused his untimely death. In 1839 he asked for a year's leave to visit Greece: 'From the beginnings of my publications I have always contemplated a systematic and detailed history of Greece. I have given twenty years to studies directed to this end ... I need a knowledge of the places, in order to compare and revise the results of my geographical and topographical studies with the reality'; translated in Gooch 1913: 40. After a visit in various parts of Greece, he died from sunstroke, while copying inscriptions at Delphi; Gehrke 1991.

[152] Janni 1968; Wittenburg 1984.

[153] For example, Müller attributes the different character of the Ionian *Stamm* to its interaction with the Near East and to the role of trade; *Die Dorier*, II, 4.

[154] This approach was severely criticised by Will 1956 in the aftermath of the defeat of Nazism and the discrediting of racialism. But to Müller's tribute, the path he opened to the exploration of regional divergences and the formation of regional and ethnic identities, has recently began to be re-explored with fascinating results; see Hall 1997, 2002; McInerney 2000.

Fustel de Coulanges, La cité

1860S TO THE SECOND WORLD WAR: RESTRUCTURING AND THE COMPETING CURRENTS

In the last decades of the nineteenth century the study of ancient history was reshaped by the influence of two contrasting broad currents. We can identify the beginnings of the first current with the works of Fustel de Coulanges[155] and Jakob Burckhardt.[156] The second current can be identified with what has been labelled the 'modernist tradition' in ancient history: the works of Eduard Meyer,[157] K. J. Beloch[158] and M. I. Rostovtzeff[159] are in this tradition, although I will argue that they share a lot with the approaches of other scholars, not usually thought of as modernists. The study of Greek history was finally dominated in the second half of the twentieth century by approaches that stem from my first current; while the second current was driven underground and has remained a minority position since. The great importance of the concept of the polis is clearly related to the emergence and final victory of the first current. I hope to show that, notwithstanding its many faults, the second current also had extremely important merits.

It must be stressed that each individual scholar did not share all the views of the others that I include under the same current; hence 'currents' and not 'schools'. The difference between the strong anti-Semitism and racialism of Beloch and the views of Meyer is well known and led to very different perceptions on issues that involved this aspect; but their overall affinities were strong, as they themselves recognised.[160] Equally important, the two different currents shared features both in their attempts to restructure the history of ancient Greece, as constructed in the previous period, and in the limitations that had been imposed on the history of ancient Greece, to which we already referred previously. Yet, I will still maintain that the second current contained seeds that might have enabled the overcoming of these limits.

---

[155] Fustel de Coulanges, *La cité.*; on Fustel, see Hartog 1988b.
[156] J. Burckhardt, *Griechische Kulturgeschichte.*; on Burckhardt, see Momigliano 1955; Christ 1972: 119–60, 1988; Janssen 1979; Gossman 2000.
[157] Christ 1972: 286–333; Momigliano 1977a, 1981; Calder and Demandt 1990.
[158] Momigliano 1966a; Christ 1972: 248–85; Polverini 1979, 1990.
[159] Momigliano 1954; Christ 1972: 334–49; Fears 1990.
[160] Polverini 1988. But both of them were extremely right-wing in their political views. Oswyn Murray has pointed out to me that there may have been something important historiographically in being right-wing in this period; after all, it was the Nazi Berve (Berve 1937) who first asked explicitly the question 'When did the polis rise?', leading to Ehrenberg's answer, which set the post-war consensus. See Canfora 1989: 63–79 (Meyer), 169–220 (Berve).

Jakob Burckhard's (handwritten)

THE FIRST CURRENT: FUSTEL AND BURCKHARDT

The British creation of a history of ancient Greece in the period 1770–1850 went hand in hand with a proliferation of *Altertumskunde* by German scholars. But there seemed to be no connections between the continuous narratives of political and military events, as presented in the politically motivated accounts of the British historians, and the static and systematic presentations of the economic, social and cultural aspects of the German *Altertumskunde*. It is not a matter of chance, I think, that there were almost no general histories of Greece written by German historians in that period.[161] This division of labour, between political narrative and *Altertumskunde*, broke down for good in the second half of the nineteenth century.

Both Fustel and Burckhardt managed to overcome this division, although they had different aims and stemmed from different traditions.[162] Jakob Burckhardt's work was the first work to introduce the very concept of the polis into the study of ancient history.[163] The aim of his *Kulturgeschichte* was to present an organic account of the interrelationships between the various cultural and social phenomena that had previously been presented in the static and unconnected manner of the *Antiquitates*. He also presented the development and change through time of Greek social, political and cultural history, in contrast to the static presentation of the *Antiquitates*.[164]

The new antiquarianism of the nineteenth century, like that of the seventeenth and eighteenth centuries, was an answer to Pyrrhonism; but unlike the earlier antiquarianism it claimed to be able to penetrate beyond phenomena into the spirit of the people and the structure of a political organisation. It was a study of antiquity revised in accordance with romantic notions of national character and the organic state, which in its turn paved the way for the sociological investigation of the ancient world introduced by Max Weber.[165]

Fustel was a direct descendant of the *Idéologues*. His work was another attempt to defend private property and the liberty of the moderns from radicalism and a false use of antiquity. Fustel's work was influenced by the anthropological discussions of the past and future of humanity, and of such issues as the origin and evolution of family, private property, customs and

---

[161] See the arguments of Funke 1996: 93–6. This is in contradistinction with the work of German scholars in Roman history, as for example Niebuhr, Nitzsch and Mommsen. The only important exception to the above rule is the *Griechische Geschichte* by Ernst Curtius. But it belongs to a quite different tradition than Niebuhr and Mommsen, and later Meyer and Beloch. See Christ 1988.

[162] Though they both shared a hostility towards source criticism and German historical philology: for such reactions, see Gossman 1983.

[163] See Gawantka 1985.   [164] Nippel 1998.   [165] Momigliano 1955: 297.

The creation of the Roman cosmopolitan Empire

religion, political institutions and the state.[166] He raised the issue of the relation between family, private property and religion, and the ancient city. He attempted to show that the original Indo-European institution of the family was based on private property and was held together by its domestic religion of the ancestral spirits. The growing unification of families into tribes, and finally cities, and the series of political revolutions that made possible the incorporation of the plebeians resulted in a continuous crisis of the ancient city, which was resolved only by the Roman conquest and the creation of the Roman cosmopolitan empire.[167]

In his account, we can already find some of the dominant characteristics of the approach to the polis still present nowadays. Fustel was influenced by the Indo-European racial discourse. The ancient city had evolved from the original Indo-European institutions: it had nothing to do with the Semitic Orient, neither was its form influenced or shaped by the varying relations to it. His ancient city had no real place in time and space. It did not really matter *when* the changes in the institutions that he had portrayed had taken place; nor was the geographical position of any importance for the evolution of the ancient city. Finally, his ancient city was unitary: it did not really matter that ancient Greek communities had very important differences between them, or in comparison to the Romans; there could have been exceptions to the rule, or varieties of the norm. The important feature was indeed that there existed an ancient city as a specific and distinct form of society and state, which could be portrayed as an organism with emergence, acme and fall.

This kind of approach can be described by two labels: functionalism and evolutionism. I use the word functionalism to describe the belief that entities like society, economy and state have their own discrete boundaries and their own laws and functions.[168] They can be portrayed in either organicist (society as an organism) or in mechanistic terms (society as a machine), but the important notion is that they form totalities with clear boundaries. I use evolutionism to describe the belief that these societies, economies and states move progressively (or regressively, which is the same thing) and wholeheartedly from one point or stage of the sequence to the next.[169] Functionalism and evolutionism are not opponents, as so often they have been portrayed.[170] In fact, one cannot exist without the other. If societies are

---

[166] We can simply mention the names of Maurer, Haxthausen and Maine; see Momigliano 1982b: 236–44; Nippel 1990b: 96–101.
[167] Momigliano 1970.   [168] See Perlin 1985a, 1994b.   [169] See Yoffee 1993.
[170] See the comments of Burrow 1967: 190–213.

Fri June 20 | 6:30 pm Perlin

well-bound entities, where each part serves the maintenance of the whole, then the only way to envisage history is through a progressive succession of different forms of societies, different stages and different types. Societies just move from one typology to the other, from one stage to the next. Functionalism and evolutionism are just interested in different aspects, the one in synchrony, the other in diachrony; but they share the same fundamental assumptions.[175]

Fustel's *Ancient City* was the introduction of these ways of thinking to ancient history.[172] In his work the ancient city was envisaged as a substance or entity that developed through a sequence of revolutions in a unidirectional way. The functionalist principle was evident in his attempt to see the multiplicity of polities and communities in their various histories as the exemplification of a single homogeneous and well-structured entity; the evolutionary principle was seen in his portrayal of the sequence of events in a unilinear development from simpler to higher forms of organisation. Fustel had a double influence: on the one hand through his student Emile Durkheim he influenced the creation of French functionalist sociology and anthropology; and on the other hand through Gustave Glotz[173] and Louis Gernet[174] the creation of the French school in ancient history.[175] Fustel was followed by generations who tried to account for the evolution of the Greek polis from its tribal origins. The modern discussion of the emergence of the polis is a direct descendant of this kind of approach.

THE SECOND CURRENT: MEYER, BELOCH AND ROSTOVTZEFF

The other current followed a very different path. It attempted to unite the narrative of the political and military events with the social, economic and cultural aspects that were treated in a systematic and static way in the *Antiquitates*. In order to do so, the scholars of this current challenged a number of key characteristics of the history of ancient Greece as it had evolved in the period 1770–1850. Their most revolutionary achievement was the emancipation of economic and social aspects from the static

---

[171] Many typologies based on these premises have been created, some more, some less, successful. The most influential is probably one *implied* by Marx: Asiatic mode of production, slave mode of production, feudalism and capitalism. Max Weber has offered various classifications according to the category studied, as e.g. between the consumer and the producer city. Durkheim offered a classification of societies with organic and with mechanic solidarity. Finally, the neo-evolutionists offered the classification of band-tribe-chiefdom-state.

[172] See Billeter 1911: 325–35.　[173] See his fundamental work *La cité grecque*, Paris, 1928.

[174] Di Donato 1990: 3–130; Humphreys 1978: 76–106.　[175] See Momigliano 1970: 325–6.

presentation of the *Antiquitates*.[176] They viewed the material culture and the human population as factors of change and readjustment for the totality of human relationships. To give one example, the study of demography was emancipated from the antiquarian researches into the populousness of ancient cities; instead, demography was treated as a factor of economic, social and political change, shaping economic development and political history. The inclusion of a whole chapter on population in Beloch's *Griechische Geschichte* was a complete revolution, if compared with the structure of Grote's *History of Greece*, in which such questions were confined to footnotes. In the same way, trade was no more relegated to the static descriptions of the *Griechische Privataltertümer*: it became a part of the narrative structure, explaining changes, causing wars, establishing relations. I will call these scholars modernists, because in their attempt to create a dynamic history, they used the social and economic patterns of modern Europe, in order to make sense of the ancient evidence.

Because of the dynamic character of their fusion of political with economic and social history, the modernists revolutionised their unit of analysis. In contrast to the approach of Fustel, the unit of analysis is not any more the individual city or the imaginary unitary entity called Greece: the modernists are interested in relationships between communities, both between Greek communities, and between Greeks and others. This opens a Mediterranean-wide vista of interrelationships with two effects: on the one hand, the traditional focus on Athens and Sparta and the exclusion of the vast majority of Greek communities shows some signs of breaking down; on the other hand, geography and the role of space becomes an important factor in the study of these interrelationships.

Meyer, who was an equally competent Orientalist and Hellenist, wrote his monumental *Geschichte des Altertums* in an attempt to study together the history of the societies of Eastern Mediterranean and trace parallel developments, interactions and relationships.[177] Meyer was clear that national history in the form of the progression of an ideal entity was not feasible:

It is therefore wrong to look at the nations for the unity of history and to abstract out of their fates the norms of historical development. An independent national history does not exist at all; rather, all peoples, which are linked together politically

---

[176] The young Moses Finley did indeed recognise this; see Nafissi 2005: 203–8.
[177] 'If anywhere, it is therefore here that there is a complete, unitary illustration, which integrates the individual histories as subordinate parts of this greater context. Such a treatment can only be synchronic'; Meyer 1907: 247.

and culturally in lasting connections, build an indissoluble unit of history, *until these connections are again dissolved due to the course of historical development* [italics mine].[178]

Everyone who has read Rostovtzeff's account of the fourth century BCE will be amazed by his attempt to bring forward the interrelationships between the Greek communities of mainland Greece, Asia Minor, the Black Sea and Magna Graecia.[179] Furthermore, he was instrumental in studying places and areas of interaction between Greeks and other cultures, from Dura in Mesopotamia to Scythia.[180] It is also notable that he wrote a *History of the Ancient World*, in which he included the history of the Near East; thus, he was the last ancient historian ever to deal with the history of Near Eastern societies.[181]

The geographical studies of German scholars at the end of the nineteenth century,[182] and their successors in British works, like those of J. L. Myres, attempted to study further the geographical background of these interrelationships, focusing on regional settings and interregional links.[183] The works of German scholars in the 1950s, such as *Die griechische Polis als historisch-geographisches Problem des Mittelmeerraumes*[184] and *Abhängige Orte im griechischen Altertum*,[185] are the last products of this current, before the domination of the other current. Thus, the modernists objected to the functionalism of the Fustelian current, by refusing to take the polis as the sole unit of analysis and by inserting Greek poleis within the wider Near Eastern and Mediterranean world.

They also argued against evolutionism. They refused to see history as the realisation of an idea, or the actualisation of a determinist pattern of evolution. Beloch and Meyer fought fiercely against the evolutionist attempts to portray a unified picture of antiquity in the form of a stage in a unilinear evolution. Different groups presented such unified pictures and evolutionary schemes. Fustel, and other anthropological historians, homogenised antiquity through the concept of the ancient city as part of the evolution of Indo-European society, or of the transition from tribe to state. The *Nationalökonomen*, such as Rodbertus and Bücher,[186] presented a homogeneous antiquity as the first, the *oikos* stage, in the evolution of the

---

[178] Meyer 1910: 41. It is significant that Meyer had a positive view of the work of Heeren, whom he viewed as his predecessor; 1907: 248.
[179] See the chapter 'The ancient world in the fourth century' in Rostovtzeff 1941.
[180] Rostovtzeff 1922, 1932. I would like to thank Oswyn Murray for pointing this out to me.
[181] Rostovtzeff 1926. David Lewis is the only effective exception to this rule.
[182] E.g. Philippson 1904.   [183] Myres 1953b.   [184] Kirsten 1956.   [185] Gschnitzer 1958.
[186] See the articles in Mommsen and Osterhammel 1989; Schneider 1990.

economy to the city-stage (Middle Ages) and the national stage (modernity). Marxists homogenised antiquity through the concept of the slave mode of production, seen as part of the evolution of society through feudalism to capitalism.[187]

On the contrary, the modernists tried to show the multiplicity of economic and social patterns prevailing in the Mediterranean world of antiquity; they showed that different areas had followed very different paths, and laid the foundations for an economic geography of the Mediterranean; their modernist inclination had the beneficial effect of driving them away from a notion of an unilinear progress of the West from antiquity through Middle Ages to modernity.[188] Meyer wrote an introduction to his *Geschichte des Altertums* called 'Elemente der Anthropologie' in an attempt to counter the theories of evolutionary anthropology.[189] He attacked fiercely the notion of an evolution from family through tribe to state, which saw the polis as an evolution from a tribal society, and the Greek *phylai* as remnants of this tribal past.[190] Characteristically, although it was Meyer who was proved correct by modern research,[191] and not the generations of evolutionist historians, such as Glotz and Gernet, scarcely anybody went back to look at what he was trying to say.[192] For this reason, the polis, as the specific Greek form of state, or as a stage in the evolution of Greek society, did not loom large on the work of the modernists.

Periodisation was an important issue in these attempts at reassessment.[193] The discovery of the Mycenaean and Minoan civilisations in the

---

[187] Ciccotti 1897. For the whole debate see Nafissi 2005: 17–54.
[188] Paradoxically, Finley came ultimately to a position very close to that of Meyer on the general historical development in antiquity. Instead of the unilinear development of one stage to the next, supported e.g. by Marxists, he came to see antiquity moving in a cyclical way from societies based on a spectrum of statuses in the archaic period to societies polarised on the free/slave line and back into a spectrum society in late antiquity; Finley 1981a: 132. See Nafissi 2005: 223–9, 243–6.
[189] See Meyer 1907: 10–17.   [190] Capogrossi Colognesi 1984.
[191] Bourriot 1976; Roussel 1976; Finley 1985a. It is notable that, although Finley rightly credits Weber with the anticipation of this discovery, the fact that Weber explicitly identifies himself with Meyer's position (1976: 379) has not provoked any discussion or reconsideration of Meyer.
[192] The exception: Nippel 1990b: 122–3, 1990a: 320–1.
[193] 'What are then the chronological and geographical limits of Greek history? Into what epochs must it be divided? We should close with the battle of Chaironeia, if Greek liberty ceased with it. But that was not the case. Greece lost, it is true, her position in the politics of the world, but still retained some of her internal independence. Several Greek states were as independent after Chaironeia as before it, and in any case it appears hardly appropriate to exclude from the political history of Greece such events as the last attempt to infuse new life into the Spartan community, and the creation of the federate states of the Achaeans and Aetolians. We must therefore go as far as the destruction of Corinth. The geographical boundaries vary at different periods . . . The want of a permanent political centre increases the difficulty of the task, but such a centre is not always absent'; Holm, *The History of Greece*, 6–7.

last decades of the nineteenth century opened a new vista for the study of
ancient history. The modernists were the first to attempt to introduce this
new world into the study of ancient history. Views obviously diverged
widely in those early years. But the modernist agenda of viewing the various
interrelationships between economic, social and political processes found
its way in this discussion too. It is clear that the perception of the new
civilisations was fundamentally influenced by the picture of the Homeric
epics. Meyer and Beloch, who wrote the first historical accounts of the
Mycenaean and Minoan civilisations, did not question that many of their
fundamental characteristics were quite alien to later Greek societies.

Still, instead of creating a fundamental gap between them, they attempted to see how economic and social processes had interacted with powers
of political consolidation and destabilisation to create a variegated picture
of Aegean history from the Minoan to the Roman period.[194] Instead of
talking about Mycenaean territorial kingdoms and Greek city-states, they
pointed out the variety of forms of political organisation in every period.
They pointed out that since the archaic period political organisation could
take the form of a small city and its territory, or a whole region united
under equal terms (Athens), or of a dominant community incorporating
the other free and/or unfree communities of a region (Sparta, Argos, Elis),
or of a region divided between many polities, but with a common political
superstructure, either under a dominant community (Thebes and Boiotia,
Opous and Locrians) or on equal terms (Achaeans, Phocians).[195] It is
impossible to talk about *the* emergence of *the* polis in this sense: one can
talk about a variety of forms of political centralisation or fragmentation,
but not about the emergence of a single unitary entity. The creation of
polities in the Minoan and Mycenaean periods are treated in the same way:
'In any case, it seems that the political fragmentation [of Crete] was
much smaller in the Minoan period, than later in the Greek period.'[196]
J. L. Myres was another characteristic figure of a scholar who could
combine archaeological fieldwork in prehistoric sites with historical geography, history of political ideas and Herodotean studies.[197]

Finally, the attempt to integrate economic, social and political history,
and to depict the interrelationships between wide areas of the Greek and
non-Greek communities, created a revolutionary approach to source use.
The study of economic and social processes, and the due attention to a wide

[194] See, in a similar way, Tritsch 1929.   [195] Meyer 1907: 301–12; Beloch 1913: 202–11.
[196] Beloch 1913: 115. Note that the palaces of Mallia and Zakros had not been found yet.
[197] Myres 1927, 1930, 1953a, 1953b.

variety of communities and regions, necessitated a move away from the restricted focus of the histories of Greece, which were constructed by the use of Greek *Hellênika*; moreover, the necessary use of quantitative data could not be served by those textual sources. The systematic use of the archaeological evidence was the outcome of this novel approach: first, the archaeological evidence was treated as a source of quantitative data that could not be provided by the literary evidence; secondly, the archaeological evidence was the only means of penetration to those Greek communities and regions that were so restrictively covered by the *Hellênika*; finally, material culture was taken seriously and independently as part of the economic, social and cultural life of the ancient Greeks.[198] One need simply look at Rostovtzeff's impressive use of archaeology in his history of the Hellenistic world to diagnose an open path, which was subsequently largely abandoned in the post-war period.

THE POST-WAR PERIOD: THE FORMATION OF THE CURRENT ORTHODOXY

This second current became a minority within ancient history in the post-war period. Offering an explanation for this is a difficult task and I admit I have no satisfactory explanation. One could point to the obvious fallacy of interpreting antiquity through an anachronistic model derived from contemporary experience, but this is not enough of an explanation: some of the modernists were moving very close to recognising the fallacious presuppositions, while maintaining the advantages of their approach.[199] On the other hand, it is clear that in other fields of history, the defeat of modernism did not lead to the extinction of the positive features identified with the second current. Pirenne's modernist account of medieval history was certainly superseded;[200] but it was succeeded by approaches that retained its positive characteristics (such as the *Annaliste* approaches); the contrast with the study of ancient history is more than impressive. One reason of obvious importance that I can put forward is the destruction of the German tradition in ancient history by the effects of the Nazi ascendancy; it cannot be a matter of chance that, in contrast with the pre-Second World War period, most important post-war developments in ancient history have come from England and France (and the USA), to the almost total absence of Germany.[201]

---

[198] See Blakeway 1932/3 and especially Dunbabin 1948.
[199] E.g. Gomme 1937; see the comments of Nafissi 2005: 218–19.
[200] Pirenne 1927.   [201] See Bowersock 1984; Christ 1999.

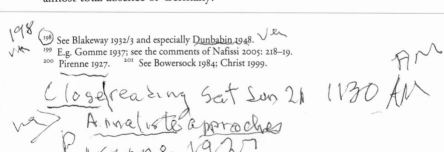

It was not until the post-war period that the concept of the polis finally reigned unchallenged in every field of ancient Greek history. The 'Paris school' made the polis the organising principle of Greek religious and cultural life;[202] Moses Finley introduced the categorical distinction between the Mycenaean redistributive societies, the Dark Ages and the age of the polis[203] and made the polis a key notion for ancient economic and social history;[204] and Victor Ehrenberg's pre-war nomination of the polis as the canonical form of the Greek state now reigned unchallenged.[205] These are the still prevailing contexts of discussion of ancient Greek history. Let us see then which are the major features of the post-war consensus.

One of the most interesting aspects of this period is the abandonment of the comprehensive and large-scale histories of Greece. No major figure in post-war ancient history has attempted to write such a comprehensive history; those histories of Greece that were written through our period, such as those by N. G. L. Hammond or H. Bengtson,[206] lack the overall vision of history, the originality and the influence of their predecessors.[207] It would be a very partial answer to argue that the growth of evidence and literature has rendered the writing of such works by a single author impossible; people with the intellectual capacities of Finley, Momigliano or Ste Croix were certainly capable of doing so, had they wished so.[208] I suggest that the main reason is the abandonment of the modernist approach: since the modernist attempt to incorporate political, economic and social history into a dynamic narrative was deemed a failure, the majority of ancient historians returned to the approaches espoused by the first current of the pre-war period. This decision left the space open for the survival of a positivist political history, largely separated from the accounts of economic and social aspects.[209]

Moreover, links between Greek history and the history of the Near East were now severed. Despite the fact that Orientalism was already strong since the conception of the history of Greece, there was still a window left open to interrelationships, parallel developments and influences. While in

---

[202] Characteristic examples: Vernant 1962; Berard 1984; Bruit Zaidman and Schmitt Pantel 1992.
[203] Finley 1957/8. [204] Finley 1973b: 123–49, 1977, 1985a.
[205] Ehrenberg 1960. It is bewildering to find out that it was not before Ehrenberg 1937 that it occurred to somebody to raise the question 'When did the Greek polis rise?'
[206] Bengtson 1950; Hammond 1959.
[207] Though it might be the case, as Robin Osborne has pointed out to me, that this situation reflects a more general trend of abandoning large-scale narratives in all fields of post-war historiography; see Furet 1984.
[208] Finley indeed attempted to do so, but abandoned the plan; see Shaw 1993.
[209] This is still the prevailing approach in e.g. Hornblower 2002; Rhodes 2006.

Start reading again Saturday Jun 21
at 1:05 PM.
Stop Saturday June 21 2 PM
2:13 PM

the age of Eduard Meyer the fast discovery of new cuneiform texts and the great progress in their decipherment and study had led to works such as the monumental *Geschichte des Altertums*, in this period the lack of interest was almost complete. Ancient historians have lost contact with developments within the field of Near Eastern studies. Meyer's conception of a fundamentally unitary history of antiquity was now decisively erased by a new Eurocentric conception of Graeco-Roman antiquity.[210]

The decipherment of the Linear B texts opened a fundamentally novel way of approach to the Mycenaean communities. One would imagine that the previous attempts to conceptualise those communities in their multiplicity and multiformity and in their varying relationships to later Greek communities would attract the interest of a great number of ancient historians; and in fact, here for the first time the opportunity to deal with archival sources was open to ancient historians. Instead, the Linear B texts were completely and without battle abandoned to the hands of philologists.[211] The result had been anticipated by Beloch:

> The difference between the philological and the historical treatment of history can be defined in this way: The philologist relates only what is in the sources and what is in as close as possible a connection with them; the historian examines his material, fills the gaps of the tradition through conclusions, and searches always further away from the events, in order to reach their causes; the philologist, as such, is incapable of doing so.[212]

The fourth feature is the abandonment of any use of the archaeological material: the pioneering efforts of Rostovtzeff in the 1930s did not find successors.[213] It was left to archaeologists to develop new ways to study material culture, while ancient historians studiously abstained; even nowadays, and after three decades of intensive surveys, their results have not yet been incorporated into the narrative of Greek history at large. The motionless and homogenising models of the polis, which proliferated in this period, made the variable and regionally diversified picture of the archaeological evidence seem irrelevant. A final feature is the abandonment

---

[210] Nafissi 2005: 225–9, 237–43.
[211] Finley was the only historian to step into the debate, but he left the field early, after managing to establish what would ultimately become the orthodox approach; see Finley 1957/8.
[212] Beloch 1913: 15.
[213] One has to make an exception for Dunbabin 1948, a work written of course before the Second World War. But his early death led to the ultimate abandonment of this kind of approach. Robin Osborne has pointed out to me how the early deaths of many British archaeologists cum historians, such as Dunbabin and Blakeway, before and after the Second World War, aborted developments that could have taken place decades earlier than they actually did.

of historical geography. The last important studies date to the 1950s: what we see afterwards is the sad story of the divorce between ancient history and geography/topography, except in the traditional sphere of *histoire évènementielle*.

We can define a number of common elements behind the contexts that we reviewed above.

The polis as a unitary entity

The first and most important characteristic of the new approach is the retention of the notion of the polis as a unitary entity and the uniting factor behind Greek history. Instead of the multilevel and multiform picture of the modernists, the polis becomes the organising principle of Greek history. Not this time in the sense of Fustel, but still with quite similar presuppositions: the polis is considered as an entity that can be defined in an absolute, if debatable, way.[214] The huge variety of Greek communities and institutions are treated as varieties of, or exceptions from, a common pattern, while anything else that cannot be accommodated within that scheme is regarded as a survival or a backward form. In the words of Austin and Vidal-Naquet: 'Admittedly, it is difficult to define criteria that would equally suit the archaic, the classical and the post-classical polis.'[215] Precisely. But the presupposition is that there *must be* an entity by that name and the only problem is to find the correct criteria to define it. Therefore, the polis is *the* form of Greek state, in contrast to the *ethnos* or the territorial monarchy; the polis is *the* form of Greek economy, in the shape of the consumer city, in contrast with the medieval producer city; the polis is *the* form of classical Greek state and society, in contrast to both earlier forms (the Mycenaean societies and states) and with contemporary ones (the Oriental states and societies). Moreover, this entity is perceived in an organic way: it has an emergence, an acme and a decline and fall. The perception of the polis as a unitary entity has often led to amazing conclusions: Nicole Loraux has gone as far as arguing that the polis can think itself and of itself, as if it is an individual person.[216]

The polis as a distinctive Greek feature

The polis is perceived as *the* Greek form of state, society and economy. In this sense it has served to create a national history for the Greeks by differentiating them from the other contemporary ethnic groups. In

---

[214] See the exhaustive collection of definitions in Sakellariou 1989: 27–154.
[215] Austin and Vidal-Naquet 1972: 51.   [216] Loraux 1991: 34.

particular, it has served the aim of differentiating and divorcing the history of Greece, the primeval Western European history, from the history of the Near East. According to the new conceptualisation, the emergence of the polis in the archaic period created an unbridgeable gap with the situation in the Near East. The incorporation of the peasants into the citizen group created a fundamentally new form of communal politics and an almost total dichotomy between free and slave, in contrast with the spectrum of statuses in the Near East.[217] Finally, Near Eastern societies were redistributive economies, where economic life was controlled by the twin institutions of the temple and the palace, while the Greek polis was a kind of society, where private property and initiative were the key features.[218] There was a controversy about the role of reciprocity, trade and non-economic motives in the Greek polis, but in any case the situation was completely different from the Near Eastern. Moses Finley reflected the thoughts of a considerable number of his colleagues, when he declared that the concept of freedom was impossible to translate in any Oriental language;[219] for him, societies with strong monarchical figures at the head of state knew only government by antechamber.[220]

The polis as a stage in Greek history

The polis is seen as a stage of Greek history, because it possessed a fundamental unity of substance. In orthodox accounts of Greek history, the story is something like this: Greek history starts with the Mycenaean societies. But it was a false start.[221] These were redistributive economies, controlled by a monarch and his palatial bureaucracy. These societies were akin to those of the Near East.[222] Therefore, to become the ancestor of the West, there has to be an unbridgeable gap in Greek history: only if the redistributive kingdoms were completely destroyed and dismantled could the later Greek societies of the poleis emerge, dominated by citizenship, rule of the law, private property and initiative etc.[223] This catastrophe has long been thought to be reflected in the destruction of the Mycenaean 'palaces' and the ensuing Dark Ages, although it has been impossible to offer a satisfactory explanation for this catastrophe and the vast majority of scholars in the last three decades have retreated to a safe agnosticism. The period between the collapse of the palaces, conventionally put *c.* 1200 BCE, and the eighth century BCE is thought of as the 'Dark Ages', where the

---

[217] Finley 1981a: 127–32.   [218] Polanyi *et al.* 1957: 12–26; Finley 1973b: 27–9.   [219] Finley 1973b: 28.
[220] Finley 1981b: 22–3.   [221] Vidal-Naquet 1990b: 19–64.   [222] Finley 1957/8.   [223] Vernant 1962.

origins of polis have been traced to different periods and places by different authors with different aims in mind.[224]

By and large, though, the polis is there at least from the seventh century onwards and it is destined to be the primary organisational form of Greek history in the archaic and classical periods.[225] In the margins of this world there exist some residues of the previous stage; these are the *ethnê*, communities that have long been conceptualised as tribal survivals in a world of poleis. But the future belongs to these survivals, since from the late classical period onwards and with the decline of the polis they become the dominant forces, either in the form of monarchies (Macedonia), or in the form of confederacies (Aetolia, Achaia).[226] Finally, the coming of Rome signals the gradual unification of the Greek world under the realm of a single power.[227]

The discourse on the 'decline of the polis' became an issue of hot controversy: a number of works were still published in the 1960s and 1970s, seeing the fourth century as the age of the decline of the polis and attempting to identify its causes.[228] But from the late 1970s onwards this discourse almost vanished.[229] It is not readily apparent why this was so; one reason was of course the realisation that there was a strong continuity in many aspects of the polis in the Hellenistic and Roman periods.[230] A. H. M. Jones' book on *The Greek City from Alexander to Justinian*[231] was an early supporter of such a view, and the post-war discovery of late antiquity further accentuated it. Scholars have progressively realised that it is impossible to think of the death of the polis in the aftermath of Chaironeia; the internal administration and life of Greek communities continued with limited changes from the classical period to late antiquity.[232] It became evident that different aspects of the economic, social and political life of the poleis had followed different paths; therefore, the homogenising account of the 'decline of the polis' was wrong in supposing that all the variables had moved in the same way. But it is a clear example of

---

[224] See the exhaustive survey in Sakellariou 1989: 293–333.
[225] Austin and Vidal-Naquet 1972: 63–177.   [226] Larsen 1968.
[227] This is the general scheme in e.g. Ehrenberg 1960.
[228] Mossé 1962; Welskopf 1974; Will *et al.* 1975: 189–244.
[229] See now Eder 1995. Significantly for the changes in academic fashion, Ober 1989 attempted to explain what he perceived as the absence of crisis in fourth-century Athens! Just compare with Mossé 1962, less than thirty years earlier.
[230] See the issue of politics: Rhodes and Lewis 1997.   [231] Jones 1940.
[232] See the points of Gauthier 1985: 1–6. On the continuity of self-government, see Dmitriev 2005.

the potency of paradigms that there has been no corresponding abandonment of the twin discourse of the 'emergence of the polis'.[233]

The polis as a solitary entity
The polis is thought of in individual terms. We do not speak of 'the rise of
poleis', but of the 'rise of *the* polis'.[234] The polis is not thought of as part of
a dynamic system of economic, social and political interrelationships and
interactions, but as a form *per se*. The result is the discarding of the place of
Greek poleis in space and time. The specific temporal and spatial configurations of those Greek communities are not given their due emphasis.
This is also due to the conception of Greek history in national terms. The
polis has substituted the national state, which historians would use if
dealing with later periods. We have already seen how this conception in
terms of national history has excluded the vast majority of Greek communities from the history of Greece. Now, the exclusion was even more
reinforced. If we can see the polis as a self-sufficient unit of analysis, then
what is the need to pay any attention to the vast majority of Greek
communities, whose economic, social and political history is only scantily
preserved, and who appear only randomly in the dominant accounts of the
Hellênika dealing with the conflicts of the 'big powers'?[235]

     This is the reason that Finley came to reject local history;[236] within the
polis approach, local history in most cases cannot be anything more than
antiquarianism of the 'tell all you know about x' form. The inability and
unwillingness of both archaeologists and ancient historians to integrate the
results of the intensive surveys within a *narrative* of economic, social and
political history of the Greek communities is another sign of this approach.
A good example is one of the most successful books on classical Greece by
Simon Hornblower.[237] The success of the book is due partly to the fact that
the author has decided to take into account the whole range of Greek
communities all over the Mediterranean, and to pay attention to the
evidence from the East. Yet, the various Greek communities of mainland
Greece, Magna Graecia, Africa and Asia Minor are treated in separate
chapters, unconnected with the main narrative, which centres as always on
political and military engagements between the 'great poleis'. The author

---

[233] Polignac 1984; Morris 1987; Mitchell and Rhodes 1997. But see now the comments of Polignac 1995.
[234] Ehrenberg 1937; Raaflaub 1993a; Snodgrass 1993.
[235] Characteristically, Finley 1970 either talks about archaic Greece in general, or deals only with
     Athens and Sparta. There is no attempt to see the interaction between communities and the wider
     system in which they participate. Contrast with Osborne 1996b.
[236] Finley 1985d: 61.   [237] Hornblower 1983, 2002.

seems to have no means of connecting the two accounts and, in that sense, the similarity with Heeren's manual of the early nineteenth century mentioned earlier, is all the more noteworthy.

This conception of the polis as an isolated form *per se* is connected with a new perception of its economic, social and political function. In economic terms, the polis is now conceived as a consumer city.[238] In contrast to the medieval city, which is a producer city, the polis does not depend on manufacture and trade for its maintenance; rather it is the place of residence for the landowners, and is maintained by rents and taxes. The conception of the polis as simply the place of residence of the *Ackerbürger*, engaged in the self-sufficient strategy of the *oikos*, undermines any attempt to look at interrelationships between communities. Each polis is an independent, self-sufficient world. The belief in a static and unchanging ancient economy, with peasants aiming at autarky and elites aiming at consumption and status, creates a chasm between an economic and social history, dealing solely with certain structural and unchanging features, and a political history that reproduces and supplements Thucydides.[239] Most accounts of the classical period of Greek history still continue narrating the political events in the good old way, while restricting economic and social developments to a single separate chapter; moreover, these developments do not seem to play any role in the political narrative.[240]

The same picture has implications for the polis as a social unit of analysis. If we portray the polis as the unique result of social struggles between landowners and peasants in the archaic period, then it becomes impossible to explain why it was only in Greece that such a kind of society supposedly emerged, while the peasants in contemporary societies of the Near East, or any other society in antiquity, indeed, failed to succeed.[241] It is equally impossible to understand regional differentiation: the champions of the prevalent anti-modernist approach have not attempted to explain what lies behind it. What makes Achaean Pellene part of an *ethnos*, while nearby Sicyon is a city-state? What makes Crete and Euboia, societies at the forefront of developments in the Geometric and early archaic period, recede to the margins of history in the classical period?[242]

---

[238] Finley 1977.
[239] This is the characteristic attitude of Finley 1973b. In his analysis of the ancient economy there is not a single factor of change as e.g. demography or trade. The whole of antiquity is simply the homogeneous structure of the ancient economy.
[240] Still the prevailing attitude in Osborne 2000.   [241] Finley 1981a: 127–8, 162–6.
[242] For Crete, see now Ericson 2005.

Finally, the conception of the polis as the social unit of analysis creates a structuralist picture of unmixed and unchanging polarities: between the polis and the aristocracy,[243] between the citizen and the metic, between the citizen-hoplite and the mercenary,[244] and so on.[245] The understanding of the polis as a self-sufficient unit of analysis makes it impossible to account for changes and transformations in any other way apart from invoking the familiar images of birth, acme and fall: the mercenary being the evidence of the decline and crisis of the polis institutions, etc.[246]

The conception of the polis as a self-sufficient unit has the same results in the examination of its political form. The traditional approach has been that the polis is fundamentally connected with the notion of autonomy. The polis can exist only as a self-governing and sovereign community. Therefore, for generations of scholars the defeat of Chaironeia marked the end of the Greek polis; according to an even older approach, the end of Greek history itself.

There is no escaping the evidence: the fourth century was the time when the Greek polis declined, unevenly, with bursts of recovery and heroic moments of struggle to save itself, to become, after Alexander, a sham polis in which the preservation of many external forms of polis life could not conceal that henceforth the Greeks lived, in Clemenceau's words, 'in the peace of decadence, accepting all sorts of servitudes as they came'.[247]

Communities which did not possess autonomy and sovereignty, such as the perioikic communities of Sparta, were treated by modern scholars as poleis only in name, despite the fact that they were recognised as poleis in antiquity.

The question of the different forms of political organisation in ancient Greece has been portrayed in the same way. The traditional exclusive dichotomy is between the polis and the *ethnos*, whereas the *ethnos* is usually understood as a tribal survival from the Dark Ages, with the population living in scattered villages and no urban centres.[248] Moreover, the political unit was not the settlement with its countryside, as in the polis, but a whole region been united under a single polity; this unity is usually thought to be due to tribal affinity and common religion, usually worship of a tribal deity in a common religious centre. If we view the polis as a self-sufficient entity,

---

[243] 'Two competing moral systems were involved: one archaic and pre-political (the guest-system of the aristocracy), and the other stemming from the polis structure (the obligations to the polis)'; Herman 1987: 3.
[244] Austin and Vidal-Naquet 1972: 157–9.
[245] A good critique of these approaches in Hammer 2004.   [246] See e.g. Marinovic 1988.
[247] Finley 1963b: 90–1.   [248] Ehrenberg 1960: 24–7; Austin and Vidal-Naquet 1972: 92–6.

then it can either be autonomous, or not a true polis; either a polis, or part of a backward *ethnos*. The complex intercommunity relations of economic, social and political collaboration, interdependence and domination are simply lost: they are substituted by a static and therefore evolutionary approach.

The emergence of the polis approach was accompanied by a complete severing of links between ancient history and other branches of the historical discipline. Until this period ancient historians not only partook of the general frames of interpretation and the intellectual exercises of their discipline, but quite often they were in the forefront of new developments. Beloch was the inventor of historical demography; Meyer created almost single-handedly the historical account of the ancient Near East; Rostovtzeff showed a pioneering use of material culture for historical synthesis. When Henri Berr and the *Annales* school reacted against *histoire évènementielle* and the domination of political history, it was certainly not these ancient historians that they had in mind;[249] in fact, ancient historians were already ahead in terms of these developments by at least a generation.

Yet, the justified reaction against their modernist assumptions took the form of looking back, instead of looking forward. The post-war period has been characterised by the emergence of new forms and new schools of history: the *Annales* school of social and economic history and the history of *mentalités*; the *Past and Present* group and history from below; the Cambridge history of political discourse and the German *Begriffsgeschichte*; world-systems theory and world history; historical anthropology, historical demography and the history of material culture; not to mention Indian *Subaltern Studies*, Italian microhistory and German *Alltagsgeschichte*. It is difficult to see what ancient history has contributed *per se* to the larger historical discipline in the post-war period;[250] nor is it possible to make sense of the projects and groupings of ancient historians in terms of the projects and groupings of the rest of their colleagues.[251] To a certain extent, this is due to the predominance of Anglo-Saxon historians: the traditional study of ancient history in Departments of Classics, instead of History,

---

[249] Dosse 1994: 7–36.

[250] The difference can be clearly perceived if one compares the large space devoted to ancient history and historians in Gooch 1913, dealing with historians in the nineteenth century, and the total absence of ancient historians in the account in Iggers 1984 of post-war European historiography.

[251] There are exceptions to my statement, of course. Some French ancient historians did participate in the *Annales* movement, though only regarding intellectual history, and not in economic or social history (P. Vidal-Naquet, M. Detienne); and the work of C. Meier and K. Raaflaub has strong links with *Begriffsgeschichte*. What is impressive is the absence of such links in the dominant Anglo-Saxon scholarship.

meant that historians of antiquity in England and, to a certain extent, in America had not established means of communication with their historian colleagues. This though does not apply to Germany, where we can clearly talk of a retrogression in the position of ancient history, compared to the situation before the Second World War. But it also fails to explain cases like that of Finley and Ste Croix, who both had a profound knowledge of and contact with the work of historians in other fields.[252]

I believe, and I hope, I will also show in the rest of this work that it is rather the post-war dominance of the polis approach that enforces this segregation.[253] From this it follows that, if we utilise the insights and achievements of the rest of our colleagues in the last five decades, we will discover why we have to abandon the polis approach; and that unless we do so, the segregation will persist.

I think the best analogy to understand this situation is provided by Peter Burke's comments on Ranke.[254] He has argued that the Rankean revolution was indeed a counter-revolution against the new history of the eighteenth century, which attempted to broaden the field of history to deal with social, economic and cultural matters. Although Ranke's new approach to sources brought a huge change in historical practices, the focus on state archives restricted history again to political history and *histoire événementielle*. The new history of the *Annales* and other similar groups in the twentieth century had to start again, where the previous movement had left off; and, in order to do this, the new history had not only to utilise the new Rankean methods, but even to 'invent' new sources for social, economic and cultural history, beyond those of the diplomatic archives.

I believe we should view ancient history in a similar light. The 'Finleyan revolution' was an important breakthrough, in terms of methodological rigour and theoretical self-reflectivity.[255] Finley launched an uncompromising attack on positivism and the cult of numbers, on any approach that believes that the evidence speaks by itself;[256] time and again he emphasised the active role of the historian as interpreter and the importance of his implicit views and bias in determining his approach to history; he recognised

---

[252] A. H. M. Jones served in the committee of *Past and Present*, while Finley edited volumes for its series. But neither of them can be thought of as offering something or gaining something crucial from the *P&P* perspective. Ste Croix drew more inspiration from Marx himself, than the work of the *P&P* Marxist historians working in other fields.

[253] Which partly explains why the segregation between ancient history and history is less so in the case of Roman history, where the empire creates a larger, pan-Mediterranean perspective: the work of Hopkins 1978 and Scheidel 1996 on historical demography are good examples.

[254] Burke 1990.   [255] Finley 1985d was and remains a landmark.   [256] Finley 1982, 1985c.

the importance of historical methodology[257] and he was pioneering in introducing model construction in ancient history.[258]

These were all fundamental contributions to the study of ancient history, and despite the heavy criticism of Finley in many respects in this work, I strongly believe that in terms of historical methodology this work belongs to the Finleyan tradition. On the other hand in very many respects, Finley's approach to Greek history was a counter-revolution and a step back from the dynamic accounts that modernist historians like Meyer, Beloch and Rostovtzeff were trying to write. Their mistaken modernist assumptions were of course fatal for the survival of their approach; but in terms of the dynamic history they attempted to write, we still have to start again from where they left off, while maintaining and applying the insights and gains of the 'Finleyan revolution'.

TOWARDS AN ALTERNATIVE: RECENT DEVELOPMENTS SINCE THE 1980S

The polis approach to Greek history, as presented above, was constructed mainly in the 1960s and 1970s, and it remained the dominant approach in the 1980s and 1990s.[259] No other overall alternative approach has appeared in front stage in the last two decades; to a large extent, the big questions and the big explanations have been left aside and most scholars have turned their attention to side issues that were left unexplored, or to new areas of research. Some still accept the polis orthodoxy unhesitatingly, while producing revolutionary works, which can potentially destroy it;[260] others have a variety of qualifications and disagreements with the orthodoxy, and have tried to present different approaches.[261]

There is an exception, which does form an alternative framework, and from which I have profited vastly. I am of course referring to the approach espoused by Nicholas Purcell and Peregrine Horden.[262] I stand in perfect agreement with their approach; and as will become obvious to the reader, my own agenda has been strongly influenced by their arguments. In a sense, this work is an attempt to focus and extend their approach: focus, in the sense that, instead of looking at the history of the whole Mediterranean, as they do, I focus on the history of the Aegean from a Mediterranean and Near Eastern perspective; extend, in the sense that I attempt to apply a

[257] Finley 1963a.   [258] Finley 1977, 1985a.
[259] See e.g. Polignac 1984; Herman 1987; Murray and Price 1990; Seaford 1994.
[260] Morris 1987; Snodgrass 1990.   [261] Osborne 1991a; Davies 1998.   [262] Horden and Purcell 2000.

similar methodology to issues not covered in their book, such as politics.
My main disagreements stem from these differences in focus and extend.

But it is quite clear that the chief inspiration for the *Corrupting Sea* does
not come from the field of ancient history; it is indeed the work of Fernand
Braudel, whose influence on ancient history has been minimal up to the
present.[263] It is impossible to present here a historiographical account of his
influence.[264] The relevance of his work will be presented in the relevant
places of the book. Instead, what I will try to do in the next few pages is to
present a number of approaches that have developed in the last two decades
within the field of ancient history; these approaches, although not challenging the current orthodoxy in its totality, nevertheless have been of great
importance for the fulfilment of such a task. In this respect, it is obvious
that my account of the last two decades is unashamedly Whig.

The most important contribution has come through the collective project
of the Copenhagen Polis Centre (CPC), founded by M. H. Hansen in the
early 1990s. Hansen, his collaborators and the many contributors to the
various conferences organised by the CPC have constructed an inventory of
the Greek poleis in the archaic and classical periods.[265] In order to achieve
this, they have attempted to trace a number of indicia of polis-ness, their
emphasis being on how ancient Greeks perceived the actual ancient poleis,
and not on modern normative criteria. In this respect, their object is clearly
positivist and anti-theoretical; yet, out of the sheer magnitude of their
survey[266] and their healthy insistence on the primacy and importance of
native perceptions, a number of very important insights have emerged.[267]
Paradoxically enough, although the CPC has been characterised by a strong
positivist methodology, and in a sense can be viewed as the quintessential
polis-centred approach, in its latest results it has moved into a more theoretically sophisticated approach. In particular, the Hansen-inspired comparative study of city-states,[268] and his attempt to define the parameters of a
city-state culture,[269] are positive steps forward. Thus, he has recognised the

---

[263] Though Greek archaeologists, as opposed to historians, have shown interest: Bintliff 1991a; Knapp
1992; Moreland 1992.
[264] See Kinser 1981; Wallerstein 1991: 187–226.   [265] See now Hansen and Nielsen 2004.
[266] See indicatively: Achaia: Morgan and Hall 1996; Aitolia: Funke 1997; Arcadia: Nielsen and Roy
1999; Boiotia: Hansen 1995d, 1996a; Chalcidike: Flensted-Jensen 2000b; Crete: Perlman 1996; Elis:
Roy 1997; Laconia: Shipley 1997; Locris: Nielsen 2000.
[267] The most important insight is the dispelling of the myth of the autonomous polis; Hansen 1995b.
Another key issue is their explosion of the categorical distinction between poleis and *ethnê* and their
showing that poleis did in fact exist in areas long considered as pre-polis, such as e.g. Arcadia;
Nielsen 2002a.
[268] Hansen 2000c.   [269] Hansen 2000a.

fact that the polis cannot be seen as a solitary and unique entity, but has to be situated within a world-systemic framework. My study would have probably been impossible without the massive empirical work of the CPC; my disagreements are a consequence of the CPC not drawing far enough the implicit conclusions of their research.

At the same time, there has emerged a keen interest in peripheral areas,[270] non-polis forms[271] and regional[272] and local studies.[273] These studies have gradually made possible a far more balanced picture of the variety of political, social and economic forms within the Aegean world;[274] moreover, and this is the key difference with the past, they tend to see the peripheral areas and the non-polis forms in their own respect, and not as primitive relics or failed attempts at normative polis status.[275]

Equally important has been the contribution of archaeology. The emergence of intensive surveys and the new social archaeology has a potentially revolutionary impact;[276] yet, it is precisely here that the dead hand of the past is particularly felt. The structuralist, static, aspatial and atemporal models of the current orthodoxy have discouraged ancient historians, with few exceptions, to take advantage of the new insights and the vast area open to them by the exploits of archaeology. In the vast majority of historical accounts it is still as if the archaeological revolution never took place. The intensive surveys have changed our perspective in three ways: by allowing us to study areas and regions for which the written evidence is meagre;[277] by showing the huge variety of possible relationships between settlements and between city and countryside;[278] finally, by showing the variety of temporal patterns in different areas and regions.[279] It is clear that the dominant approach to the polis had not prepared ancient historians for such findings.

In terms of the study of material culture, Ian Morris in a number of studies has pointed to the formation and maintenance of regional groupings in the Aegean and the mainland from the Dark Ages to the classical period.[280] Having defined four groups (central Greece and the Aegean, western Greece, northern Greece and Crete), he has argued that social, economic and political processes are articulated with varying or contrasting

[270] Morgan 2003.   [271] Cabanes 1976, 1983; Beck 1997.
[272] See the work of Freitag 2000 on the gulf of Corinth; and Reger 1994; Brun 1996 on the Cyclades.
[273] Salmon 1984 on Corinth; Shipley 1988 on Samos; Osborne 1985 on Athens.
[274] See the studies of Ruschenbusch 1983, 1985; also Nixon and Price 1990.
[275] Gehrke 1986. See also the articles in Brock and Hodkinson 2000.
[276] The pioneer figure in both cases is of course Anthony Snodgrass; see Snodgrass 1980, 1990.
[277] Jameson *et al.* 1994.   [278] Osborne 1987: 113–36.   [279] Alcock 1993.
[280] Morris 1997b, 1998b, 2000.

ways in each region; that changes occur in each region with different pace, differing directions and differing results; and that the novel middling communities of the archaic period are particularly present and strong in his central and Aegean region. The value of his scheme for the purposes of our approach cannot be stressed enough.

Finally, it is important to stress the contribution of French and Italian scholarship.[281] I need to start by noting the much stronger interest in the history of historiography among French and Italian scholars;[282] despite the presence of Arnaldo Momigliano, by and large Anglo-Saxon scholars have shown a minimal interest in these issues over the years.[283] The Paris school had of course a pioneering role in enforcing the polis-centred approach on the study of ancient history. But it is interesting to note that during the 1990s some of the key members of the school came to challenge from a variety of standpoints certain of its fundamental tenets. Nicole Loraux argued that the structuralist and functionalist postulates of the anthropological study of the polis ended up in homogenising and excluding conflict from the understanding of the polis;[284] while Marcel Detienne came to advocate the pursuit of comparative history, in order to challenge some of the unexamined postulates that we accept in ancient history.[285] On the other hand, it is important to note that the Finleyan orthodoxy never went unchallenged in France; most of the stimulating criticisms of the model of the consumer city have come indeed from French scholars.[286] The influence of alternative historical traditions has been quite strong here; it is the influence of Braudel that has made French scholars much more open to Mediterranean approaches to Greek history.[287]

French and Italian scholars have been much more alert to the role of space in history than their Anglo-Saxon colleagues;[288] historical geography[289] and the study of the relationship between community and territory

---

[281] I owe to Nicholas Purcell the emphasis on a specifically Italian approach to ancient history.

[282] See Cambiano 1984a, 1984b; Canfora 1987; Hartog 1988b; di Donato 1990; Vidal-Naquet 1995; Ampolo 1997; Avlami 2000a. One should add here the strong interest among German historians: Christ 1972, 1996b; Nippel 1980, 1990b; Gawantka 1985.

[283] Sally Humphreys and Oswyn Murray, both connected to Momigliano, are the obvious Anglo-Saxon exceptions.

[284] Loraux 1991, 2002: 45–62; interestingly enough, she makes a point about Aristotle's conception of the polis, which is similar to the approach espoused here.

[285] Detienne 2000, 2005.   [286] Descat 1995; Bresson 2000b.

[287] See e.g. Brun 1996; Nicolet 2000. The influence of Marxism has been strong in the important Giardina and Schiavone 1981, unfortunately rarely consulted by Greek historians.

[288] Polignac 1984, which otherwise accepts much of the structuralist understanding of the polis, is a good example of the enhanced role of spatial issues in French scholarship.

[289] Leveau 1984; Rougemont 1990.

have been two of their most important contributions.[290] French and Italian scholars have devoted much more attention to the wider Greek world[291] and its relationship with Near Eastern and Western Mediterranean cultures;[292] they have been pioneers in the study of urbanisation[293] and the division and exploitation of the territory in the colonial world of the Western Mediterranean and the Black Sea.[294] These studies, by showing the sheer diversity of Greek poleis, have done much to undermine the dominant model. A final tribute is in place: the publication of the collective *I Greci. Storia, cultura, arte, societa* under the direction of Salvatore Settis[295] has been probably the most innovative collective work in ancient history in recent years; its emphasis upon the interaction between Greeks and the other peoples of the Mediterranean and the historiography of the study of ancient history are particularly welcome. Many of the approaches espoused in this collective work are further explored here.

To sum up: the history of ancient Greece was formulated in an era of the emergence of nationalism and the national states, in an era of Western ascent and imperialism, and the emergence of Orientalism. In the present era of globalisation, both from those above and from those below, the nineteenth century postulates that dominated the formation of our discipline should be reviewed anew. What is to be done? This historiographical account will be followed by three explorations: the one is to look back at the Greek, and in particular the Aristotelian, approach to the polis and Greek history; I will argue that it can offer a much better alternative to the current orthodoxy. The second is a criticism of the present orthodoxy and its treatment of the polis as an entity, manifested in its Orientalism (the Greek polis vs. Oriental despotism) and Eurocentrism (the ancient consumer city vs. the European producer city). Finally, I attempt to sketch an alternative approach by utilising both the Aristotelian approach and the historical criticism of the current orthodoxy. Going beyond Eurocentric perceptions of Greek history, I offer an analysis of the Greek poleis as parts of a changing *système-monde*.

---

[290] Bonias *et al.* 1990; Rousset 1999.
[291] The annual *Convegno di studi sulla Magna Grecia* have been a key institution in this respect, unfortunately little noticed in Anglo-Saxon scholarship: see *Magna Grecia*; *Problemi*.
[292] Elayi 1988; Debord 1999; Briant 2002; see the special issue of *REA* 1985.
[293] Greco and Torelli 1983.   [294] See the articles in Osanna 1992; Brunet 1999; *Problemi*.
[295] Settis 1996, 1997, 2001.

CHAPTER 2

The ancient discourses on the polis

It is time to discuss how the ancient Greeks themselves thought about the polis, to see if their thought can support the modern uses that have been made out of it. My discussion will focus on Aristotle's *Politics*, since this text has provided most of the ideas underlying the conceptualisation of the polis.[1] Aristotle does not represent the *communis opinio* of ancient Greeks, but his text is the only complete ancient Greek text surviving that gives us a context of ancient discourses on the polis.[2] I will attempt to understand Aristotle's work on its own terms and in its own context; I will then try to show that many of his ideas face in a different direction from that of much modern research and many an orthodox view.

But there is an obvious limit to this attempt. The aims of Aristotle, or, put in different words, the discursive presuppositions of his genre, are very different from my own and my own genre's, which is of course history. Aristotle had an impressive knowledge, and made impressive use of the past, but his approach is not a historical one.[3] Robert Nisbet, in a book written long ago, has shown the unbridgeable gap between the vision of history and the vision of developmental and evolutionary approaches to the past; moreover, he has shown that the general premises of this evolutionary and developmental approach to the past, which can be clearly recognised in

---

[1] I owe much to the work of Sakellariou 1989: especially 214–82, whose discussion of Aristotle's views on the polis is by far the best I have seen. The modest reference to his work in my footnotes does not reflect the importance of his influence.

[2] For the few things we know about Stoic ideas on the polis, see Schofield 1991; Murray 2005.

[3] I have always been amazed by his acute (but reactionary) defence of past experience, as for example in *Politics*, 1264a, 1–5: 'let us remember that we should not disregard the experience of ages; in the multitude of years these things, if they were good, would certainly not have been unknown; for almost everything has been found out, although sometimes they are not put together; in other cases men do not use the knowledge which they have'. See also 1267b, 1–2. I have followed most closely the translation of *Politics* by H. Rackham in the Loeb series, but since I have made changes and alterations it should be better to take the responsibility for them.

Aristotle, are still shared by the body of social and anthropological thinking of Europe, even in the twentieth century.[4]

History plays no role in Aristotle's work; in fact, the past is divided into two parts: one is the evolving of events (wars, political decisions, dynasties, famines, etc.); the other is *physis*, the evolution of entities according to their inner natural predestination.[5] This does not mean that the existing reality is identical to its nature; accidental events can corrupt it, arrest its development or transform it in various ways. These accidental events of the past are important for assessing the actual nature of the entity and its natural course. Aristotle's work should be read in this way. When he differentiates between natural and unnatural exchange,[6] or when he postulates that a city must be *eusynoptos*,[7] he is not implying that ancient Greeks actually despised unnatural exchange, or that every Greek polis was actually *eusynoptos*; he was well aware that, in reality, things were quite different, and he could occasionally provide excellent arguments of why this was so. But these were corruptions or aberrations of the natural course, and played only a secondary and incidental role in his work.[8] His work indeed had two aims: to understand the natural course of things and define the ideal conditions of the natural course; and to give suggestions and prescriptions for the existing realities that would direct them as much as possible towards the natural course.[9]

My aims as a historian are fundamentally different. The historical discipline in the last century managed to overcome the ancient division between a *histoire événementielle* and a natural history. Therefore, one cannot follow Aristotle all the way through. Aristotle (and, indeed, any other Greek writer) can give invaluable glimpses of the political, social and economic interrelations between Greek communities. But the patterns and processes, which the modern historian will wish to reconstruct, are not always to be found *per se* in the ancient authors, for two reasons: first, because, processes of the *longue durée* almost always elude the notice of contemporaries, and the significance and outcome of many actions and processes can be really understood only *a posteriori*; but more importantly,

---

[4] Nisbet 1969.

[5] For Aristotle's perception of the accidental and the necessary, see in particular *Metaphysics*, 1064b, 15 – 1065b, 4. His clear point is that 'a science of the accidental is not possible'; hence, history cannot exist as a science, unless it is *natural history*, exploring the evolving of the necessary natural growth of things.

[6] *Politics*, 1257a–b.   [7] *Politics*, 1327a, 1–3.

[8] 'But then we must look for the intentions of nature in things which retain their nature and not in things which are corrupted'; *Politics*, 1254a, 35–6.

[9] *Politics*, 1288b, 22–36.

because the discursive rules and the *outillage mentale* of ancient authors are quite different from those employed by a twenty-first-century historian.

On the other hand, modern Western historians have been far too confident that their own analytical tools and concepts are sufficient to understand and write about societies in the past, or non-Western societies in the present. The concepts and discourses of people in the past, or of contemporary non-Western people, are treated as historical sources, but rarely as models of analysis equally valid and stimulating as those of the modern historian. Post-colonialism and ethnohistory have revealed the extent to which native understanding of their society and history have enormous value; they have shown how circumscribed and ethnocentric are many of the Western concepts that Western scholars take as universal categories of analysis.[10] Accordingly, I will argue here that modern historians should take Aristotle's categories of analysis seriously. I hasten to add that it is not a matter of discarding modern notions and using ancient ones; rather, it is an effort to use some of the ancient approaches, in order to overcome the limits of the modern concepts, and construct a historical understanding of the past. Nor is this one more attempt to show that 'our ancestors the Greeks' have invented and conceived everything. Rather, it is the case that our concepts and categories are not necessarily any better, or any more natural, than those of past actors; and that sometimes, the notions of past actors have more value than those of our contemporaries, even for the present. I am happy to note that a historian of India has reached conclusions similar to my own.[11]

I should here apologise for my direct conversation with Aristotle, bypassing most of modern scholarship. The reason is not mere intellectual laziness. Most scholars working on ancient philosophy are interested in very different things from what interests me in this context; I hope it is equally legitimate to bypass their questions and ask my own. Ancient historians have had a double reaction to Aristotle; unsurprisingly, from Fustel onwards, they have been all too ready to accept Aristotle's evolutionary account of the emergence of the polis, and to prioritise one only of Aristotle's conceptualisations of the polis, while disregarding the others. I will try to show why some uses of Aristotle's concepts are wrong and how stimulating for historical analysis and narrative are some of his other concepts, which have been largely ignored.

---

[10] Chakrabarty 2000.   [11] Inden 1990.

THE ARISTOTELIAN DEFINITIONS OF THE POLIS

The identification of the polis with a community of citizens has a very ancient pedigree. Already in the poetry of the archaic period we hear that the polis is the men, not the walls of the city.[12] This indeed is one of the central questions of Aristotle's *Politics*:

> But the polis is a composite thing, in the same sense as any other of the things that are wholes, but consist of many parts; it is therefore clear that we must first inquire into the nature of the citizen; for the polis is a *plêthos* of citizens, so that we have to consider who is entitled to be a citizen and what is a citizen.[13]

This is the **first** Aristotelian definition of the polis in my classification. Modern scholars, therefore, have followed this seemingly unproblematic hint of the ancient sources; they have identified the emergence of the polis with the emergence of a community of citizens, after the fall of the redistributive monarchies of the Mycenaean world and the demise of the exclusive and hierarchic control of the aristocracies portrayed in the Homeric epics. This reconstruction was always open to challenge from two sides: the picture of the epics could be reinterpreted so as to show that a community of citizens was already present in the epics;[14] but this was obviously mainly a matter of chronology and not of essence. The second problem was somewhat more substantial; if the polis was defined as a community of citizens, then it was quite difficult to locate the moment of the decline of the polis, given that in this organicist approach the emergence necessitated a corresponding decline. It was always fairly clear that at least until the late Roman empire the Greek poleis were still communities of citizens, although other elements might have changed drastically indeed.[15] The recognition of this problem has tempted the majority of scholars to accept the continuity of polis as a phenomenon beyond the end of the classical period.

I have already pointed out the problems created by this ontological approach to the polis; Aristotle offers us an alternative way of conceptualising the polis that has been largely ignored.[16] This is the identification of polis as a form of *koinônia*, called here the **second** definition of the polis, found already in the beginning of the *Politics*:

> From these two *koinôniai* (i.e. male and female, master and slave) then is first composed the household ... the *koinônia* therefore that comes about in the course

---

[12] E.g. Alcaeus, fr. 112.   [13] *Politics*, 1274b, 39 – 1275a, 1.   [14] Raaflaub 1997.
[15] Already Jones 1940.   [16] My approach here has similarities with Ober 1993.

of nature for everyday purposes is the household ... On the other hand, the primary *koinônia* made up of several households for the satisfaction of not merely daily needs is the *kômê*.[17]

The *koinônia* finally composed of several *kômai* is the polis; it has at last attained the limit of virtually complete *autarkeia*, and thus, while it comes into existence for the sake of life, it exists for the good life. Hence every polis exists by nature, in as much as the first *koinôniai* so exist; for the polis is the end of all other *koinôniai*.[18]

Here then we have a teleological definition of the polis as a form of *koinônia*. Aristotle wishes to establish the naturalness of the *politikê koinônia* by giving it the status of the *telos* of every other primary *koinônia* in offering the opportunity to achieve the *autarkeia* and the good life. In the course of his discussion there emerges a **third** way of defining the polis.

And not only does a polis consists of a multitude of human beings, it consists of human beings differing in kind; the polis cannot be constituted by a collection of persons all alike.[19]

For we agree that every polis possesses not one part (*meros*), but several ... One of these parts (*merê*) therefore is the *plêthos* of people which are concerned with *trophê*, the so-called peasants, and second is what is called the *banausoi*, the mechanic class; and third is a commercial class, and fourth is the class of manual labourers, and the fifth class is the one to defend the polis in war ... and the class that plays a part in judicial justice, and in addition to these the deliberative class, deliberation being a part of political intelligence ... and a seventh class is the one that offers *liturgies* (services) to the community by means of its property, the class that we call the rich. And an eighth is the class of public servants, that is those who serve in the magistracies, inasmuch as without rulers it is impossible for a polis to exist.[20]

And we must also further consider how many there are of these things referred to that are indispensable for the existence of the polis; for among them will be the things which we pronounce to be parts of the polis, owing to which their presence is essential. We must therefore consider the list of *erga* that a polis requires: for from these it will become clear. First then a polis must have a supply of *trophê*; second crafts (since life needs many tools), third arms ... also a certain abundance of money, in order that they may have enough both for their internal needs and for requirements of war; fifth, a primary need, the service of gods, termed a priesthood, and sixth in number and most necessary of all, a provision for deciding questions of interests and of rights between the citizens. These are then the *erga* that virtually every polis requires (for the polis is not a chance *plêthos* of people, but one *autarkês* for the needs of life, as we say, and if any of these *erga* happens to be wanting, it is impossible for that *koinônia* to be absolutely *autarkês*).[21]

---

[17] *Politics*, 1252b, 16–17. [18] *Politics*, 1252b, 28–32.
[19] *Politics*, 1261a, 23–5. [20] *Politics*, 1290b, 24 – 1291a, 36. [21] *Politics*, 1328b, 3–19.

Aristotle has now offered up to us three definitions of the polis. The first one defines the polis as a *plêthos* of *politai*, citizens; the second one defines it as a sort of *koinônia*, indeed as an agglomeration of various *koinôniai*; the third one defines it as an indispensable unity of *merê*, parts. Is there a contradiction between all these three different definitions, or can they be reconciled? I think they can, provided we are reminded of Aristotle's account of the aims of the polis. As we already saw, these are *autarkeia* and the good life that depends on *autarkeia*. Since *autarkeia* is the precondition of the good life, the various *koinôniai* and the various parts (*merê*) of the polis are there to ensure its fulfilment. But it is necessary to pause here and rethink the meaning of this term, which has consciously remained untranslated until now.

One of the most important misconceptions about Aristotle's thought is to render *autarkeia* simply as self-sufficiency, in the form of the ability of the polis to produce anything it needs by its own means and without exchange or dependence on anybody else.[22] This is clearly not the whole case. Aristotle defines it as 'that which on its own makes life worthy of choice and lacking in nothing'.[23] The emphasis in his use of the word in this sense is not therefore on self-production, but on the procurement by the polis of the goods and services necessary for its aims and its reproduction.[24] Moreover, the relation between *autarkeia* and independence is not straightforward. Aristotle comments 'for how can a polis that is by nature slavish have any title to the name? The polis is *autarkês*, but the slave is not *autarkês*.'[25] The point here is not that a slavish polis cannot produce everything it needs by its own means, but that a slavish community has no independent will to take decisions of how to procure anything in need.[26]

To unite both senses then, *autarkeia* refers to the ability of one to provide for all their needs irrespective of the means employed.[27] The stress is on the *ability* (or if you prefer capacity) to provide: when Pericles in the

---

[22] 'Very much the same holds true about its territory i.e. of the polis. As to the question what particular kind of land it ought to have, it is clear that everybody would commend that which is most self-sufficing and such is necessarily that which bears every sort of produce, (for *autarkeia* means having a supply of everything and lacking nothing)'; *Politics*, 1326b, 27–30. But even here it is quite clear that this is simply the most commendable situation; as Aristotle will make clear in the next few lines, even his ideal polis has to import what she lacks, and export what it has in abundance.

[23] *Nicomachean Ethics*, 1097b, 14–15.   [24] Meikle 1995: 44–5.   [25] *Politics*, 1291a, 9–10.

[26] 'But on the other hand the polis was formed not for the sake of life only, but rather for the good life, for otherwise a polis could consist of slaves and of lower animals, but as it is this cannot happen, because they do not share in happiness and purposive life (*zên kata proairesin*)'; *Politics*, 1280a, 31–4.

[27] Josiah Ober defines *autarkeia* as including foreign trade, but excluding dependence upon any foreign power; see Ober 1993: n. 15. See also Mayhew 1997: 38–48.

Funeral Oration describes Athens as *tois pasi autarkestatên*,[28] he is not of course implying that Athens was in a position to produce everything that she needed; in fact, he will go on to stress that 'our city is so great that all the products of all the earth flow in upon us, and ours is the happy lot to gather in the good fruits of our own soil with no more home-felt security of enjoyment than we do those of other lands'.[29] What Pericles is willing to convey is the sense that Athens has the ability, the power, to provide itself with everything that it is in need of, and in that sense it is self-sufficient.[30] The belief that the polis, even in its ideal form, was supposed to be self-sufficient and without the need for exchange, was not espoused by ancient Greeks.[31] Aristotle clearly takes exchange for granted in the definition of the ideal polis.

[I]t is advantageous in respect of both security and the supply of necessary commodities that the polis and the *chôra* should have access to the sea ... and the importation of commodities that they do not happen to have in their own country and the export of their surplus products are things indispensable; for the polis ought to engage in commerce for its own interest and not for the interest of others (*autêi gar emporikên, all' ou tois allois dei einai tên polin*).[32]

To come back to the various Aristotelian definitions of the polis, the purpose of the various *koinôniai* that are subsumed by the polis, or of the various parts (*merê*) of the polis, is to ensure this *autarkeia*. Let us deal with the *koinôniai* first. What is their role according to Aristotle?

The sum of *koinôniai* are parts as it were of the *politikê* (*koinônia*); travellers for instance associate together for some advantage, namely to procure something that they need for the purposes of life; but the *politikê koinônia* too, it is believed, was originally formed and continues to be maintained for the benefit of its members; this indeed is the aim of the lawgivers, and they call just that which is to the common benefit. Thus, the other *koinôniai* aim at some particular benefit; for example sailors combine to seek the profits of seafaring with a view to making money or something of the kind, fellow soldiers at what is advantageous in war, whether it is wealth or victory or the taking of a city that they seek, and members of *phratries* and *demes* act similarly ... all the *koinôniai* then seem to be part of the *politikê koinônia*.[33]

The other *koinôniai* are a constituent part of the *koinôniai* of the polis – for example that of the members of a *phratry*, or priestly colleges (*orgeônes*), or *chrêmatistikai koinôniai*.[34]

---

[28] Thucydides, II, 36.   [29] Thucydides, II, 38.   [30] See Raaflaub 2004: 184–7.
[31] See Bresson 1987.   [32] *Politics*, 1327a, 18–29.
[33] *Nicomachean Ethics*, 1160a, 8–29. I follow the translation of W. D. Ross.
[34] *Eudemian Ethics*, 1241b, 25–7.

From this it follows that there is a gap between our first and our second definition. The first one defines the polis as the *plêthos* of its citizens; the second one defines the polis as a sort of *koinônia* that includes every other *koinônia*. According to the first definition, only citizens are part of the polis; according to the second definition, the partners and members in every *koinônia*, which is subsumed by the polis, are members of the polis. The same holds true concerning the parts (*merê*). The various people who provide the polis with its necessary *erga* are not therefore necessarily citizens. The second (the *koinôniai*) and the third (the *merê*) definition seem then to be very similar. Both classifications aim at satisfying the *autarkeia* of the community: the *koinôniai* is a classification viewed from the point of the relationships or associations between the various sorts of people necessary for *autarkeia*; the *merê* is a classification viewed from the point of the various functions needed to establish the *autarkeia*.

What is the connection then between these two categories and the citizens? I think that Aristotle makes it quite clear that since the aim of the polis is the good life, the citizen is the one who alone is capable of participating in the good life. Aristotle does indeed give a more restricted definition of the citizen, as the one who participates in the deliberative or judicial administration of the polis.[35] But the problem with this definition, as Aristotle is well aware, is that it does not allow us to comprehend who is entitled to be a citizen, since it is clear that the entitlement to citizenship varies widely between the various poleis. This is the reason I believe that this restricted definition does not help us much; and therefore I prefer to emphasise the alternative Aristotelian definitions. We should prefer relational definitions to the axiomatic one based on the participation in deliberative/judicial definition.[36] Aristotle's analysis and epistemology is pluralist and capable to accept and incorporate diversity; but its necessary corollary is the concept of hierarchy, in order to rank people according to their needs, rights and capacities.[37]

But since, just as with all other natural organisms those things that are indispensable for the existence of the whole are not parts of the whole organisation, it is also clear that not all the things that are necessary for poleis to possess are to be counted as parts of the polis ... And the polis is one form of *koinônia* of *homoioi*, and its object is the best life that is possible. And since the greatest good is happiness, and this is some perfect activity or employment of virtue, and since it has so come about that it is possible for some men to participate in it,

---

[35] *Politics*, 1275a, 1 – 1275b, 22.   [36] The same point is raised by Hedrick 1994: 294–7.
[37] See Saxonhouse 1992: 189–95.

but for others only to a small extent or not at all, it is clear that this is the cause for there arising different kinds and varieties of poleis and several forms of *politeiai*.[38]

That is the reason behind the several different forms of definition of the citizen. Different poleis adopt different criteria for defining the citizen according to different relations among their constituent parts.

As there are several forms of *politeiai*, it follows that there are several forms of citizen, and especially of the citizen in the subject position (*archomenou*); hence under one form of *politeia* citizenship will be necessarily extended to the artisan and the hired labourer, while under other forms this is impossible, for instance in any constitution that is of the form entitled aristocratic, and in which the honours are bestowed according to goodness and to merit, since a person living a life of manual toil, or as a hired labourer, cannot practice the pursuits in which goodness is exercised. In oligarchies, on the other hand, though it is impossible for a hired labourer to be a citizen (since qualification for admission to office is high), it is possible for an artisan; for even the general mass of the craftsmen is rich ... But under many *politeiai* the law draws recruits even from foreigners; for in some democracies the son of a citizen mother is a citizen, and the same holds true about illegitimate children among many. Nevertheless, inasmuch as such persons are adopted as citizens owing to a lack of citizens of legitimate birth (for they introduce this kind of legislation because of underpopulation), when a polis becomes well off for numbers, it gradually divests itself first of the sons of a slave father or mother, then of those whose mothers only are citizens, and finally allows as citizens only those whose both parents are *astoi*.[39]

Therefore, the definition of the polis as a community of citizens must be qualified. Aristotle presents us with a situation where a polis can exclude a substantial part of the native male population (apart from the always-excluded women, children, slaves and metics):

But one of the difficulties as to what constitutes a citizen is left. Is it truly the case that a citizen is a person that has the right to share office in the government, or are the mechanics (*banausoi*) also to be counted as citizens? If these persons also are to be counted who have no share in offices, it is not possible for every citizen to possess the citizen's virtue; for this man is a citizen. *If on the other hand no one of these is a*

[38] *Politics*, 1328a, 22–41. 'And a polis is a *koinônia* of *genê* and *kômai* in a perfect and *autarkês* life, which in our view constitutes a happy and noble life; the *politikê koinônia* must therefore be deemed to exist for the sake of noble actions, not merely for living in common. Hence, those who contribute most to such a *koinônia*, have a larger part in the polis than those who are their equals or superiors in freedom and birth but not their equals in civic virtue, or than those who surpass them in wealth, but are surpassed by them in virtue'; *Politics*, 1281a, 1–8.
[39] *Politics*, 1278a, 15–35. For a radical though controversial reinterpretation of the meaning of *astos*, see Cohen 2000: 49–78.

citizen, in what class is he to be ranked? For he is not a resident alien (metoikos), nor a foreigner (xenos) [emphasis mine].[40]

I think it is quite characteristic that Aristotle does not come up with a term as an answer to his own question. One can come, through Aristotle's analysis, to a spectrum analysis of the citizen body.[41] The polis consists of all those who contribute to its *autarkeia*; the citizens are those who take advantage of the *autarkeia* to achieve the good life; since different people and groups participate in varying ways in these two aspects, the citizen group can be extended along a spectrum with various nuances. Finally, this is the reason that the **fourth** definition of the polis by Aristotle, as a 'koinônia politôn politeias',[42] as a participation of citizens in the constitution, must be qualified and not be taken as an absolute definition. It is a definition that concerns only the part of the polis that has political rights and participates in political procedures: it can exclude, apart from the usual slaves, metics and women, the part of the citizen population that has no political rights.

THE POLIS OF ARISTOTLE AND THE HISTORICAL GREEK POLEIS

It is now time to put to ourselves a decisive question: what is the relation between the polis as the central notion of Aristotle's *Politics* and the actual poleis of historical reality? If until now Aristotle has proved an illuminating guide, can we follow him all the way through in our analysis of the actual historical realities? If we take Aristotle as a guide to the historical Greek poleis, the answer must be decisively negative. The reason is that Aristotle's analysis of the polis cannot be totally separated from his whole philosophical approach. In a sense, Aristotle is not dealing with real historical entities. His definition of man as a *politikon zôon* is the clearest witness to that:

From these it is evident that the polis is part of the natural order (*tôn physei esti*) and that man is by nature a political animal, and a man that is by nature and not merely by fortune citiless, is either an inferior human or above humanity.[43]

It is clear therefore that the polis is also prior by nature to the individual; for if each individual when separate is not *autarkês*, he must be related to the whole polis as other parts are to their whole, while a man who is incapable of *koinônein* (entering into a *koinônia*), or who due to his *autarkeia* has no need to do so, is no part of a polis, so that he must be either a beast or a god.[44]

[40] *Politics*, 1277b, 33–9.   [41] See Mossé 1979.   [42] *Politics*, 1276b, 1–2.
[43] *Politics*, 1253a, 2–5.   [44] *Politics*, 1253a, 25–9.

From this it is quite clear that everybody, with the exception of beasts and gods, should be part of a polis; and this clearly conflicts with historical reality.[45] In Aristotle's time there were innumerable communities that could not be classified as poleis: to come back to one of his own examples, how is one to classify Babylon, since he has negated its status as polis? It is obviously neither a household, nor a *kômê*, nor a *symmachia*.[46] This is the reason that older translators of the *Politics* have rendered polis with the more general term 'state', since it was quite clear that Aristotle was referring to a human reality more general than the particular historical experience of the Greek polis. But this is a wrong answer to a real problem: the reason behind the conflation of a generalised human reality with the particular historical experience of the Greek polis is Aristotle's definition of the polis as a *koinônia* with the aim of *autarkeia* and the good life.

Aristotle seems to have a biological definition of the polis in two respects: on the one hand, the polis is *like* an organism, coming into life into elementary form, but already with the seeds of its future growth;[47] on the other hand, *like* an organism, it is a composite whole made up of various parts in varying relationships.[48] The reason for this biological model is Aristotle's philosophy and his polemical aims: his philosophy of *telos* necessitating an examination of things according to their supposed aim; his conception of *physis* as the development of things according to their inherent predisposition;[49] and his clearly stated attempt to deny the theory of the social contract and prove that 'social' relationships are based on biological necessities and are therefore natural.[50]

But does Aristotle think that the polis *is* a natural organism with its own *telos*? If this were the case, it would have clearly been very problematic for his argument. If the polis were a natural organism, then one would normally expect its completion in a healthy, well-functioning form. But since Aristotle explicitly argues that no existing polis has a well-ordered

---

[45] See also the comments of Murray 1993.

[46] *Politics*, 1276a, 27–30. If we follow the rhetoric of the passage we might characterise Babylon as an *ethnos*. The absurdity, *by modern criteria*, of characterizing Babylon as an *ethnos*, is I hope clear.

[47] 'And therefore, every polis exists by nature, inasmuch as the first *koinôniai* so exist; for the polis is the end of the other *koinôniai*, since that which each thing is when its growth is completed, we speak as being the nature of each thing, for instance of a man, a horse or a household'; *Politics*, 1252b, 30–3. See also 1253a, 19–39.

[48] See the brilliant comparisons of Aristotle in *Politics*, 1290b, 21 – 1291a, 40.

[49] See Nisbet 1969.

[50] For a discussion of the biological substructure of Aristotle's discussion in *Politics* see Kullmann 1992. The attempt in Ober 1993 to argue that Aristotle sees the formation of the polis as a form of qualified social contract is stimulating, but it does not really negate the above point, as Ober himself seems to acknowledge.

form,[51] then it would follow that nature has created an organism which usually does not reach its fulfilment. What is even more interesting is that Aristotle does not seem to be troubled at all about viewing the polis as a natural organism that is almost always in an unnatural state. A similar question concerns whether the polis has its own *telos*. Every natural organism is an end in itself and fulfils its own purpose; but according to Aristotle, the polis does not exist for its own sake, as e.g. the state in the German philosophy of the nineteenth century.[52] The polis exists for the sake of the good life, i.e. it is a means to an end beyond itself, rather than the end itself.[53]

Based on these two observations, Bernard Yack has argued that Aristotle does not view the polis as a natural organism with a *telos* of its own.[54] Aristotle could clearly differentiate between things that have a nature and things that exist or take place according to nature, but have no nature by themselves.[55] The polis is not a natural organism with a *telos* of its own, but rather a form of community (*koinônia*) that aims to fulfil the good life; the polis is a means to an end and not its own *telos*. On the other hand, 'the impulse towards this kind of community exists in all men by nature'.[56] There is a nice passage that shows the similarities and the differences between natural organisms and the polis:

We should consider the organisation of an animal to resemble that of a polis well governed by laws. For once order is established in a polis, there is no need of a separate monarch to preside over every activity; each man does his own work as assigned, and one thing follows another because of habit. In animals this same thing happens because of nature: specifically because it is part of them, since they are so ordered, is naturally disposed to do its own task.[57]

These findings point to two important conclusions. Aristotle's concept of the polis is atemporal and cannot be used to trace the historical development of the Greek polis.

What Aristotle was interested in was, not the *history* of the state, but, if we may use here a term that becomes of immense importance in the eighteenth century, the *natural history* of the state: the manifestation or actualisation of conditions that are regarded as inherent, as potential, in the institution from the start.[58]

It might have been helpful if Aristotle had analysed the polis in relation to other, alternative forms of political (not of course *politikai*) *koinôniai*, or

---

[51] *Politics*, 1260, b35.   [52] See Meinecke 1957: 343–433; Iggers 1968: 90–123.
[53] *Politics*, 1252b, 29; 1281a, 2.   [54] Yack 1993: 88–102.   [55] See e.g. *Physics*, 192, b30–6.
[56] *Politics*, 1253, a30.   [57] *On the Motion of Animals*, 703, a28–b2.   [58] Nisbet 1969: 31–2.

if he had accorded organic status to *ethnê*, territorial monarchies and other
forms of polities.[59] But given Aristotle's methodology this was unnecessary.
This is the reason that the question of the *decline* of the Polis is impossible
to be conceptualised within the Aristotelian discursive framework. It is like
talking about the decline of the Apple tree. Obviously, a specific apple tree
comes into life from its seed, comes into its full growth and dies; but the
Apple tree, as genus, cannot decline or die. A particular polis can come into
existence, grow and decline, but the Polis as defined by Aristotle cannot
decline: it simply exists. The Polis is a cycle that never ends.

We have therefore to counter strongly the identification of the concept
of the polis in Aristotle with what modern scholars have identified as *the
Greek* polis; i.e. a particular stage of Greek history and a distinctly Greek
form of society, economy and state. The perception of the polis in Aristotle
puts it completely outside history. And indeed, this is the perception of the
Greeks in general. With the exception of primitive conditions, where
people are living in scattered small groups (as e.g. after the deluge) without
any form of political and communal organisation, Greeks perceived that
their whole historical existence since the establishment of agriculture and
the building of nucleated settlements had taken place within poleis.[60] The
idea of the emergence of the polis or indeed of its decline was completely
alien to the Greeks.[61] Moreover, the idea of the polis as a specifically Greek
institution is not supported by Greek texts. Aristotle talked of Carthage in
terms of the polis[62] and included among his 158 *politeiai* the constitutions
of the Carthaginians and the Lycians.[63] Wilfried Gawantka has rightly
commented that the notion of *the Greek* polis (*hê hellênikê polis*) is one for
which there is no evidence in the Greek texts.[64]

What is the Aristotelian and more general Greek concept of the polis
then? I will argue that we have to make a clear differentiation between two
uses of the polis by the ancient Greeks. **One use of the term refers to
specific and particular communities, i.e. poleis.** A study of the use of the
word for actual historical communities has demonstrated that polis is used
with two interrelated meanings. It describes (a) a nucleated settlement
without any inference to its size (it can vary from small settlements of a few

---

[59] See, on the other hand, Lehmann 2000.
[60] See e.g. Plato, *Nomoi*, III, 676a–682c; *Protagoras*, 322a–e.
[61] Thucydides' attempt to demean the scale of the Trojan war in favour of 'his' Peloponnesian war by
comparing Mycenae and 'the poleis of that age' to his contemporary poleis (I, 10.1) betrays a
complete absence of the notion of the emergence of polis in the period in between. See Snodgrass
1986: 47–9; see also Haubold 2005.
[62] *Politics*, 1272b, 24 – 1273b, 27.   [63] See also Keen 2002 on other non-Greek poleis.
[64] Gawantka 1985: 106–10.

hundred inhabitants to large urban centres),[65] and (b) a community of citizens with local self-government. To link the two meanings, it has been observed that the use of the word to describe a nucleated settlement is confined to settlements that act as the political centres of communities of citizens with local self-government.[66] This minimum definition can be all encompassing, but it needs to be qualified in some important respects.[67] First, it must be stressed that it is a *minimum* definition: a polis can comprise much more than a single nucleated settlement of a community of citizens with local self-government, but no settlement or community described as polis fails to qualify for this definition. Second, our definition leaves open the question of rule and external relationships: a polis can be governed by one, a few or many persons; it can have autonomy, or be under the rule of a dominant polis in a single state (Laconia), in a hegemonic league (Athenian league) or in a hegemonic *koinon* (Boiotia), or finally under the rule of a king (Ionia); alternatively it can be part on equal terms in a *sympoliteia* or a *koinon*.

The other use of polis by the Greeks is to refer to the human community in general, in a sense that encompasses and amalgamates the three modern divisions of society, economy and state.[68] Aristotle differentiates between the despotic *koinônia*, as that between the master and the slave, where relationships exist for the benefit of the despot, and the political community, where the aim is the benefit of both the rulers and the ruled:

For there is such a thing as being naturally fitted to be controlled by a master (*desposton*), and in another case to be governed by a *basileus* (*basileuton*) and in another to live in the *politeia* (i.e. the third proper constitution) (*politikon*) and a different government is just and expedient for different people; but there is no such thing as natural fitness for tyranny (*tyrannikon*), nor for any other of the forms of government that are divergences, for these come about against nature . . . but first we must define what constitutes fitness for *basileia* (*basileuton*), what for aristocracy (*aristokratikon*) and what for *politeia* (*politikon*).[69]

Here a clear differentiation is drawn between the bond between master and slave (and Aristotle thought that it was the barbarians who were naturally predisposed to play the role of the slave), the *politeiai* (constitutions) of *basileia* and *politeia* and the degenerated *politeia* of tyranny. Although Aristotle believed that the barbarians are by nature disposed to live in a

---

[65] Ruschenbusch 1985. For the similar use of the concept of the city in the Near East, see Flemming 2004: 235–6.
[66] Hansen 1995a, 1995b, 2004b.   [67] See the comments of Lévy 1990: 54–8.
[68] See Lévy 1990: 65–6.   [69] *Politics*, 1287b, 36–41.

despotic community, there is nothing that obstructs the possibility that there could be barbarians who live in a *politikê koinônia* and Greeks who live in a despotic community.[70]

It is true that Aristotle denied the *politikos bios* to both European and Asiatic barbarians, based on the effects of the climate.[71] But to understand this, we have to pay attention to the particular context of this passage. It belongs to Book VII, which deals with the nature and arrangement of the *politeia aristê*. Aristotle is interested in the situations that furnish the right sort of citizens for his ideal *politeia*; in the same way he excludes manual workers, artisans and traders from his *aristê politeia* a few lines earlier. It is thus mistaken to infer that Aristotle argued that citizens and poleis could only be found among the Greeks. It is the sort of citizens for his ideal *politeia* that he is interested in, and not of the polis in general, or the poleis in particular. It is the ideal *politikos bios* that he denies to the barbarians, not actual life within a polis. Therefore, his negation could work at a most general level of abstraction; it left considerable space for nuances and variances when applied to particular cases, where Greek communities existed side by side with non-Greek ones, and this I take to be the reason that Aristotle felt no discomfiture in accepting barbarian Carthage as a polis.

In this sense both the words polis and *politês* were abstracted from their reference to members of a specific self-proclaimed polis, and were used indiscriminately to describe any political community and its members.[72] Herodotus uses the words polis and *politês* even for communities that he explicitly describes as not being poleis.

> There was among the Medians a clever man called Deiokes. Deiokes was enamoured of *tyrannis* and thus he set about gaining it. The Medians at that time living *kata kômas* [in villages], he was a notable man in his own village, and he began to profess and practice justice more constantly and zealously than ever ... Then the Medians of the same *kôme*, seeing his dealings, chose him to be their judge and he (for he coveted sovereign power) was honest and just. By so acting he won no small praise from the *poliêtai* [the fellow members of the community], insomuch that when the men from the other *kômai* learned that Deiokes alone gave righteous judgments ... and having obtained the power, he constrained the Medians to

---

[70] 'Everybody, I believe gives the name of *dynasteia* to the *politeia* (constitution) which then existed and still continues to exist today among both Greek and barbarians in many quarters; and Homer mentions its existence in connection with the *oikêsis* of the Cyclopes etc.'; Plato, *Nomoi*, III, 680B.

[71] *Politics*, 1327b, 20–33.

[72] For the use of polis to describe barbarian communities in tragedy, see Aeschylus, *Persae*, 511–12; Euripides, *Bacchae*, 171; *Iphigenia in Tauris*, 464, 595; *Medea*, 166; *Phoenissae*, 214. See Easterling 2005: 53.

create one single *polisma* [city] and make this the object of their chief attention disregarding the others [i.e. the *kômai* they used to live in].[73]

It is clear that Herodotus uses the term *poliêtai* to denote the members of communities that he explicitly describes as *kômai*, denying their status as poleis and narrating the *post hoc* creation of a *polisma* by Deiokes: *poliêtai* here describes the members of the community in general, and not the citizens of a self-proclaimed polis. Cases like this abound in Herodotus. Croesus tells Cambyses that he kills 'andras seôytou poliêtas', 'members of your own community';[74] Mycerinus, the Pharaoh of Egypt, 'was clement towards the *poliêtai*', i.e. his fellow Egyptians;[75] the Magoi tell Astyages that

if kingship devolves to this boy [Cyrus] who is Persian, we Medians will be enslaved by the Persians and will become worthless outcasts. But as long as you are king, being *poliêtês* [i.e. belonging to the same community with us], we have our share of power and great honour is paid us by you.[76]

Aristotle uses the term *politikôs* to describe even relationships between animals,[77] making it clear that the concept of the polis and cognate terms are divorced from reference to specific poleis. Egyptians for example are 'reputed to be the most ancient people, and they always had laws and political system (*politikên taxin*)'.[78] His inclusion of the *basileia* of the barbarians among the proper constitutions of the *politikê koinônia*[79] shows again that the polis is conceived as human society in general, and not in the specific terms of individual poleis.

Disregarding for the time being the use of the term polis to refer to specific poleis, let us concentrate on the second use of the term. If it is a mistake to take the polis of Aristotle's *Politics* as *the* Greek polis, then what is one to make of it? I will argue that the polis, as used in this second sense and context, should be understood as a discursive paradigm. Modern scholars have scorned Aristotle and the rest of the Greeks for failing to understand that his emphasis on the polis on the eve of Alexander's conquest of Asia, the creation of the Hellenistic world and the subordination of the poleis to monarchies and dynasts were anachronistic. This again shows how distant is the modern perception of the polis from the ancient perceptions. What modern scholars usually see as the decline of the polis,

---

[73] Herodotus, I, 96–8.   [74] Herodotus, III, 36.   [75] Herodotus, II, 129.   [76] Herodotus, I, 120.

[77] 'A man is a *politikon zôon* **more** than any bee and any gregarious animal [emphasis mine]'; *Politics*, 1253a, 7–8. See also his definition of *politika zôa* in *Historia Animalium*, 487b 33 – 488a13. We are even told that ravens and crows tend to live in poleis; ibid., 617b 13–14. See Hansen 1996b: 199–200.

[78] *Politics*, 1329b, 30.   [79] *Politics*, 1285a, 15–30.

i.e. its loss of the ability to play a key role in interstate politics and its loss of independence in foreign policy, is emphatically absent from Aristotle's discussion in the *Politics*. This was rightly so, for two reasons. First because this phenomenon was nothing new; the vast majority of the poleis were always in that condition and it was merely the few great poleis aspiring to hegemony that found themselves in this dependent situation only in the Hellenistic period; secondly, because the polis, in the form of human community in general that is discussed in the *Politics*, is only fleetingly interested in the vagaries of fluid interstate power balances.

A final example will make it clear, I hope. In his *Politics*, Aristotle has not much to say about 'Polisübergreifende Politik'.[80] The reason is not difficult to understand: first, Aristotle considers the polis as a *koinônia*; and in the same way he examines relationships between poleis, as forming another kind of *koinônia*. Every *koinônia* according to Aristotle is held together by *philia* (friendship) between the partners. In his *Nicomachean Ethics* he defines the possible forms of *philia* as falling under three categories: friendship for utility, for pleasure and for the sake of the partner's good.[81] In his view then relationships between poleis can only aim at the first form of friendship and must be deemed as inferior to the form of friendship that takes place among the citizens. Moreover, in his seventh book on the ideal *politeia*, he tries to establish the best *bios*, both for the polis and the individual. Arguing that war is only a means to an end for the polis,[82] and not an absolute end, he argues against the subjugation of other poleis as not forming part of the aims of the polis.

This is precisely the reason that modern analysis of the polis has ignored this part of Aristotle's thought on the polis and has introduced other sets of criteria that are completely absent from Aristotle's definitions.[83] This was a step in the correct direction. But we still have to face the challenge presented by Aristotle's dynamic approach to the constituent parts of the polis; a processual approach differentiating between various factors and levels. The next chapter of this work will be devoted to an attempt to save this part of our intellectual inheritance and build on it a historical understanding of the polis.

---

[80] For the following, see Winterling 1995.   [81] *Nichomachean Ethics*, 1156a, 6 – 1256b, 24.

[82] *Nichomachean Ethics*, 1333a, 35.

[83] This of course is not to say that Aristotle, or many other contemporaries, indeed, did not notice the importance of these criteria. The *Politics* are full of such comments e.g. about the growth of cities through trade and the movement of population; 1327a, 12–16. But the philosophical form of his treatment of the polis does not allow these criteria to enter his definition.

CHAPTER 3

Making use of Aristotle: concepts and models

The Aristotelian treatment of the polis has been sketched above. It is now time to put a number of questions and arrive at a number of conclusions that will provide our guidelines for the rest of this study. The problem with the modern scholarship on the polis is that it has discarded the binary use of the term by the Greeks, in order to arrive at a single, 'essentialist' or ideal-type definition of the polis. In doing this, it has been forced to disregard most of the ancient uses of the term to describe particular historical communities, because those uses do not fit with what the polis 'ought to be', according to the preferred definition; on the other hand, the nature of the political discourse of the ancient Greeks on the polis has often been misrepresented and its main insights ignored. Accordingly, our task is to argue for a novel study of the Greek poleis by paying new attention to both the Greek contexts of using the term. In this final chapter of the first part I try to abstract some basic concepts, models and insights from the political discourse of the Greeks. These basic concepts and models will be used in the coming chapters, in order to review and think again about the vast number of different historical Greek poleis.

I will argue that Aristotle's approach in particular, and other ancient Greek approaches in general, can be used to construct an alternative modern approach to the study of Greek communities: we could use their perceptions to challenge the objectivity and usefulness of our own perceptions. And what is more, we could use their perceptions to construct novel, *historical* conceptualisations and perceptions of the past. The great validity of Aristotle's approach to the polis rests on the dynamic and interrelated basis of his perceptions: the polis is viewed as a composite whole, the interlinking node of a variety of processes and relationships. And although he turns his attention to the issue of how the polis can take advantage of these processes and relationships, instead of analysing the processes and relationships themselves, we can take advantage of his insight for our own aims. In the following I stress three central issues: his analysis of the polis as a set of *koinôniai*; his analysis of the polis as a composition of *merê*; and his analysis of the interrelationship between the polis and its external environment. I will also add a fourth that does not stem from Aristotle directly, but from the Aristotelian tradition of constitutional theory, as exemplified by Polybius;[1] namely, the polis and interstate relationships.

THE POLEIS AND THE *KOINÔNIAI*

Since the most fundamental *koinôniai* are the ones between male and female, master and slave and parent and children, then women, slaves and children are necessarily part of the polis. How does Aristotle conceive of these *koinôniai*?

It seems that Aristotle wavered between two concepts of the *koinônia*, a broader and a narrower. The broader embraced combinations of people in any kind of inter-relationship, not excluding temporary and non-structured ones. The narrower concept was limited to associations of partners who were tied by friendship (solidarity), had some common interests, pursued some common end and obeyed common rules ... the term 'society' is quite inadequate to render either the broader or the narrower concept expressed by *koinônia*: 'union', 'association' and 'community' are suitable to the narrower, but misleading for the broader.[2]

The first great advantage of Aristotle's concept of *koinôniai* is its ability to overcome static polarities and divisions, such as those between masters and slaves, citizens and metics, men and women, Greeks and barbarians. Of course, these distinctions did exist and they did play an important role;[3] but the problem is that we have made of them unsurpassable states of being, while in reality these concepts are images and identities that are defined by constant challenge and renegotiation, depending on the context; moreover, they might make sense in some contexts, but they might be completely irrelevant in others. Aristotle's great discovery was indeed diversity and multiplicity, where other Greek thinkers were trying to see the underlying unity behind the apparent diversity; at the same time he used the concept of hierarchy to subordinate diversity to his normative ideas. We can keep his explorations of diversity, without therefore accepting his concept of hierarchy.[4] The advantage of his concept, then, is that it allows us to pay attention to the concrete experience of people in the various forms of *koinôniai* in which they associate. Greek and barbarian indeed; but what

---

[1] See von Fritz 1954; Nippel 1980: 142–56.   [2] Sakellariou 1989: 219.
[3] For the role of these polarities in Greek historians, see Cartledge 2002.
[4] See Loraux 1991; Saxonhouse 1992.

is the perception of such a polarity, when they both participate in a *koinônia* aboard a ship? Free and slave; but what happens when they both participate in a *koinônia* for work (e.g. working in the shipyards) under the same conditions? Citizen and metic: but what happens when they drink together and converse in a tavern or a barber's shop? Men and women, finally: but what happens when they participate in a *koinônia* of cult?

A further advantage is conceptual flexibility. In contrast with the modern conception of isomorphism between society, economy and the state, the concept of *koinôniai* recognises that the boundaries of different *koinôniai* are different, and not necessarily overlapping. The boundaries of a household are very different from that of guest-friendship, or a trading agreement, or a religious or scholarly community, or a group of *systratiôtai* (military comrades). All these relationships, which are described as *koinôniai* by Aristotle, are part of the *politikê koinônia*. Aristotle is clearly aware that these *koinôniai* have boundaries that reach beyond the boundaries of the individual polis and have their own regularities and rules; but he (and the whole tradition of civic Humanism) is interested in them only to the extent that, and as long as, they serve the aims of the polis, i.e. *autarkeia* and the good life.

We can argue that the *politikê koinônia* in the sense of human community is more a 'set of sets' than a clearly defined organism. To take the polis as *the* unit of analysis, when analysing the social (or therefore the economic, political or cultural) history of the ancient Greeks is misleading. The boundaries and the aims of each *koinônia* will differ substantially from one polis to another, and in different points in time. But the value of talking about *koinôniai* in plural, instead of talking about society in the singular, is precisely to relativise and contextualise the content of this 'set of sets'. The usual juxtaposition of the citizen-hoplite and the mercenary, and the identification of the growing number and importance of mercenaries with a supposed decline and crisis of the polis, is an example of this kind of failure to understand the polis as a set of sets.[5] Military *koinôniai* (*systratiôtai*) are part of the *politikê koinônia*, but they are not subsumed by it: their orientation and boundaries can take a variety of forms, which do not necessarily coincide with that of the polis.[6]

Finally, the Aristotelian concept of *koinônia* gives us the possibility to overcome a linear conception of time. According to this conception, which accepts a structuralist and isomorphic conception of society, economy and

[5] Marinovic 1988.   [6] I have dealt with these issues in Vlassopoulos 2003.

state, history is a linear progression from one period to the other, from one stage to the next: we move from the archaic society to the classical and so on.[7] But in reality things are never like this; traditionalist historians recognise that by talking of survivals and archaic features. As long as our unit of analysis is a unified entity with tight boundaries, we cannot do otherwise, but conceive it within a linear notion of time. But the Aristotelian *koinôniai* allow us to grasp the plurality, diversity and **non-reducibility** of the component parts of the polis. Instead of the linear time that traditional history uses, we can substitute the multiplicity of time-scales and durations of historical time. If, instead of our entities emerging, growing and declining, and moving in a linear pattern of progress (or regression), we substitute an image of a variety of levels, in a variety of spatial configurations and with a variety of temporal scales, conjunctures and rhythms, our approach must necessarily change.

THE POLEIS AND THE MERÊ

Aristotle's definition of the polis through an analysis of its *merê* offers a powerful alternative to the modern historical conceptualisations. The modern approach is that there exist separate fields of human activities and that the analytical categories to conceptualise and study them are natural; when historians or other social scientists are confronted with societies, where such distinctions are not evident, then they attempt to explain why the fields were mixed, or why one field was preponderant over the others.[8] This is to a large extent the nature of the anti-modernist stance in ancient economic history: it attempts to explain why there was no separate field of the economy in antiquity; but by this it takes for granted that a separate field of the economy ought to exist, as it supposedly exists in our modern society.[9] What most historians seldom do is to challenge the naturalness of the concepts they employ and their applicability even in their own society.

Aristotle's conception refuses to make such a distinction between the variety of human needs and acts: they form an inseparable whole, although they are satisfied and enacted in different ways in different communities. Aristotle has a holistic notion of *autarkeia*. Instead of an artificial division between economy, society and politics, Aristotle stresses the interconnect-edness of all the functions and processes necessary for the production, reproduction and well being of a human community. He includes in the

---

[7] For a criticism of these approaches, see Yoffee 1993.   [8] Roseberry 1989.   [9] Contra, Sahlins 1976.

functions of the polis necessary to establish the *autarkeia* much that we would not classify as part of the economy: the administration of justice, the waging of war or the cult of the gods. But we have already dealt with this aspect.

Moreover, his conception has another advantage: instead of talking about abstract, but quasi-personified entities (the economy, the society, the state), Aristotle focuses on the actual human groups that perform such functions and activities. He makes it clear that the groups that serve the needs of the community are not exclusive of each other: 'Different functions appear to be often combined in the same individual; for example, the soldier may also be a farmer, or an artisan; or again the counsellor a judge.'[10] With his definition then we have two advantages. The first one is that we can see people in the co-existing multiplicity of their roles. The second one is the chance to raise the question: how many roles do people share in a single community at a certain period, and how are these roles expanded, reduced or transformed?

But we can also make another more important remark. Aristotle has a conception of the polis as a varying agglomeration of multiple ingredients and argues that the different combinations of the various elements give a different shape to the community; this gives us the chance to overcome reifications and abstractions that have created a number of problems for the study of ancient history. The discourse on *the* Greek polis presents a homogenising picture. On the contrary, Aristotle creates a different and variegated picture; his discussion of the various Greek constitutions provides an illuminating example. He insists that there are various kinds of democracies and oligarchies, because of the varying nature of the parts of the population that support each form of constitution:

Now the reason of there being several forms of constitution is that every polis has a considerable number of *merê*. For in the first place we see that all the poleis are composed of households, and then again that of this multitude some must necessarily be rich and some poor and some between the two, and also of the rich and the poor the former class is heavy-armed and the latter without armour. And we see that one portion of the common people (*dêmos*) is agricultural, another engaged in trade, and another mechanic. And the upper classes have distinctions also corresponding both to their wealth and the *megethê* of their property.[11]

Now it has been stated before *what kind of democracy is suited to what kind of polis*, and similarly *which of the kinds of oligarchy is suited to what kind of populace*; ... In

[10] *Politics*, 1291b, 3–5. [11] *Politics*, 1289b, 27–35.

fact there are two causes for there being several kinds of democracy, first the one stated before, *the fact that the populations are different* (for we find one multitude engaged in agriculture and another consisting of handicraftsmen and day-labourers, and when the first of these is added to the second and again the third to both of them it not only makes a difference in that the quality of the democracy becomes better or worse but also by its becoming different in kind) [emphasis mine].[12]

Aristotle's comments here are clearly opposing the modern orthodoxy of a Greek polis as a community of peasants and with marginal numbers of artisans, workers and traders. He argues that different poleis consist of different proportions of the *merê*.[13] Moreover, he insists that there are different sorts of non-agricultural populations in different *poleis*:

For there are several classes both of the people and of those called the notables; for instance, classes of the people are, one the farmers, another the class dealing with the crafts, another the commercial class occupied in buying and selling and another the one occupied with the sea – and this is divided into the classes concerned with naval warfare, with trade, with ferrying passengers and with fishing (for *each of these classes is extremely numerous in various places*, for instance fishermen at Taras and Byzantium, crews of triremes at Athens, merchant seamen at Aegina and Chios, ferrymen at Tenedos) [emphasis mine].[14]

But if we accept Aristotle's point that different poleis are constituted by different proportions of the *merê*, how are we to explain the existence of these different proportions? What is the reason that fishermen abound in Taras and not in Athens, merchant seamen in Aegina and not in Taras? The point in Aristotle is **not** about the specialisation of labour, which is indispensable for every human community passing a certain limit of population and wealth/power differentiation. Those communities, where the population comprises substantial numbers of craftsmen, traders and wage labourers, cannot be explained away by their internal specialisation of labour. The populations of the various poleis are different, because they have different places and occupy different roles in an inter-polis division of labour. Aristotle's conception of different forms of *merê*, poleis and *politeiai* is predicated on the existence of a 'world-system' of poleis and other communities, whose workings shape the internal distribution and specialisation of the population of each individual polis. Therefore, the notion of the polis as a self-contained economic or social unit, as portrayed for example in ideal-type constructions, such as the consumer city, does not accord well with the evidence of Aristotle.

---

[12] *Politics*, 1317a, 12–29.   [13] See Gehrke 1986.   [14] *Politics*, 1291b, 17–27; see also 1290b, 37–1291a, 10.

Of course, what Aristotle does in his *Politics* is to analyse this system of relationships and processes from the point of view of the benefit of the political community and its members. Whether Aristotle chose to develop this understanding or not is unimportant in the present context; we can appropriate his insight for our own aims. His approach should be appreciated and utilised as much as possible. It implies that the polis cannot be understood as an entity or an essence; the polis, each individual historic polis, forms the nexus, in specific temporal and spatial conjunctures, of a variety and multiformity of processes and relations that are beyond each individual polis. In other words: each polis is part of a wider system agglomerating relations and processes and cannot be analysed as an isolated entity.

THE POLIS, THE STATE AND INTERSTATE RELATIONSHIPS

My third issue is best exemplified by Polybius in his famous sixth book.

By constructing therefore his constitution in this manner and out of these elements, Lycurgus secured the absolute safety of the whole territory of Laconia, and left to the Spartans themselves a lasting heritage of freedom. But as regards the annexation of neighbouring territories, supremacy in Greece and generally speaking an ambitious policy, he seems to me to have made absolutely no provision for such contingencies, either in particular enactments or in the general arrangement of the state.[15]

[A]nd here a conspicuous defect in their constitution revealed itself. For as long as they aspired to rule over their neighbours or over the Peloponnesians alone, they found the supplies and the resources furnished by Laconia itself adequate, as they had all they required ready to hand, and quickly returned home whether by land or by sea. But once they began to undertake naval expeditions and to make military campaigns outside the Peloponnese, it was evident that neither their iron currency, nor the exchange of their crops for commodities which they lacked, would suffice for their needs, since these enterprises demanded a currency in universal circulation and supplies drawn from abroad.[16]

But what is the purpose of this digression? It is to show from the actual evidence of facts, that for the purpose of remaining in secure possession of their won territory and maintaining their freedom the legislation of Lycurgus is amply sufficient, and to those who maintain this to be the *telos* (aim) of the *politeia* we must admit that there is not and never was any system or constitution superior to that of Lycurgus. But if anyone is ambitious of greater things, and esteems it finer

---

[15] Polybius, VI, 48, 5–7. I follow the translation of W. R. Paton in the Loeb series with slight adaptations.
[16] Polybius, VI, 49, 6–9.

and more glorious than that to be the leader of many men and to rule and lord it over many and have the eyes of all the world turned to him, it must be admitted that from this point of view the Laconian constitution (*politeuma*) is defective, while that of Rome is superior and better framed for the attainment of power; this is indeed evident from the actual course of events.[17]

What comes out of these lengthy quotations of Polybius is that the search for *the* essence of *the* Greek polis glosses over the fundamental difference between hegemonic and middling/small polities. The Lacedaimonian constitution was perfectly adapted to the needs of a self-centred polis, which aimed at its simple reproduction; but it was not enough for the policies of a hegemonic polis, which aimed at annexation of foreign territories and world supremacy. The aims and therefore the internal and external arrangements and relationships of these two different categories of communities were totally different. A constitution (i.e. the internal relationships of groups, the management of resources, etc.) that is absolutely fine for a middling and small polis can be a serious obstacle for the development of a hegemonic one. It is wrong to put them together under the same label of the state: the two categories of polities, although they will share a number of functions, do not have the same aims, or the same arrangements.

Therefore, to lumber Athens and Koressos under the same rubric as being specimens of *the* Greek polis is simply misleading. We have grown up under the illusion of the post-war UN image, where every state seemed to participate on a more or less equal basis, having total control and sovereignty over its internal and external affairs. The tragic events we live through serve to remind us what was always clear to the ancients: a hegemonic state can take over actions of its own, interfering with the sovereignty of other states, taking control of processes that in other periods are under the control of each small or middle polity. A general and achronic definition of the city-state mixes hegemonic and 'Normalpoleis' together; moreover, it fails to recognise that the extent to which hegemonic and 'normal' polities have control over their internal and external processes and arrangements is context-, conjuncture- and period-specific.

Finally, one has to make a clear differentiation between the strategies, techniques, arrangements and relationships that a hegemonic polis ought to enter in order to qualify for the title, and those needed by the middling and small poleis. There is no reason to believe that the pace, the time scale, the intensity and the spatial arrangement of the 'hegemonic' techniques, arrangements and relationships would change, consolidate and expand in

[17] Polybius, VI, 50.

the same way as those in use by the middling and small poleis. The failure to differentiate between them has had a pernicious effect on the study of ancient history.

THE POLIS AND THE EXTERNAL ENVIRONMENT

I come now to my last proposition. Is an ideal-type construction of the polis feasible? Or is there something fundamentally mistaken with this approach? I will argue that ideal-type constructions attempt to abstract reality from its temporal and spatial parameter and conjuncture; and that Aristotle offers a powerful warning against this methodology and intuitions towards an alternative one. In Book II of *Politics* he argues against the idealisation of the Cretan *politeia*. And, in order to do this, he attacks precisely an ideal-type construction that abstracts from the spatial and temporal position of each polis. According to him, the power configurations within Cretan poleis cannot be studied *in vacuo*. Class relationships, or relationships within the elite, take place within a spatial background, which cannot be abstracted; in this case the Cretan geopolitical position puts Cretan elites and their subjects in a very different situation from that of other poleis in different geopolitical settings.

Now it is a thing admitted that a polis that is to be well governed must be provided with leisure from menial occupations; but how this is to be provided is not easy to discern. The *penestai* in Thessaly repeatedly rose against the Thessalians, and so did the helots against the Laconians, where they are like an enemy constantly sitting in wait for their disasters [i.e. of the Spartans]. Nothing of this kind has hitherto occurred in Crete, the reason perhaps being that the neighbouring poleis, although they fight each other, in no instance ally themselves with the rebels, because as they themselves possess *perioikoi*, this would not be for their interest; whereas the Laconians were entirely surrounded by hostile neighbours, Argives, Messenians and Arcadians; for with the Thessalians, too, they [the *penestai*] originally began rising, because they [the Thessalians] were still at war with their neighbours, the Achaeans, Perrhaibians and Magnesians.[18]

And the fact that the *dêmos* [the common people] quietly tolerate their exclusion [from power] is no proof that the arrangement is a sound one; for the *Kosmoi* unlike the *Ephors* have no chance of making some profit, as they live in an island remote from any people to corrupt them.[19]

And it is a precarious position for the polis to be in, when those who wish to attack it also have the power to do so. But, as has been said, it is saved by its locality; for distance has had the same effect as *xenêlasia* [the expulsion of

---

[18] *Politics*, 1269a, 34 – 1269b, 7.   [19] *Politics*, 1272a, 39 – 1272b, 1.

foreigners]. A result of this is that with the Cretans the *perioikoi* [the dependent population] stand firm, whereas the helots often revolt; for the Cretans take no part in foreign empire (*exôterikê archê*), and also the island has only lately been invaded by warfare from abroad, rendering manifest the weakness of the legal system there.[20]

As the last lines indicate, the temporal conjuncture is clearly important. The spatial configuration does not exist in a temporal eternal continuity. Rather, the temporal conjuncture gives the spatial configuration its varying influence and importance. To talk then about *the Greek* polis in general, or even about individual poleis, without paying attention to their position within a spatially and temporally arranged system of power and resource relationships, is seriously misleading. The development of the Cretan poleis cannot be understood as part of the development of the Greek polis in general, or from a kind of internalist analysis. It should also be stressed that the island position is not a factor of isolation *per se*; it functions like this only in specific circumstances and conjunctures. We know all too well from the remarks of ancient authors how an island can find itself either in a position of complete dependence[21] or of potential world dominance[22] according to the circumstances: Aristotle himself in the passage above tells us how a change in power relations has introduced warfare with states outside the island and destabilised its structures.

The study of Athenian democracy is a good example of how the disregarding of the world environment misguides scholars. Josiah Ober, in his highly influential *Mass and Elite in Democratic Athens* attempts to explain the apparent socio-political stability of Athenian democracy, in contrast with the constant turmoil in most Greek poleis. He turns down empire and slavery as the explanations of such stability, in order to argue that the cause was the accommodation of the masses and the elite through a public ideology constructed on terms set down by the demos.[23] Ober is perfectly right to refuse to accept the profits of empire or slavery as sufficient explanations. And yet, he fails to ask some more fundamental

---

[20] *Politics*, 1272b, 16–22.   [21] Ps-Xenophon, *Athênaiôn Politeia*, II, 2.

[22] 'Also the island [Crete] appears to be designed by nature and well situated to rule the Greeks (*archên Hellênikên*); it lies across the whole of the sea, round which almost all Greeks are settled; for Crete is only a short distance from the Peloponnese in one direction, and from the part of Asia around Triopion and from Rhodes. Owing to this Minos won the empire of the sea (*thalassês archê*) and some of the islands he subjected and in others he settled colonies': Aristotle, *Politics*, 1271b, 33–9. Instead of talking about the transition from the Minoan and Mycenaean redistributive monarchies to the Greek poleis, it would be more profitable to contemplate why it was that Crete was never again in a position to exploit its advantageous geographical position after the Minoan period.

[23] Ober 1989: 17–35.

questions, precisely because he treats Athens as an ideal type of a Greek polis. We can agree that the Athenian empire and the profits from it might have been a necessary but were hardly a sufficient reason for the creation and maintenance of democracy. But one can argue that the real importance of the empire, or, better, of the hegemonic position of Athens within the political arena of classical Greece, was the absence of external interference with the running of Athenian politics.

This situation was, and still is, clearly exceptional. For the vast majority of Greek democracies in antiquity, and for modern democracies nowadays, the greatest problem has been that they were never allowed to conduct their own internal politics on their own terms. For most of Athenian history, the question that the speaker in Lysias XXXIV puts, namely how can we retain universal male citizen suffrage at the aftermath of the fall of the Thirty, when Sparta opposes it, was non-existing.[24] For every Greek democracy outside Athens the perennial issue was how to maintain a democracy in an international environment, where oligarchs could always hope on external help, in order to overthrow a democracy; or, in general, a democratic regime had always to find a *modus vivendi* with the great powers of each age. It is of course far from accidental that, every time Athenian democracy was overthrown, it was due to external interference (508/7, 404/3, 322, 317 BCE), or, more generally, external circumstances (411/0 BCE). Athens was the exception to a normal rule of turmoil, to an important extent because its hegemonic position ruled out, most of the time, external help in the overthrowing of the democratic regime. Is it a matter of chance that Western scholars, who have never had the experience of foreign interference and imperialist imposition of regime change, have taken for granted what is clearly highly exceptional? I would not think so.

The study then of how spatial arrangements interlink and interact with temporal conjunctures and economic, social and political processes has not yet even started for ancient history. But it is a desideratum that has an illustrious ancestry, as I hope to have shown.

There is another aspect here that stems again from the sixth book of Polybius, but has equally strong Aristotelian connotations.

The *politeia* of the Carthaginians seems to me to have been originally well contrived as regards its most distinctive points ... But at the time, when they entered on the Hannibalic war, the Carthaginian *politeia* had degenerated and that of Rome was better. For as every body or *politeia* or action has its natural periods first of growth, then of prime and finally of decay, and as everything in them is at

---

[24] Lysias, XXXIV, 6–11.

its best, when they are in their prime, it was for this reason that the difference between the two *politeumata* manifested itself at this time. For by as much as the power and prosperity of Carthage had been earlier than that of Rome, by so much had Carthage already begun to decline.[25]

No matter the organicist metaphor of growth, prime and decay, the essential idea is that of conjuncture. Time matters in history, and *when* things take place, cannot be abstracted from our models and conceptualisations. In the case of interstate relationships, as in any other form of relationships indeed, the polities that interact might be at different or varying time scales and conjunctures; the conjuncture of their interaction is absolutely crucial.

A short summary of the Aristotelian contribution is in place. I have argued that the Aristotelian concept of *koinôniai* allows us to see the polis not as a bounded entity, but as the agglomeration of a variety of associations and relationships, ranging from beyond the boundaries of a polis (merchant associations, mercenaries) to just a small nucleus within it (a local cult group). These *koinôniai* have their own varying aims and their own specific temporal and spatial configurations, which do not necessarily coincide with the aims and the configurations of the specific polis. The Aristotelian concept of the parts allows us to see the needs of production and reproduction of a human community in its totality and interrelationship, and not as segregated and distinct levels, such as the modern concepts of society, economy and state. At the same time it makes it clear that the production and the reproduction of the needs of a polis depends on its place within a larger 'world-system'; therefore, the polis should not be viewed as an independent and self-sufficient entity. The Polybian contribution shows that there exists a fundamental gap between hegemonic and non-hegemonic poleis; and that we should not try to gloss over this basic difference in terms of internal arrangements and external aims, in order to arrive to a homogenising definition of *the* polis. Finally, the Cretan comments of Aristotle show that the polis cannot be abstracted from its spatial and temporal configuration; any definition which tries to abstract from them is destined to be misleading.

---

[25] Polybius, VI, 51.

PART II

Rethinking the contexts. The polis as an entity: a critique

The purpose of the following two chapters is to review and criticise a particular way of approaching ancient history, and history in general. I want to criticise the approach that sees the Greek polis as an entity, and history as a succession or juxtaposition of entities, variously called the West, Greece, Rome, the Orient, antiquity, etc. This will be attempted in a number of case studies. They attempt to criticise some deeply entrenched postulates of social theory and history writing. Charles Tilly has called them 'the pernicious postulates of twentieth century social thought', and I reproduce below some that I deem relevant:[1]

'Society' is a thing apart; the world as a whole divides into distinct 'societies', each having its more or less autonomous culture, government, economy and solidarity.
'Social change' is a coherent general phenomenon, explicable *en bloc*.
The main processes of large-scale social change take distinct societies through a succession of standard stages, each more advanced than the previous stage.[1]

The following chapters attempt to show that all these postulates have indeed pernicious results. Societies are not entities with clear and distinct boundaries. This image results in the dichotomy between internal structure and external influence, leaving perennially unresolved problems. Instead, I will argue that we need to view societies as always parts of wider systems: this will allow us to resolve the dichotomy between internal and external. At the same time, societies, economies, cultures and states do not have necessarily the same boundaries, as the dominant image of the national state helps to reinforce; instead, they have varying boundaries, which depend on the historical context and their place within those larger systems.[2] Moreover, societies (or economies, or states, or cultures) are not homogeneous: they are composed of a variety of levels, and they

---

[1] Tilly 1984: 11.   [2] See the points of Davies 2001: 20–2.

include a variety of institutions and groups, which do not necessarily have the same aims, the same arrangements and the same time scales. For all these reasons, historical time is not linear. There exist various durations of historical time; and different processes, institutions, networks and groups have their own temporal scale. In this way, we can avoid the perennial dichotomy between structure and change, and understand how structure and change co-exist and interact at the same time as interlinking time scales.

Therefore, instead of a homogeneous and solitary entity (society, economy, culture, state) moving in a linear fashion from one stage to the next, we have to envisage a multiplicity of levels, processes, institutions and groups, with various boundaries, various time scales and various interconnections forming parts of wider world-systems, and moving in a variety of directions concurrently.[3] This is no consolation to those who feel comfortable with grand, linear metahistories, such as the main Eurocentric narratives. Yet, the alternative proposed here is not a post-modern 'histoire en miettes'. Instead of the intellectual safety of abstract theoretical anticipations (societies emerge and move from structural stability to crisis), or Eurocentric metahistories (Greek history is the beginning of the history of the West), I argue that only specific and contextual historical analysis can show how societies, economies, cultures and states fit together, how they form and dissolve world-systems and how the variety of time scales translates into historical development. Ancient Greek history needs to be rewritten from such a perspective; but it will not be rewritten in the present context. This is impossible before the shortcomings of the dominant approaches are pointed out, and an alternative conceptual framework is clearly articulated. This is the only aim of the chapters that follow.

The chapter on the Near East is a critique of the old discourse on the Greek polis and the Oriental despotism, which is of course basically a discourse on the Western origins of democracy and liberty, and a denigration of the stagnant and despotic Others. It shows how misleading it is to depict Near Eastern societies as despotisms, and to present the Greek poleis as a unique phenomenon. It also tries to show that politics should be seen as an agglomeration of various levels, which are not necessarily organised in the same way: the authoritarian high politics of diplomacy and war can differ considerably from popular politics organised on very different principles. Finally, it shows why we have to discard the notion of

---

[3] For a criticism of such a homogenising conception of modernity, see Yack 1997.

the sovereign state, and why our understanding of politics or democracy has to take into account the larger world-system and its conjunctures.

The next case study concerns the comparison between the ancient Greek polis and the medieval/early modern European city; this comparison is basically a discourse on why the Rest (ancient Greeks and Romans in this case) did not follow the path of the West to economic progress, capitalism and industrialisation. I try to show how misleading it is to look at economic history with a Eurocentric bias. I also point out that such a dichotomy rests on a simplistic and outdated depiction of both Greek poleis and medieval and modern European cities; and I argue that the orthodox approach fails to realise the different levels of the economy and the fact that economies are parts of wider world-systems. Finally, the last five chapters present and articulate an alternative framework and its conceptual tools. There is a separate introduction at that place.

CHAPTER 4

East and West, Greece and the East: the polis vs. Oriental despotism

As we have already discussed, the polis has functioned as a boundary mark to separate the history of the Greek communities from those of the Near East. This was accomplished through the construction of a contrast between the Greek polis as a community of citizens and Oriental despotism. This contrast is well entrenched in modern scholarship and will be challenged in this chapter, in an attempt to show that the juxtaposition misconstrues what it is to be compared and completely misrepresents the Near Eastern realities. There is then a clear need to reconsider this old dichotomy. Do we have any predecessors in our task?

There has already been some promising work, trying to overcome Orientalist dichotomies, but it has been mainly concerned with cultural and religious history;[1] social, economic and political history has only recently begun to benefit from such a novel approach and still to a limited extent.[2] Moreover, this kind of work has a certain limit. It argues for Oriental influences in ancient Greek culture and religion; it does not challenge directly the meaning of the two juxtaposed entities, and it does not attempt to write a 'connected history'.[3] I am trying to do something more challenging, yet still limited: my aim is a change of perspective. Instead of being the self-referent ancestor of the West, Greek history can be viewed within the changing history of the Eastern Mediterranean. We can view Greek history from the reference point of the Near East and the Mediterranean, both in earlier and later phases, and not form an imaginary European viewpoint. If Oriental despotism is no more than a Eurocentric

---

[1] Burkert 1992; Miller 1997; West 1997.
[2] Hornblower 1982 is one exception in political history; see also the articles in Raaflaub 1993b. On economic history, see Andreau *et al.* 1994, 1997. The various *Achaemenid History Workshops* did much to revise the history of the Persian empire, but had a very limited effect on the writing of Greek history.
[3] A criticism echoed in Dougherty and Kurke 2003b: 2–5. For an agenda of 'connected histories', see Subrahmanyam 1997; see also Samman 2001.

myth, then Greek history and the Greek polis can be viewed from a totally altered standpoint.[4] But unfortunately, I will not follow the even more promising task of writing a 'connected history' in this study. The lack of research and methodological tools makes it currently impossible; nevertheless, for the time being, the results of changing perspective will hopefully be sufficiently rewarding.

A final note on methodology is due. We are dependent on the nature of our documentation. Our recourse to the history of the Near East depends, archaeological evidence apart, on inscriptions on hard materials and, overwhelmingly, on clay tablets. Clay tablets were only one of the writing mediums used in the Near East and their use declines gradually both geographically, as one moves from Mesopotamia to the Levant and the Mediterranean, and chronologically, as one approaches the first millennium, when clay tablets in Akkadian were substituted by parchment in Aramaic. Therefore, we know the least about the societies that were closer to the ancient Greeks, both geographically (Asia Minor, Levant, Phoenicia) and chronologically (the first millennium BCE). This progressive lack of evidence as we approach the Greek world, geographically and chronologically, is a bewildering problem that can be only partly overcome.[5] But since in this work I do not aim to write a connected history of the Eastern Mediterranean, the absence of evidence for the contemporary Near Eastern communities is not an insuperable problem; our comparative study of conceptual and methodological issues is equally valid, whether we deal with the third millennium or the first.

I note also that Herodotus and other Greek authors have little to say about the societies of the Levant, while they said a lot about Egypt, Persia and Scythia; can we take this as a sign that the Greeks perceived the great similarities between the Levant and their own societies, and therefore restricted their comparative discourses to Egypt, Persia and Scythia, which presented obvious and discursively exploitable differences to their own societies?[6] I risk an affirmative answer and leave it at that; but it would certainly reward further study.

A second issue of documentation is equally important. It is impossible to offer a Near Eastern definition of liberty, politics or citizenship. We have no texts discussing explicitly these concepts, no Near Eastern *Politics*.

---

[4] See the points of Flemming 2004: xi–xv.
[5] The sad lack of written sources for Phoenician cities in the archaic and classical periods is clearly visible in Elayi 1987.
[6] Hartog 1986, 1988a.

Therefore, it is impossible to give a systematic treatment to the subjects we are interested in. We are very much dependent on the fragmentary and partial character of our sources. The only way to study citizenship or self-government is by tracing the implicit uses of words and practices, as reflected in administrative and economic documents, or literary texts.[7] But let us be frank about the implications of this: it is not a particularity of the Near East, reflecting the unimportance or non-existence of these phenomena there. On the contrary, it is the normal situation with the vast majority of Greek communities. How many public decrees of the citizenry do we have during the classical period from such important poleis as Corinth, Thebes, Samos or Sparta, not to mention the vast number of small poleis? Very few indeed.[8] And even when we have them, how often can we establish who had the right of citizenship and on what terms? Indeed, the absence of this kind of evidence has induced scholars to assume implicitly, when speaking about the Greek polis in general, a situation of general adult male suffrage, as in Athens, despite the clear statements of Aristotle to the contrary.[9] In fact, in the odd case where we do have some evidence, it points to directions that look as far away from the Athenian model as possible. A famous fifth-century inscription from Locris is an illuminating example: we find the groups (clans?) of the Perkothariai and the Mysacheis, present in all Locrian communities and possessing their own special laws and privileges, apart from the other citizens.[10]

We should not, then, make too much of the absence of Near Eastern explicit evidence on citizenship and citizen life. In fact, only the preservation of Aristotle's *Politics* allows us to talk about Greek citizenship and the Greek polis in more general terms, and not simply about the specific but exceptional features of Athens and Sparta. This then is not a novel practice, since it is the only procedure left to the scholar who wishes to study the same issues in the vast majority of Greek societies apart from Athens and Sparta. What we are going to do is to ask specific questions according to the material available. This procedure, although it cannot lead to a comprehensive and total account of Near Eastern views and realities concerning citizenship, community and self-government, will, I hope, trace enough substantiated points to vindicate our case. In the following I will focus on

[7] On the methodological issues involved, see van de Mieroop 1997a, 1997b, 1999a.
[8] See the collection of Rhodes with Lewis 1997.
[9] *Politics*, 1278a, 15–35. I have been hard-pressed to find any article discussing rights of citizenship outside Athens and Sparta: but see Ostwald 2000.
[10] Meiggs and Lewis 1969: nos. 20, 22–8. See Koerner 1993: 172–202; van Effenterre and Ruzé 1994: 178–85.

three aspects: a political identity focused on the city; citizenship; and self-government.

GENERAL ISSUES

The power of Orientalism is certainly felt in the discipline of ancient history. To speak about citizenship and self-government in the ancient Near East would raise a substantial number of eyebrows. Moses Finley reflected the prejudices of a considerable number of his colleagues when he declared that the concept of freedom was impossible to translate in any Oriental language.[11] In the face of these well-established views, I will argue that citizenship, self-government and identification with a polis were common property in many parts of the ancient Near East. In other words, I will try to show that a minimum definition of the polis can be successfully applied to the Near East.

Before proceeding further, however, I am obliged to deal with these well-entrenched preconceptions. I will deal with the belief that the concept of liberty was unknown in the Near East and that the distinctions between slave and free were blurred.

Concerning the first statement of Finley, it is difficult to understand how he could rest so much and so often on such a self-contradictory point. The Greeks had no word for religion, but surely nobody believes that they had no gods and cult practices. The fact is that they did not organise and categorise mentally their cult and beliefs in the same way that Western Europeans from the early modern period on do.[12] So, the fact that the peoples of the Near East did not categorise their social relationships in the same way that the Greeks did does not imply that the only way to understand the relationship between slavery and freedom is to use the discourse of liberty, and that every civilisation that does not use this discourse has no relations of freedom.[13] It is an old habit of Eurocentrist thought to posit the path of Western European history, from antiquity to the present, as the natural order of things.

That said, slavery and freedom are important for the questions of citizenship and self-government. If one accepts the absence of clear distinctions between slavery and freedom propounded by Finley, it is difficult

---

[11] Finley 1973b: 28.
[12] For the Greek attitude, see Vegetti 1995; for the European construction of the category of religion, see Asad 1993: 27–54.
[13] On the Near Eastern attitudes to freedom, see the interesting Snell 2001.

to imagine any kind of meaningful citizenship or self-government. But the distinction between slave and free is clear in the Near Eastern sources. In Mesopotamia, where our sources are more plentiful and clear, one can distinguish the following categories: (a) the free citizens, (b) free persons who did not have citizenship and could not own land within the city (usually military colonists and other free persons connected with the king), (c) semi-dependent but not slave populations, which were usually the labour force of the palace and the temples, and finally (d) slaves.[14]

The distinction between the categories was clear and in most cases a person could not pass from one category to the other: a citizen could not be legally enslaved, a liberated slave could not become a citizen, and so on.[15] The Neo-Babylonian records of slave sales provide a good illustration. The seller had to guarantee that the slave under sale was neither of the status of a royal slave (*arad-šarrūtu*),[16] nor of that of a free person (*mār-banûtu*).[17] Each category had clear rights, privileges and obligations: a slave could not participate in the assembly of the citizens nor could he buy a 'prebend', i.e. acquire rights that would enable him to get part of the temple income, a right reserved only for citizens. 'The claim to citizenship and its privileges in a Mesopotamian city was based not solely on a person's having been born there of free parents, but also on ownership of real estate inside the city's walls.'[18] This is one explanation of the custom of houses or house lots described as *ezibtu*, 'left over'. When economic necessity forced the owner to sell his house, he would retain a small lot in order to retain his citizen rights. Citizens could not be conscripted for the army or corvée. They had also no restriction of movement and could dispose of their work-power in any way they liked. We even hear of strikes in cases where temple officials did not have the assets to pay the free workers and the workers refused to resume work, until they were paid for their labour.[19]

One can add many more examples, but I believe the situation is clear; the free citizens were clearly demarcated from other categories, although both within the citizen body and within the dependent and slave populations there existed important differences.[20] The situation was similar to the Greek world, where wealthy archons were at a different level from poor citizen peasants, and slaves with considerable property under their control differed from slaves in the mines.[21] A final note: the existence of citizenship

---

[14] Dandamaev 1974. [15] Greengus 1995.
[16] In order to avoid any problem with the royal authorities. [17] Dandamaev 1984: 182–3.
[18] Oppenheim 1969: 15. [19] Dandamaev 1987.
[20] Dandamaev 1984: 67–80. [21] Cohen 2000: 130–54.

in the Near Eastern cities is a reality recognised by the Greeks themselves. I will not point again to the existence of the Aristotelian *politeiai* of the Lycians and the Carthaginians. I want to draw attention to an inscription of the Athenian polis honouring the king of the Phoenician city of Sidon.[22] The decree presents a number of privileges for 'those who have political rights (*politeuousi*) at Sidon and live there', i.e. in other words, the citizens of Sidon. It is important to note that for the Athenians the existence of kingship did not exclude *per se* the existence of citizenship, even in a 'barbarian' Near Eastern state.

CITY IDENTITY

It is well established that one can recognise what Hansen has termed city-state cultures in many parts of the ancient Near East, especially Mesopotamia, Syria and Phoenicia.[23] The reference to Phoenician cities in Neo-Assyrian documents of the first millennium is a good example. Some times reference to a Phoenician city is given by means of the name of the city or the ethnic (Tyre, Tyrians), plus a determinative sign standing for the concept of city; in other cases by means of toponym or ethnic, plus the sign standing for country; finally in other cases with toponym or ethnic, plus the sign standing for people; we have here the concepts of city, state and community, like in Greek poleis.[24] In these regions the primary political unit was a city (*ālum* in Akkadian), functioning as a political centre and controlling a smaller or larger territory.[25]

Of course, a city-state could expand and create a macro-state or even an empire, but for a very large part of their millennial history these imperial expansions were unstable and prone to collapse; there was a repeated cycle of centralisation and collapse, and usually no city was able to create an empire anew.[26] Moreover, even when a city-state created an empire and dominated others, this did not usually mean annexation and consolidation; instead the dominated city-states continued as separate political entities, but their rulers either became vassals of the dominant ruler, or were deposed and replaced by rulers nominated by the dominant ruler.[27]

It was only in the middle of the second millennium, and after more than 1,500 years of city-state systems, that Babylonia and Assyria were transformed into unified kingdoms and the cities became mere administrative

[22] Tod 1948: 116–19. [23] Hansen 2000a, 2000c.
[24] See Elayi 1987: 40–1; see also Flemming 2004: 190. [25] Van de Mieroop 1997b.
[26] Stone 1997. [27] Larsen 2000a.

municipalities with only local self-governance. In any case, these consolidations never occurred in Syria and Phoenicia, where the city-states continued to function as political entities, whether under an overlord or without one. The term 'Phoenicians' for example is an outsider term; the Phoenicians always defined themselves as citizens of individual cities, for example Tyrians, Sidonians, Byblians, etc.[28]

Even within the unified kingdom of Babylonia the only political identification available was with the cities: there was no overall political identity. A subject of the king of Babylonia was always a citizen of a city (or a member of a tribal group), never a citizen of Babylonia. There was not even a word to describe the whole realm, but only words for the particular regions (Sumer, Akkad, Sealand); the king was simply 'the king of Babylon', as always identified with the chief city.[29] People gave their children names derived from the name of their city, celebrating their identification with it. City identification was not simply sentimental: in judicial cases, for example, involving citizens of different cities, judges from both cities would join to pass sentence.[30] In certain cases the city as community was distinguished from the person of the king: in a Phoenician inscription, the king of Sidon and his son announce that they will add the cities of Dor and Joppe 'to the frontiers of the territory that belongs to Sidonians for ever'.[31] The territory is described as belonging to the civic community, not to the king himself.

One of the most important aspects of city identity were the privileges accompanying city status.

The residents were granted a large degree of independence, especially exemption from royal taxation, corvée and military duties, which were the primary areas of interaction between the king and his subjects. Also the physical integrity of the citizens was guaranteed and their blood could not be shed by the king or his representatives. The freedom from taxation and service was thought to be the result of divine protection over the cities, indicated by the Akkadian word *kidinnu*, a divinely enforced security, which was probably symbolised by an emblem set up in a prominent place in the cities.[32]

The concept of *kidinnu* is already mentioned in texts of the second millennium. But it was only in the first millennium, when the kingdom of Babylonia disintegrated and the new Assyrian empire needed to secure its place in the south, that the citizens of Babylonian cities got the chance to

---

[28] Elayi 1987: 1–2.   [29] Brinkman 1984.   [30] See the case in Sippar, Harris 1975: 127–8.
[31] Elayi 1987: 42.   [32] Van de Mieroop 1997b: 135.

enhance and protect better their rights. The Assyrian kings felt it was decisively important to guarantee the *kidinnu* of Babylonian cities, in order to foster their relationship with the Babylonians, as their numerous references in their letters prove.[33] In a famous letter of the citizens of Babylon to the Assyrian king Ashurbanipal, they state:

So likewise have we (been concerned with the protection) of those who inhabit our wide country, be it but a woman from Elam, from Tabalu, or from Ahlame. The kings our lords (said) in giving us (their) advice, 'The gods have given to you [Babylonians] keen understanding and a great spirit, for yours is a cosmopolitan race, since Babylon is the bond of the lands. Every man entering the city, no matter who he may be, his *kidinnutu* is assured. And "Allotment of a house of Babylon" is the name of the (new) citizen. *No dog that enters therein is slain* . . . as to the *women* that (are in Babylon) their *kidinnutu* (are safeguarded) with us'. [emphasis mine][34]

In the so-called *Tale of the Poor Man of Nippur*, the 'mayor' (*hazannu*) of Nippur protests against being beaten by a supposed royal emissary by arguing: 'My lord, do not destroy a man of Nippur; with the blood (of a man) of *kidinnu* sacred to (the god) Enlil do not desecrate your hands.'[35] In the Neo-Babylonian and Persian periods, the changing geopolitical circumstances led to a decline in the importance of *kidinnu*; the Persian kings did not need the Babylonian cities as allies in an unstable world with enemy neighbour kingdoms and polities; they now ruled a consolidated territory, and the rationale for recognising the rights of the Mesopotamian citizens was gone.

SELF-GOVERNMENT

This brings us to the question of self-government, and in fact it is impossible to disentangle the question of citizenship from the question of self-government, because our only way to understand what a citizen is, is by observing what he does. We can address three aspects: political deliberation and the administration of city life, the settlement of disputes and the representation of the community to higher authorities. For all three issues, it is important to pay attention to a fourth one: the agencies through which the citizens organised their activities. We can clearly identify the key ones: magistrates and assemblies, in a perfect Aristotelian match.[36]

---

[33] See Waterman 1930: no. 301; Reviv 1988.   [34] Pfeiffer 1935: no. 62.
[35] Reviv 1988: 291.   [36] *Politics*, 1275a 1 – 1275b 21.

MAGISTRATES AND ASSEMBLIES

Magistrates had an important role in Near Eastern cities.[37] It is important here to make a division. Some magistrates were clearly appointed by external powers, usually foreign kings that happened to possess control of the particular city at the moment (such as the Persian temple overseers).[38] They were basically overseers of the higher authority, as every imperial authority has always done (such as the Athenian,[39] Spartan[40] or Ptolemaic[41] *phrourarchoi* and overseers) and they were not normally citizens of the city they ruled. Second, there were city officials (like the chief magistrate of the city, the so-called 'mayor', *hazannu*) in whose appointment, due to their important role, the foreign authority (the king) would have an interest: the interest ranged from outright external nomination (imposition) to discreet supervision of local selection.

These letters indicate that the local community were supposed in normal situations to have suggested a candidate, and it was for the Assyrian king to ratify and accept their choice ... Despite the commonly used terminology 'governor' for these offices, we are dealing with a system that should really be described as vassalage rather than as imperial provincial administration. The local elites provided the candidates for leadership, they suggested to the Assyrians who could be acceptable to them and they were directly involved in determining such matters as political allegiance.[42]

Finally, there were a lot of (mainly lower) officials who were selected by the citizens, without any obvious external interference.

Assemblies were the second important agent of city life. We have Assyrian evidence concerning the assembly of the city wards (*babtum*) and the city or temple assembly (*puhrum*). How did the city assemblies function? Our clearest evidence comes from the Assyrian colonies in Anatolia, in the first part of the second millennium BCE. The thousands of tablets of correspondence between the Assyrian colonist traders and their relatives and trade partners back in the metropolis of Assur allow us to reconstruct in sufficient detail the citizen structures of both the colonies and to a certain extent the metropolis. Assur did have a king, but his role was rather circumscribed, until at the end of the eighteenth century BCE the leader of an Amorite tribe managed to become king of Assur, extend the

---

[37] Van de Mieroop 1999b.
[38] Third-second millennium Babylonia: Stone 1997; Assyrian Babylonia: Brinkman 1979; Persian Babylonia: Dandamaev 1977; Seleucid Babylonia: van der Spek 1987.
[39] Meiggs 1972: 205–19.   [40] Cartledge 1987: 90–8.   [41] Bagnall 1976.   [42] Larsen 2000a: 123.

royal authority and create an extensive territorial kingdom.[43] But before that, city life seems to revolve around the citizen body and its assemblies. We know that the city had an annual eponymous archon (*limmum*), who was usually a member of the high aristocracy and was chosen by lot. The office was of profound importance, since it had financial functions (collection of debts and export taxes), and was an ideological counterpart to the king; in fact, excavators of Assur have found two rows of stelae, the one dedicated by kings and queens, the other by eponymous archons after they had served their term.[44]

Among the citizen group one can differentiate between the city conceived as the totality of the citizens (*ālum*), and the group called the elders (*šībūtu*); we find in the texts expressions like 'the city and the elders' (much like the common Greek expression *edoxe têi boulêi kai tôi dêmôi/têi polei*, though with priority reversed). In the texts from the Old Assyrian colonies, we find a classification between 'big' and 'small' men. According to the so-called 'Statutes' of the colony of Kanesh,

> a lawsuit involving at least two parties is brought to the attention of the council of the 'big men' who will investigate it. They may apparently either dismiss it, or pass it on to the assembly, ordering the secretary of the colony to convene that body. The decision to pass the matter on and have the primary assembly convened must be taken by a majority of the 'big men' ... My interpretation leads to the conclusion that the colonial administration was based on a bi-cameral system, and the relationship between the two 'chambers' corresponds closely to what may be found in other similar systems, for instance in the Greek city-states.[45]

In many cases these assemblies have powers completely independent of the co-existing city kings. A case from eighteenth-century Syria is revealing. Zimri-Lim, the king of Mari, orders two individuals from the city of Urgiš to release the property they had unlawfully seized. The two individuals do not go back to Terru, the king of Urgiš, to settle the dispute; instead 'they went to Urgiš and called for a meeting (*puhrum*). The Urgišites then responded: We shall release everything from the encampment.'[46] We see here the citizens bypassing the authority of the king and using their collective decision-making body in order to decide about the issue. It is interesting to note that the word for meeting (*puhrum*) is used for the gathering itself, which does not speak. When the people speak, it is as a town, as the Urgišites.

It is very difficult to determine who actually participated in the assembly. A scribal exercise dating from the second millennium gives us the

[43] Larsen 2000b.   [44] Larsen 1976: 192–217.   [45] Larsen 1976: 294–5.   [46] Flemming 2004: 198.

record of a trial for homicide, judged by 'the assembly of Nippur'. Among the people who spoke out in the assembly we find a bird-catcher, a potter, two gardeners and a soldier. The fact that this record served as an exercise probably implies that the composition of such an assembly was fairly conventional. It shows that a wide variety of professions not only had the right but also the time to sit in the assembly.[47]

The participant in the assembly clearly took on a public profile, and was vulnerable to humiliation by his fellow citizens. Fear of this is expressed in prayers to gods: 'Do not abandon me, my lord, to the assembly, where there are many who wish me ill. Do not let me come to harm in the assembly.'[48]

The citizen body was divided internally in two ways. The first way that is encountered in the biggest part of Mesopotamian history is the division in city wards. The city wards had their own assemblies and their own officials. But what is most interesting for the historian of ancient Greece is a novel division of the first millennium BCE. While previously a Mesopotamian citizen was identified only by his name and his father's name or his occupation, from the beginning of the first millennium the Mesopotamians started to attach to their names a third name of an ancestor. It is well established that these names were not names of actual ancestors, since there was only a restricted number of them, and they were shared by far too many people to be their real ancestors. So, the conclusion that a growing number of scholars reach is that they were fictional kinship groups,[49] similar to the equally fictional groups of tribes and *phratries* of the Greek poleis.[50] If this conclusion is accepted, and obviously there is much work to be done in this direction, then the similarities in the time of emergence and in the function between the Greek and Mesopotamian cities are really stimulating.

POLITICAL DELIBERATION

After having reviewed the agencies of political action, it is time to look at the practices of self-government. Our first aspect is political deliberation. We have abundant evidence to show that political deliberation was an important aspect of Near Eastern civic life. I will have recourse to three cases, the Syro–Palestinian cities of the late second millennium BCE, as depicted through the royal correspondence found in Amarna, in Egypt, the

[47] Van de Mieroop 1997b: 122–3.   [48] Van de Mieroop 1997b: 127.
[49] Van de Mieroop 1997b: 107–10; see also Larsen 2000a: 121.
[50] For the fictional character of the Greek *phylai*, see Bourriot 1976; Roussel 1976.

eighteenth-century BCE Syrian communities reflected in the archives of
Mari, and the Babylonian cities, as depicted in their correspondence with
the Assyrian suzerain in the period 800–600 BCE. These cases are chosen
not only in terms of the abundance of evidence, but also because political
instability and continuous realignments allow us to make visible a number
of issues which are usually not mentioned in the sources in periods of
stability.

The Syrian and Palestinian cities were usually governed by local kings,
although sometimes the kings were killed, or there were no kings at all, and
the cities negotiated on their own terms with the other political powers. The
men of the city of Keilah, a city where no king is mentioned, play one ruler
off against the other and change alliances within a short period.[51] Rib-Addi,
the king of Byblos, actually goes as far as mentioning the internal opposition
of the citizens of Byblos towards his foreign policy of alignment with Egypt:

When the people of Gubla [Byblos] saw this (they said) 'How long shall we
contain the son of Abdi-Ashirta [an enemy king]? Our money is completely gone
for the war.' Then they moved against me, but I killed them. They said, 'How long
can you go on killing us? Where will you get people to live in the city?' So I wrote
to the palace for troops, but no troops were given to me. Then the city said,
'Abandon him. Let's join Aziru' [a king hostile to Egypt]. I said, 'How could I join
him and abandon the king, my lord?' Then my brother spoke and swore to the
city. They had a discussion and the *lords of the city* [the term probably means the
property owners] were joined to the sons of Abdi-Ashirta.[52]

In the archives of Mari we find a large number of cases of collective
political decision-making. Here I only reproduce some eloquent accounts,
which concern the double city of Isqâ-and-Qâ and the city of Tuttul:

I heard the following news of the Isqâ-and-Qâites. 'They have been called up (for
service), (with) a ten-day provisioning. They are going to (join) the reinforcements
of Hammurabi.' When I heard this information, I wrote to Yamrus-el and the
elders of Isqâ-and-Qâ, and the (household) heads of Qâ-and-Isqâ assembled
before me – a group of 200 as one man. In their meeting, I addressed them as
follows.[53]

The *tahtamum*, an institutionalised form of council seems to have considerable power to represent the community and resist the wishes of royal
magistrates:

Regarding my lords' *sirum*-tax that is levied on the Tuttulites, just as I seated the
tahtamum-council once, twice, even three times and I made my request to them,

[51] Moran 1992: nos. 280, 289, 290.   [52] Moran 1992: nos. 138, 221–2.   [53] Flemming 2004: 185.

these men have written once, even twice, to Imar.[54] I seated the *tahtamum* (to have a thousand trees cut) and I spoke to them (about it), (but) they did not comply.[55]

A case from eighth-century Babylonia is equally revealing. Babylon was now under the control of a Chaldean king, and the Assyrians were trying to negotiate with the Babylonians to regain control of the city. The Assyrian envoys reported that they had to conduct their interview with the Babylonian officials outside the main city-gate, not being invited into the city; Babylonians, presumably members of the council of elders, came out of the gate to talk to the Assyrians, and we are told that people representing the Chaldean king were present during the talks, although they are not reported to participate in the discussions. Later we hear about a group of ten and another group of five that although present in the city did not come to take part in the negotiations.[56] Another very interesting case is presented from the seventh century, when Babylon was under the control of the rebel brother of the Assyrian king. We have a number of letters of the Assyrian king addressing the Babylonians and trying to convince them to secede from his rebel brother. The interesting question is where the letters were delivered and to whom, since it would be difficult to hold such an assembly in Babylon, while the rebel king was still residing there.[57] It is clear nevertheless that the citizens had procedures of public deliberation and rulers took this very seriously in their political plans.

SETTLEMENT OF DISPUTES

The settlement of disputes in the ancient Near East has seldom been approached from any angle except the legalistic. Therefore, most discussion centres on the issues found in the 'law codes' and not the actual procedures and the day-to-day settlement of disputes within the society.[58] Nevertheless, in the vast majority of cases the settlement of disputes is a concern and a right of the self-governing community. Contrary to many other societies, where the administration of justice is in the hands of a state apparatus, or the exclusive prerogative of an elite; in ancient Mesopotamia most cases were judged by courts comprising members of the citizen body. We must note here that alongside popular courts there existed royal judges appointed by the king. But they dealt only with cases involving royal officials, or members of the private household of the king, and in exceptional circumstances with cases of capital punishment that had political

[54] Flemming 2004: 189.   [55] Flemming 2004: 211.   [56] Larsen 2000a: 124–5.
[57] Waterman 1930: no. 301; see Larsen 2000a: 124.   [58] See the comments of Yoffee 2000.

significance.[59] Otherwise, each Mesopotamian citizen had the right to be judged by his peers, and we even have cases involving citizens from two different cities, where it was considered necessary to have judges from both cities to decide the case. Who were members of these courts? We have some explicit mentions, where we can identify as members of the court ordinary citizens, for example butchers, artisans, soldiers serving the temple, etc. Moreover, to cite one example, a study of Neo-Babylonian court decisions shows that we know the names of 264 court 'judges', 47 of whom are city governors, scribes and high officials of temples and 217 of whom are not given a profession in the actual court proceedings. Nevertheless, many of them are known from other sources to be artisans, bakers, brewers, butchers, tenants of temple- and privately owned fields, etc.[60]

It should be obvious, then, that ordinary citizens participated in the law courts and had the right to pass judgement on their peers. When we remember that according to Aristotle popular courts were one of the most important features of political life, it is easier to understand why we clearly have to disagree with Finley's claim that

all the [Greco-Roman] city-states had in common one feature, the incorporation of peasants, craftsmen and shopkeepers into the political community as members, as citizens ... they were not at first members with full rights ... but even limited recognition was *without precedent in history* ... Any account of Greek or Roman politics must properly acknowledge that *radical socio-political innovation* [emphasis mine].[61]

REPRESENTATION TO AUTHORITIES

Representation of the city to higher authorities was a third important aspect. It is clear from our sources that cities could represent themselves as a collectivity with its own distinct identity.

Reference to [collective ethnics such as] the 'Terqa-ites, Imarites, Ekallatumites' and so on appears to reflect a standard perspective on the town as a political unit that deals with political units outside itself. Such external affairs seem to inspire this unadorned expression of collective town action, regardless of which individual leaders or representative groups are in fact involved.[62]

---

[59] Like e.g. the Athenians transferring cases of capital punishment with political significance from their dependent poleis of the Delian league to Athens, although the vast majority of cases were still under the jurisdiction of the courts of each individual city; Meiggs 1972: 220–33.
[60] Dandamayev 1981.   [61] Finley 1983: 15.   [62] Flemming 2004: 184.

This practice and the accompanying ideology of collective representation is directly paralleled in ancient Greek sources, whether literary texts or inscriptions.[63]

My examples come again from Syria–Palestine in the Amarna age and Neo-Assyrian Babylonia. In the first case, we have letters like the one sent by the 'city and the elders of Irqata' to their Egyptian overlord,[64] where there was no surviving king and the civic institutions of Irqata considered themselves competent to approach the Pharaoh directly; or the letters sent by 'Ilirabih [a local potentate] and (the town of) Byblos'.[65] From the first millennium we possess many letters of Mesopotamian cities to the Assyrian kings. The letters usually open with the formula 'the people of PN, big and small [or elders and young]', i.e. they represent the whole community.[66] A letter of the Assyrian king Ashurbanipal to the people of Nippur is highly illuminating.

The king has to explain that when fifteen elders of Nippur recently had been at Nineveh, and only half of them had been admitted to an audience with Ashurbanipal, this was not due to ill will on his part: 'It is the fault of the *shandabakku*, who is your governor, and secondly of the palace overseer who did not allow you to enter in my presence. I swear by Ashur (and) my gods that I did not know that half of your number entered before me and the rest did not.' Even the Assyrian king had to be polite towards these men, and their role as representatives of the city was clearly taken very seriously.[67]

We even have a case where the citizens of Ur write as a collectivity to Ashurbanipal to defend the acts of their mayor (*hazannu*);[68] we see that the citizen body has the ability to address the higher authorities independently of the magistrates ratified by the king.

Finally, another important aspect of Mesopotamian cities was institutions and practices for communal sharing of community resources. We are well acquainted with them in the case of Greek poleis and institutions and practices such as the *theôrika*, or the assembly and court pay. But these are viewed as a peculiarity of the community of citizens of the Greek polis. The most well-known example from Mesopotamia is the 'temple prebend'.[69] A prebend was a portion of the general temple income that was granted to individuals.

---

[63] See Pope 1988.   [64] Moran 1992: no. 100; Reviv 1969: 287.
[65] Reviv 1969: 289.   [66] Waterman 1930: nos. 210, 942, 1274; see also nos. 296, 297, 518.
[67] Larsen 2000a: 125, citing the document in Waterman 1930: no. 287.
[68] Waterman 1930: no. 1274.
[69] For a fascinating analogy, see J. L. Borges' 'The lottery in Babylon' in *Labyrinths. Selected Stories and Other Writings*, New York, 1964, 30–5.

In third-millennium Babylonia, temple offices were held by what could be called anachronistically professional priests, members of the cultic and administrative personnel of the temple, whose livelihood depended on their temple employment. But, in the early second millennium, temple offices became a commodity that could be inherited, traded and divided, because it guaranteed the holder a financial reward. Thus we see that the office of temple sweeper, for instance, could be held for as little as a quarter of a day per year, which meant that the owner received a very small fraction of the income assigned to the function. A system was established in which individuals could buy themselves a place within the temple organisation, for which they probably did not have to provide any labour, but which guaranteed them an income.[70]

It is quite probable that the reader might react by arguing that all these were simply *ad hoc* attempts to gain more particular and specific rights, and do not represent any principled struggle or discourse. But such an argument precisely shows how distorting the Occidentalist discourse can be; its essentialism transforms concrete struggles of real people into abstract entities such as Democracy or Freedom, without place in particular space or time. And indeed this is particularly what has happened with our accounts of Greek democracy: we almost always deal with a conception of democracy as the a-temporal ideal type of Athenian democracy.[71] Democracy is viewed as an internal institutional arrangement of each separate society, without paying attention to the specific conjunctures of the power politics of a whole system.[72] Such approaches tend to forget that the strength of Athenian democracy depended to a great extent on its imperial place within the Greek political world-system, which made outside interference and subordination irrelevant for most of the time in the classical period. And naturally enough, when in the Hellenistic period Athens ceases to be a hegemonic polis, scholars lose interest: most, if not all, accounts of Athenian democracy finish at 322 BCE. We know now,

---

[70] Van de Mieroop 1997b: 111.

[71] See e.g. the words of Christian Meier: 'the result was that the *Greeks* came to occupy a unique position in the world, one in which the citizens exercised *unprecedented* control over their conditions of life [emphasis mine]': Meier 1990: 1; who exactly are the Greeks who had unprecedented control over their conditions of life, if not Athenians in their hegemonic period? For Aristotle's view on this issue, see Winterling 1995.

[72] Again, this is not an academic issue. The Occidentalist discourses identify liberal parliamentary democracy as the universal norm and then find out that the vast majority of humanity is not living under such a norm, only to denigrate these 'non-modern', 'traditional' 'authoritarian' societies for failing to catch up with the Western norm. But it would be worth asking whether it is precisely the absence of this kind of democracy from the greatest part of the world-system that makes feasible its existence in a small part of the core of the system. The absence of thinking in terms of systems and processes and its substitution by essentialist norms is a very real problem. See Held 1995.

thanks to Christian Habicht among others, how false such an approach is.[73] But the argument that Athens remained a democracy up to the Roman period should raise the wider issue of the political struggles of the vast majority of Greek communities that had to put up with continuous interference and subordination from outside powers, already from the archaic period: what is it to be a democracy when you are under the control of an imperial or hegemonic power, even if that is Athens? This was the crucial issue for the vast majority of the Greeks, in all periods. In this way, the experience of the Near Eastern subaltern classes and communities is very helpful in rethinking our categories. Political struggles, ideologies and institutions take place in specific historical conjunctures; they cannot be subsumed by the Occidentalist game of the (re)discovery of 'politics' or democracy by the West in its various incarnations.

CONCLUSIONS

It is time to come to conclusions. I hope that it has become clear that the stereotypes about the Near Eastern societies, economies and polities are in need of radical deconstruction; the juxtaposition between the world of the Greek polis and the redistributive bureaucratic monarchies of the Orient is grossly misleading. But how does this affect our perception of the Greek communities and their history?

One lesson is our perception of politics. The Orientalist notion of 'government by antechamber' with its concomitant theory of the Greek invention of politics is very simplistic;[74] it rests on a very restricted notion of politics, with a top-down perspective. It effectively equates politics with institutions and with foreign policy; and any polity that does not have self-proclaimed 'participatory' institutions, and where foreign policies depend on the decisions of a small unaccounted group or an individual, is thought of as pre-political or despotic.[75] The claim is problematic for our own modern democracies: foreign policy is still conducted by small unaccounted groups, as the clear gap between official policies and popular will in most Western countries in the case of the recent war against Iraq

---

[73] Habicht 1997.
[74] See the characteristic Occidentalist words of Meier: 'By developing the political, the Greeks became the eye of the needle through which the whole of the world history [*sic*!] had to pass before it could arrive at the modern European stage'; Meier 1990: 2.
[75] See the comments of Liverani 1993.

shows. Does that mean that our countries are governed by antechamber?[76]
If decisions about foreign policy and war were taken by an unaccountable
Near Eastern monarch and its advisers, and if theoretically he had absolute
power to enforce his decisions, nevertheless his power affected only very
restricted aspects of the life of his subjects; for the majority of issues, his
subjects were governed by their own institutions and practices, which were
of a very different nature.[77]

Instead of this restricted approach, we could view politics as the variety
of debates, institutions, practices and struggles that humans engage with, in
order to accomplish the production and reproduction of their lives. It is
neither given nor unavoidable that every one of these debates, institutions,
practices and struggles must be arranged in the same way and with the same
rules, follow the same path and implicate the same groups and arrangements.[78] Our Near Eastern evidence shows clearly that the rules of high
politics do not apply to the workings of popular politics; different groupings take place in regard to different practices and institutions, etc.[79]

The second lesson is that in order to do this, we have to broaden our
restrictive emphasis on institutions; we have to view politics as a *field*,
encompassing a variety of levels, activities and identities in a variety of
relationships.

The political field is not defined by institutional and territorial boundaries, but
rather is constituted by groups who are engaged in political activity . . . In thinking
about what we mean by a political field, it might be helpful to imagine a battlefield. A battlefield is not defined by particular boundaries, but instead is constituted by the activity. The boundaries of the battlefield can expand and contract
and the composition of the field can change, as new groups enter and exit . . .
Through this conception, one might identify a number of activities as political . . .
These activities are not necessarily directed towards a functional equilibrium, but
exist as a field of tensions in which individuals may be motivated by interest, by
concerns with the public good, and by different outlooks on the goals of community life. It may well be that in the study of such activities we encounter

---

[76] The implementation of the British nuclear armoury is another case in point. Nobody has ever voted
for it, not even the whole cabinet knew about it, or decided on the plans to create it; Thompson 1985.
Is Britain governed by antechamber, or is our Orientalist perception wrong?

[77] The 'myth of absolutism' has met recently with equally strong criticisms in the case of early modern
Europe, for the same reasons; see Henshall 1992.

[78] For a similar perspective, applied to nineteenth-century Latin America, see Forment 2003. Forment
argues for a distinction between high politics, controlled by caudillos and other forms of authoritarian power, and the large number of associations working on very different principles. See also
Muhlberger and Paine 1993 for early modern Europe.

[79] For a similar perception of the politics of medieval and early modern India, see Perlin 1985b; Inden
1990: 5–36.

institutions. But these institutions should be regarded as instances of political processes – a particular set of formalised relationships that emerge from, are constituted by, and continue to be altered through political activity.[80]

These remarks raise again the validity of the Aristotelian notion of social and political life: a huge variety of *koinôniai*, ranging from the temporary and the informal to the highly institutionalised.[81] If not, we face the danger of permanently excluding from our narratives of politics women, slaves and aliens. These might not formally participate in institutions (although this is quite debatable in a number of cases),[82] but they certainly participated in politics in the wider sense of the word that we have tried to delineate. Otherwise, it is difficult to understand why, for example, metics and slaves fought along with citizens for the restoration of Athenian democracy in 403 BCE: why should they care, if politics was the exclusive privilege of the citizens?[83] But the most important problem is that without this perspective, the policies, aims and approaches of the subaltern classes are completely written off our mental map. The lower classes in societies lacking participating institutions in the arena of high politics are then portrayed as docile subjects of a totalitarian despotism, incapable of collective action and agency.[84]

To give an example, M. I. Finley has asserted that

> whatever the facts may be about [democracies in early Mesopotamia], their impact on history, on later societies, was null. The Greeks, and only the Greeks, discovered democracy in that sense, precisely as Christopher Columbus, not some Viking seaman, discovered America.[85]

I cannot disagree more with his statement, and this for two reasons. First, talking about the discovery of democracy makes the assumption that democracy is a physical entity that exists objectively, in the same way that America has existed, since its last major geological formation some millions of years ago. The notion that a concept or an institution exists objectively in its ether, like a Platonic Idea, waiting to be discovered by the first brilliant mind to succeed, is, I hope, manifestly contestable. But I have a

---

[80] Hammer 2002: 26–7. See also Wood 2002: 5–23.   [81] *Eudemian Ethics*, 1241b, 25–7.

[82] Metics for example participated in the army, some festivals and processions, and aspects of deme life. See Jones 1999; Adak 2003.

[83] See the arguments of Middleton 1982.

[84] Again, these are not academic arguments. The recent war to implement 'democracy' rests on an Orientalist notion of docile masses unable to determine by their own actions their own future. Accordingly, Oriental dictatorships and despotisms can only change through the 'beneficing' intrusion of the West: Ali 2002.

[85] Finley 1973a: 14.

more serious disagreement, which is again implicit in Finley's comparison. What does it mean to say that America was discovered by Columbus and not by a Viking seaman? Obviously, one is not talking about its native inhabitants, who did not have to discover it, since they lived there. It clearly means discovery for the West, which is envisaged in our passage as the agent and object of history.

Finley claims that it is the Greek conceptualisation of democracy that has been used by Western Europeans to construct their own notions, institutions and practices. Fair enough, but this cannot be a claim about history in general, about humanity in general, but rather about the history of appropriation by Western Europeans (whether of America or of democracy). This is the reason that most definitions of democracy are problematic. They ultimately end up with criteria that do not fit every case, and with complaints or admissions of a misfit between definitions and realities. 'Only what has no history can be defined' Nietzsche aphorised and he was correct.[86] I prefer to keep close to Aristotle in viewing democracy (politics) as a struggle, as a process;[87] and a process or a struggle cannot be invented; it can only be waged (by various people, in various periods and contexts, with various aims and with varying outcomes).

Finally, we should better abandon the mechanistic approach of the sovereign state. One of the gravest mistakes in approaching the Greek poleis is to view them as another incarnation of the modern Western idea of the sovereign state, with clear and well-defined boundaries, possessing absolute and exclusive control of territory, population and force/power. In reality, every community consists of a variety of groups with varying ambitions, means and capacities. In order to satisfy these ambitions and to use the means and capacities, these various groups participate in politics, i.e. in processes, practices, institutions, debates and struggles. But the setting is not given: instead of thinking in terms of the mythical sovereign state, in reality polities always participate in political world-systems or imperial formations.[88]

Our Near Eastern evidence shows this clearly: a variety of polities co-exist under hierarchic relationships ranging from the village community

---

[86] See the points of Geuss 2001: 6–7.   [87] See Rancière 1999.

[88] David Held has asked this particular question in terms of the modern world. Definitions of democracy and the state depend on the questionable notion of the sovereignty of the state and its control of the economic, social and political means of production and reproduction. But this is obviously not the case in a world where multinationals, world markets, imperial powers, international organizations and transnational unions play a fundamental role. Accordingly we have to adjust our theories of the state and democracy to account for the global context of human societies and polities; Held 1995: 23–7.

to the empire. Therefore, the ambitions, means and capacities of the various groups of each community depend, change and interact with the context and conjuncture of this community within the political world-system or imperial formation of the moment. We cannot accept, for example, a definition of the sovereign state as the holder of the monopoly of military power: in reality, it might be a citizen army, a city magnate or tyrant raising his own forces, a mercenary commander, a federation of troops, etc. It is important to consider all these options as co-existing alternatives and not read them as signs of crisis or decline (always from the perspective of the sovereign state). This is a message that we have to keep in mind in understanding our own current reality.

Moreover, we have to pay particular attention to the contextual political environment instead of isolated analyses. We have seen how between 1000 and 500 BCE the collapse of the Babylonian imperial formation, the highly unstable situation of Babylonia and the emergence of Assyrian power have crucial implications for political changes: the resurgence of city-state forms, the emergence of civic subdivisions such as the tribes, in order to differentiate the old Babylonian citizens from the new Chaldean inroads, and the exploitation of the needs of Assyrian strategic policies by the citizens of Babylonia, in order to extract civic privileges and concessions.[89] The unification of Mesopotamia and adjacent areas under Persian rule led to the erosion of these privileges and concessions, since the environment changed now completely, from a multipolar to a unipolar system. The Persians had no more need of such balances and checks, and the map was redrawn in different ways.[90] These findings suggest that we cannot study popular politics in isolation from variations and changes in the wider system of states. The emergence of Greek democracy, for example, should be seen not simply as part of the internal development of each Greek polis, but also in relation with the elaboration and changes in the political world-system in which Greek poleis participated.[91] We still lack such an environmental analysis of Greek politics.[92]

---

[89] Larsen 2000a.
[90] Aegean history should be viewed within a similar prism: a unity of Aegean history based on a multipolar environment from the second millennium up to the creation of a unipolar environment by the Romans which will actually last for centuries later. In such a way the Occidentalist 'Greek mirage' can be deconstructed by regaining its historicity.
[91] For such an approach regarding early modern popular politics, see Te Brake 1998.
[92] The concept of 'peer–polity interaction' is very similar, but has yet to be employed in a detailed study in ancient history; see Snodgrass 1986; Herring 1991. For an analysis of Hellenistic poleis following such a line, see Gauthier 1987/9; Ma 2003.

Most approaches that have tried to bring closer the Greek world and the Orient, have effectively argued for the secondary importance or the minimisation of politics in such a comparative agenda; in contrast, I argue here that politics is a key issue in such an agenda, for both sides. The lower classes of the Near Eastern societies had neither control on foreign policies, nor a 'democratic' ideology,[93] but they tried to exploit the niches available and take advantage of existing institutions, creating their own counter-practices and counter-institutions.[94]

This is not to deny the particularity and distinctiveness of Greek politics in favour of an assimilated Mediterranean or Near Eastern world. The vast majority of the Near Eastern political experiences and practices that we have examined would be considered oligarchic by most ancient Greeks; democratic politics, in the ancient Greek understanding of the term, seem rather absent. But we have to remember that democracy was only a variant among the wider subject of ancient Greek poleis constitutions, and oligarchies of various sorts did constitute the mainstream of Greek political experience.

Therefore, my argument is for recognising diversity within a larger unity. But the burden of my argument is that we have drawn our arguments and our explanations of Greek distinctiveness in the wrong way. Phenomena such as the city as a community of citizens, the city as a form of identity, the communal sharing of community resources, the distinct rights of citizens, or self-government, are not distinctive features of the Greek world that can explain its particularity. We have to look elsewhere and not in an Orientalist binary opposition between a free West and a despotic Orient. Secondly, instead of viewing the polis (in the sense of a community of citizens), or democracy, as the teleological and 'classical' outcome of the evolution of Greek political life, we should rather study how a variety of processes and activities coalesced into the formation of Greek polities and democracies. If we see democracy as the continuous outcome of a struggle and not simply as a particular institutional form of high politics, then it would not emerge as the miracle, which it is often presented as.

---

[93] Though see qualifications in Finet 1975.
[94] For such an agenda, see Thompson 1993a; Perlin 1985b; Chandavarkar 1998.

CHAPTER 5

The consumer city: ancient vs. medieval/modern

We can now move to see how the concept of the polis has functioned in discussions of ancient economic history. The debate on the polis as a consumer city is an offshoot of an old discourse. It is based on a certain reading of the history of medieval and modern Europe, and the origins of capitalism and modernity. The central desideratum of this discourse is to explain how Europe moved towards modernity, how capitalism emerged and why previous eras and civilisations, or contemporary non-European ones, failed to move towards modernity and capitalism. There have been of course many answers to these questions; but one that became particularly influential was the idea that it was the medieval European city and its urban classes that opened the path to capitalism and modernity.[1] In this approach, the medieval city, separated from the feudal countryside, as 'a non-feudal island in a feudal sea',[2] composed mainly of merchants and artisans, fostered the expansion of trade and manufacture, revolutionised the stagnant countryside, and ultimately led to capitalism and modernity. The work of the Belgian historian Henri Pirenne in the early decades of the twentieth century gave particular prominence to such ideas.[3] The debate has been going on since then, but, as we will later see, this way of looking at the issue, and the viewing of the medieval city as the answer to the question, have been largely discarded.

The validity of this comparison between ancient and modern economies for the study of ancient economic history was forcefully argued for by M. I. Finley in the 1960s and 1970s;[4] since then, it has remained dominant,

[1] The idea started to be used in historiography in the aftermath of the French Revolution. Thierry and Guizot presented the medieval communes and the bourgeoisie as the ancestors of the class who made the Revolution. See Comninel 1987: 5–76.
[2] Postan 1975: 239.   [3] Pirenne 1927.
[4] Finley 1973b: 121–49, 1977. A similar approach was concurrently advanced in Austin and Vidal-Naquet 1972: 129–49.

123

in particular in the study of Greek economic history,[5] if for no other reason than no other consistent and influential alternative model has yet emerged.[6] Finley presented his ideas as a borrowing from the work of Max Weber, though there exist very important differences between his approach and that of Weber, as we will shortly see. Finley adopted two 'Weberian' ideal types: the consumer and the producer city. The consumer city is 'one which pays for its maintenance (*Lebensunterhalt*) ... not with its own products, because it does not need to. It derives its maintenance rather on the basis of a legal claim (*Rechtstitel*), such as taxes or rents, without having to deliver return values.'[7]

On the contrary, the producer city is a city deriving its means of maintenance from the productive activities of its inhabitants, i.e. trade and manufacture. The medieval city was separated from its countryside both economically and politically; on the contrary, the ancient polis ignored any distinction between urban and country dweller, and accorded citizenship and political/economic participation on equal terms to both (it is not that everybody in the polis was equal, but that inequalities were not based on the distinction between city and countryside). Therefore, according to Finley, the ancient city should be seen as a consumer city, while the medieval and modern city was a producer city. In contrast to the medieval city, the polis did not depend on manufacture and trade for its mainte- nance; rather it was the place of residence for the landowners, and it lived by rents and taxes. Moreover, the polis had no economic policy. In contrast with the medieval city, which fostered the interests of its producers, and therefore contributed to the development and growth of manufacture and trade, the ancient polis cared only for the interests of its members as consumers; it could not boost economic growth and development.[8]

According to Finley, then, despite exceptions and deviations, and accepting that in reality things were much more complicated than his ideal types, most ancient cities could be understood as consumer cities, while most medieval/modern cities could be seen as producer cities. Moreover, it is this difference between the character of ancient and the character of medieval/modern cities which explains the difference between

[5] There have been a number of dissenting voices, to a greater or lesser extent, in the field of Roman history: Hopkins 1983; Jongman 1988; de Ligt 1991; Wallace-Hadrill 1991; Pleket 1993; Mattingly *et al.* 2001. But in Greek history, Finleyan orthodoxy has found far less opposition. From the few exceptions, one should mention Osborne 1991b; Descat 1995; Bresson 2000b.
[6] For such an *aporia*, see Cornell and Lomas 1995; Whittaker 1995; Cartledge 1998; Parkins and Smith 1998; Salmon 1999. But see also Davies 1998; Horden and Purcell 2000: 89–122; Hansen 2004a.
[7] This definition by Werner Sombart is cited in Finley 1977: 13.
[8] Originally argued by Hasebroek 1933; Finley 1985a.

the ancient and the medieval/modern economy, and the inability of ancient economy to move towards capitalism.[9]

It is interesting to note, before moving on to see to what extent such an analysis is justified, how much Finley has simplified and transformed his Weberian borrowings.[10] Weber suggested that a general typology of the city from an economic perspective could distinguish between four types: the consumer city (*Konsumentenstadt*), defined in the same way as Finley; the producer city (*Produzentenstadt*), defined as a city maintained by its own manufacture; the merchant city (*Handelsstadt*), defined as a city maintained by its commerce; and what he called *Ackerbürgerstadt*, which he defined as a city which, 'while serving as place of market traffic and centres of typically urban trade, is sharply separated by the presence of a broad stratum of resident burghers satisfying a large part of their food needs through cultivation and even producing food for sale'.[11] Finley assimilated Weber's *Handelsstadt* and *Produzentenstadt* into his producer city, which seems reasonable enough in the context; but his assimilation of *Konsummentenstadt* and *Ackerbürgerstadt* into his consumer city not only assimilated two categories, which it would be valuable to keep separate, but also violated clearly Weber's understanding.[12]

On the one hand, Weber differentiated between three types of *Konsummentenstädte*: the city of the prince, depending on the court of a prince, or on princely concessions; the city of rentiers who spend there their income acquired outside the city (rents, taxes, income from offices); and finally the city of rentiers who derive their income from rents on urban property; the latter form of cities originated in the trade and commerce consolidated in the hands of an urban aristocracy. Weber explicitly argued that this last category of cities existed in antiquity, and they were only superficially *Konsummentenstädte*, but really *Handelsstädte*, the rents of which represented a tribute of acquisitors to the owners of houses.[13] Therefore, Weber clearly thought that not all ancient cities were consumer cities. On the other hand, Weber did argue that the majority of ancient cities were *Ackerbürgerstädte*; yet, when talking about the transition from

---

[9] For this inability of the ancient economy to 'take off', see the characteristic words of Finley: 'hypothetically, had the Roman empire encompassed the civilised world, as the panegyrists said, there is no reason why Europe, western Asia and northern Africa should not still, today, be ruled by Roman emperors, America still belong to the red Indians'; Finley 1973b: 176.

[10] For Finley's selective and partly misleading borrowing of Weber's concepts, see Descat 2000. For a wider discussion, see Nafissi 2005.

[11] Weber 1958: 70–1.   [12] For the following, see Bruhns 1985.   [13] Weber 1958: 68–9.

an *Ackerbürgerstadt* into consumer, producer or merchant cities, he clearly differentiated between ancient cities and consumer cities.[14]

What interests us here is that Weber never equated his ideal types of cities with particular periods, as Finley did; and he was willing to accept that a multiplicity of different forms of cities existed in every period or civilisation, while Finley reduced all ancient cities into a single type. Finley's juxtaposition of the ancient city to the medieval/modern one seems to owe more to Pirenne's understanding of the role and function of the medieval city than to Weber. Finley effectively revived in the 1970s Pirenne's conception of the medieval city, as the motor of economic development and progress, to juxtapose it to the ancient city, precisely at the point when historians of medieval and modern economies were leaving behind this conception and this whole approach to economic history.[15] The theory of proto-industrialisation,[16] Brenner's theories of class struggle and the importance of capitalist agriculture[17] and Wallerstein's[18] and Braudel's[19] world-systems theory changed the landscape of economic history; in combination, they showed, from a variety of different perspectives, that the economic and social history of medieval and early modern Europe could not be understood by using the medieval/modern city as the key explanation of economic development and change. It is not far off the mark to argue that the consumer city approach turned ancient history backwards, instead of forwards. Characteristically for the state of the field of ancient history, ancient historians managed largely to ignore in their debates what economic historians in other fields have been doing for three decades.

To return to the polis as a consumer city, this comparison and opposition between the ancient and the medieval/modern city and economy is heavily influenced by Eurocentric assumptions. To start with, the comparison is lop-sided: it compares the cities and economies of the ancient Mediterranean, not with those of medieval/modern Mediterranean, but with those of medieval/modern north-western Europe. Why have generations of scholars thought that this comparison is valid? Why have they never attempted to compare the ancient Mediterranean with later periods of its history?[20] Why have they never attempted to compare ancient

---

[14] Weber 1958: 71–4. For Weber's conception of Greek cities, see Capogrossi Colognesi 1990: 197–222.
[15] See Prak 2001b.   [16] Kriedte *et al.* 1981.   [17] Brenner 1977, 1982.   [18] Wallerstein 1974.
[19] Braudel 1981–4.
[20] Given the majestic work of Braudel 1972 on the early modern Mediterranean, one would expect that such a comparison would be highly profitable and vigorously pursued. Yet, characteristically for the state of research in ancient history, it never took place. It is hoped that the work of Horden and Purcell 2000 will lead to such a change in perspective; see Harris 2005.

Mediterranean cities and economies with any other, non-European, pre-industrial economies? What enables this certain sort of comparisons, and renders invisible any other possible comparison, is the study of ancient history from the perspective of Europe.[21] The economic and social development of medieval and modern Europe is taken to be the universal path of historical development and modernity.[22] Seen within this discourse, it is possible to ask why ancient cities and economies did not develop in the same way, and to attempt to explain the divergence by means of a comparative analysis.

In the following pages, many of the Eurocentric assumptions behind this comparison will be criticised. The comparison rests on a distinction between the ancient and the medieval/modern economy, a distinction which makes sense only from a certain European perspective. It reifies complex processes with different levels and temporal and spatial frameworks, in order to render them as part of the genealogy of Europe. Why should we talk of an 'ancient economy' or a 'medieval economy', instead of accepting that every economy in any period comprises a number of levels and sectors, which can develop in very different and even opposing ways?

Moreover, this approach takes the cities and economies of medieval and modern Europe as the standard, against which the cities and economies of all other periods and areas have to be judged. The result is easy to imagine; let us cite David Washbrook's observation: 'South Asian economic and social history was written more to explain why the region did not develop like Europe, or perhaps did not develop at all, rather than to account for the changes and developments, which did actually take place.'[23] Substitute ancient for South Asian and this is perfectly applicable to ancient history – precisely for the same reasons.[24] Furthermore, this approach separates ancient Greek cities and economies, and medieval and modern European ones, from their place within larger contemporary systems, and from their relations with other non-Western societies. They are seen as autonomous and solitary entities, developing alone, again in order to form part of a genealogy of Europe. Finally, the genealogy of the West, which moves in a linear fashion from antiquity, through the Middle Ages, to modernity, is responsible for the disappearance of historical conjuncture. In the following pages we will explore how these Eurocentric agendas are pursued in the study of the economic and social history of the Greek poleis.

---

[21] On the uses of comparisons in ancient history, see Detienne 2000.
[22] See the similar problems discussed by Aymard 1982.
[23] Washbrook 1988: 62.   [24] See, characteristically, Finley 1973b: 137–8.

LEGAL VS. ECONOMIC DEFINITIONS

The differentiation between the ancient city, which is seen as less a city than a place of residence for landowners, and the medieval and early modern city, which is portrayed as functioning as a 'proper' place of trade and manufacture, is problematic; in both cases there exists an important chasm between economic and legal/social definitions of the city. A great number of medieval cities were cities only in name; they had acquired the right to be cities, and have their own wall or jurisdiction, but they were little more than big villages.[25] To say, then, that the ancient city was simply the place of residence for the landowners, while the medieval city was the centre of trade and manufacture, is misleading. Many medieval cities were mere villages or small towns with merely a legal claim to the status of city, while many trade and manufacture centres never acquired the legal status of a city.[26] Therefore, if one seeks a valid comparison, one should compare either legal/social definitions by contemporaries or economic definitions constructed by the historian himself. We should compare ancient centres of manufacture and trade with medieval centres, and not ancient poleis with medieval and modern cities.

THE DISTRIBUTION OF POPULATION

Contrary to the general belief among ancient historians, many medieval cities had substantial populations of peasants and agricultural workers. A classic example is the city of Romans in 1579/80, as portrayed in Le Roy Ladurie's marvellous book; 36 per cent of the city population were agricultural workers, while the city included an important number of landowners and merchants who had acquired land and the status of nobility.[27] Braudel offers another late example:

Things had barely changed in 1722, when a treatise on economy deplores the fact that artisans instead of peasants were concerning themselves with agriculture in the small towns and princedoms of Germany. It would be better if everyone 'kept in his own station'. Towns would be cleaner and healthier, if they were cleared of

---

[25] 'In Germany as a whole in the late middle ages, 3,000 places are reckoned to have been granted the status of cities: their average population was no more than 400 individuals'; Braudel 1981: 482.

[26] 'Mere size was no test: many genuine cities were no bigger than villages in population or area. And the economy did not enter into consideration at all, apart from the requirement that the material goods indispensable for civilised amenities had to be available somehow'; Finley 1973b: 124. The same holds true about medieval cities.

[27] Le Roy Ladurie 1980: 5–20.

livestock and their 'piles of dung'. The solution would be 'to ban all farming in the towns, and to put it in the hands of those suited to it'. Craftsmen would be able to sell goods to the peasants; peasants would be sure of selling the regular equivalent to townspeople, and everyone would be better off.[28]

Moreover, in many cases in medieval Europe, and in most cases in later periods, the landowning elites resided in the city, living off their agricultural income, and took part in its economic life and administration. An account of medieval Italy is telling:

Many urban immigrants were or became landholders, great, middling or small; landownership, and for the wealthy, a country villa, was the first ambition of all urban classes; and over a widening area around the cities an increasing, even dominant, share of land together with livestock was held or acquired by townsmen ... The towns concentrated agrarian as well as mercantile wealth. And in varying degrees, *communes* and *universitates*, founded by *possessores*, reaffirmed their character as communities of landowners. In urban sources of all kinds the typical *civis* was figured as a landowner ... A substantial, even major part, of urban legislation was devoted with other agrarian matters to the protection, management and consolidation of citizen estates.[29]

At Milan, in 1266, in a chance list of some 2,000 citizens all without exception were registered owners in the *contado*. At San Gimignano in 1314 61.8 per cent of all property owners, holding 84 per cent of all land, were resident townsmen.[30]

Finally, many medieval cities attempted, and some managed to acquire substantial territorial possessions (such as the Italian *contado*).[31] As a result, taxes and rents from these rural areas belonging to the cities were an essential part of urban income. Therefore, it is quite misleading that medieval cities acquired their means of subsistence by exchanging their manufactured goods, and by the profits of their trade.

To recapitulate: it is true that the majority of medieval/early modern cities were not *Ackerbürgerstädte*. Peasants mainly resided outside cities, in the *contado*; in this respect, they resemble those Hellenistic and Roman cities in the Near East with Greek proprietors living in the city and the native peasants in the countryside;[32] but they certainly differ from most Greek cities, where the vast majority of peasants resided in the polis centre, and had political rights in the civic community.[33] It is equally true that, on average, merchants and craftsmen formed a much larger

---

[28] Braudel 1981: 488.   [29] Jones 1997: 280.
[30] Jones 1997: 286. For other Italian cities, see Griffiths 1981: 98–101.
[31] Berengo 1999: 111–70.   [32] Ste Croix 1981: 9–19.
[33] For the proportion of the population living in urban settlements in ancient Greece, see Hansen 2004a: 11–16; for peasants living in cities, see *ibid.*: 16–18.

proportion of, and had a much more pronounced role in, medieval/early
modern cities than was the case in ancient ones. But it is impossible
to argue that medieval/early modern cities were producer cities, while
ancient cities were consumer cities. In both, a large proportion of urban
residents were substantial landowners; rents and taxes formed a considerable part of their income; and a large part of the countryside belonged
to urban residents. Therefore, Weber was correct in differentiating
between consumer city and *Ackerbürgerstadt*, and Finley and his followers
were wrong in collapsing them in a single category.[34] The result is natural:
'The comparison of the ancient and medieval cities and their elites is a
lopsided one: discussion of the ancient city naturally embraces the society
as a whole, while discussion of the medieval city excludes the countryside,
its elites and values.'[35]

But even if one concedes that the ancient city acquired its means of
subsistence by rents or taxes from agricultural production, this is no answer
to the question of how the substantial proportion of non-agricultural
population of the big cities managed to procure its necessities. The *thêtikon*
(wage labourers), *agoraion* (merchants) and *banausikon* (artisans), which
are emphatically mentioned by Aristotle in his analysis of the ancient
polis,[36] could procure their necessities only by exchanging their products
with the landowners and peasants. Why should one not expect, *prima facie*,
that they would seek to enlarge their share, by producing new luxuries or
cheaper products? The same holds true for medieval artisans, workers and
merchants. The place of residence of the landowners is more a matter of
conjuncture than a stable factor.

EXPORTS—IMPORTS

Let us move to the question of the role of production for export. According
to Finley, 'The agrarian European feudal world provided the medieval
cities with the external markets that ancient cities lacked. The kings, lords
and church dignitaries, living on their manors or in small agglomerations,
created a fundamentally different town–country relationship from that of
their highly urbanised land-owning predecessors.'[37] Finley believed that
manufacture in ancient cities was only for the local market, while in

---

[34] See the similar conclusion of Hansen 2004a, which seems though to impute on Weber what was
Finley's misapplication.
[35] Wallace-Hadrill 1991: 243.   [36] Aristotle, *Politics*, 1291a, 1–7, 1291b, 17–28, 1296b, 25–31, 1329a, 35–9.
[37] Finley 1973b: 140–1.

medieval cities it was destined for export. He cites Xenophon saying 'of all the activities I know, silver mining is the only one in which expansion arouses no envy ... if there are more coppersmiths, for example, copper-work becomes cheap and the coppersmiths retire. The same is true in the iron trade',[38] and he comments: 'In both passages Xenophon thinks of manufacture only for the local market; otherwise, his remarks make no sense'.[39]

But in every society before the Industrial Revolution and the emergence of capitalist production, most of the production was geared towards the local market. This is true for both the ancient and the medieval cities. Compare this account of the medieval Italian cities north of Rome:

> But even in these more vigorous regions, despite high-sounding claims, the economic activity of the vast majority of towns was limited principally to local enterprise and markets. They evolved no notable export industry, and produced no mercantile plutocracy of 'ricchi populari merchatanti'. The typical guilds were minor corporations engaged in basic trades, victualling, clothing, building ... More important, in the great majority of towns, which did combine some export industry with commerce or banking, there is much to indicate that, notwithstanding contemporary views, industrialisation was marginal, capitalism in all its forms of limited development, and international enterprise, whatever its prestige and power, based in a system much more devoted to local than long-distance exchange. The bulk of the commercial population were simply retailers and artisans trading with town and country.[40]

The medieval system of guilds would never have existed if the above description were wrong. Attempts to regulate the number of artisans and their employees, their wages and the price of their products would have never been feasible, if most of the production was not destined for the local market. After all, the regulations of the guilds tried exactly to ensure that 'copperwork would not become too cheap and the coppersmiths would have to retire'.[41] When in later periods, as in the eighteenth century, production was much more controlled by merchants with exportation in mind, the old cities with their inflexible guilds and regulations were found to be a great obstacle. Therefore, production turned to the countryside, where peasant craftsmen were not protected by the guild regulations.[42] It is not by chance that Manchester, the birthplace of modern capitalism, was never a medieval city with guilds, but a city under feudal control.[43] In fact, to come back to ancient cities, one could even say that, in the absence of

---

[38] *Ways and Means*, IV, 3–6.   [39] Finley 1973b: 135.   [40] Jones 1997: 272–4.
[41] See the comments of Barel 1977: 412–22.   [42] Braudel 1982: 297–316; Kriedte 1983: 9–17; Berg 1985.
[43] See Merrington 1976: 188–9.

guild regulations, the ancient world was more favourable to trade and manufacture than the medieval cities.

This is not to say that all production was for local consumption. Finley himself admitted that some manufactured goods were destined for export in the ancient world;[44] and the same holds true about the medieval world.[45] But to understand which products, from what materials, in which areas, for which markets, in which periods were destined for export is not a matter of juxtaposing two ideal types. One has to look at patterns, trends and rhythms of consumption,[46] at communication and transportation networks, at relations within world-systems, at relations of exploitation and power, at mentalities, and so on.[47] To accomplish this task, it is important to differentiate between time scales, between regions and between levels of production, exchange and consumption.[48] It is here that the differentiation of Braudel between material culture, market (or economy) and capitalism is most helpful;[49] it helps to understand how self-consumption is concurrently linked with local market production and long-distance trade.

It also seems relevant here to suggest that different areas, different eras and different world-systems seem to give primary importance to different goods for large-scale, long-distance exchange. Metals played a particularly important role in the exchange systems of the Bronze Age Near East and the Mediterranean.[50] The ox-hide ingot, the standardised form of trading copper in the Bronze Age, is only imaginable with an intensity of exchange that is not to be found in later societies; interestingly, the ox-hide ingot is unique to the Bronze Age.[51] On the other hand, textiles and spices, and later coffee and sugar, were the chief items of large-scale trade in the medieval and early modern world-system.

Metals, textiles and spices as items of large-scale exchange seem to be of much lesser importance in classical antiquity.[52] Is it a matter of chance that the clay amphora, the container of processed agricultural goods, such as olive and wine, is the chief indicator of large-scale exchange in classical

---

[44] Finley, 1973b: 136–7.
[45] Most products were destined for local production. It was only a few manufactured goods, mainly textiles, which entered long-distance trade.
[46] See Foxhall 1998.
[47] See Mintz 1985 on the whole process of production, exchange, consumption and the social and cultural consequences of the use of sugar in the early modern world. For ancient history, see Vandermersch 1994 on the production, exchange and consumption of wine of Sicily and Magna Grecia in the fourth and third centuries BC.
[48] Wallerstein has introduced the notion of commodity chains, in order to describe and study these interrelated phenomena; see the articles in *Review*, 23, 2000.
[49] Braudel 1982: 455–7.   [50] Gale 1991.   [51] See Treister 1996: 97–103.
[52] Horden and Purcell 2000: 346–50.

antiquity?[53] Can we argue that the chief items of large-scale, long-distance trade in ancient Greek history were processed agricultural goods, and not manufactured goods or raw materials? And what are the implications of this for the nature of production, exchange and consumption, and the form and role of ancient cities within their economic world-systems? These are admittedly no more than suggestive questions; but they have a number of implications that can lead to very important conclusions. They imply that there is a reciprocal relationship between the character of each world-system, its cities and its forms of exchange on the one hand, and the chief items of large-scale trade on the other.

A last point remains. According to Finley,

the ancient–medieval contrast is closely linked with the difference in the quantity and significance of production for export in the two worlds. The local peasantry remained a constant: men with the small holdings that we have examined, even free citizen-peasants, represent the lowest and most inelastic possible market for urban production ... What is true of peasants with respect to level of demand (though not periodicity) is no less true of the urban plebs. Production can therefore leap upward to the extent, and only to the extent, that there are export markets.[54]

The idea of the constancy of demand of peasants and the urban masses is now clearly discarded by medieval/early modern economic historians.[55] I can see no compelling reason for which it should be *a priori* maintained for ancient history. Moreover, if we exclude the urban and the rural plebs, then the purchasers of exported goods were the landowning elites. Did the medieval landowners have a different or greater purchasing capacity or willingness than the ancient landowners? This is quite hard to accept *prima facie*. And one would expect that it would be more profitable for the economy of a city if it benefited directly from the consumption and spending of the landowning elite, as in the case of the ancient city,[56] than in the ideal type of the medieval one.[57]

THE PLACE OF CITIES WITHIN WIDER SYSTEMS

The belief that medieval cities were centres of interregional trade and manufacture, and that it was through their role and agency that capitalism

---

[53] Horden and Purcell 2000: 372–5. For the history of wine production, exchange and consumption, and its networks, see Unwin 1991.
[54] Finley, 1973b: 138.   [55] See e.g. de Vries 1994.   [56] Osborne 1991a.
[57] For the importance of elite consumption for early modern Indian cities and towns, see Bayly 1991: 110–62.

emerged, has been discredited by historical work in the last few decades. I will here refer only to one approach to the issue, the so-called Brenner debate.[58] This debate has centred around the work of Robert Brenner, who argued that the transition from feudalism to capitalism cannot be understood as the result of the progressive role of cities; the relations between peasants and landowners in the countryside were a much more important issue, as revealed in the different outcomes in countries that had all shared the feature of the producer city. Brenner pointed out that the role of cities is impossible to understand if abstracted from the totality of interrelationships in which they partake.[59]

Neville Morley has shown us the validity of this remark in the case of Rome.[60] Rome has been the archetype of the consumer city, a parasite on the whole of the empire, drawing its means of maintenance from state taxes and the income of the big aristocrat landowners. Morley shows that even the consumer city *par excellence* creates processes that transform the economic and social structures of the whole Italian peninsula. The demography of a population, which needs constant immigration just to ensure the maintenance of the population at the same level, had a profound effect on the demographic structure of the whole Italy; the provision of staples, wine, oil and meat to Rome transformed the forms of land exploitation, the settlement types and the cultivation forms in whole regions of Italy.

If this is true of Rome, the parasitic city *par excellence*, then this is even truer for those cities that could not depend on the privileges of being the imperial capital for their maintenance and growth. In 401/0 BCE, in the aftermath of the loss of empire and the civil war, Athens imported commodities worth 1,800 talents.[61] How did Athens pay for these commodities, given the lack of tribute, the drain of resources expended during the war and the cessation of mining in Laurium?[62] Should we classify Athens as a producer city, or is there something wrong with the model in the first place? The value of the producer city as an explanation of the emergence of capitalism has been severely curtailed; its twin, the consumer city, should suffer similarly as an explanation of ancient economic development.

In fact, the history of early modern Europe provides many examples showing how problematic is the distinction between consumer and producer cities. We see a producer city, such as Venice, conquering the whole Terraferma; in the seventeenth and eighteenth centuries its merchants turn

---

[58] Aston and Philpin 1985. [59] Brenner 1977, 1982. [60] Morley 1996.
[61] This calculation is based on Andocides, *On the Mysteries*, 133–4. [62] See Hansen 2004: 23–5.

from trade to the countryside, and re-feudalise it.[63] We see a city like Antwerp, governed by its landed aristocracy, becoming the centre of European trade and money exchange in the sixteenth century.[64] We see a consumer city like London transforming the whole English economy, but without advancing its own production.[65] We see at the same time an old feudal 'consumer' city, such as Manchester, without guilds or city-charters, becoming, because of these absences, the birthplace of industrial capitalism.[66]

In all these cases, how does the classification of producer vs. consumer city help us to understand and explain? Morley in his study shows persuasively that what differentiates seventeenth-century London from sixteenth-century Madrid is not their consumer or producer identity, but the totality of interactions and interrelationships of each city with the English and Spanish economy respectively.[67] The mistake in the comparison between consumer and producer cities is ontological thinking: the abstraction of an entity (the city) from the whole complex of relations, processes and functions in which they partake, and their non-contextual juxtaposition.

CITIES WITHIN SYSTEMS

We can argue that the distinction between consumer and producer cities does not allow us to grasp the role that a consumer city will play within a larger economic system; its role may vary enormously, from parasite to stimulator, based on its place and articulation within this larger economic system. But how about producer cities? Even if one accepts that ancient consumer cities did not have only negative and parasitic roles, is it still not

---

[63] Woolf 1968. 'In summary, the intensive farming methods, for which Northern Italy was famous, continued in use, but in a very much altered environment. The decline of the urban economy forced most peasant agriculture into a less market-oriented posture. This, together with the spread of sharecropping, made the social and political setting decidedly more "feudal" – to use that word in its nineteenth-century polemical sense – than it had been in the sixteenth century. Agriculture now bore directly much more of the burden of maintaining the privileged classes of Italian society in their accustomed style'; de Vries 1976: 55.

[64] 'Nor, another disadvantage, was the city governed either in 1500 or later by her merchants. The aldermen belonged to a handful of the families, which composed the tiny landed aristocracy, and they retained their power for several centuries. In theory, they were even forbidden to have dealings in trade – a rather curious prohibition, but one frequently repeated, no doubt because it was not always observed. Lastly, Antwerp did not have her own native merchants of international standing: foreigners dominated the scene – Hanseatic traders, English, French and above all southern merchants: Portuguese, Spanish and Italian'; Braudel 1984: 145. I think it would be stimulating to compare this picture with ancient centres like Athens, Rhodes and Delos.

[65] Wrigley 1967.   [66] Merrington 1976: 188–9.   [67] Morley 1996: 25–31.

true that there were few ancient producer cities?[68] Is it not true that there
were many more medieval/modern producer cities, and that this makes all
the difference between ancient and medieval/modern economies?

There were indeed ancient cities that based their wealth on trade, such as
Aegina or Chios; Finley believed that they were exceptions.[69] But how less
exceptional are the medieval cities that he had in mind, like Venice or
Genoa? According to the figures of Paul Bairoch, out of *c.* 1,450 cities and
towns in late medieval Europe with a population of more than 2,000,
62 per cent were small towns of 2,000–6,000 inhabitants with highly local
functions (i.e. providing a market for the exchange of local agricultural and
manufactured products), 22 per cent were regional centres with populations between 4,000 and 12,000 and a bare 14 per cent were the cities with a
population of more than 8,000 inhabitants and more than regional importance, with commercial, manufacturing or administrative focus, such as
Venice, Bruges or Paris.[70]

Of course, there are many more merchant cities in the medieval than in
the ancient Greek world. But an analysis must take into account the world-
system in which they participated.[71] The medieval world had two key areas
of 'producer' cities, northern Italy and Flanders; these cities were heavily
involved in long-distance trade and manufacture of goods, mostly textiles.
But the emergence of the 'producer' cities in these areas, and in this period,
is comprehensible only if viewed through the working of the medieval
world-system, and not through an atemporal and aspatial ideal-type construction. They emerged as part of a concentric world-system, bringing
together areas from the Baltic Sea to China, a system made possible by the
Mongol empire.[72] But this was hardly the case for most medieval cities,
which had a very different function and role, as already discussed.

Ancient poleis too must be seen in their various roles within a
Mediterranean world-system and not as isolated ideal types.[73] Given that
Greek cities participated in a much smaller world,[74] where most of Europe

[68] For an attempt to look at the Roman city of Leptiminus as a producer city, see Mattingly *et al.* 2001.
[69] Finley 1973b: 131.   [70] Bairoch 1988: 164–9. See also de Vries 1984.
[71] For the world-system of medieval cities, see Abu-Lughod 1989: 51–134.
[72] On world-systems, see Wallerstein 1974, 1991; Braudel 1982, 1984; Nitz 1993; but also Stein 1999.
[73] A similar point, from a somewhat different perspective, is argued in Horden and Purcell 2000: 89–122.
[74] 'The [European] continent can be divided into two: on one side an ancient region, long exploited by men and history and enriched by its efforts; on the other a new Europe, for long centuries uncivilised. The great achievement of the middle ages was the colonization, education, development and urbanization of this uncultivated Europe- as far as the Elbe, the Oder and the Vistula, as far as England, Ireland, Scotland and the Scandinavian countries'; Braudel 1982: 569.

was still highly underdeveloped,[75] is it not natural that medieval trade and manufacture were on a much higher scale and importance? The small number of cities like Aegina and Chios might relate to their small niche within a world-system that is controlled by others. These are only suggestions, since we still lack a study of the workings of the world-systems of antiquity, but there seems to be plenty of value in exploring them further.[76]

THE ROLE OF THE CITY IN PRE-INDUSTRIAL TIMES

But there seems to be a point at which we can be more positive about ancient cities, and which has usually been totally ignored. Finley's definition of the consumer city rests on a predetermined notion of the city and its proper economic role. The supposed separation between city and countryside, and the identification of city with trade and manufacture, is not a manifest reality. Before the Industrial Revolution, there was no reason why the city had to be the centre of manufacturing production.

From 1500 to 1800 or so, merchant capital remained mobile and dispersed. A large portion of production went into food and textiles, and increases in production generally occurred through the multiplication of small, dispersed, merchant-connected units of production, such as households and shops. Capital frequently moved to the location of labour, rather than vice versa. Consequence: a finely articulated hierarchy of markets from local to international, with local markets that corresponded to the geography of labour. The nineteenth and twentieth century brought expansion and concentration of capital in a limited number of (mainly urban) locations, movement of labour to those locations, increasing commercial production of consumer durables and services, and a sharpening division between agricultural countryside, and service plus industrial production in cities.[77]

The frustrated expectation of seeing ancient cities as centres of manufacture emanates from a misconceived premise. The location of manufacturing production in the cities, to the exclusion of the countryside, is *historically contingent*; it was found only in a few parts of the late medieval European world-system before the Industrial Revolution. When one is reminded of how manufacture moved again to the countryside in the

---

[75] One should not forget that any account of the emergence of the medieval cities starts with the great movement for land clearing and reclamation that preceded and accompanied this emergence. The creation of a new, huge north-western European agricultural world is the basis of the emergence of the new medieval cities. See Bartlett 1993.

[76] Sherratt and Sherratt 1993 move in this direction, but in a highly schematic way.

[77] Tilly 1989: 170.

following early modern period, one should realise that this premise should not be taken as the norm and the measure of every other system of cities in the past.[78] Most manufacturing production in the past was destined for local consumption and exchange. There was no apparent reason, apart from the dependent changes in consumptive fashion, why a particular city should develop a specialisation in the production of a manufactured product, and depend on its interregional exchange.

One should start the other way round. Exchange mechanisms of significant intensity were primarily instituted because of natural shortages in primary necessities, such as agricultural products, metals, timber or other raw materials. Consider the Old Oligarch:

If some city is rich in ship-timber, where will it distribute it without the consent of the rulers of the sea? Again, if some city is rich in iron, copper or flax, where will it distribute it without the consent of the rulers of the sea? However, it is from these very things that I have my ships: timber from one place, iron from another, copper from another, flax from another, wax from another. In addition they will forbid export to wherever any of our enemies are, on pain of been unable to use the sea. And I, without doing anything, have all this from the land because of the sea; yet no other polis has even two of these things: the same polis does not have timber and flax, but wherever there is flax in abundance, the land is smooth and timberless. There is not even copper and iron from the same polis, not any two or three other things in a single polis, but there is one product here and another there.[79]

These regional specialisations were not indeed random. Demosthenes provides a nice illustration of interregional exchange in the fourth century:

Now, men of the jury, take thought in your own minds, whether you ever knew or heard of any people importing wine by way of trade from Pontus to Athens, and especially wine from Cos. The very opposite is, of course, the case. Wine is carried to Pontus from places around us (*ek tôn topôn tôn peri hêmas*), from Peparethos, and Cos and Thasos and Mende, and from all sorts of other poleis; whereas the things imported here from Pontus are quite different.[80]

The specialisation of a whole area (the Black Sea) in wheat production[81] led a number of poleis (island poleis or coastal poleis of the north Aegean) to decide to exploit their crucial geographical position within maritime

---

[78] This is the famous phenomenon of proto-industrialisation; see the classic Kriedte *et al.* 1981; Prak 2001a: 123–58.

[79] *Constitution of the Athenians*, ii, 11–12. I have followed the translation by G. Bowersock in the Loeb series.

[80] Demosthenes, XXXV, 35. I have followed, with alterations, the translation of A. T. Murray in the Loeb series.

[81] Ščeglov 1990.

networks, in order to specialise in more cash-raising crops, such as the vine, instead of wheat.

Contrary to modern geographical theory, commodity production has been centred neither on the places where raw materials have been produced, nor on the places where finished products were consumed. Rather, it is located within the medium of communication itself. Here too the islands have an important role, because of their communications, which allow them a special place in the network of connectivity and redistribution, and thus enable them to maintain unexpectedly high populations.[82]

Specialisation in the production of manufactured goods was an opportunistic activity predicated on this more normal exchange of agricultural goods. This understanding goes back to Adam Smith. The whole Book III of *The Wealth of Nations* is devoted to elaborating the two ways of the advancement of trade in Europe since the Middle Ages. The first way, urban manufacture for export, is characterised by Smith as abnormal, the result of specific European conjunctures; while he thinks as natural and particularly welcome the development of manufacture, which is based on the procession of the natural products of the countryside, a development that is dependent on the prior development of agriculture.[83]

This suggestion is strengthened by Fernand Braudel; he argued that the wine and the olive are the Mediterranean equivalents of the rural industry of north Europe:

However, it is unlikely that these rural industries in the Mediterranean ever attained anything like the importance they had already acquired in England, or in northern Europe; they never took the form of a whole group of rural centres under the control of urban merchants, as was so frequently the case in France in the eighteenth century ... If correct, this observation would prove two things: first, that the Mediterranean countryside possessed an inherently better balance of resources than so many northern regions (and possibly this is true, for vines and olives were often the equivalent of rural industries of the northern countries – arboriculture balanced the peasant budget).[84]

In fact, Xenophon's text speaks of people rich in natural products coming to Athens to sell their products, but in the case of manufacture it talks of the craftsmen moving *themselves* to Athens:

---

[82] Horden and Purcell 2000: 346.

[83] See Smith 1976: 376–427. I strongly believe there is much value in looking back at Smith's remarks in constructing a historical economics for ancient history. Garlan 1999b develops such an approach for ancient history.

[84] Braudel 1972: 429.

For if the state is tranquil, what class of men will not need her? Shipowners and merchants will head the list. Then there will be those rich in corn and wine and oil and cattle; men possessed of brains and money to invest; craftsmen and professors and philosophers; poets and the people who make use of their works; those to whom anything sacred or secular appeals that is worth seeing or hearing. Besides, where will those who want to buy or sell many things quickly meet with better success in their efforts than at Athens?[85]

The mobility of craftsmen, more than the mobility of the products, may be quite an important factor in ancient economic processes. 'It is essential to stress that Mediterranean redistribution is closely tied to the mobility of the producer: the wandering craftsman is a key figure. That is one of the reasons why the search for 'industry' in the ancient world is rather absurd.'[86] The consumer city model, in trying to judge ancient cities by a flawed standard, fails to note what is most interesting about their development. The issues raised above suggest that we should pay much more attention to the Mediterranean nature of ancient Greek poleis,[87] instead of amalgamating them as ancient cities, to be compared with medieval and modern European ones. There seem to be particular characteristics of Mediterranean cities and Mediterranean economies which have been greatly obscured by the Eurocentric habit of comparing ancient cities and economies only with later medieval and modern north European cities and economies to the exclusion of Mediterranean comparisons.[88] The various functions of cities within Mediterranean economies in various periods of their history is an avenue that seems particularly promising.[89]

CONCLUSION

To recapitulate: the consumer city model shows a number of severe problems. The distinction between an 'ancient' economy and a medieval/early modern one is highly schematic; this is not to say that there are no important differences, but they have neither been properly located, nor correctly interpreted. The perception of ancient cities as unitary entities through a single perspective is misleading; and the consumer city model does not give us a plurality of interpretative models suitable for

[85] Xenophon, *Ways and Means*, V, 3–4. [86] Horden and Purcell 2000: 346.
[87] A point will be made in later chapters for their particular Aegean character as well. The Aegean archipelago, as a system bringing together closely knit islands and mainland coasts, is unique in the Mediterranean. Similar island systems are only to be found in few other places in the world: the Indonesian archipelago is probably the only other similarly important system. For island systems, see the fascinating Broodbank 2002.
[88] See the comments of Bresson 2005. [89] See the articles in Nicolet 2000.

understanding the variety of Greek poleis. Moreover, the consumer city model conceives ancient poleis as isolated entities; it does not allow us to grasp the interaction and interdependence of ancient poleis within their world-system. We have already seen how the Aristotelian definition of the polis, as consisting of various parts (*merê*), points to such a different conceptualisation. Equally, its *a priori* conception of the role of the city in a pre-industrial setting obscures the actual patterns of relationship between cities, hinterlands and wider networks in antiquity.

Finally no economy should be understood as a homogeneous entity: every economy is constituted by a variety of processes on different time scales;[90] it is spatially and socially connected with other regions and districts in concrete and contextual conjunctures; it is constituted by various *co-existing* levels and spheres of economic, social, political and mental activities.[91] We have to construct our own, positive models of ancient cities, ancient agriculture, manufacture and trade. Such an attempt forms the next part of this study.

---

[90] I refer to Braudellian multiple durations of historical time. Speaking about cities and their demography and size, we can distinguish between the time of the event (a war, a famine, a plague), the time of the conjuncture (is the city in the phase of expansion or contraction? Is family size growing, stable or declining?), and the time of the *longue durée* (nucleated or dispersed forms of settlements). Can a model of the Athenian city work without taking all three time scales into account?

[91] In ancient cities, e.g., there is concurrent production for the household, for the local market and for long-distance trade; production by the use of household labour, wage labour, dependent labour. In the same way, there is concurrent exchange by reciprocity, redistribution and trade. Finally, there is concurrent self-consumption, conspicuous private consumption and conspicuous public consumption. We have to understand in what ways all these various levels and spheres co-exist and interact, and for whose benefit. See Davies 1998.

PART III

Beyond the polis: the polis as part of a système-monde

Until now this work has pursued three goals. The first was to show how the dominant approach to the study of Greek history emerged, how the polis emerged as the key organising principle, what other alternative approaches have been sidelined and how wider discursive issues fundamentally shaped the course of scholarship on Greek history. Following this, I attempted to look back at how ancient Greeks discoursed about their poleis, paying particular attention to the various Aristotelian conceptualisations of the polis, and arguing that their analytical value is still relevant for modern historians. Finally, I have presented a critique of the current orthodoxy on the study of Greek polis: an orthodoxy that views the Greek polis as a unitary and solitary entity, to be juxtaposed to other similar entities. I pursued this critique in two case studies: the opposition of Greek polis to Oriental despotism; and the opposition of the Greek polis as consumer city versus the medieval/early modern European producer city.

The question has probably long arrived at the reader's mind: if the criticism has been successful, what is there to substitute those approaches criticised? How can we write Greek history from an alternative approach? How can Greek history be integrated with the history of the Near East and the wider Mediterranean? It is indeed legitimate to expect a positive example of what such a history would look like. But the reader, who expects to find in the following pages an alternative narrative of Greek history, will be utterly disappointed. The reason is not intellectual laziness; rather, there are some important limitations to any step forward.

The first is a limitation imposed by the absence of the necessary scholarly work from the perspective espoused in the present study. This is not to minimise the achievements of other scholars; it is only to argue that the dominance of the Eurocentric perspective and the limited interest to approaches and findings forged outside the discipline of ancient history make certain questions and certain research agendas impossible to pursue. Everybody of course has the right to pursue whichever questions seem relevant to him or her; but from the perspective outlined in this study, there remains an enormous amount of work that has not been accomplished to date. Some gaps and limits have been already pointed out; more will follow in the coming pages; until such work is accomplished, it is impossible to attempt a consolidated alternative account. Moreover, if previous approaches have been criticised for their methodological and analytical procedures, what is now needed is an alternative analytical and methodological framework. Before attempting to write an alternative narrative of Greek history, we need analytical tools that will enable us to do so. The last part of this work is devoted to the exploration of such an alternative analytical workshop. If it succeeds in convincing the reader that such an analytical framework has methodological and analytical consistency, it accords well with the evidence on ancient Greek history that we have available, and provides new insights and new ways of looking at the evidence, then its aims will have been accomplished. It remains for future works to apply the method and tools in order to construct positive historical narrative.

The task of creating such an analytical framework has been particularly difficult and hazardous, but at the same time challenging. Many influences behind the approach fostered here lie outside ancient history. In a sense, the approach and its tools had to be constructed from a continuous dialogue with various other disciplines: early modern and modern European history, world-systems theory, post-colonialism and political theory. Talking about a dialogue implies what will become clear later on: my attempt was not merely to borrow or to adopt approaches that have developed outside the field of ancient history. In fact, I have tried to modify these approaches for the particular needs of the study of ancient history, and in a number of cases I have come to criticise some approaches for failing to account for the evidence of Greek history; in these cases, the study of Greek history can even contribute towards a rethinking and adapting some central tenets of these approaches.

In contrast to the approaches criticised in the previous chapters, my attempt here is to show that the polis should be treated not as an independent entity, but as part of a system. What kind of system? Until now I have been using the word 'world-system' to convey this meaning. But the term has been charged with a number of meanings with which I would like to dissociate my use of it. In this respect, the somewhat awkward term 'système-monde', borrowed from Fernand Braudel, will serve us better; a *système-monde* does not encompass the whole world; instead it is a world in itself, based on the interdependence and interaction between its various communities, groups and regions.[1] The *système-monde* can be as small (e.g. the Aegean), or as large (the Mediterranean), as our analytic focus requires; it depends on the parameters under study, the time scale and a number of other issues. My use of the *système-monde* conveys as much meaning as this; the specific parameters must be spelled out for each particular system under study. It is important therefore to dissociate from my concept of the *système-monde* other attached notions, such as centre and periphery, unequal exchange and, of course, capitalism. These concepts are relevant for some *systèmes-mondes*; but they are not necessary accompaniments of every *système-monde*;[2] and I do not find them relevant in the systems under study here. Therefore, the limited general parameters I am trying to set out in the following chapters concern three issues: (a) that the polis is a part of a larger system (b) that there exists a multiplicity of co-existing temporal and spatial levels within that system and (c) that the poleis should be analysed within the 'environment' created by the system and its multiple levels.

[1] Braudel 1984: 21–70.
[2] Janet Abu-Lughod has argued that the medieval world-system had no centre, no hegemonic power, but consisted instead of a number of concentric cycles; Abu-Lughod 1989: 3–40. See also Stein 1999: 3–81.

CHAPTER 6

The polis as a unit of analysis: poleis and koinôniai

It has been a commonplace that societies, states and cultures are the units of analysis that historians have to use. I will restrict myself to the treatment of the notion of society in this context. Since the nineteenth century, it has been accepted wisdom that societies are distinct entities with their own rules, laws and borders, and they are the units of analysis that historians use. One could study the relations or interactions between different societies, but one still studies relations and interactions between distinct and definable entities. Is this view justified? I believe not, and in fact it has had a very pernicious influence on the study of Greek history. We hear about the contrast between aristocracy and the polis; between polis and the *ethnos*; between the citizen-hoplite and the mercenary; between Greece and the East. These distinctions emanate from a static and internalist view of society. I want then to pose two distinct yet interrelated questions: can we speak of the polis as a kind of society? And is the polis an adequate framework for the analysis of the social history of ancient Greek communities?

What is ancient Greek society then? Let us accept for a moment the usual view that a society is coterminous with the boundaries of a polity. What is Athenian society? Is it the society of the Athenian polis? There are reasons to doubt it. For, to start with, are the Phrygian and Lydian metics, who fight as Athenian hoplites to the dismay of Xenophon, part of Athenian society?[1] Are the Athenian *cleruchs* of Skyros, Imbros, Lemnos, Chersonese, Samos part of Athenian society?[2] What about the Athenian mercenaries in Asia Minor or Egypt?[3] Maybe one could think that it is possible to give a simple, affirmative or negative answer to these questions. But in reality, Athenian society is dependent on a variety of communities, networks and institutions that go beyond the Athenian polis. To put it in

[1] *Ways and Means*, II, 3; Adak 2003: 67–72. [2] Gauthier 1973; Cargill 1995.
[3] Pritchett 1974: 59–116.

the manner of Aristotle, would Athenian society be the same, if they did not exist?[4]

(a) The metics were not a dispensable part of Athenian society.[5] Their role was very important in many respects. To give just one example, they furnished some thousands of hoplites, a considerable contribution to the Athenian army.[6] The existence and continuous maintenance of a sizeable metic population is predicated upon networks of human mobility, networks of mobility of goods sufficient to provide the means of maintenance for such a big population, and finally a port that is able to command all these resources and networks.[7]

(b) Peisistratos managed to return to Athens by using the profits from his dealings with the mines of the Pangaion;[8] Thucydides had the right of working the gold mines in Thrace and consequently strong relationships and influence with the aristocracy of the area;[9] Alcibiades, after his fall from Athenian favour, retreated to his *teichê* (forts) in the Chersonese.[10] These were possessions acquired through institutions and maintained through social relations (you need workers to work the mines, and a system of relations to control their labour and dispose the product). Would Athenian society be the same if these possessions, institutions and relations did not exist?

(c) Classical Athenian society would be unthinkable without a huge number of slaves that were regularly imported. The importation of slaves is predicated upon two factors: social relations in the export communities that can maintain a steady supply of human beings subordinated enough to become commodities; and a network sophisticated enough to guarantee the maintenance of the link between importers and exporters. If the history of the American colonies is impossible to understand without the history of the creation and maintenance of the networks of supply and the 'internal' dynamics of the African communities of supply,[11] how are we to understand Athenian society without these considerations? In the beginning of the *Republic*, Socrates goes down to Piraeus to celebrate the introduction of

---

[4] For an account of Athenian society that goes beyond the usual citizen-centred approach, see Cohen 2000.

[5] Whitehead 1977.   [6] Thucydides, II, 13, 7; 3,000 metic hoplites in II, 31, 2.

[7] For mobility of goods and people, see Purcell 1990; Horden and Purcell 2000: 342–400.

[8] Herodotus, I, 61–4; Aristotle, *Athênaiôn Politeia*, 15; Lavelle 1992.   [9] Thucydides, IV, 105.

[10] Xenophon, *Hellenica*, I, v, 17, II, i, 25.

[11] For such a perspective, see Wolf 1982: 195–231; Kelley 2002.

the Thracian cult of Bendis; how does this introduction reflect on the innumerable Thracian slaves in Athens?[12]

(d) The fleet was vital for the maintenance of the Athenian empire and of the Athenian society. But the fleet depended among others on a large number of rowers. It should by now be clear enough that a large part of the rowers were *not* Athenian citizens, their slaves or metics, but foreigners from various Aegean communities;[13] otherwise, the Lacedaimonian advice to Cyrus to offer a drachma as daily pay, in order to recruit the Athenian sailors, would be incomprehensible.[14] So, the Athenian navy depended on the availability of a huge amount of surplus labour from all over the Aegean communities; and this availability was itself dependent upon a variety of social relations, networks and institutions.[15]

People might raise the argument that this is an analysis that fits Athens well, but Athens is obviously an atypical case, which can be hardly used to generalise about Greek poleis. Indeed, but the argument is precisely that from Athens to an inland community of Arcadia there is a whole spectrum of possible interrelationships and interdependencies between communities, large and small, coastal and inland. But let me give another example from the tiny polis of Arcesine in the Cycladic island of Amorgos. Arcesine was one of the three poleis on Amorgos. Nevertheless, in the 'Athenian Tribute Lists' the three poleis appear as a single entity (*Amorgioi*) paying one talent of tribute to Athens.[16] If this one talent is divided between the three poleis, then all of them are part of the vast group of 'small spenders', communities paying less than one talent as tribute. As Lucia Nixon and Simon Price have shown, the assessments in the Tribute Lists are based not on territory or population, but on the total amount of resources and wealth available to the community.[17]

The three island poleis therefore do not seem to have any special kind of resources, and their wealth should resemble that of the vast majority of other Greek small poleis. Yet, we have a number of inscriptions from the late fourth century, recording loans contracted by the polis of Arcesine from a variety of lenders coming from other Cycladic islands.[18] What is

---

[12] *Republic*, 327a; see Parker 1996: 170–5. [13] Van Wees 1995. [14] Xenophon, *Hellenica*, I, v, 4.
[15] To put it the other way round: would Aegean societies be the same in the absence of huge imperial fleets in need of surplus labour? How would they maintain their populations and their social *modi vivendi*? I think this is a very clear example where the existence of networks of mobility and means of employing surplus labour influence social relations.
[16] See Meiggs 1972: Appendix 14, Carian District. [17] Nixon and Price 1990.
[18] On these inscriptions, see Gauthier 1980.

notable in these inscriptions is that the loans are secured on the public and private property (which is divided into real estate and 'maritime' wealth) of both the citizens of Arcesine and the 'oikountes en Arkesinêi', i.e. the metics of Arcesine. It is even more notable that the property of those metics is important enough to be cited as surety in all the loans recorded, and in all cases where there is mention of the sureties in each inscription. How could a tiny polis of a small Aegean island with no particular resources or wealth 'acquire' such an important community of metics? Is this not a clear case that the vast majority of the Aegean communities participated in networks of relations, which render the notion of a distinct and bounded society problematic?[19]

I argue then that a specific society (Athenian society), or even Greek society as a whole, cannot be the one and only unit of analysis.[20] Beyond the individual polity lies a unit of analysis, which, to use Immanuel Wallerstein's words, is the world-system: 'It is a world-system, not because it encompasses the whole world, but because it is *larger than any juridically defined political unit*' (emphasis mine).[21] Every society is an interdependent part of this system, although obviously of varying grades of influence, power or subordination within the system. Greek society as a distinct entity with clear borders is a chimera. Societies are not something that is given; they are not observable and distinct realities. Rather, society, to use a Braudellian phrase, is 'a set of sets': 'For the historian, who is bound so closely to the concrete world, total society can only be a sum of living realities, *whether or not* these are related to each other: to him it is not a single container, but several containers – and their contents.'[22] It is the empirical and contextual interlinking and interdependence of varying communities, polities, institutions and networks.

We will now look at the context of society and examine the polis as a community of citizens and as a kind of society. Can the Greek polis be thought as a form of society? Is it adequate to think of a Greek polis as a community of citizens? Let us start with the polis as a kind of community. Now, this is really a very helpful concept in thinking about the polis.[23] But it is necessary to qualify this concept in two ways.

First, in many cases the polis does not comprise only a community of citizens; I am not referring here to slaves, 'serfs', women, metics and

---

[19] See further Brun 1996: 163–82.
[20] See the similar concerns of Pocock 1975b regarding the subject of British history.
[21] Wallerstein 1974: 15. See also Wallerstein 1991: 229–72.
[22] Braudel 1982: 458.   [23] See e.g. Walter 1993.

citizens with lesser rights, although mentioning them is very helpful in avoiding the pitfall of creating a monolithic picture dominated by citizens.[24] I am mainly referring to cases where the polity comprises both a community of citizens, and dependent but free communities with various statuses and in various relationships to the dominant community of citizens. The *Lacedaimonian* polis was an indivisible unity of the community of *Spartan* citizens and the dependent communities of the *perioikoi*, each with its own constitution and citizenship.[25] One can cite similar examples from Elis, Crete and Locris. We have a law of the Hypocnemidian (East) Locrians, regulating their relationships with their colonists to the Western Locrian polis of Naupaktos.[26] From this document it is clear that the East Locrians form a *koinon* of communities with their own laws and magistrates, which are explicitly called poleis. Nevertheless, political decisions are taken in the name of and by the citizens of the dominant polis of Opous.[27] So, the state of Opous is not simply its community of citizens, but a composite polity.

But it is neither simply a matter of juridical relations, nor a matter concerning some backward areas of Greece. Let us consider the case of relations between *mêtropoleis* and *apoikiai*. A. J. Graham wrote long ago a very stimulating book about them. His healthy British empiricism enabled him to avoid the pitfalls of the traditional German legalistic approach to the question; instead of trying to define in any possible way the legal relations and obligations between them, he was more interested in seeing the repercussions of these relations in the real lives of ancient people.[28]

The result is very stimulating. Poleis like Thasos held a direct control over the political, social and economic relations of their *apoikiai*, despite the fact that the *apoikiai* were themselves poleis with distinct capacities and obligations: as an example, Thasos legislated to prevent stasis in its *apoikiai*.[29] Poleis like Corinth created *apoikiai* in crucial places for the maintenance of their wide links and even sent magistrates to some of these *apoikiai*.[30] Poleis like Miletus created a huge network of *apoikiai* in their field of interest in the Black Sea, which allowed a plethora of potential strategies for its own citizens: the decrees allowing equal political, economic and religious participation to Milesian citizens in the various Milesian *apoikiai* show the importance of these practices.[31] Finally, one

---

[24] See, with caution, the approach of Cohen 2000.   [25] Shipley 1997; Hall 2000.
[26] Meiggs and Lewis 1969: no. 20.   [27] Nielsen 2000.   [28] Graham 1983.   [29] Graham 1983: 83–4.
[30] Magistrates in Poteidaia: Thucydides, 1, 56.2; Graham 1983: 135–7. See Fornis 1997.
[31] Relations between Miletus and Olbia: Tod 1948: no 195; Graham 1983: 98–117.

sees the great advantages of imperial control: Athenian *apoikiai* and *cleru-chies*, long- and short-term Athenian settlements abroad.[32] They proved important enough to force the Athenians to withdraw from one war (the King's Peace in 387 BCE)[33] and participate in another (the Lamian war in 322 BCE).[34] The widespread cases of island *peraiai* (island communities possessing territories on the mainland) serves to remind us of the impor-tance of these issues.[35]

In all these cases, the precise legal relations are not very important. What is important is that we see the polis reaching outwards beyond its own territory and having control beyond its own citizens. We should not indeed belittle the importance of these relations due to the relative absence of evidence. The discovery of a single inscription with the Athenian law imposing a grain tax of 8.5 per cent on the three *cleruchies* of Lemnos, Imbros and Skyros,[36] a reality totally unexpected from the pre-existing evidence, shows the importance of these relations for our poleis.

Second, the fact that the polis *is* a community of citizens does not mean that it is actually *governed* by a community of citizens.[37] According to the Greek political philosophers a polis can be governed by a single person, a few, or many, without any discrimination to its status as polis. One can mention the innumerable cases where the internal and external power struggles resulted in more or less permanent tyrannies, which have misleadingly been divided between an original 'age of tyrants' and recurr-ing later tyrannies. The coinages of the Sicilian tyrants are inscribed with the name of the community of citizens, not with their own name or with the name of a kingdom (as in the United Kingdom of GB and NI). The Athenian treaty with Dionysius I of Syracuse in 367 BCE is characteristic: the treaty is between the Athenians and Dionysius and his descendants. Dionysius is described as 'archon of Sicily'. Yet the oath is to be taken not by Dionysius alone, but along with 'the archons and the *boule* of the Syracusans, and the *strategoi* and *trierarchoi*'.[38] Although the oath is between the Athenians and Dionysius, archon of Sicily, the various archons and the council of Syracuse are made part to the oath.

---

[32] Cargill 1995.
[33] The fear of losing the *cleruchies* of Lêmnos, Imbros and Skyros were already crucial in the peace negotiations of 392 BCE and the Athenian capitulation in 387 was meant to preserve them, as in fact it did; Xenophon, *Hellenica*, IV, viii, 15.
[34] In order to save the *cleruchy* of Samos from being returned to the Samians; Diodorus, XVIII, 8, 7.
[35] Brunet 1997; Funke 1999.   [36] Stroud 1998.
[37] A characteristic attitude in Morris 1991: 27: 'If the citizens became subjects, their community ceased to be a polis.'
[38] Tod 1948: no. 136.

The distinction between the monarch and the polis is hard to make in this context, because monarchy and even the existence of a macro-state, encompassing the major part of Sicily, does not exclude the existence of the community of citizens and its archons and governing bodies. Besides the case of Cyrene and its well-known kingship,[39] one can usefully turn to the situation in Cyprus. Even if the references of Isocrates to the Cypriote kingdoms as poleis are rejected as part of political propaganda,[40] the famous bronze tablet of Idalion is illuminating: there, besides the king one will find straightforward references to the polis, in the explicit sense of civic community.[41]

To recapitulate; it is important not to miss the fact that many poleis were much more than simply a community of citizens. Many hegemonic poleis managed to incorporate within their boundaries a multiformity of free or unfree communities of various statuses. No definition of the polis can use as a criterion a feature that applies only to a minority; but on the other hand it is important not to miss this reality under homogenising statements. This is highly significant, when we remember that polities with multiple and hierarchic levels of participation are universally encountered both in other places (like the Near East), and in other periods of Aegean history (like the Mycenaean polities). Instead of creating stages of Greek history, we could study in parallel these hierarchic polities and attempt to trace processes of consolidation and fragmentation.

Moreover, we must recognise the fact that the organisation of power *within* Greek communities is fluid and multiform; instead of creating stage histories and treating the large number of examples to the contrary as exceptions, we can concentrate on the mechanics and processes of power consolidation and fission in various forms of political communities and in their *longue durée*.[42] Of course one could dismiss these features as exceptions.[43] But we have to bear in mind not only that the number of exceptions will be inconveniently high and that we are going to make exceptions of many of the most important poleis; it is also that an ideal-type construction like this makes it impossible to understand change and transformation, the processes of power and territory consolidation/fragmentation.

We will now come to the concept of polis as a kind of society. Nothing can be more unhelpful than this. To quote James Whitley's words,

The polis is usually thought of as a unique and specific social form, which presupposes an antecedent state of uniformity ... If the concept of city-state is

[39] Mitchell 2000.   [40] Isokrates, *Euagoras*, 49–50, 52–7; *Nikokles*, 9, 19, 24, 31.
[41] Demand 1996, 1997.   [42] See e.g. Morris 1991.   [43] See, characteristically, Runciman 1990: 348.

to retain any validity at all, it should be seen as an institution. It was never a type of society, the defining principle of Greek life and thought, whose most representative example was fifth-century Athens. Rather, it was a successful institution, with very limited functions, which managed to accommodate itself to a very great range of social formations. The term polis should delimit a range of institutional forms; it is not to be identified with Greek society in any stage of its development.[44]

The 'rise', 'acme' or 'decline' of the polis is not the 'rise', 'acme' or 'decline' of a single type of society; rather, different communities or different regions developed in different or divergent ways; the fact that the variety of these communities were identified as poleis should not lead us to think of them as sharing a common social form.

To give an illuminating example, W. G. Runciman[45] has tried to demonstrate that what the various kinds of poleis shared was an evolutionary dead-end: whether democracies or oligarchies, they were far too democratic to expand in any systematic, consolidated and long-term way; thus, they were destined to be dominated by larger entities like territorial states,[46] whether kingdoms (Macedonia) or republics (Rome). They could not transform internally; they had to be dominated in order to change. It is fairly obvious that this view is related to the view of polis as a form of society. Runciman's statement is sophisticated, but can stand only by ignoring a large number of contrary cases.

The Greek poleis of Sicily were incorporated into a territorial state under the domination of the tyrants and kings of Syracuse.[47] In Crete, the archaic period with the legendary hundred poleis was followed by a process of territorial consolidation, whereby in the Hellenistic period a few cities came to dominate large parts of the island; Gortyn came to control the whole central-south Crete, Knossos the central-north, Hierapytna the east, etc.[48] During the archaic and early classical periods, Sparta, Elis and Argos were able to acquire or conquer in a more or less permanent way, and by various methods, large territories, controlling between them more than 60 per cent of the Peloponnese.[49] Greek poleis participating in regional *koina* and *ethnê* (the Aetolian and Achaean poleis and *phylai*) managed to transform their state organisation and incorporate by various means an astonishing number of communities, creating trans-regional forms of

[44] Whitley 1991: 194.   [45] Runciman 1990: 364–7.
[46] For the territorial state, or, to adopt Hansen's more appropriate term, the macro-state, see Hansen 2000a: 16.
[47] Davies 1978: 187–97, 246–9.   [48] Chaniotis 1996: 27–8; Hansen and Nielsen 2004: 1144–95.
[49] See Hansen and Nielsen 2004: 70–4 (size of territories), 489–504, 540–6 (Elis), 547–98 (Sparta), 598–619 (Argos).

organisation.[50] And if one is reminded of the Athenian involvement in the Aegean, Sicily and Egypt, the creation of colonies and *cleruchies* and the acquisition of landholdings in foreign lands by the Athenian elite, one is left to wonder what would have happened if the Athenians had been successful on one of their fronts. As J. K. Davies put it,

> its failure (the Athenian expedition to Sicily) decided the war and thereby determined that Greek history would not go the way of Italian history. There a dominant power, Rome, commanded preponderant resources, and ultimately merged its sovereignty in a larger scale entity. Greece was to continue to be polycentric, competitive, spoiling, and subject to influence and pressure from outside.[51]

So there was neither an evolutionary dead-end, nor a single response to matters of internal and external relationships. We cannot use the polis as a form of society in these general terms.

To summarise: the polis cannot be taken as the sole unit of analysis for Greek history. Greek poleis were always, but in varying degrees and ways, part of a wider world, which needs further analytical tools in order to be conceptualised. At the same time, Greek poleis cannot be taken as simply a form of society, or as a community of citizens. Greek poleis have formed very different societies, including very variable elements; many of them have included many more people than their community of citizens. What is to be done?

---

[50] Aitolia: Funke 1997; Scholten 2000. Achaia: Larsen 1968: 215–40; Morgan 2000, 2001.
[51] Davies 1978: 133. See also the similar critique of Runciman by Morris 1997b.

CHAPTER 7

Poleis and space

After our discussion of whether the polis should be treated as the sole unit of analysis for Greek history, it is time to attempt to define alternative units of analysis and research tools. In this section we are going to look at the spatial side of Greek poleis. Unfortunately, the location of Greek poleis within space has been one of the most neglected sides of the study of Greek history. The most characteristic index of this attitude is the habit of depicting Greek poleis as simple dots on the map, without showing the extent of their territories. I must be obviously mistaken, and yet the only map I can locate that attempts to portray Greek communities as territorial entities is in the publication of Müller's *Die Dorier* in 1824. In the words of Archibald, 'the usual representation of historical communities as dots in a white void reinforces the static impression of isolated, nucleated oases'.[1]

Another very common problem with the use of maps in the study of Greek history is the misleading depiction of poleis territories. The case of Athens is characteristic: all maps in general works of Greek history, and most even in specialised studies, depict only Attica as the territory of the Athenian polis. I know no map of the territory of the polis of the Athenians which attempts to depict the overseas settlements of the Athenian polis (*cleruchies* and other dependent communities). In fact, one has to go all the way back to Kahrstedt's book of 1934, titled *Staatsgebiet und Staatsangehörige in Athen*,[2] to find a spatially aware analysis of Athens, which puts together the citizens, the metics, the *cleruchs* and the perioikic communities (Oropos, Eleutherai). Generations of readers and scholars get accustomed to the idea that you can simply ignore these communities, when thinking and writing about Athens. Of course, it is not simply the case that the *cleruchies* are not depicted, because they were temporary acquisitions; some of them were indeed (Eretria, Samos), although the Athenians went into war with the Macedonians for them, a war that

---

[1] Archibald 2002: 49.   [2] Kahrstedt 1934.

abolished Athenian democracy for many years. But many, and some of the most important ones (Lemnos, Imbros, Skyros), were part of the Athenian polis for the whole of the classical period, even down to Roman times.[3] Could one ignore Venetian overseas settlements in maps of Venetian history? I doubt it.

In the following pages, I attempt to look at the spatial aspect of Greek poleis from three viewpoints in descending order: the first is the larger spatial unit, what until now I have called 'the world-system'; the second is an intermediate level that we can call 'region'; and the third is the spatial configuration of each Greek polis, in regard to both its spatial arrangement within its own boundaries, and its arrangement with the two larger levels that we have defined. A final point I want to make is that these levels of analysis should not be reified; they should be viewed as dynamic arrangements and configurations, and not as new analytical entities substituting the polis-entity.

POLEIS AND TERRITORIES

Varieties of poleis territories: a classification

Starting from the third level, it is of course well known that each polis (e.g. the polis of the Corinthians) comprised a political centre (Corinth) and a territory (Corinthia). In this respect it would be wrong to argue that the spatial aspect of the polis has been neglected. The problem rather lies in the understanding of this relationship. In reality, this relationship shows enormous variations.[4] In the following lines I attempt to classify three basic different forms of relationship between a polis and the exploitation of its territory and resources.

There were poleis that depended on the exploitation of their territory *for their own* subsistence and reproduction; in this case we are dealing with agricultural communities mainly involved in cerealiculture, and secondarily in the production of those other agricultural staples (oil, wine, fruits) and animal products that were necessary for their own needs.[5] Of course, they would still have to import a number of commodities not locally available (metals, salt, slaves), but their economic and social arrangements were geared primarily towards self-production and self-consumption. A large number of mainland and inland Greek poleis belonged to this category.

[3] Their study is now much easier thanks to Cargill 1995.
[4] See Gehrke 1986: 96–176; Osborne 1987: 113–36.   [5] See Gehrke 1986: 97–116, 150–63.

The second category comprised poleis that depended again on the exploitation of their territory for their subsistence and reproduction; but the crucial difference with the first category was that the exploitation of their resources was geared to a large extent towards staple commodities that were meant for *exchange* (wine, oil, fish, wood, metals) and not simply for self-consumption.[6] This is not of course to say that their economies were monocultures, devoted to the cultivation of a single crop, as the West Indies sugar economies, or modern African monoculture economies.[7] Such monoculture economies were, and still are, usually the result of outside imperial imposition; this was rarely the case with ancient Greek poleis.[8] The poleis of this category would of course devote a substantial area of their land to cereals and other crops, which would be locally consumed; but their commercial crops had extremely important effects on their settlement patterns, communications,[9] network systems, credit and commercial arrangements[10] and social institutions and practices.[11]

The case of Sicilian Acragas is characteristic: although literary sources tell us that the cultivation of cereals played an important role in its economy,[12] here is Diodorus' account of its state in the late fifth century:

> At this time, so it happened, that the polis and the *chôra* of the Acragantines enjoyed great prosperity ... Their vineyards excelled in their great extent and beauty and the greater part of their territory was planted in olive trees from which they gathered an abundant harvest and sold to Carthage; for since Libya at that time was **not yet** planted in fruit trees, the inhabitants of the territory belonging to Acragas took in exchange for their products the wealth of Libya and accumulated fortunes of unbelievable size ... and Polycleitus in his *Histories* describes the wine cellar in the house [of an Acragantine] as still existing ... there were in it, he states, three hundred great *pithoi* hewn out of the very rock, each of them with a capacity of one thousand amphoras, and beside them was a wine-vat, plastered with stucco and with a capacity of one thousand amphoras.[13]

As one can surmise, concentration on the exploitation of resources for exchange[14] had as a corollary a greater or lesser reliance, depending on the

---

[6] The point is old: see Morel 1983: 558; but it has not yet managed to reach the Anglo-Saxon literature on Greek history. The influence of Finleyism is surely responsible. See the reorienting comments of Osborne 1996a; also Gehrke 1986: 116–49.

[7] See Wolf 1982: 310–53.   [8] But see Horden and Purcell 2000: 284–7.

[9] Bonias *et al.* 1990 on Thasos.   [10] Etienne 1985.

[11] In the case of Thasos, e.g., one can see how the leading families of this *cité commer çante* invested in the cultivation of vines and the construction of rural kilns for the *emballage* and exchange of wine; see Garlan 1999b.

[12] References in Nenci 1993.   [13] Diodorus, XIII, 81, 4–83, 3.

[14] Exploitation of mines should be included here; for the effects of the Laurion mines on the landscape use of South Attica and Athens in general, see Osborne 1985: 93–126, 1991b; Rihll 2001.

case, on the constant importation of cereals for the subsistence of these poleis. In contrast to primitivist expectations of autarky, there exists evidence enough that many Aegean communities were importing cereals on a regular basis;[15] thus, through interdependence for vital necessities, relations between different poleis were further accentuated.

Furthermore, the construction of pottery kilns in the countryside, in order to facilitate the collection and exchange of the commercial staples, is a characteristic feature of these exchange mechanisms. The best-analysed example is that of Thasos;[16] but pottery kilns in the countryside, particularly near the seashore, have also been found in Peparethos,[17] Cnidos,[18] Paros and Naxos,[19] and Samothrace;[20] they are all communities whose trademark amphoras are found widely distributed over all the Mediterranean and the Black Sea.

The example of Cnidos is particularly interesting. A variety of coastal pottery kilns have been found; but most impressive is the large complex of amphora workshops in the inland location of Resadiye; this shows that simplistic dichotomies between agriculture and manufacture and between city and countryside do not apply usefully to the patterns of Greek history.[21] We have already commented on this, but let us repeat once more: there is no inherent reason for which manufactural production should be restricted to the city, to the exclusion of the countryside. If anything, European proto-industrialisation in the countryside shows why we should avoid such crude simplifications.[22]

Finally, it is characteristic of these poleis with commercial exploitation of their territory that there is a very lively market in land and other forms of real property;[23] to an important extent, land is treated as a means of extracting surplus and not simply subsistence.

An important group in between these two categories are those poleis which, though devoted to cereal cultivation to a great extent, were able to export regularly large quantities of cereals; thus, although these poleis might cover their subsistence needs by their own means, their regular large exportable surpluses put them on a different level with the self-centred poleis of the first category, and much closer to the outward-looking

---

[15] See Bresson 2000a. [16] Picon and Garlan 1986.
[17] Doulgéri-Intzessiloglou and Garlan 1990. On the wine of Peparethos and its exportation, see Demosthenes, XXXV, 35.
[18] Empereur *et al.* 1999. [19] Empereur and Picon 1986. [20] Karadima-Matsa 1994.
[21] See Garlan 1999b. [22] Kriedte *et al.* 1981. [23] See the case of the Cyclades: Etienne 1985.

poleis of the second one.[24] These poleis were mainly situated in the wider Greek world (e.g. Sicilian poleis,[25] Olbia,[26] Cyrene[27]).

Lastly, a third category comprises those communities that based their subsistence and reproduction not primarily on the exploitation of their territory, but to a great extent on redistribution, service and position: **redistribution** in the sense that they were involved in the movement and exchange of commodities mainly produced by others;[28] **service** in the sense that their members earned their living by working for others, as sailors,[29] mercenaries[30] or craftsmen; **position** in the sense that these communities exploited their exalted place within material[31] and cultural[32] geographies. One could of course add poleis that depended on **manufacture**, but it is very difficult to find such communities, before the late Hellenistic and Roman period.[33]

My purpose in constructing the above classification is not to present another ideal-type classification of poleis. Instead, it is a classification of **relationships** between poleis and their territories. It is obvious that for some poleis, at some periods or even in their whole history, a specific form of exploitation of the territory and its resources was dominant, if not the only one existing. But most of the time, and for most of the poleis, there was a variety of overlapping relationships, whether a single one was clearly dominant or not. Therefore, the aim is to use this classification in order to study the changing forms of relationships between poleis and their territories, and not to reduce the poleis as static personifications of the ideal types. Let me give an example: the Arcadian polis of Mantineia was an inland community, which seems to belong among those poleis that depended on the exploitation of their territory for their own use.[34] And yet, we know that many of its citizens made a living by fighting abroad as mercenaries;[35] it is not then simply a self-focused community that we are dealing with. What I want to stress is the relativity and inherent mutability of such relationships, which can only be studied for specific communities, at specific conjunctures and in specific contexts.

---

[24] See de Angelis 2000, 2002.   [25] Carter 1990; Fantasia 1993; Nenci 1993.   [26] Ščeglov 1990.
[27] Rhodes and Osborne 2003: 486–93. See Laronde 1996.
[28] Gehrke 1986: 172–6. The most characteristic case is of course Aegina; see Figueira 1981.
[29] Rauh 2003: 146–68.   [30] For Arcadian mercenaries, see Roy 1999.
[31] E.g. poleis in strategic locations, such as Byzantium: Polybius, IV, 38–44.
[32] E.g. poleis sanctuaries, such as Delphi and Delos; Reger 1994; Gehrke 1986: 166–72.
[33] For manufacture in Roman cities, see Morel 1985. Though, according to Socrates, most of the Megarians made a living from their manufacture of garments; Xenophon, *Memorabilia*, II, viii, 6.
[34] For all the following references to Mantineia, see Hodkinson and Hodkinson 1981.
[35] Roy 1999: 346–9.

It must be quite clear from the above exposition that space plays a fundamental role in the history of Greek poleis. This can be qualified in a number of senses. To a great extent, the difference between the two first categories of poleis is geographical: the poleis of the first category would be usually found in inland areas of the Peloponnese, Boiotia and the rest of mainland Greece (Sparta, Phleious, Tegea, Thebes); while coastal and island communities figured prominently among the second category. All the big producers of transport amphorae, the clearest indication of the exchange orientation of the second category, were island (Rhodes, Thasos, Cos, Chios) or coastal communities (Cnidos, Sinope, Heracleia Pontica, Mende).

But it is not simply a difference between inland and coastal communities. A note of Polybius is very revealing in this respect. He is describing the Illyrian expeditions to plunder Elis and Messenia, and he comments: 'The Illyrians were all the time ravaging these areas; because of the length of the coasts, and of the fact that the cities who rule these areas are located inland (*mesogeious einai tas dynasteuousas poleis*), the help to these people against the Illyrians came from afar and slowly.'[36] Elis and Messenia were two areas that belonged firmly in the first category of poleis, exploiting their territory for their own use; and despite the fact that they possessed long coasts, it was the way they exploited their territory which determined the location of the cities and their relationship with the sea. Topography on its own determined nothing.

Furthermore, the communities that depended on redistribution, service or position are even more revealing of the inadequacy of a purely topographical approach. Making a living out of redistribution, service or position does not depend on any simple geographical determinism (there is no purely geographical reason for which Aegina should have been a commercial polis; though there are of course purely geographical reasons for which Orchomenos in Arcadia could not have been); it depends on exploiting advantageous conjunctures; on the nature of interactions and of the wider system; and on the nature of the actors themselves. There is no intrinsic reason why islands should be wealthy nodes of communication and agricultural export; they could equally be impoverished and isolated places of exile.[37] Equally, there is no intrinsic reason for which inland or mountainous communities should be geared towards self-production and -consumption.[38]

---

[36] *Histories*, II, 5.
[37] For the variety of Greek images of insularity, see Vilatte 1991; for the variety of possibilities of Aegean islands, see Brun 1996; for the Aegean islands as impoverished isolated refuges in post-antique times, see Vacalopoulos 1976; Slot 1982; Sanders 1996.
[38] Greek inland mountainous communities were centres of mobile craftsmen and traders in Ottoman Greece; see Tsotsoros 1986; Asdrachas 2003: 357–67.

It is not simply topography, but the *historical configuration* of spatial *relationships* that play a determining role in human history: 'connectivity is not a matter of physical geography, but of the patterns of human mobility'.[39] It is important then to draw attention to two different aspects of the spatial configuration of the poleis. The first is the location of poleis within networks of power, culture or redistribution of goods and people. The second is the effects of networks on spatial arrangements and the exploitation of territory.

Poleis and networks

Very revealing is the case of the six poleis of Lesbos, analysed by Alain Bresson.[40] He shows that the two most powerful poleis, Methymna and Mytilene, did not possess larger territories, or more fertile lands, than the rest of the island's poleis; rather, their dynamism depended on their position on the part of the island facing the Asia Minor coast, and their ability to exploit the Eastern Mediterranean traffic that passed between the eastern coast of Lesbos and Asia Minor, towards the Straits to the north, and towards Rhodes and Egypt to the south.

Another example is Corcyra. We know that the production of wine and other staples was a very important activity for the island; the beginnings of the notorious civil war were due to the punishment of the leaders of the oligarchs with a huge fine for cutting stakes for their vines in the sacred grounds of Zeus.[41] But Corcyra was not simply a community of agricultural producers. According to Thucydides, 'Indeed it was only shortly before the Persian war and the death of Darius the successor of Cambyses, that the Sicilian tyrants and the Corcyraeans acquired any large number of galleys. For after these there were no navies of any account in Hellas till the expedition of Xerxes.'[42] Thucydides says that at the outbreak of the Peloponnesian war, Corcyra had a fleet of 110–20 triremes,[43] which was manned to an important extent with slaves.[44] Since we do not have any evidence that the Corcyraeans used their fleet in order to conquer territory, or to exact tribute (i.e. what the Athenians did), then the obvious question is what was the reason for maintaining such a large fleet. It looks probable that the purpose was to guard the Adriatic Sea *traffique* from piracy.[45] We see here how the placing of this community within a network changes its internal arrangements – in this case the

---

[39] Horden and Purcell 2000: 395; see also 53–88.   [40] Bresson 1983.   [41] Thucydides, III, 70.4.
[42] Thucydides, I, 14.2.   [43] Thucydides, I, 25.4, I, 54.2.   [44] Thucydides, I, 55.1   [45] Kiechle 1979.

creation of a large fleet, with all the huge logistical, social, economic and political issues which the creation of a Greek fleet raised.[46]

The North Aegean island of Peparethos (modern Skopelos), offers a further example. It is telling that in the fifth century this island polis paid an annual tribute of three talents to the Delian League; this puts it among the small list of the 'big spenders'.[47] What is even more interesting is the fact that the tribute of Peparethos was eighteen times larger than that of the neighbouring island of Ikos (1,000 drachmas) and twelve times more than that of Alonesos (1,500 drachmas);[48] these differences cannot be explained simply by larger agricultural territory or enhanced fertility. It looks probable that it is Peparethos' wine production for long-distance trade that makes the difference. Peparethos had a strategic position among the maritime routes that led to the Black Sea; for traders sailing there, buying en route the wine of Peparethos to exchange for the grain of the Black Sea, was a favourable option, as the passage from Demosthenes already quoted demonstrates.[49] The construction of amphora kilns in the coastal countryside of Peparethos, in order to take advantage of this trade, is now securely attested.[50]

Poleis, networks and spatial arrangements

This attempt to exploit the routes of long-distance exchange has important repercussions for the spatial arrangement of the polis. The Cyclades offer some very characteristic examples.[51] In the fourth century, we see a movement of the centres of some island poleis from the interior towards the coast. Tenos actually constructed a whole new city centre on the coast in the middle of the fourth century;[52] Cythnos, where the old centre is not so far away from the coast to require the movement of the whole settlement to the sea, constructed Athenian-style 'long walls' to connect the new fortified port with the old centre.[53] The move to the coast is even more impressive if one considers the resurgence of piracy in the fourth-century Aegean.[54]

In contrast to later periods of Cycladic history, in antiquity the centres of the Aegean islands were largely located on the coast; and it is only those little and poor islands, such as Pholegandros and Sikinos, whose life

[46] Gabrielsen 2001a.   [47] See Nixon and Price 1990.   [48] Bruneau 1987.
[49] Demosthenes, XXXV, 35.
[50] Doulgéri-Intzessiloglou and Garlan 1990. We even have a classical shipwreck off nearby Alonesos, full with amphoras from Peparethos, to make the case even clearer; Hadjidaki 1996.
[51] See Brun 1996: 144–53.   [52] Etienne 1990: 16–22.   [53] Mazarakis 1993.
[54] Tenos itself was sacked by Alexander of Pherai; Demosthenes, L, 5.

depended on the exploitation of their own territory for their own use, where we find the ancient polis centres located inland.[55] A similar example is that of Cnidos, another coastal polis famous for its wine production and exchange; the archaic centre of the polis was located in the interior of the Cnidian peninsula, an excellent location for the exploitation of the agricultural land; but in the late fifth to early fourth centuries, a new centre was constructed on the tip of the peninsula, where there was no agricultural potential: the clear aim was to capture the maritime traffic between the Straits and Egypt.[56]

The relationship of various poleis to these exchange networks is of clear importance. But there exist other networks, apart from those of exchange; and the repercussions of the insertion of the poleis into these networks are not simply in terms of settlement patterns. There are profound political and social implications; the most significant example is the case of the insertion of large, inland, mainly agricultural polities into high politics and the networks of redistribution and mobilisation. Athens and Rome are two characteristic examples of communities with inland centres and no important ports which opted, or were forced, to build large and important *avant-ports* (Piraeus, Ostia) in the period of their history when they entered high politics and redistributive networks.[57] High politics in antiquity was to an important extent dependent on naval power;[58] and naval power depended not only on the construction of port facilities, but also on networks of mobilisation for the manpower that would build and man the fleet,[59] and on networks of redistribution that would provide the necessary materials for the construction of the fleet,[60] and the cereals for the maintenance of the excessive workforce that the navy brought into existence.[61]

To restrict ourselves to Athens, it is impossible to stress enough that, before the fifth century, the Athenians had no important port and their centre was located inland. The contrast with the early development of the port of Oropos, which was not originally part of the Athenian polis, although at times dominated by it, is telling.[62] The creation of the port of Piraeus was a decisive step in the history of the polis; but what has attracted little attention is the fact that the Athenians refused to move their centre to the sea, as the other poleis we have already discussed did (a decision that would have been feasible in the aftermath of the Persian

[55] Brun 1996: 152–3.   [56] Berges 1994.   [57] See Tchernia and Viviers 2000.   [58] Gabrielsen 2001a.
[59] Amit 1965.   [60] Timber: Meiggs 1982: 116–53.
[61] Garnsey 1988: 89–164, though minimising the amounts to be imported.
[62] See Mazarakis-Ainian 1998.

destruction).[63] So, Athenian history was characterised by a polarity between an inland centre and an *avant-port*.[64] This was not the case with many of the poleis with an exchange-oriented territory (think of Thasos, Corcyra, Chios, where port and polis-centre coincide) and most of the poleis based on redistribution, service or location (Aegina, Byzantium, Rhodes).[65]

It is wrong therefore to take Athens as the typical case of the commercial city, and then be surprised, for example by the low status of traders, and the reluctance of the Athenians to enter personally into commerce. Athens was not a commercial polis from origin: it managed to attract and contain the networks and relationships which were already established by other poleis and their people. It is to these poleis, as described above, that we should turn our attention if we want to study the importance of exchange in social and political structure.

Settlement, territory and exploitation

The study of the territory of Greek poleis proves then to be of great importance; there have been very significant advances in the study of the territories of Greek colonies, in both the Black Sea and Magna Graecia–Sicily,[66] and the last two decades have seen the beginning of the study of the territories of the Greek poleis of the Aegean and the mainland.[67] There are two very important issues that scholarly research has not fully addressed yet. The one concerns scale: the exploitation and settlement of the territory of a polis will obviously depend on the scale of this territory. This is not simply a question of a simplistic dichotomy, whereas a small polis territory could be exploited from the single nucleated settlement of the polis, while a large territory would necessitate the existence of villages or isolated farmsteads. The important issue concerns the *relationships* between these various forms of settlements and between various forms of exploitation.

---

[63] Garland 1987: 2–4, is the only study I know who asks the question what the history of Athens would have been, had she decided to relocate its centre to Piraeus, instead of building the Long Walls.

[64] 'Also states sometimes enter on faction for geographical reasons, when the nature of the country is not suited for there being a single city, as for example at Clazomenae the people near Chytrum are in feud with the inhabitants of the island, and the Colophonians and the Notians; and at Athens the population is not uniformly democratic in spirit, but the inhabitants of Piraeus are more so than those of the city'; Aristotle, *Politics*, 1303b, 8–13. See Roy 1998.

[65] Though Corinth shows a pattern similar to Athens.

[66] On Magna Grecia–Sicily: Lepore 1968; Osanna 1992. On the Black Sea: Kryjickij 1999; Wasowicz 1999 summarising previous work.

[67] Brunet 1999.

We know of a variety of ways of exploiting the territory from the experience of the poleis of the colonial world. In the case of the cities of East Crimea (Bosporus) we see two opposing ways at work: Pantikapaion, on the European side of the Bosporus, seems to have taken control of the inland territory through the creation of secondary large settlements (dependent or autonomous poleis and villages) and without building scattered farmsteads in the hinterland;[68] on the other hand, the poleis on the Asiatic part of the Bosporus seem to have resorted to the creation of rural farmsteads, a large number of which were constructed already in the archaic period.[69] Graham Shipley has noted a similar disparity between the island poleis of Samos and Chios.[70] In Samos there is a very prominent polis centre, but there is an almost complete lack of any kind of material evidence from the western part of the island; there is only one large sanctuary (the Heraion) and no rural and peripheral ones; in Chios, on the other hand, there is a large number of peripheral settlements and important rural sanctuaries to go along with the polis centre.[71]

The other important issue is the relationship between the settlement patterns and the kind of exploitation of its territory that a polis employs. Robin Osborne has argued that the isolated farmsteads with towers, which are predominant in South Attica,[72] are the result of the subsistence needs created by the exploitation of the nearby mines with their huge concentrated workforce; he argues though that in the rest of Attica the dominant pattern of settlement was nucleated settlements (*demoi* villages).[73] We have here a clear case where a specific pattern of exploitation leads to a specific pattern of settlement in a specific conjuncture. But the question has not been asked in these more general terms yet about the totality of Greek poleis and their territories.

POLEIS AND REGIONS

This is probably the least studied aspect of Greek history. Unfortunately, the absence of work in this field poses clear limits to the remarks that follow. The region is a geographical area that shows certain common traits, common patterns and forms of interaction between the various communities, territories and groups that comprise it. A region might share a

---

[68] Maslennikov 2001.   [69] Kuznetsov 2001.   [70] Shipley 1987: 231–47.
[71] For Chios, see Yalouris 1986.   [72] Lohmann 1992, 1993.
[73] Osborne 1991b, 1996a. Whether one accepts his argument for the rest of Attica or not (contra Lohmann 1995) is irrelevant to his justified point about southern Attica.

common perception of identity, but this is not a necessary characteristic: the communities of Ionia shared a large number of cultural practices and institutions;[74] but the communities and polities of the North Aegean did not share any common identity, although they did form a distinct region. Moreover, a region might be politically unified in some periods, but again this is not necessary: Thessaly had a form of political unity that varied in its intensity from period to period,[75] Arcadia was united politically only for a very short period in the fourth century[76] and the Cyclades were never politically unified, except by being under the same suzerain from time to time.[77]

The use of the individual polity (usually the polis) as the only analytical category for the study of Greek history has resulted in the fact that ancient historians have not constructed analytical tools to study patterns, processes and forms of interaction that involve a number of polities concurrently. The few, marginalised studies that exist almost always concern regions that had a political or/and cultural unity; even then, most of the studies that exist are usually devoted either to topography and a traditionalist *histoire évènementielle*,[78] or to cults and institutions.[79] The region as a geographical category is largely absent.[80] It is characteristic that although the North Aegean was one of the most crucial regions for Greek history,[81] there is still no study of the communities of the region as a unity, clearly because it did not have the political or cultural unity that would render it a traditional subject. There are separate studies for Chalcidike, Thrace, coastal Macedonia and the islands of Thasos and Samothrace, but no study of the region as a whole; and most of these studies have the limitations that we have noted.

The exception to the above negative comments is indeed to be found in archaeology. The study of material culture has long made necessary the use of alternative units of analysis, apart from the polis; it was clear that the production of many artefacts and buildings showed similar features over wider areas.[82] Eastern Greek pottery is a good example; it describes the products of a wider area with sufficient similarities in production and distribution to be classed together.[83] We can also document the opposite phenomenon; Mendaian wine, titled so from the city of Mende in

---

[74] Graf 1985.   [75] Archibald 2000.   [76] Nielsen 2002a: 121–57.   [77] Brun 1996.
[78] See Isaac 1986 on Thrace; Zahrnt 1971 on Chalcidike.
[79] See e.g. Schachter 1981–94.
[80] There are three effective exceptions, none of which, interestingly, is Anglo-Saxon: Vinogradov 1987 on the Black Sea; Brun 1996 on Cyclades; and Freitag 2001 on the Corinthian Gulf. See also the comments of Morgan 2003: 213–22.
[81] The importance of the region as a whole is stressed in Heskel 1997, which is restricted, though, to the reconstruction of the political history of a few years.
[82] Shapiro 1996.   [83] Cook and Dupont 1998.

Chalkidike, has been found to be a brand name for the wines of the wider Chalkidike region and not simply for Mende.[84]

Other archaeologists have more recently extended the notion of archaeological regions to include other issues apart from production; they have noted the existence of regional practices in the use and consumption of material culture, in the fields of houses, burials and temple construction. Ian Morris in a number of studies has pointed to the formation and maintenance of regional groupings in the Aegean and the mainland from the Dark Ages to the archaic period.[85] Having defined four groups (Central Greece and the Aegean, Western Greece, Northern Greece, Crete), he has argued that social, economic and political processes are articulated with varying or contrasting ways in each region; that changes occur in each region at a different pace, in differing directions and with differing results; and that the novel middling communities of the archaic period are particularly present and strong in his Central and Aegean region.

What still remains a desideratum, though, is a study of the creation, maintenance, breaking up and reinvention of these regional practices.[86] What is it that makes a region that is not politically or ethnically unified, like the Western Peloponnese, follow similar practices in burials and temple construction?[87] What forms of links and what kind of linking actors does it take for such regional practices to evolve? What forms of communication and what intensity of communication?[88] How do these regional systems break up? What creates regional convergence in certain issues and divergence in others? And let me repeat my usual complaint; we need such studies to be extended to the classical period and beyond.

POLEIS AND THE *SYSTÈME-MONDE*

It is now time to analyse the last level of our spatial analysis. It is important to clear up some important misconceptions which are often associated with this notion.[89] The first is that a *système-monde* implies by necessity a distinction between a dominant core and an exploited periphery (and semi-periphery). Therefore, if it is impossible to find a clear distinction

---

[84] Papadopoulos and Paspalas 1999.   [85] Morris 1997b, 1998b, 2000.
[86] One study in this direction is Morgan 1990.   [87] Morris 1998b: 54–5.
[88] 'What is the minimum average number of annual sailings between one city and another to promote similar religious architecture in both?'; and 'what density of traffic can be postulated to account for the spread of more or less canonical temple design across the whole Greek Mediterranean?'; Purcell 1990: 37.
[89] Cf. Shipley 1993.

between a centre and an exploited periphery, then there existed no *système-monde*. A dominant centre and an exploited periphery is only one possible form of a *système-monde*. The modern *système-monde* is undoubtedly structured in a centre-periphery form, but this does not mean that every *système-monde* in the past had the same characteristics, or that there were no *systèmes-mondes* before the emergence of the modern one. One can envisage a variety of different forms: Janet Abu-Lughod has convincingly argued that the medieval *système-monde* of the thirteenth and fourteenth centuries CE had a form of concentric circles, instead of a single centre and periphery.[90] 'In fact, we can accept Wallerstein's minimum definition that [a system] is a world-system, not because it encompasses the whole world, but because it is larger than any juridically defined political unit.'[91] If so, the crucial issue is that a single community or polity (a Greek polis) cannot be a self-sufficient unit of analysis.[92] By using the term *système-monde*, I am trying to portray and analyse a larger frame of historical reference. I will argue that there are various forms of interactions and processes that one could call *systèmes-mondes*; they range from low- to high-intensity systems; and from anarchic to centrally organised. There need then be two primary qualifications: a *système-monde* does not necessarily encompass the whole world; there can be several co-existing world-systems; and the extent of each of them can change from period to period and so can only be historically reconstructed. And a *système-monde* is a system, but not necessarily a highly structured and coherent one; again, its intensity can be described only in concrete historical analysis, and not in *a priori* theory. So, a *système-monde* can indeed be a (highly structured) system of the (whole) world, as it is nowadays; but it can also take historically contingent forms varying in extent, structure and intensity. In the following pages, I am trying to delineate three general aspects of such *systèmes-mondes*.

World environment: bordering space, bordering communities

The first aspect is that all communities and polities occupy a space and border on other communities and polities. We cannot abstract the nature of the space they occupy and the nature of the communities and polities they border on from an analysis of the historical development of the communities under study.[93]

---

[90] Abu-Lughod 1989.   [91] Wallerstein 1974: 15.   [92] Wallerstein 1991: 229–72.
[93] See Abulafia 2005.

The nature of space

The Etruscan civilisation of city-states is in many ways comparable with the Greek system of poleis;[94] but the Greek system was centred around the Aegean archipelago of islands, while the Etruscan system lacked island communities. Also, in most of the cases the main centres of Etruscan polities were situated in the interior, while many of them constructed *avant-ports* to facilitate their maritime connections; this was very different from the situation of many Greek poleis, as we saw. In what specific ways was the history of the Etruscan city-states different from that of Greek poleis because of the different geographical environment? What specific results and developments can we attribute to this? The same questions could be asked for Greek history; we should not take its coastal nature as given and unproblematic, in particular when one thinks of the later rise of some inland powers (Macedonia), and the apparent inability of other inland powers (e.g. Epirus) to dominate Greek history. These questions are usually not asked, though it seems that a comparative study from such a perspective would yield highly stimulating results.

The nature of bordering communities

Greek history would have been very different if many Greek communities had not bordered on a large and powerful empire such as the Persian one. And different communities developed in very different ways, because of the nature of communities on which they bordered. Can one explain the different historical development of the communities of Western Greece by this fact? One should not speak about slow-motion *ethnê* and dynamic poleis, unless one pays attention to the larger spatial setting of these communities.

Greek communities then occupied a specific space and bordered on specific communities; they were part of a historically specific larger system, which cannot be abstracted from a study of their history.[95] Marshall Sahlins has developed the concept of *complementary schismogenesis* to account for

---

[94] Torelli 2000.
[95] Let me offer examples from modern history: can one understand the nature of medieval and early modern English kingship and state apart from the fact that it did not have to fight constant border wars, like French or Spanish kings had to do, due to English insularity? Can one understand American history apart from the fact that the States had never to fear invasion or war by a powerful neighbour? International relations studies have devoted a lot of attention to these issues, although their restricted temporal vista (modern and contemporary history) and their many anti-historical assumptions often limit the usefulness of such work for ancient historians. For more promising studies, see Hobden 1998; Buzan and Little 2000; Hobden and Hobson 2001.

the different, yet closely related, developments of Athens and Sparta.[96] Contrary to scholarly accounts which explain changes and developments in both societies as purely the result of internal causes, he argues that many of the Spartan distinguishing features (as e.g. Spartan *xenêlasia*, the severe oppression of the helots, the decision to forgo naval power in the aftermath of the Persian wars) can be explained as a result of a schismogenic opposition with their adversaries, primarily Athens, but also Argos and Arcadia. Thus, the concept of complementary schismogenesis can help us to understand the development of Greek poleis in relation to their external environment.

A first, elementary perception of a *système-monde*, then, simply pays attention to the nature of space within larger spatial unities and to the nature of the neighbouring communities. The nature of these relations, whether sporadic or highly intensified, has a formative effect on the development of a community, a polity, a culture. One could possibly speak of a world environment in the case of the looser and less intense relations; and of a *système-monde* in the case of the more constant and intensified relations.

World processes: processes beyond control

But we need intensified interactions and exchanges in order to speak of a *système-monde* of a more elevated level. In this second sense, which exists side by side with the first one, a *système-monde* exists because there appear processes, exchanges and interactions that link many groups, communities and polities; and these processes, exchanges and interactions, moving people, goods and ideas, range beyond the boundaries of a single group, community or polity. There is also a further elaboration of these issues in the next chapter, dealing with poleis and polities.[97]

We can roughly distinguish between three different world processes: processes moving people; processes moving goods and processes moving ideas/technologies.[98] We barely need to add that the three processes are not necessarily to be distinguished; it can often be the case that the same agents might move people, goods and ideas/technologies at the same time. Alternatively, as Horden and Purcell note,

in very many cases the connectivity is generated by 'mobilities', the primary cause of which is not redistribution. In these instances the patterns of redistribution, the opportunities for the special intensification of production offered by connectivity,

---

[96] See Sahlins 2004: 69–82.   [97] Chapter 8, 190–202.
[98] See Charpin and Joannès 1992 for a similar perspective on the Near East.

will be shaped neither by supply, nor by demand, but by the accidents of channels of human mobility.[99]

While the migration of merchants from Heracleia Pontica to Athens was the result of processes of moving goods or ideas,[100] the migration of Ionian craftsmen on the eve of the Persian conquest discussed below was caused to an important extent by the political upheavals of the Persian conquest and the Ionian Revolt;[101] but of course the Ionian migration had important effects on the processes of moving goods and ideas/technologies. Therefore, the relationship between the three processes cannot be established *a priori*, and needs to be contextually studied.

Movements of goods

The movement of goods in long-distance exchanges is well attested for antiquity. One of the most illuminating images is Polybius' description of the Black Sea:

The Pontus therefore being rich in what the rest of the world requires for the support of life, the Byzantines are absolute masters of all such things. For those commodities which are the first necessaries of existence, cattle and slaves, are confessedly supplied by the districts round the Pontus in greater profusion, and of better quality, than by any others: and for luxuries, they supply us with honey, wax, and salt-fish in great abundance; while they take our superfluous stock of olive oil and every kind of wine. In the matter of corn there is a mutual interchange, supplying or taking it, as it happens to be convenient.[102]

We see here two important issues. The one is interdependence: the Aegean is dependent on the importation of cattle and slaves from the Black Sea; while the Black Sea is dependent on the importation of wine and oil from the Aegean. The archaeological record gives abundant evidence to verify this picture: the huge amount of amphoras from various Aegean communities found in the Black Sea region testifies to the intensity of these links.[103] The second issue is the distinction between luxuries and necessities. This distinction is important, but needs to be contextualised. The distinction between what constitutes a luxury and what a necessity cannot be established *a priori*. There are few goods that belong certainly to the one category or the other; for the vast majority, there is a spectrum of positions that they can

---

[99] Horden and Purcell 2000: 396.
[100] On Heracleots in Athens, see Osborne and Byrne 1996: 72–94.
[101] For the mixed character of the Ionian migration, see Gras 1991.   [102] Polybius, IV, 38.
[103] See Garlan 1999a.

occupy. Given sufficient demand, a luxury can become a necessity;[104] the modern history of sugar is a good example in this respect.[105] But it is also the cultural patterns of consumption which determine what kinds of goods are deemed necessary for a certain mode of life.[106]

A history of the mobility of goods in the Mediterranean *système-monde* would have to address a number of interrelated issues. The first one is the relationship between production, demand and consumption, which we underlined above. The second is the degree of interdependence. Robin Osborne has argued that already in the archaic period the distribution of different products of different Athenian pottery workshops over the Mediterranean shows marked and consistent patterns, which can be explained as production targeting specific markets; in this respect he thinks it is possible to speak of a conglomeration of interdependent markets.[107] The question is to what extent this model can be extended to other goods. It is certainly the case that many goods circulated primarily within local networks and their production and prices reflect local needs.[108] We need models that will take into account the various levels of mobility, how different levels will shape the circulation of goods and in which circumstances and conjunctures certain goods would move from one level to another.[109] To give an example, grain could be produced for local consumption, but in certain circumstances it could move to a regional or even international level; alternatively, grain could be produced directly for regional or international networks of exchange.[110] Production is not tantamount to capacity to produce: when a scholar asks 'Chian wine was once the island's main source of wealth and reputation. Why is it then that now Chian wine is not so famous?',[111] he points to the constant changes in the production and movement of goods that come a long way towards undermining the model of static pre-modern agriculture that until recently was the scholarly orthodoxy.[112] The relationship with consumption patterns and network connections is equally important in this respect.

This introduces the issue of long-term changes in the mobility of goods. Unfortunately, from the time Rostovtzeff wrote his magnificent chapter on the economic development of the Mediterranean world in the fourth century,[113] there have been few attempts to trace the developments in the

---

[104] See the insightful comments of Vallet and Villard 1963: 263–5. [105] Mintz 1985.
[106] Foxhall 1998.   [107] Osborne 1996c.
[108] See Reger 1994 on goods and prices in Hellenistic Delos.
[109] Davies 1998. See the fundamental insights of Braudel 1982.   [110] Bresson 2000a.
[111] Sarikakis 1986: 127.   [112] See Vlassopoulos n.d.; Sutton 2000: 41–70.
[113] Rostovtzeff 1941: 74–125.

movement of goods. Partly, this is the result of the influence of Finleyism; an approach that denied economic development in antiquity, describing a static ancient economy for more than a thousand years.[114] Yet, there is clear evidence of changes in the movement of commodities. To give one example, the development of the wine production of South Italy and Sicily in the late classical and Hellenistic period created a reorientation of patterns of exchange; the importation of wines from the Aegean took a very different form.[115]

Finally, of utmost importance are the networks through which goods circulate. Diaspora trade is a good example: it is often the case in world history that trade between two communities is conducted by a diaspora community of merchants, often coming from a third community, which physically relocates and controls the movement of goods through its agents.[116] Diaspora communities are diverse; sometimes they have a single common origin, often they have mixed and ever-changing backgrounds; often they are stateless communities, in a few cases they have the active support of their community of origin. In other circumstances the movement of goods is based on itinerant communities.

At the same time one encounters the *emporion*, a form of regulated settlement housing the communities of exchange common to many different Mediterranean communities; the *emporion* is a settlement usually organised and maintained by the host community.[117] We see therefore on the one hand various diaspora communities (e.g. Phoenician or Aeginetan traders) scattered over wide areas and creating and maintaining links of solidarity and support; on the other hand, *emporia*, where the various diaspora communities are brought together in relationships of collaboration, conflict or exploitation both between themselves and with the host community.[118] There have been some recent and very fascinating attempts to study the *emporia*, but much yet remains to be done.[119]

Movement of people

At the level of moving of people, things are more complicated. Some of these movements are forced and without the will of the people moved; slavery is perhaps the best example of this category of movement.[120] The story of the reciprocal effects of the movement of slaves on both their

---

[114] Notably, in Finley 1973b there is no discussion of factors of change.   [115] Vandermersch 1994.
[116] Curtin 1984: 1–12; Kuhrt 1998.   [117] Bresson and Rouillard 1993.
[118] On the Phoenician diaspora communities and their place within the *emporia*, see Baslez 1986, 1987, 1988, 1996.
[119] Bresson 1993; Gras 1993; Hansen 1997e; also Möller 2000.   [120] Horden and Purcell 2000: 388–91.

communities of origin and their communities of destination remains wholly to be written. We have studied very little the effects on Greek culture and history of those hundreds of thousands of slaves, who lived through the ages among Greek communities, apart from doing the necessary dirty work; given the huge number of comparative examples that suggest the strong influence of slaves on their host communities,[121] there is a lot of work to be done in assessing what such a contribution might be for ancient Greece.[122]

One hears of Thracians visiting Mytilene in order to ransom some other Thracians (relatives?), who have been sold into slavery.[123] What did the liberated slaves bring back to their country from their experience of slavery? The father of the defendant in a speech of Demosthenes supposedly acquired his foreign accent from being captured during the Deceleian war and being sold as a slave in Leucas;[124] what else did he acquire and what did an Athenian slave contribute to the society of Leucas? In the beginning of the *Politeia*, Socrates goes down to Piraeus to celebrate the introduction of the Thracian cult of Bendis, and is clearly impressed by the procession of the Thracians.[125] Did the procession include both free Thracian metics and Thracian slaves? How did an Athenian converse with his Thracian slave when going back home after the event? The boor described by Theophrastus announces and discusses all of his affairs with his slaves;[126] what advice did they give him, based on their cultural background?

Beyond slavery, mobility of people ranges across a wide spectrum of options from the more to the less voluntary.[127] Migration in the face of danger is the option closest to the forced movement of slavery. The migration of thousands of Ionians to the West during the latter half of the sixth century due to the Persian conquest is one of the most important developments in archaic history that still waits to be taken seriously into account.[128] The migration and the catastrophes that surrounded it changed Ionia decisively; one wonders what would have become of Miletus, this great colonising power of the archaic period, if it did not have to suffer the haemorrhage of destruction and forced migration brought by fifty years of

---

[121] See e.g. Bastide 1978; Sobel 1987; Gilroy 1993; Dubois 2004.
[122] For a recent attempt, see Morris 1998a. One does not need to agree with his conclusions in order to appraise the novelty and importance of asking these questions.
[123] Antiphon, *On the Murder of Herodes*, 20.   [124] Demosthenes, *Against Euboulides*, 18.
[125] *Politeia*, 327a; see Parker 1996: 170–5.   [126] *Characters*, IV, 3.
[127] See Horden and Purcell 2000: 377–89.
[128] It is largely absent from e.g. Osborne 1996b; but see Gras 1991; Lombardo 2000.

Persian rule.[129] At the same time it changed the West in important ways, bringing new architectural styles,[130] new philosophical schools and political ideas[131] and new forms of colonial enterprises, like that of the Phoceans.[132]

But we have also migrations of people that seem more voluntary than forced. The migration of Athenian potters to southern Italy in the late fifth-century BCE and their role in creating an innovative new style of pottery is well known to archaeologists.[133] On the contrary, it is absent as a fact from discussions of classical history. What prompted these potters to migrate? How common was this kind of activity? What else did they bring with them, apart from their contribution to late classical southern Italian pottery?

Unfortunately, the study of mobility in the Mediterranean of the first millennium is marred by approaches focused on colonisation as an official act. According to this approach, mobility is only important in the archaic period, when it is organised by the poleis in the form of colonies, and again in the Hellenistic period, this time organised by the Hellenistic monarchs; consequently, mobility disappears from historical accounts dealing with the classical period, which was purportedly not a period of crisis, at least in the fifth century.[134] Fortunately, this view is now contested by a growing number of scholars. Concerning the archaic colonisation movement, they view it more as a result of individual mobility and private opportunistic enterprises.

The 'private enterprise' which is widely and surely rightly assumed to have been responsible for the settlement at Pithekoussai, should be envisaged as responsible also for the vast majority of eighth- and seventh-century settlements, as shown by the way they attract pottery and metalwork from a wide, but usually peculiar, variety of Greek and Italian areas, by their varied layouts and the fact that regular grids are demonstrably later in several cases, and by the marked discontinuities with which the settlement history at many of these sites is visited.[135]

I think there is no need to restrict this comment to the archaic period, which is not to deny that from the fifth century onwards we have clear cases of colonising ventures that are centrally directed by the political authorities of the metropolis. But it is highly suggestive that even in these centrally administered cases, the colonisers still come from various directions;[136] the

---

[129] Davies 1997a: 139; Ehrhardt 1983.   [130] Barletta 1983.   [131] Von Fritz 1940; Mele 1982.
[132] Lepore 1970; Morel 1966, 1975, 1982.   [133] MacDonald 1981; see also Papadopoulos 1997b.
[134] A rare attempt to see mobility in its larger dimensions is McKechnie 1989, although he is still not completely outside the view that sees mobility as a crisis phenomenon.
[135] Osborne 1998: 268; see also Gras 1991.
[136] This was already recognised by the early literature of colonisation in the eighteenth century; see Vlassopoulos forthcoming. Another good illustration that the development of historiography is never linear.

Athenian colony in Amphipolis and the re-colonisation of Sybaris are ample testimony to widespread personal mobility in the ancient Mediterranean.[137]

The time has come to see colonisation as simply one form of mobility:[138] we need to study the colonist along with the mercenary,[139] the sailor,[140] the trader,[141] the craftsman,[142] the doctor, the sophist[143] and the exile;[144] the story of mobility in these larger terms remains still to be written.[145]

It is also important to abandon the Hellenocentric accounts of Greek mobility.[146] It is indeed the case that in the Dark Ages and the archaic period the Phoenicians have an accepted role in accounts of Greek mobility and colonisation,[147] though ethnocentric approaches are strong even here. What is truly remarkable is the complete disappearance of Phoenicians and other Mediterranean peoples in accounts of Greek history of the classical period; in this period Mediterranean peoples feature only to the extent that they come into political conflict with the Greeks or fall under their control. Xenophon's Ischomachus and his contemporary Athenians were impressed by the arrival of a huge Phoenician ship in the port of Piraeus, which must have been the event of the year; he discussed extensively with the crew the organisation of activities and the arrangement of material aboard the ship;[148] what else did they discuss and what else did Ischomachus learn?

A fascinating example, showing how misleading is the standard approach, is Athenogenes, an Egyptian metic, involved in selling perfumes in late fourth-century Athens.[149] The cunning Athenogenes arranges in collaboration with Antigone, a prostitute, to sell to a wealthy young Athenian citizen two male slaves along with their perfume workshop, which is though heavily indebted. The details of the story are not of direct concern here, but what happens later on is quite revealing (§§ 29–31):

---

[137] See the various articles in Sordi 1994. The reply to Osborne's claims in Malkin 2002 is highly stimulating. Many of his points are indeed strong, in particular his historiographical points. Malkin is in favour of keeping the terminology of colonial foundation, although he too agrees that colonisation from above, as a state action, should be abandoned. Instead he offers a model of colonisation from below, which could be accommodated with Osborne's argument. His comparison of Greek colonisation from below with modern Jewish kibbutzim in Palestine is a highly stimulating idea; one can only deplore and protest that some modern people should have to face the ancient fate of Killyrioi and Mariandynoi.

[138] Despite the arguments of Purcell 1990, few have heeded this direction in classical history.

[139] I have argued in favour of this approach in Vlassopoulos 2003; Tagliamonte 1994.

[140] Rauh 2003: 146–68. [141] Velissaropoulos 1980; Reed 2003. [142] Burford 1969.

[143] For the mobility of doctors and sophists, see Thomas 2000: 9–16. The issue of mobile intellectuals is unfortunately little explored until very recently; but see now Montiglio 2005.

[144] Seibert 1979. [145] But see Giangiulio 1996, characteristically for the archaic period.

[146] See Papadopoulos 1997a. [147] Shaw 1989; Docter and Niemeier 1995; Hoffman 1997.

[148] *Oeconomicus*, viii, 11–14. [149] Hypereides, *Against Athenogenes*.

During the war against Philip, he left the city just before the battle and did not serve with you at Chaeroneia. Instead, he moved to Troezen, disregarding the law, which says that a man who moves in wartime shall be indicted and summarily arrested if he returns. The reason for the move, it seems, was this: he thought that the city of Troezen would survive, whereas he had passed a sentence of death on ours ... He is so degraded and so true to type wherever he is, that even after his arrival at Troezen, when they had made him a citizen, he became the tool of Mnesias the Argive and, after being made a magistrate by him, expelled the citizens from the city.

An Egyptian perfume seller has the obligation to fight for Athens, along with thousands of other foreigners living in Athens; instead he escapes, goes to a tiny obscure place like Troezen, is enrolled as a citizen, even becomes a magistrate.[150] How common was such an event? If we judge from the tone of the passage, it does not seem very extraordinary; the moral outrage is against his disenfranchising citizens, not in his becoming one. What did Athenogenes carry from his Egyptian cultural baggage when he became a citizen and a magistrate? We need a larger horizon.[151]

Movement of ideas/technologies

Finally, there comes the movement of ideas and technologies. And to some extent it has been better studied than the previous issues. We have excellent studies of the spread of Orphism from the Western to Eastern Mediterranean and the Black Sea;[152] of the idea, the practices and the accoutrements of the symposium in its spread from the Near East to Greece and the Western Mediterranean;[153] of the spread of the technology of constructing and employing triremes, instead of the much smaller pentekonters, from the Eastern to the Western Mediterranean during the late archaic period;[154] of the spread of new techniques of siege and fortification from the experiments of Greek tyrants in Sicily and Magna Graecia to the exploits of Philip and Alexander in mainland Greece and Asia Minor.[155]

The real issue here is that although individual issues are rather well studied, we are missing the larger picture. We lack studies of the interconnections between the different processes of moving ideas/technologies.

---

[150] See Whitehead 2000: 287–8, 339–41.
[151] Our colleagues studying the Bronze Age Aegean have been more open-minded in this respect: see Knapp 1993; Cline 1995.
[152] See the articles in Tortorelli-Ghidini *et al.* 2000.   [153] Dentzer 1982.   [154] Wallinga 1993: 103–29.
[155] Garlan 1974.

To what extent is the transfer of an idea predicated or accompanied by the transfer of a technology? And what are the networks and the agents through which ideas/technologies spread? Does the spread of Orphism pass through the same networks and the same agents that spread perfume vases?

The case of Zopyrus of Heracleia/Tarentum is a fascinating illustration of these issues.[156] Zopyrus, a figure of the late fifth to early fourth century BCE, is credited with authorship of the Pythagorean work *Krater*; but he is also credited with designs and innovations in the field of war engines. This is not very surprising, given the connection between Pythagoreans and science;[157] but what is more fascinating are the network connections. For in the fourth century Dionysius of Syracuse was distinguished for his successful attraction of specialist craftsmen, which led to important break-throughs in the art of siege warfare,[158] and Zopyrus of Tarentum could be plausibly linked to him; but Zopyrus is also credited with devising a catapult for the Milesians. The only plausible context for this service is the Syracusan expedition to help the Spartans during the latter stage of the Peloponnesian war.[159] And thus we see one man spreading the art of siege warfare from Syracuse to Miletus; but this same man is connected to the spread of Pythagorean religious and philosophic ideas. If the networks that move religious and military ideas and technologies seem to go together in this case, how far can we extend this example?

Many times, the most difficult problem is the identification of the agents of this process. The elite chamber tombs of Scythia and Thrace provide an interesting illustration of this issue:[160] they show many strong similarities, despite the huge distance between the two areas; they also seem to transfer the idea of the symposium to the context of the grave, given their icono-graphy, spatial arrangement, reclining couches, etc. Gocha Tsetskhladze has argued that it was Ionian craftsmen from the Ionian colonies in the Black Sea and Thrace respectively who built these graves for the local elites; given that chamber tombs of a very similar construction were very popular in various regions of Asia Minor adjacent to Ionia (Phrygia, Lydia), it is plausible to argue that we have here a good case in which we can identify a group of people spreading an idea and a technology, and linking together Asia Minor, Thrace and the Black Sea.

I will end this section by noting what for me is the most frustrating lack of study: the movement of political ideas and practices. It is here again that the conception of the polis as an autonomous entity had one of its most

---

[156] For what follows, see Kingsley 1995: 143–58.   [157] See e.g. Huffman 2005.
[158] Diodorus, XIV, 41–3.   [159] Thucydides, VIII, 26–39.   [160] For what follows, Tsetskhladze 1998b.

malign effects. For it has made people think that political developments in each polis were the result of purely internal developments (the political history of Athens) or large metahistorical processes (the development of *the* polis). The exchange of ideas and experiences and the physical relocation of political agents, through the all too common exiles, have not received adequate treatment. There have been a few short studies of the movement of political ideas, which are worth referring to here. Anthony Snodgrass and Irad Malkin have argued that it was the experience of establishing communities in the colonial world which gave birth to the idea of the polis in the mainland;[161] and David Lewis and Wolfgang Schuller have studied to what extent we can see the diffusion of Athenian democratic institutions to the rest of the Greek world.[162]

This lack of interest is particularly unfortunate; for one of the most fascinating discoveries of recent works in social and political history is the international character of social and political movements even in pre-modern times. To give just one example, Peter Linebaugh and Markus Rediker have given us a wonderful account of the revolutionary Atlantic in the seventeenth and eighteenth centuries, showing how people from various nations and races, from Britain, Ireland, Europe, Africa and the Americas, created movements of resistance and solidarity and fostered new ideologies and arguments for their struggles.[163] We do know that the culture of the upper classes in Athens was indeed international: foreigners like Herodotus, Lysias, Dinarchus and Anaxagoras had an important role in the formation of Athenian culture;[164] Plato's dialogues show in an exemplary way how upper-class Athenians mixed with foreigners on equal terms in discussing politics, philosophy and the arts. The blending of philosophy and mathematics with aristocratic politics in south Italy created the anti-democratic theory of arithmetic and geometric equality, which finally found its way to Athens.[165] But what about the lower classes? If we are now able to see the international character of pre-modern movements, and we can easily observe the important role of foreign intellectuals in the world of the Athenian elite, should we not suppose that something similar was taking place among the common people? Should we not suppose that the creation and maintenance of democratic politics in classical Athens did owe something to the huge number of foreigners living among the Athenians?

---

[161] Snodgrass 1980: 119–22; Malkin 1994a.
[162] Schuller 1979; Lewis 1997; see also Robinson 1997 on early democracies outside Athens and Rhodes and Lewis 1997.
[163] Linebaugh and Rediker 2000. See also Durey 1997; Tise 1998.
[164] See now Thomas 2000 on the Ionian intellectual diaspora.   [165] Harvey 1965/6.

In 355 BCE Dion overthrew the tyranny of Dionysius the Younger in Syracuse. What followed was a popular movement that took advantage of Dion's success and attempted to proceed in a far more radical direction than Dion imagined or wished. A meeting of the assembly came to decide the redistribution of all property in the city: the ideological justification of this measure was that 'the first beginning of liberty was equality, and of slavery poverty for the propertiless'.[166] In the end, the attempt of the elite to annul the decision of the assembly proved successful. But what interests me here is the articulation of a democratic lower-class ideology, which posits equality of wealth as a precondition of democracy, and attempts a practical redistribution of wealth.[167] If a poor Syracusan found himself living as a metic in Athens, in the aftermath of this popular explosion, and following this radical democratic ideology, how would he converse and discuss with lower-class Athenians? Or alternatively, if Athenians happened to be staying or living in Syracuse during these incidents, how would they convey to their compatriots these events and their underlying ideological debate? Or, in the final instance, how would lower-class Athenians react to the news of such developments in Syracuse? We have adopted a deeply Athenocentric stance, and we seldom think about the repercussions of developments, events and debates outside Athens on the Athenians themselves.[168]

WORLD CENTRES: CENTRES, PERIPHERIES AND NETWORKS

Mediterranean history knows many centres. There are sanctuaries, religious centres which bring together communities, forge links of common identity, disseminate practices and ideologies; the role of Delphi and Olympia in this respect is too well known to require much discussion here.[169] There are the already mentioned *emporia*: those nodes that organise, attract and direct the mobility of goods, people and ideas/technologies. There are centres of cultural, scientific and academic practices: they range widely, from the courts of Sicilian tyrants[170] or an Anatolian dynast,[171] to the philosophical schools of fourth-century Athens,[172] or the Cnidian and

[166] Plutarch, *Life of Dion*, 37.5   [167] For this event, see Fuks 1984.
[168] Franco Venturi has written a masterpiece, in which he looks at the Enlightenment through the prism of contemporary reactions to events taking place all over Europe and the Atlantic, stressing in particular the importance of the implications of events taking place in the periphery of Europe for the development of Enlightenment thought. See volumes III–IV of his *Settecento riformatore*, translated as Venturi 1989, 1991. If writing such a work for ancient history is impossible, due to the lack of sources, the approach is still illuminating.
[169] On their emergence, see Morgan 1990. See also Rougemont 1992; Sanchez 2001.
[170] Dunbabin 1948: 298–9.   [171] Hornblower 1982: 332–51.   [172] Ostwald and Lynch 1994.

Coan centres of medicine.[173] And there are of course political centres, but these are extensively discussed in chapter 8, and are omitted from the discussion here. What should be clear from this discussion is that the creation of centres of processes defies the polis-centred approach, which sees the poleis as autonomous entities, and necessitates a world-system approach.

Athens in the classical period is a good example. Athens managed to take control of the international commerce in cereals and based its subsistence and reproduction on the successful maintenance of this control. No wonder of course that every time this control came under pressure, or was destroyed, the Athenians found themselves in a very difficult situation. Moreover, Athens exploited to a large extent, as we already described above, the international movement in manpower, goods and ideas. From artistic production and intellectual exchange, to servile labour and the rowers of Athenian fleets, Athens depended on overwhelmingly and successfully attracting huge numbers of foreigners, both Greek and non-Greek. Isocrates has put it nicely:

Moreover, she [Athens] has established her polity in general in such a spirit of welcome to strangers and friendliness to all men that it adapts itself both to those who lack means, and to those who wish to enjoy the means which they possess, and that it fails to be of service neither to those who are prosperous, nor to those who are unfortunate in their own cities; nay, both classes find with us what they desire, the former the most delightful pastimes, the latter the securest refuge. Again, since the different populations did not in any case possess a country that was self-sufficing, each lacking in some things and producing others in excess of their needs, and since they were greatly at a loss, where they would dispose of their surplus, and whence they would import what they lacked, in these difficulties also our polis came to the rescue; for she established the Piraeus as a market in the centre of Hellas – a market of such abundance that the articles which it is difficult to get, one here, one there, from the rest of the world, all these it is easy to procure from Athens.[174]

Byzantium offers some good illustrations of what a centre could look like.

As far as the sea is concerned, Byzantium occupies a position the most secure and in every way the most advantageous of any town in our quarter of the world: while in regard to the land, its situation is in both respects the most unfavourable. By sea it so completely commands the entrance to the Pontus that no merchant can sail in or out against its will. The Pontus therefore being rich in what the rest of the world requires for the support of life, the Byzantines are absolute masters of all such things ... The Byzantines themselves probably feel the advantages of the situation, in the supplies of the necessaries of life, more than any one else; for their

---

[173] Sherwin-White 1978: 256–89.   [174] Isocrates, *Panegyricus*, 41–3.

superfluity finds a ready means of export, and what they lack is readily imported, with profit to themselves, and without difficulty or danger: but other people too, as I have said, get a great many commodities by their means.[175]

Byzantium gained from its favourable condition in two ways: it was able to control the traffic to the Black Sea and thus to profit from taxes, dues and the invisible profits of a commercial port. The Rhodian war with Byzantium (220–19 BCE) over the Byzantine imposition of taxes on trade through the Straits illustrates this capacity; it also shows the inevitable conflict when another emerging centre had to protect its own interests: the huge numbers of Rhodian amphoras in the Black Sea give ample testimony of what was at stake.[176]

On the other hand, Byzantium profited from being able to exploit its position in order to import commodities easily and export its surpluses with assurance; one could see that given the guaranteed customers due to the passing ships, there was gain in intensifying agricultural production. The Byzantines had to pay a high price for this, as Polybius narrates, being in continual warfare with the Thracians, and later on with the Gauls, in order to protect their precious and fertile territory.[177] Finally, it would be wrong to assume that the Byzantines had a passive role, simply exploiting their ideal geographical position and profiting from networks maintained by others. The war between Byzantium and Callatis in the Black Sea around 260 BCE shows their active policies: the war erupted when Callatis decided to restrict the *emporium* of Tomis to her own traders; obviously that threatened the interests of Byzantine traders.[178] We can see here warfare caused by the attempts to enforce 'mercantilist' policies.

It is also relevant to mention here the creation of zones of influence. Many communities found themselves in a position to impose their control over wider areas and create zones of influence, within which they exercised forms of control that varied widely in intensity. One such example is the creation of commercial zones of influence. The case of Carthage and her creation of a commercial zone within which trade was restricted to Carthaginian merchants is well known.[179] But many Greek communities had similar practices: Thasos created her one zone in the north Aegean; Olynthus in Chalcidike; Sinope in the Black Sea; Massalia in the Western Mediterranean.[180] We see here purposive attempts to forge a region around

---

[175] Polybius, IV, 38.
[176] 10,000 Rhodian stamps have been catalogued from the Black Sea: Badal'janc 1999.
[177] Polybius, IV, 45. [178] See Vinogradov 1987: 41–4, but with a different interpretation than mine.
[179] See the treaties with Rome mentioned by Polybius I, 82.6, III, 23.2, XXXI, 21.1.
[180] Bresson 1993: 201–14.

a dominant centre; it is an interesting question to what extent the creation of these commercial zones had a wider effect on other aspects.

The examples I am using here are all well known to ancient historians; but what we are missing is a combined study of the variety of social, economic, political and cultural centres of the wider Greek world. Such a study will have to raise a number of important issues.

The first issue is the relationship between all these different forms of centres. The archaic period is one in which these various centres tend to be distinct and separate; but during the fifth century Athens emerged as a political, economic and cultural centre at the same time. Unfortunately, this has led to the standard Athenocentric image of classical Greek history by obscuring the existence of other centres during the same period.[181] At the same time there has been little study of the wider phenomenon at hand: what are the connections between different forms of centres?[182] How does a centre of one kind transform itself into a multiple centre? It applies equally well to classical Athens and to Hellenistic Delos, a religious centre becoming the chief commercial centre of the Eastern Mediterranean.[183]

The second issue is scale. The Mediterranean had thousands of *emporia* in the various periods of its history; although we still lack studies of the development of each of these *emporia* through time, their distribution and functions, etc., what is even more important is to recognise the development in the scale and power of these centres. We can distinguish between local *emporia*, pooling the goods of the local areas; regional *emporia*, based on interregional exchange; and international *emporia*, which function as places of international exchange.[184] The creation of the last order of centres is one of the most important developments in Mediterranean history.[185] It is well reflected in the difference between the diverse cargoes found in archaic and classical shipwrecks and the homogeneous cargoes that characterise Roman shipwrecks; evidence, among other things, of the emergence of international centres of exchange, which make it feasible for many traders to bypass the *cabotage* of local and regional *emporia*, and have direct access to the large international centres. But there are still cases in earlier periods that point to the same directions: the many findings of Rhodian vases in Sicily during the period 650–550 BCE contrast sharply with their almost complete absence from south Italy; can we take this as evidence of

---

[181] See the protests of Thomas 2000: 9–16.   [182] But see Engberg-Pedersen 1993.
[183] See Rauh 1993. For Hellenistic Rhodes becoming both a commercial and cultural centre, see Rossetti and Furiani 1993; Gabrielsen 1997.
[184] See the points of Bresson 1993: 199.
[185] For a survey of late Hellenistic maritime centres, see Rauh 2003: 33–92.

direct networks between Rhodes and Sicily, which bypass south Italy?[186] The case of Rhegion and Zancle, the cities in the straits of Sicily, provides another interesting example. The vases found in them show similar patterns with those found in Etruria, in particular in the preponderance of first quality Attic pottery; but they contrast sharply with the findings in the cities of the Gulf of Taranto and in Sicily; we see here again the role of the emergence of a centre mediating between two areas of international exchange, and the different position of cities remaining outside this network.[187]

The emergence of Gravisca in the Western Mediterranean and Naucratis in the Eastern Mediterranean during the late archaic period illustrates well the change in magnitude and scope.[188] The creation of these international commercial centres, from Athens to Rhodes, Alexandria and Delos is of the utmost importance.[189]

A third issue is control and competition. A centre can attempt not only to attract, but actually to control the activities and processes on which it is based; moreover, it might try to transform its controlling power in one field into power in other fields; or, alternatively, its role as a centre in one field might necessitate the creation of centres in other fields too. There is an obvious difference between attracting and controlling; between the Athenian control on the movement of cereals and the Athenian attraction of manpower. The reason they are treated together here is not because I want to minimise the difference. Rather, it is because I want to draw attention to a spectrum of reactions and forms of control that an emerging centre might use in order to exploit for its own benefit these international networks.

A recent discovery of a lead weight from the western Black Sea, dating to the late fifth century, is a good illustration of the issues involved;[190] the weight bears the owl, emblem of Athenian coinage, on the one side, and the tunna, emblem of the coinage of Cyzicus, on the other. Its weight seems to aim at a synchronisation of the Attic with the Cyzicene standard, two of the most important standards in this period, and can even be synchronised with the Aeginetan one; was it a result of the needs created by the intensification of links within the *système-monde* that brought together the Aegean world and the Black Sea, or of Athenian imperial imposition, as seen in the notorious Standards Decree? The former seems more probable, but the variety of possible answers shows well the complexity of the issue at hand here.

---

[186] See Vallet 1963: 316.   [187] Vallet and Villard 1963: 268.   [188] Giangiulio 1996: 519–21.
[189] See the approaches in Nicolet 2000.   [190] For the following, see Meyer and Moreno 2004.

What needs to be stressed is that the three levels I have distinguished are dissimilar *and* co-existing. They have different temporalities and different properties, but these levels are not superimposed on each other, like the floors of a house, but rather interpenetrating.

Epilogue

This whole discussion of the poleis as part of a *système-monde* had a double aim. On the one hand it was necessary to emphasise that viewing the polis as a solitary entity is deeply misleading; we have to see Greek poleis as interdependent parts, in varying ways, of a wider *système-monde*; and I have tried to suggest a number of ways and a number of concepts than can allow us to study them from such a perspective. On the other hand, there was a wider claim: our general histories of Greece are overtly Athenocentric and Hellenocentric.

The modern treatments of Greek history oscillate between two attitudes, which I find equally problematic. The one is to take Athenian history, society, economy and culture as equivalent to Greek history, society, economy and culture.[191] The polis-centred approach has played a fundamental role in this respect. Athens provides a good example of the rise, acme and decline of the polis (rising through the archaic period, having a golden age during the classical, falling in relative obscurity in the Hellenistic), which accords well with the standard periodisation; Athens became a democracy, so its history accords well with the teleological account of the development of democracy from monarchy through aristocracy and tyranny; it also allows the common enough identification of polis and democracy, and the wiping off the mental map of the various oligarchic experiences that constituted the rule of Greek history; Athens was an independent power and lost its autonomy only in the Hellenistic period, which helps to equate the concepts of polis and autonomy; at the same time, Athens was a political, economic and cultural centre, which enforces the view that the polis had its own entrenched economy, polity, society and culture, and misses the wider processes and centres on which the vast majority of poleis were constantly dependent.

It would be unfair to imply that all scholars have adopted an Athenocentric perspective. As a matter of fact, the tradition of taking the Greek world as a whole and using evidence from a wide number of Greek communities is equally old and common. One problem with this approach

---

[191] See e.g. Dillon 2004, where Greek stands for Athenian.

is that it usually still accepts the general polis-centred framework, which largely determines what will be the questions to be asked and what will constitute facts and events for modern historical accounts; consequently, much remains still outside its grasp, even when adopting a wider Greek perspective. But the more important problem is that of accepting the wider Greek world as a matter of fact; everybody who spoke Greek is somehow part of Greek culture and civilisation. The assumption behind this approach is that culture and society are closed, homogeneous, bounded entities. Greek culture is understood as a closed, bounded entity juxtaposed to other closed, bounded entities.

This has a double negative effect: it has failed to create methodological and analytical tools in order to study the variety of Greek cultures, their links and forms of interaction; between the individual polity and a reified Greek world or culture there exist no concepts to analyse the intermediate levels, the variety of links between them, and the ways in which the variety of communities and levels, scattered all over the Mediterranean, came to form a single system with its own rules. It has also created problematic reifications: Greek history is written as a national history, and is separated from other national histories in the Mediterranean (e.g. Egyptian or Persian). Even when scholars take into account the interactions between Greeks and other peoples, they tend to understand this as an interaction between two closed, bounded entities.

I have spent much effort in this book in order to show why these assumptions are methodologically and historically mistaken and misleading. Fortunately enough, there have been other voices with the same protests. A recent volume edited by Carol Dougherty and Leslie Kurke has tried to make a very similar point.[192]

In an important way, if there is any point talking about the unity of the Greek world, fragmented in a huge number of different polities, scattered all over the Mediterranean and the Black Sea, it must be emphasised that this unity was created and maintained by the huge numbers of mobile people: sailors, traders, soldiers, artists, physicians, poets, intellectuals. As Filippo Cassola has put it, 'these activities [of these thousands of mobile people] were enough to create a connective network which embraced the whole Greek world and caused an exchange of experiences that guaranteed not the homogeneity of the culture, but the reciprocal comprehension and the reciprocal interest among all the inhabited centres'.[193] But if we accept that this is the case, it is important to recognise that the networks of

---

[192] Dougherty and Kurke 2003a.   [193] Cassola 1996: 10.

mobilising and moving these people were not controlled only by Greeks and did not involve only Greeks.

Athenian monumental funerary art of the classical period provides a good example.[194] One of the most impressive monuments of fourth-century Athenian art is the funerary monument of Nikeratos, a metic from the city of Istria in the Black Sea; the monument is clearly inspired and imitates the famous Mausoleum of Halicarnassus. But the creation of this new form of funerary art, which fuses together Greek temple architecture and Greek sculpture with Near Eastern decoration themes and funerary monuments, is neither simply an imitation, nor another illustration of Athenian creativity; it was based on long experimentation between Greek and non-Greek artistic practices that took place in the wider Mediterranean Greek world.

Greek artists in Sinope (the Black Sea), Cyrene (North Africa) and the Greek cities of Asia Minor, working for both Greek and non-Greek customers, experimented for a long period, fusing the tradition of Greek public art with the various non-Greek traditions of monumental tombs, which were to be seen in their adjacent areas. In the fourth century this experimentation found its way to Athens, creating one of the most impressive artistic achievements of the Greek world. We see here clearly the interaction between various components of Greek and other Mediterranean cultures; the role of the wider Greek world as a laboratory of experimentation and interaction; the introduction of the new practices to Athens; and the role of metics in Athenian culture. But I am thinking of the ships that carried these artists, or anybody else who helped to transmit these practices from the wider Mediterranean to Athens; what else did these ships carry? What else did these people carry in their heads?

One of the most importance consequences of such an approach would be to reclaim the history of the wider Greek world, in Magna Graecia, in Sicily, in Cyrenaica, in Asia Minor, in the Black Sea, and to insert it into our main accounts of Greek history. The polis-centred approach has managed to marginalise all these communities of the wider Greek world, since they do not fit its criteria: they lack clear lines of evolution from rise, through acme to decline; they show different periodisations from that accepted in Greek history; for most of their history they were under the control of other powers; the categorical distinctions between insider and outsider, male and female, Greek and barbarian, so important to the polis approach, seem less important. Moses Finley characteristically talked about 'the failure of the Sicilian Greeks to make a success of the city-state way of life'.[195]

---

[194] For the following, see Hagemajer Allen 2003.   [195] Finley 1979: 48.

But there is no need to resort to such marginalisations. The wider Greek world was an essential part of the Greek *système-monde*; not simply in matters of economics (one could think how different fifth-century Aegean would have been without the vital exchange networks with the Black Sea), but in all possible respects. To give just one example, 'A map designed to note the birthplaces of important pre-Socratic philosophers and fifth-century BC sophists would leave the entire mainland of Greece south of Thrace entirely empty [with the single exception of Hippias of Elis].'[196] Another important consequence of this would be the undermining of many generalisations about Greek history. James Redfield has tried to do this about the Epizephyrean Locrians of southern Italy, creating a third model of Greek culture next to that of Athens and Sparta, by arguing that Locrian society was culturally distinct, because of the particular position it allotted to women.[197] It has become a topos that the Greeks made a categorical distinction between Greeks and barbarians, as many of our Athenocentric sources suggest (though by no means all); but the evidence from Magna Graecia, for example, where many non-Greeks managed to acquire citizenship in the Greek poleis, shows that 'not all Greeks predicated their view of the world on the dichotomy between Greek and non-Greek'.[198]

In conclusion: the world-system approach can allow us to uncover a novel Greek history, taking into account the totality of Greek communities and to insert Greek history within the history of the wider Mediterranean and the Black Sea.

[196] Tarrant 1990: 621.   [197] Redfield 2003.   [198] Lomas 2000: 175.

CHAPTER 8

Poleis and polities

Perhaps the greatest problem in the study of the Greek poleis has been the way it has been perceived and treated as a solitary entity. No definition or study of the Greek polis has yet attempted to incorporate the fact that every historical Greek polis was part of a system of interactions between poleis, *ethnê*, *koina* and non-Greek communities and polities. The *historical* institutional environment of the Greek poleis has usually been discarded by recourse to two complementary strategies. The one is the well-known Occidentalist practice of evolutionism:[1] different forms of polities are classified as steps in the evolutionary ladder, with 'archaic' forms of *ethnê* co-existing with progressive classical poleis and 'old-fashioned' Greek poleis co-existing with 'modern' Hellenistic kingdoms and *koina*. At the same time, the other Occidentalist discourse on the origins and history of the West creates a dichotomy between a Greece of the polis and an Orient, each with its own separate history, although they might from time to time interact in the well-known billiard game. One of the most malignant results of these approaches is the abandonment of political history to the most traditionalist *histoire évènementielle*. The static, evolutionist and reified definitions of the polis leave little space for a processual and theoretical approach to Greek political and military history.[2]

Our aim here is to overcome these well-entrenched practices and view Greek poleis as part of a *système-monde* of polities in the wider context of the Eastern Mediterranean and the Near East. The variety of Greek polities was not an assemblage of specimens from different evolutionary boxes: they co-existed, they interacted and they interlinked in ways that shaped

---

[1] See in general, Chakrabarty 2000: 237–55.

[2] Ste Croix 1972: 89–166 laid the foundations for such a study; but his explanations were not wholly successful and the focus of the book was anyway somewhat more restricted. Cartledge 1987: in particular 180–330 is the most successful approach we ever had yet, following in the steps of Ste Croix' book in very many ways. But much is still to be accomplished. The introduction in Balcer 1984 is very ambitious, but the book accomplishes rather little.

decisively their collective history. At the same time, the historical development of Greek communities took place within a wider international environment and (dis)equilibrium. We have to introduce then a number of key concepts to deal with our subject.

POLEIS AND SOVEREIGNTY

It has been thought that one of the *sine qua non* characteristics of the polis is its autonomy, the right to conduct its external relationships in its own terms and by its own decisions. This can no longer be tenable. The work of the Copenhagen Polis Centre has demonstrated, beyond reasonable doubt, that autonomy, in the sense of political independence in external relationships, was never part of the Greek concept of the polis, both on theoretical and on practical terms.[3] On theoretical terms, Greek thinkers never discuss the concept of autonomy, when they attempt to define the essence of the polis.[4] Moreover, the Greeks found no problem in calling poleis a variety of communities and settlements that were obviously not able to conduct their own external relationships on their own terms.[5]

There were poleis that were part of a larger state, ruled by a dominant polis in terms of external and sometimes internal relationships.[6] Examples abound: one can cite the poleis of the *perioikoi* of Sparta,[7] which along with the Spartans constituted the Lacedaimonians;[8] the perioikic poleis of Elis;[9] the dependent poleis of various Arcadian poleis,[10] like Mantineia and Orchomenos; and the dependent poleis of Cretan poleis, like Gortyn, Praisos and Eleutherna.[11] To give an example from Crete, we have a treaty between the Praisians and the community of the Stalitai. The Stalitai have a number of military and financial obligations towards the polis of Praisos that make clear its dependent status. On the other hand, the Stalitai have the right to impose their own taxes; they have their own laws and magistrates; and they are provided with a right on their land (*chôra*), city (*polis*) and some unspecified islands. A first observation concerns the fact that Stalai are to have control of a clearly demarcated territory, as any independent polis would. The second observation concerns the use of the term polis to describe Stalai. In case someone assumes that the designation of

---

[3] Hansen 1995b.   [4] See Sakellariou 1989: 213–90 on Aristotle's discussion of definitions of the polis.
[5] On sovereignty, polis-status and coinage, see Martin 1985.
[6] The best though not exhaustive introduction to dependent communities in ancient Greece is still Gschnitzer 1958.
[7] Shipley 1997; Hansen 2004c.   [8] Hall 2000.   [9] Roy 1997.   [10] Nielsen 1996b.
[11] Perlman 1996.

polis refers to Stalai only in the sense of urban settlement, it is important to stress that later in the inscription, Stalai and Setaia are referred to as poleis in the *explicit sense of political community*.[12]

There were poleis that formed a regional polity,[13] what the Greeks called *ethnos* or *koinon*.[14] The *ethnos* was long misleadingly identified by modern scholarship as an alternative to polis, an archaic tribal state flourishing in areas with no poleis. This too is untenable.[15] Regions with a distinct identity could form *koina* with poleis as participants (e.g. the Boiotian poleis),[16] but even in cases like Achaia and Arcadia, the *ethnos* comprised both poleis (Mantineia, Tegea, Pellene) and *phylai*, sub-regional entities, which were still formed by small poleis (the 'tribal' communities of Mainalians, Parrhasians, Kynourians).[17] The poleis that participated in these *koina* or *ethnê*, both on equal terms, or under the hegemony of dominant poleis, still thought of themselves, and were recognised by others, as poleis.[18]

Finally, on practical grounds, many poleis were for long periods of their history under the rule of other states, whether other poleis (Athens,[19] Spartan *decarchies*[20]); non-Greek imperial powers (the Ionian poleis and Persia[21]); or Greek kings and tyrants (the Sicilian poleis and the tyrants of Gela and Syracuse,[22] the poleis of Troad and Greek tyrants[23]). Still, they thought of themselves, and were recognised by others, as poleis. A definition of polis as an autonomous state would exclude, on both theoretical and practical grounds, the vast majority of archaic and classical communities and settlements, which were recognised by the Greeks as such.

It would be more useful to divide the Greek poleis in three general categories: hegemonic poleis (e.g. Athens, Sparta), middling or regionally powerful poleis (e.g. Thasos, Samos, Tegea) and small poleis (Koressos, Plataea). This is not an ideal-type construction, nor does it intend to be all-inclusive. It simply attempts to draw attention to the different capacities, resources, potentialities and aspirations of each different category, which

---

[12] *Inscriptiones Creticae*, III, vi, 7B, ll. 17–18: 'ean de pou allai prostaxêi ho kosmos ho Praisiôn hopoterai [ôn] tam poleôn [= Stalai and Setaia], houtoi pleontôn'. It is obvious from this passage that when the Gortynians wanted to refer to a community of people they had no other term to describe it than simply 'polis'. Perlman 1996: 257–8 seems to miss this point. Chaniotis 1996: 385–93, on the other hand, acknowledges this use of polis in the sense of community of members.

[13] We can define as regional polity a polity consisting of a number of communities of a region with equal or unequal status.

[14] Beck 1997.   [15] See already the remarks of Giovannini 1971: 71–93.

[16] Hansen 1995d, 1996a, 1997c.   [17] Arcadia: Nielsen 1996a; Achaia: Morgan and Hall 1996.

[18] In general, see Morgan 2003.   [19] Meiggs 1972: 205–54.   [20] Cartledge 1987: 90–4.

[21] Tuplin 1987.   [22] Hansen and Nielsen 2004: 172–248.

[23] Xenophon, *Hellenica*, III, i, 10–27; Hansen and Nielsen 2004: 1000–17.

cannot be subsumed under the generalising umbrella of the city-state. We have already drawn attention to the comments of Polybius to this effect. A hegemonic polis might form a variety of relationships with a middling or small polis, ranging from alliance or opposition to domination, or even incorporation.[24] Our models and concepts need to take account of this important difference and its various configurations.

POLEIS, *ETHNÊ*, *KOINA*

My use of the word polity implies a decision to bypass the old distinction between polis, *ethnos* and *koinon*. The organisational forms of Greek polities are not specimens from different stages of a supposed evolution. Rather, they have to be seen in two complementary ways: the organisational form is dependent on the aims, capacities, resources and aspirations of the polity; and it also depends on its place and its possibilities within a wider *système-monde*.

We have already commented that a large number of poleis participated in *ethnê* and *koina*. What is more, the old myth of an urbanised world of poleis and the village-dominated world of *ethnê* should finally be laid to rest. Poleis in the sense of nucleated settlements are widely encountered in the regions dominated by *ethnê*, and their sizes are directly comparable to those of the vast majority of the other poleis (some even reach the size of real urban centres).[25] To give an example from Achaia, which for most of its history formed an *ethnos* and a *koinon*, the twelve *merides*, already described by Herodotus,[26] were centred on nucleated settlements that would perfectly qualify as political centres of poleis.[27] In the words of Fritz Gschnitzer,

the poleis appear everywhere, even in the regions of *ethnê*, as the subjects of the social relationships, the communities of social life; on the other hand, the *ethnê* were the real political units, the subjects of international law, and only outside the areas organised as *ethnê* were the poleis playing this role. The coincidence of both forms, of social and political unity, was therefore not the general rule, but rather the characteristic of a specific type of political order, i.e. the independent polis, or, more precisely, the independent *Normalpolis*.[28]

Moreover, since the polis is usually envisaged as a community of citizens, it is impossible to differentiate the polis from the *ethnos* on this account. Older approaches to the *ethnos* envisaged it as a remnant of a tribal

[24] See Amit 1973.   [25] Jost 1986, 1999.   [26] Herodotus, I, 145.   [27] Morgan 2000.
[28] Gschnitzer 1991: 433.

past in less-developed areas of the Greek world.[29] These approaches have been successfully refuted in the last three decades, by showing that the internal divisions of the Greek poleis (the *phylai*, etc.) were not remnants of a tribal organisation of society, which persisted in the *ethnê*, but artificial creations of the archaic period.[30] In the same way, the supposed tribal affinities of the *ethnos* are fictive; the Greeks of the *ethnê* were capable of inventing and forging ties of political, social and religious kinship, as the Greeks of poleis were.[31] The *ethnos* is now envisaged not as an alternative to the polis, but as a complex organisational linking of political forms and communities both above and below the polis.[32] Many *ethnê* had their own assemblies, and although they could comprise communities with their own citizenship, they also had their own citizenship, which they could confer to individuals.[33]

The distinction between polis and *ethnos* as forms of political and social organisation is a mirage of modern scholarship. In fact, a more meaningful classification would distinguish between **Normalpoleis**, with a single nucleated settlement acting as political centre, **Großpoleis**, consisting of a nucleated settlement acting as political centre and a number of other settlements, either demes (villages) or dependent poleis, and **regional polities** (*ethnê*), consisting of poleis (nucleated settlements), or *kômai* (villages).[34] But my point again is not to substitute a two-fold division with a three-fold one. The point is that the differing forms of political organisation should be viewed both as synchronic alternatives and in their diachronic development and interaction; and that we should study processes of formation and fragmentation, instead of putting labels and pushing our conceptual objects into the appropriate collector's box. A recent study shows eloquently why polis and *koinon* should not be juxtaposed, but seen in their interdependence: studying the processes by which poleis are abandoned in the late classical and Hellenistic periods it shows that it was often the existence of links of *syngeneia* and the links forged in a *koinon* that allowed poleis under threat to survive in exile, regroup under more favourable conditions, stand their ground or be absorbed within other communities.[35] The role of the *koinon* in promoting social resilience to local, lower-level stresses such as population shortage, disease and poverty should be taken seriously into consideration.

---

[29] See Ehrenberg 1960: 24–7; Snodgrass 1980: 42–4.   [30] Bourriot 1976; Roussel 1976; Finley 1985a.
[31] Davies 2000.   [32] See the comments of Archibald 2000; see also Morgan 2000.
[33] Davies 2000.   [34] Gschnitzer 1991: 439–42. See also the comments of Hansen 2004a.
[35] Mackil 2004.

We should abandon the teleological conception of history, where the *ethnos* is destined to be succeeded by the city-state and the city-state by the monarchies and the *koina* of the Hellenistic period. We should view all forms of political communities as co-existing alternatives, with differing or different aims and abilities, or even as organisational forms with different scales that do not necessarily exclude each other. We should look at the totality of political structures available to past actors in order to understand how they came into existence; how they were shaped by past actors; how they antagonised each other for the actors' allegiances; how they interacted with and acted on social and economic processes; and finally why some of them in specific temporal and spatial contexts were more successful than others.

A fascinating example of how to do so is offered by Hendrik Spruyt in his book with the characteristic title *The Sovereign State and its Competitors: An Analysis of System Change*.[36] He has studied the various forms of political organisation in early modern Europe, and argues against the teleological view, where the feudal kingdoms and principalities were destined to be substituted by the sovereign national states. He tries to show how a variety of political forms were devised to cope with the crisis of the medieval world and how different actors in different periods and regions opted for different solutions (France and the territorial state of the Capetids, Germany and the city leagues like Hansa, Italy and the city-states). He illustrates how the different forms were part of an interrelated system and interacted with each other, and how economic and political processes influenced and were influenced by the political ones. Finally, he tries to show how, in the specific political, economic and social conjuncture of early modern Europe, the national state came out as the most successful solution to the challenges of the period. The obsession with the polis and the neglect of the other forms of political communities ensures that we will create a misleading picture.[37]

POLEIS, NETWORKS AND THE *SYSTÈME-MONDE*

Given our differentiation between various levels of polities, the working of the political *système-monde* is dependent upon flows of resources and networks for its production and redistribution. This can be further qualified: on the one hand flows of resources and networks of production and distribution have their own logic and time scale, which is independent from that of the political *système-monde*. The logic of and reasons for

---

[36] Spruyt 1994.   [37] See the comments and articles in Brock and Hodkinson 2000.

migration or commodity production in one area does not necessarily emanate from the needs and workings of the political *système-monde*. The polities try to harness and take advantage of these independent flows and networks for their own aims; a good example is provided by the behaviour of Lysander at the end of the fifth century BCE:

> When he came to Ephesus, he found the city well disposed to him and very zealous in the Spartan cause, although it was then in a low state of prosperity and in danger of becoming utterly barbarised by the admixture of Persian customs, since it was enveloped by Lydia, and the King's generals made it their headquarters. He therefore pitched his camp there, and ordered the merchant vessels from every quarter to land their cargoes there, and made preparations for the building of triremes. Thus he revived the traffic of their harbours, and the business of their market, and filled their houses and workshops with profits, so that from that time on, and through his efforts, the city had hopes of achieving the stateliness and grandeur, which it now enjoys.[38]

The power and prosperity of Ephesus derives from attracting to the city the flow of resources in wider processes. Equally, the form of and the changes in the political *système-monde* are partially dependent on unpredictable, chaotic and uncontrollable changes in these flows and networks. But at the same time, polities attempt to channel and control these flows and networks and in this way they redirect them in substantial ways. McKechnie has presented a compelling case that the rise and dominance of late classical and Hellenistic potentates and kings was based on the exploitation of an already existing large pool of 'outsiders in the Greek cities'; it was the displacement of large numbers of individuals that allowed the potentates to consolidate their power by taking advantage of it.[39] So there is a *dialectique* between the system and the flows and networks.[40]

This is probably one of the most neglected issues in current research. The maintenance, reproduction and expansion of each Greek polity depended on these flows and networks; but the form, the degree and the extent of these relations are predicated on its position and status within the *système-monde*. An inland, agricultural, small polis would have minimal recourse to the flows and networks: its inland position would severely restrict its ability to take advantage of networks of connectivity to provide, for example, its cereals, in order to specialise in other activities apart from merely auto-consuming cereal culture; its low status would not urge it to pursue serious power

---

[38] Plutarch, *Life of Lysander*, 3.2–3.   [39] McKechnie 1989: 1–3.
[40] The globalisation of financial flows in the modern world is an apt example. No government can bring under its control these world flows; but they can always try to harness and take advantage of them, and their practices have the effect of redirecting these flows; see Arrighi 1994.

strategies, which would force it to enter the networks for resources (e.g. timber for shipbuilding) and manpower (e.g. rowers, mercenaries).

But at the same time, its small and precarious position may make it seriously dependent on the networks and flows of the political *système-monde*: a substantial proportion of citizens of small Arcadian communities gained their subsistence from mercenary service abroad;[41] hence, their small communities were dependent on international networks of mobilisation of military manpower and their fortunes.[42] These networks could take people very far away indeed; Arcadian mercenaries fought for Cyrus, the Persian claimant to the throne, all the way to Mesopotamia;[43] and there are fourth-century inscriptions from the Black Sea, ranging from honorary monuments of Arcadian mercenaries for King Leycon of the Bosporan kingdom to grave inscriptions and proxeny decrees for other Arcadians.[44] At the same time, a small community might find itself in a state of dependency in the political *système-monde*, forced to become a dependent polis, or dissolved into a larger political entity.

Meanwhile, for regional and hegemonic polities, the workings of this system were even more critical. For hegemonic poleis, the situation is quite clear: in order to exercise hegemony, it was necessary to have control over money, resources and manpower.[45] Money could be provided by subjects or allies, acquired through exploitation of local resources (e.g. the Athenian mines), or gained through commandment of exchange networks. Resources could actually be locally procured, but, in the vast majority of cases, they needed to be imported, such as the timber needed for any serious naval strategy.[46] Manpower was crucial: mercenary and metic soldiers, rowers and sailors for military aspects and a huge workforce to guarantee the necessary networks of provision and exchange. The boast of Jason of Pherae that he could very easily provide the crews of his navy with native *penestai*[47] was formidable: in most other cases, navies depended on the availability and importation of a huge workforce.

---

[41] Roy 1999; in the fourth century 'more Arcadian hoplites served as mercenaries abroad than *several* of the strongest Arcadian poleis could muster'; Nielsen 2002b: 81.

[42] Of course, here again we meet the case that polities would try to take advantage of these networks. After the formation of the Arcadian *koinon* in the 360s the Arcadians tried to use this huge mercenary force, which international networks had long since created, for their own aims; hence the creation of the standing army of the *Eparitoi* and the concomitant problems of securing the resources for its maintenance; Roy 2000: 316–21. In the end the peripheral position of the Arcadian communities made sure that the experiment had to be abandoned.

[43] Roy 1967.   [44] See Vinogradov 1987: 30–2.

[45] See Gabrielsen 2001a on naval warfare and the Greek poleis.   [46] Meiggs 1982: 116–53.

[47] Xenophon, *Hellenica*, VI, i, 11–12.

Our difficulty in grasping these realities seems to stem from two factors: on the one hand, the fact that no polity could take full control of these flows and networks has encouraged scholars with Occidentalist expectations to disregard them almost completely: scholars, who expected to find mercantilist state policies to control exchange, currency and exports, great commercial-cum-state companies controlling international trade and clear-cut centres and peripheries were obviously disappointed; hence the easy step to forget the whole issue, and build models inherently incapable of taking it into account.[48] The second problem of course is documentary: the absence of archival resources that would allow us to reconstruct the flows and networks of resources and manpower, as scholars of medieval and modern European history have managed to do.

We must then attempt to redress this imbalance in our accounts. Vincent Gabrielsen has stressed the importance of manpower and labour mobilisation for the power strategies of various polities:

Migratory movements, gravitating above all towards flourishing urban centres (whether in the East or in the West) must be considered as an economic activity of the first order, since they essentially meant the relocation and exploitation of a valuable resource, manpower: by this I mean the supply and use of the physical *and* mental energies of people of free status. Already in classical times, city-states, always eager to supplement their citizen populations (periodically or permanently) with external supplies of human potential, had become aware of three hard facts: 1) that manpower was a perennially scarce resource; 2) that like certain other types of resource (e.g. strategic ones) it sometimes could not be obtained, even if one possessed the necessary purchasing power; and 3) that its indispensability for not only the military but also the civil aggrandisement of states made it worth competing for – often fiercely.[49]

This has implications for the nature and the extent of the political *système-monde* that we are examining. All too often, treatments of the Greek political system have included only polities from mainland Greece and excluded the rest of Greek and non-Greek communities in the rest of the Mediterranean. The justification would probably be that the direct political–military links between Greek communities of the mainland and other polities have been quite secondary and restricted. This is true to a certain extent, although the intensity of such links has been probably undervalued. But once we understand that even the workings of the mainland political system depend on flows of resources, which have a Mediterranean-wide extent, then it becomes important to think in these

---

[48] Finley 1973b: 154–76.   [49] Gabrielsen 2001b: 221.

wider terms. One could enquire, for example, about the connection between the migration of thousands of Greeks to a repopulated Sicily after the expedition of Timoleon[50] and the defeat of the Greek poleis from Macedonia: did the draining of Greek poleis from available manpower play a role in their defeat?

POLITIES, THE *SYSTÈME-MONDE* AND FORMS OF CHANGE

If we recognise that polities are not individual entities, but parts of a political *système-monde*, then we need to differentiate clearly between the different forms of interaction and change within such a system. The treatment of the polis as an individual, yet unitary, entity has helped to obscure and confuse the variety of different forms.

Following Robert Gilpin,[51] we can define three forms of change. The first concerns 'the nature of the actors or diverse entities that compose an international system', and could be called **actor change**. It concerns changes like the change from the archaic political system composed of Greek polities, to the classical one composed of Greek polities and a large empire (Persia), to the Hellenistic one with the emergence and domination of the large Hellenistic kingdoms. The second type of change is 'a change in the form of control or governance of an international system; this type of change will be called **systemic change**' (e.g. the change from the tripolar balance between Athens, Sparta and Persia in the fifth century, to the anarchic balance of the evolving fourth century). The third form of change is that 'a change may take place in the form of regular interactions or processes among the entities in an ongoing international system; this type of change will be labelled simply **interaction change**'. Under this label we can include, for example, the change from mainly cultural and scattered political and military exchanges between Greek polities in the archaic period to a new form of relationships, where a border conflict in one region might lead to a general war between all the Greek polities.[52]

The failure to differentiate between different forms of change in the political *système-monde* creates acute problems. An example is the notorious discussion of the decline of the polis, and the crisis and demise of Athens in the late fourth century.[53] J. K. Davies has treated this discourse with his

---

[50] Talbert 1974: 146–60.
[51] Gilpin 1981: 39–40; I have modified the names he gives to different forms of change.
[52] See the case of Locrians and Phocians in the 390s and the eruption of the Corinthian war; *Hellenica Oxyrhynchia*, XIII, 3–4.
[53] A classic treatment is Mossé 1962; the issue is re-examined in Eder 1995.

usual lucidity. He argues that linking the two issues and arguing that the defeat of Athens by Macedonia is an aspect of the general decline of the polis is unconvincing, because

> it oscillates between being propositions about an individual polis and propositions about the city-state system as a whole. That would be legitimate, if, and only if, they were organisms of the same kind with the same sort of purpose. In fact they are not, though the distinction is obscured by our pernicious habit of using the terms 'Athens' or 'Sparta', when we are actually referring to 'the resources of land, money and manpower controlled by Athens or Sparta at any one particular moment'.[54]

The reasons that Athens loses its hegemonic position seem to have less to do with a general crisis of the polis, or of the Athenian polis, and more with changing relationships in changing conjunctures of interstate relationships.

> [This brings us] to the concert of powers of the fourth century, where the pace of change was rapid, to Athens' disadvantage, viz. that of technology transfer. She had been ahead of the game in a Greek context alike in some aspects of military technology (especially naval warfare and siege warfare), and in administrative technology (running an Empire). Those competitive advantages were gradually eroded, not because Athenians forgot the skills, but because others copied them and/or developed their own techniques . . . what probably matters more is what is less visible, the ways in which a Philip, or a Jason, or a Mausolus did for their own areas what Athens had done for the Aegean in the fifth century. That had comprised imposing a serious fiscal regime with the administrative expertise to run it, putting hardware in the ground in the form of roads and forts and new towns, and, in general, so harnessing resources, as to turn this or that geographical expression into a unified polity. It is this development, which comprises the main external environmental pressure on fourth-century Athens, rather than the ambitions or blocking capabilities of Thebes or Sparta, not least because this development took place above all within the areas, which Athens had regarded as her sphere of influence – Thessaly, Macedonia, Thrace, W. Asia Minor and Sicily.[55]

Time matters in history and *when* things take place cannot be abstracted from our models and conceptualisations. In the case of interstate relationships, as in any other form of relationships indeed, the polities that interact might be at different or varying time scales and conjunctures, and the conjuncture of their interaction is absolutely crucial.

The problem becomes manifest when, for example, Moses Finley talks about 'the failure of the Sicilian Greeks to make a success of the city-state way of life'.[56] As if there was a model of city-state life that can be found at

---

[54] Davies 1995: 34.   [55] Davies 1995: 35.   [56] Finley 1979: 48.

some part of mainland Greece and could be imitated. We deal here again with an evolutionist view of the past: there was a form of Greek society and it had to develop into its fifth-century form, from which it could only decline from the fourth century onwards. In reality what happened was that a multiplicity of regional and interregional divergent paths was put in shadow by the unprecedented rise of the Athenian *archê* and its deadly antagonism with Sparta. It is mainly due to Thucydides that we tend to perceive the fifth century through the sole prism of the antagonism between two imperial poleis, while at the same time elevating this temporary fifth-century conjuncture into 'classical Greece', which is the measure of normality; a standpoint from which everything else was either an archaic precursor, or a proto-Hellenistic decline.

Instead, one could see the sixth century in all its divergent plurality: poleis enlarging their own territory and subjugating the defeated populations (Sparta);[57] poleis dominating whole regions by driving away the former inhabitants (Argos);[58] poleis dominating whole regions by incorporating them within their polity (Elis);[59] communities expanding by creating dependent *apoikiai* supporting networks of interests in particular areas (Thasos, Corinth, Miletus);[60] tyrants attempting to take control of whole areas of the Aegean (Polycrates of Samos,[61] Histiaius of Miletus[62]); tyrants creating *apoikiai* and controlling networks of communities (the Cypselids of Corinth,[63] Peisistratos[64]); citizen magnates carving out their own principalities in a variety of relationships to their polis (Miltiades and the Chersonese[65]). The same variety is to be seen in the fourth century, after the bipolar antagonism fades out: creation of federal polities, with communities sharing rights of marriage and property (the Chalcidian *koinon*);[66] *ethnê* incorporating other communities (the Achaeans and Calydon in 389 BCE);[67] kings creating federal polities under their rule (Molossian kings and the Epeirote *koinon*);[68] magnates taking control of large polities to create their own *archê* (Jason of Pherae);[69] magnates creating their own principalities (Mausolus, Caria and the Greek poleis);[70] citizens creating their own networks and links of wealth, power and territorial acquisitions in varying relations to their poleis (Iphicrates,

[57] Shipley 1997. [58] Pierart 1997. [59] Roy 1997. [60] Graham 1983: 71–153.
[61] Herodotus, III, 39.
[62] Histiaius and Myrcinus in Thrace: Herodotus, V, 11; 23–25; Aristagoras at Myrcinus: V, 126.
[63] Salmon 1984: 209–17. [64] Berve 1967: 61–3. [65] Loukopoulou 1989: 67–94.
[66] Xenophon, *Hellenica*, V, ii, 19; see Zahrnt 1971. [67] Xenophon, *Hellenica*, IV, vi, 1.
[68] Davies 2000. [69] Diodorus, XV, 60, 1–4; Xenophon, *Hellenica*, VI, i, 4–16.
[70] Hornblower 1982: 107–37.

Chabrias,[71] Agesilaus, Archidamus[72]); and of course the old story of expansion through annexing territory (Elis), dominating other communities within a federal structure (Thebes) and creating *cleruchies* (Athens) is still going on.

I hope that there is little need in the present context for pointing out that the very same processes continue to take place throughout the fifth century, although of course the central bipolar antagonism is dominant. And of course, if seen through this background, the 'anomalous' histories of the communities of Magna Graecia, Libya, Asia Minor and the Black Sea, which cannot fit into the ideal pattern of 'classical Greece', take a very different colour. Instead of being then the classical ideal that every period should be measured against, the fifth century becomes a highly stimulating conjuncture: instead of writing teleological accounts of how Greek history was predetermined to lead to the fifth-century 'classical world' and its fourth-century evolving decline, the fifth-century pattern becomes itself a highly idiosyncratic pattern in need of explanation.[73] Why and how were the divergent and variable pictures of the sixth and the fourth century bisected by the bipolar one of the fifth century? Instead of the linear and Athenocentric narrative that moves from the rise of the polis in the archaic period, its acme in the classical and its decline and substitution from Hellenistic monarchies and koina, we need a new historical narrative that would take into account the issues discussed above.[74]

---

[71] See Pritchett 1974, who tends to minimise their personal strategies and motives.
[72] On Agesilaus and Archidamus, see Cartledge 1987: 314–30.
[73] See the comments of Ma 2003: 36–7.
[74] Davies 1978, 1997a provides good examples of how to accomplish it.

CHAPTER 9

Poleis and time

The aim of this chapter is to provide a temporal framework for the study of Greek history; it will serve as an accompaniment to the analytical and spatial frameworks that have been presented in previous chapters. We have seen how Eurocentrism has shaped the construction of the temporalities within which Greek history has been studied in the last two centuries. Chapter 5 aimed to show that the temporality that juxtaposes antiquity and modernity, or sees antiquity only through the prism of the emergence of modernity, is deeply problematic and misleading. In what follows, I explore a variety of different temporal frameworks for the study of Greek history.

THE CONSEQUENCES OF EUROCENTRIST TEMPORALITIES

The construction of Greek history as a field within a Eurocentric perspective had a double effect. On the one hand, the incorporation of Greek history within a Eurocentric metanarrative necessitated the construction of Greek history as an entity with beginning, acme and end; it needed a homogenised national narrative; on the other hand, Greek history existed as an entity only from the perspective of how it functioned as a stage in the evolution of the West.

I will deal with this second issue first. We can call this perspective the tunnel vision of time.[1] It is the idea that there is a sort of linear trajectory in history, which moves ultimately to modernity. It is the image of a train (a veritable *Orient Express* as a matter of fact), which passes from various stations, while keeping moving forward to reach modernity (from Mesopotamia, to Greece, to Rome, to medieval Italy, to Holland, to industrial England, etc.). The stations have no importance, no history of themselves: their sole function is to receive and facilitate the train of

[1] For the term, see Blaut 1993: 3–8.

progress in its journey to modernity.[2] The history of the stations, after the
train has departed, is a parochial history, left to specialists, and with little
impact on perceptions of what is going on within the tunnel, where the
train moves.[3]

We have seen how this temporal perspective works in the chapter on the
consumer city. It is the Eurocentric tunnel vision that legitimises a comparison between ancient Mediterranean cities and medieval/early modern
Western ones. The result is the abstraction of ancient Greek history from
the continuous history of the Aegean and the Eastern Mediterranean. The
impact of this abstraction has been tremendous. One of its effects is the
misunderstanding and misrepresentation of many features of Greek history.[4] Greek colonisation is a good example. The Greek settlement expansion in Asia Minor, the Black Sea, southern Italy and Sicily in the archaic
period has not been a unique feature of Mediterranean history; in fact, it is
impressive to note that Aegean Greeks turn to the same areas (Asia Minor,
the Black Sea, Egypt along with the Balkans) in a new phase of outward
expansion in the eighteenth and nineteenth centuries AD.[5] It is of course
true that many features of the ancient Greek colonisation are different from
the more recent expansion (ancient Greek colonies were often autonomous
polities, eighteenth-century *paroikies* were never so); but I hope there is no
need to argue extensively that ancient Greek colonisation will appear quite
different from its present colouring, if approached from a Mediterranean
historical perspective.[6]

We need to provide the study of ancient history with other temporal
perspectives, apart from the Eurocentric one. Until fairly recently, the only
temporal perspectives of historical change that existed were deeply
Eurocentric: history was presented as the development that led to the rise
of the West and the creation of modernity. The rest of past or modern non-
Western societies either had to construct a temporal framework on the
basis of the Eurocentric model, or were denied any change and development and were presented as static and stagnant.

The attempts to write the economic, social and political history of the
Greek communities revolved around varying and opposing attitudes to the
Western paradigm. Before the Second World War, the prevailing attitude
was that of the modernists, who turned Greek history into a forerunner of

---

[2] For a non-teleological account of European history, see Fontana 1995.
[3] For such a perspective on the Near East, see Larsen 1989.
[4] I have dealt with these issues extensively in Vlassopoulos n.d.
[5] Tsoukalas 1977: 269–371; Kardasis 2001.   [6] See Jacoby 1994.

the Western paradigm; the obvious misfit between their accounts and the actual facts in turn boosted the primitivist approach, which offered a different account, but was again based on the Western paradigm: if ancient Greek history did not look like what the Western paradigm spelled, then it was a story of failures, stagnation and vicious circles.

Hypothetically, had the Roman Empire encompassed the civilised world, as the panegyrists said, there is no reason why Europe, western Asia, and northern Africa should not still, today, be ruled by Roman emperors, America still belong to the red Indians.[7]
    A vicious circle of evils was in full swing. The ancient world was hastened to its end by its social and political structure, its deeply embedded and institutionalised value system, and, underpinning the whole, the organisation and exploitation of its productive forces. There, if one wishes, is an economic explanation of the end of the ancient world.[8]

Both primitivists and modernists were mistaken, though for different reasons that have been already analysed.[9]
    But recent work in historical scholarship offers us a way out of the impasse. The discovery that the early modern East had its own clear historical development, and not simply stagnation and vicious circles, although this historical development did not follow the Western path, opens extremely stimulating new vistas.[10] The expansion of markets, the extension of money use, the growth of commercial manufactures, the development of sophisticated financial networks, the rise of influential capitalists and of more bureaucratised state forms were found not only in Europe, but also in South Asia, China and West Africa.[11] Nevertheless, the interconnections between these different aspects of change were different in the early modern East with that of early modern Europe; they also had clearly different results.[12]
    The collective impact of all the above is to challenge the logic of the Western paradigm itself: the idea that what emerged in nineteenth-century Western Europe was somehow a natural and necessary outcome of human development; a goal which humanity was ultimately destined to reach; a state which previous periods and other civilisations failed to reach and only the modern West with its peculiar innate characteristics managed to reach first; a condition that will ultimately diffuse globally assimilating 'archaic', 'traditional' and other anomalies. In the words of an Indian historian,

---

[7] Finley 1973b: 176.   [8] Finley 1973b: 176.   [9] See the critique of Nafissi 2005: 235–83.
[10] Prakash 1990; Wong 1997; Bayly 2002.
[11] See Perlin 1994a; Wong 1997; Brook and Blue 1999; Pomeranz 2000.   [12] Washbrook 1988.

of course these [scholarly] developments are of great moment for historians of South Asia. What has been less apparent is the challenge they pose for historians of Europe, for the ideas South Asianists are coming to reject form the basis of the classic antithesis between Europe and Asia. This antithesis, which opposes a dynamic Europe to a static and traditional South Asia, undergirds the historiography of Europe. Its rejection, therefore, is nothing less than a call for a wholesale rethinking of the European past.[13]

These discoveries are of direct relevance to the study of Greek history. We can now envisage a Greek history that will not be an account of how close the Greeks approximated the modern Europeans, or why they failed to do so more; rather, it is now starting to be possible to write an account based on what and how Greeks actually did what they have done. We can start looking into Greek history as a historical development that does not necessarily lead to the rise of the West, but has possibly led to, and shared elements with, the historical development of societies outside the West.[14] It is unambiguous that in such a novel historiographical attempt our problems stem from the fact that 'while the Eurocentric account of human development was overly linear, its very linearity meant it could be presented as a narrative. In contrast, the polycentric account of human history is by its very nature non-linear, and thus more difficult to present in narrative form.'[15] There is no clear suggestion as to how one could overcome this problem; but there is certainly a growing discussion among historians in other fields, and ancient historians would only gain by paying attention and contributing to them.[16] We probably live through a period, where current reality and scholarly work put into question the premises of the whole modern enterprise of historiography; but in the same time they offer us the, or a, way out of the impasse.

Let us come now to the construction of Greek history as a unified narrative. This was deeply problematic, as Greeks had no national centre, no national state and were scattered all over the Mediterranean and the Black Sea. The solution was the construction of Greek history as a form of quasi-national history, as the history of an entity (ancient Greece) that could be juxtaposed to other entities (Rome).

There were important differences between different understandings of Greek history as a form of national history, depending on whether one conceived such a history as a history of a geographical area (Greece, in whichever way one defines it), of an imaginary entity (like e.g. when we talk

---

[13] Parthasarathi 1998: 105–6.   [14] See Nafissi 2005: 257–62.   [15] Birken 1999: 18.
[16] Bender 2000a; Guha 2002; Stuchtey and Fuchs 2003.

of Greece and Rome) or of a people (the Greeks). To give just one example, a history of Greece conceived as an imaginary entity can finish with the battle of Chaironeia in 338 BCE (as with Grote for example), because such an imaginary entity can have a certain end, according to how it is defined; but it can hardly be so with a history of the Greeks, since Greek-speaking populations continued living for many centuries after Chaironeia (and in a certain sense, still live nowadays). It is characteristic that, with very few exceptions, no Western scholar has ever attempted to write a history of the Greeks;[17] the history of Greece has a certain end (whether the classical, or the Hellenistic period) and then is followed by the history of Rome. We do not study the Greeks from the perspective of how a particular people developed throughout history, but from some point onwards (whether the Hellenistic or the Roman period) we subsume them under the history of another imaginary entity (whether *Hellenismus*, or Rome). But I do not want to enter here into a discussion of the ambiguities and contradictions between a Eurocentric *History of Greece* and an ethnocentric *History of the Greek Nation*.[18]

During the nineteenth century, the construction of modern national identities and the struggles to create new national states legitimated a national reading of Greek history.[19] Greek history was seen from the perspective of the resistance to foreign aggression and the striving for national unity and the creation of a national state.[20] The apparent inability or failure of the Greeks to create such a unity and state was the subject of long and heated discussions.[21] But after the First World War almost all the nationalities in Europe acquired their own state, and borders and territories remained largely the same till the 1990s; the defeat of Nazi Germany in the Second World War was a severe blow to nationalist and racialist readings of history. Therefore, from the 1950s onwards the old metanarrative of the striving for unity and unification came to lose much of its power, though it was never completely superseded.[22] It was now the polis that played the prominent role in a national account of Greek history. The polis was adjustable to a narrative of emergence, acme and decline; it also had the advantage of bringing together social, economic, cultural and political history.

---

[17] See Miliori 2000. The most notable exception is of course George Finlay.
[18] For a discussion of these issues, see Kyrtatas 2002: 91–131.
[19] The relationship between nationalism and the writing of history is treated in Thiesse 1999.
[20] Funke 1996.   [21] See e.g. Mathieu 1925.
[22] Will 1956 is a good indication of the changing attitudes.

There are many different aspect of this periodisation, which are deeply problematic. Greek communities were scattered all over the Mediterranean, and had a variety of historical trajectories; yet, the need to have a single unified and homogeneous national evolution results in the exclusion of the vast majority of these communities from standard accounts of Greek history, and their segregation into local studies of little value and influence to the rest of the discipline. Had we tried, though, to bring into pieces our linear time, and understand that the time scale of the large imperial polis is very different from the time scale of the small and middling one, we would have altered our accounts for both periods. In the words of John Davies,

Greek history, unfolded as it did through a multitude of regional and civic micro-histories most of which were only spasmodically documented, if at all, presented – as Roman history did not – the acute technical problem of interweaving different narratives in different theatres in such a way as to show both their independence and their degrees of interlocking. That in turn set the challenge of balancing the affairs and agendas of the bigger players (Athens above all, but also Sparta and Macedon and Syracuse) on the one hand against those of the small fry, and on the other against the looming presence of the Achaemenid Persian empire, its predecessors, and its successors. Indeed, but for the powerful influence of the Hellenocentric cultural tradition, it would be tempting – and indeed more rational – to write most Greek politico-military history as a subset of Persian history.[23]

Moreover, periodisation has to be connected with spatial issues.[24] Every community has a place in space, which cannot be abstracted from its history; a social, political and economic history that ignores the spatial parameters of each process is bound to be inconclusive and misleading; furthermore, space means that the old distinction between internal and external factors and influences is illusory; internal and external have meaning only if we specify what is the unit of analysis. Giving a community a place in space means that by necessity it is related to other communities that occupy concurrently the bounding space; that the interaction with those other communities is not a secondary or external factor, but delimits the field of processes and networks which take place. This means that every approach, such as the consumer city one, which tries to define its phenomenon as a solitary entity, as if it could exist alone and not in relation to other entities, is seriously handicapped. The vast majority of definitions and approaches to the polis suffer from precisely this handicap: they define the polis as a solitary entity, as if a polis could exist alone and not only in a system of interactions with other polities and communities that define the

---

[23] Davies 2002: 228.   [24] See the approach of Berlin 1980.

field of interactions and processes in between them. We cannot write Greek history properly unless it is a history in space: i.e. of a part of a wider Mediterranean and Near Eastern world.

The difference between a 'progressive' and fast-developing southern and eastern Aegean (central Greece, the Peloponnese, Aegean islands) and a more 'backward' and slowly developing western and northern mainland (Aetolia, Epirus, Macedonia) is well known to scholars;[25] in fact, it is interesting to note that this regional divergence spans the gap between Mycenaean and archaic/classical history.[26] This divergence has been explained in evolutionary terms: between more primitive *ethnos* regions, representing a stagnation into an earlier phase of development, and poleis regions, which have moved one step forward in the evolutionary ladder.[27]

We have already shown why this distinction between *ethnê* and poleis is highly misleading.[28] What should be stressed here is the role of space: is it a matter of chance that it is the communities coming into contact and a variety of relationships with the more advanced and complex societies and polities of the Eastern Mediterranean that develop more complex political, social and economic arrangements? And the lack of those intensified contacts and pressures in the west and north leads to less intensive and complex arrangements? In other words, a periodisation of Greek history has to take into account the varying spatial arrangements, which different regions of the Aegean and other regions inhabited by Greek communities have with each other and with non-Greek regions.

LINEAR TIME

Ancient historians have accepted a single linear temporality and period-isation: we usually divide ancient Greek history in the Mycenaean, Dark Age, archaic, classical, Hellenistic and Roman periods. This periodisation goes back to Winckelmann's attempt to periodise the history of Greek art.[29] It was subsequently adopted in political history, where periods were divided by significant events: the Persian wars divided the archaic from the classical period, the battle of Chaironeia or the death of Alexander the classical from the Hellenistic, the battle of Pydna or Actium the Hellenistic from the Roman.[30] In the course of time the original restriction of

[25] See Bintliff 1997. [26] See Halstead 1994. [27] Ehrenberg 1960: 24–7.
[28] See chapter 8. [29] Haskell 1991; Potts 1994: 11–46.
[30] Unfortunately, there is very little historiographical work on the periodisation of Greek history; for the construction of the Hellenistic period, see Bichler 1983; Canfora 1987.

historical narrative to political and military history was superseded: social, cultural and economic aspects were emancipated from the static and achronic accounts of the *Antiquitates*, and came to be presented as inter-related phenomena characterising every period and being part of historical development. Thus, the original politically oriented periodisation came to encompass social, economic and cultural history.[31] Thus came a period-isation scheme that divided political, social, economic and cultural history in the same distinct and autonomous periods. At the same time, the discovery of the Mycenaean civilisation and the Dark Ages added new periods to the scheme, which were created by not solely political criteria.[32]

We still cling to a nineteenth-century form of periodisation, without trying to construct any alternative schemes. The current scheme was based on the concept of the *Zeitgeist*, positing that every period was defined by a certain spirit; on a functionalist understanding that all aspects of human life ought to cohere and form an equilibrium;[33] and on an evolutionist percep-tion that all aspects of human communities move at the same pace in the same direction.[34] Few scholars would probably accept explicitly these pre-suppositions nowadays. And yet, no alternative periodisation has emerged.

My argument is that these presuppositions are mistaken. Functionalism is wrong, because the imaginary whole does not exist: it is not the case that every institution, practice or process serves the same aim in the same direction: they occupy different levels, in different contexts and with differ-ent temporal and spatial scales.[35] Mercenary service and citizen service, or polis ideology/policy and aristocratic ideology/policy are not incompatible practices undermining each other, as in a functionalist analysis, or successive stages of rise/decline, as in an evolutionary one: they are merely differing fields of activities in different levels and contexts. (This does not mean that all practices are always compatible: but only a historical analysis can show how and when they are brought into collision.) Some scholars have expressed this through the concept of heterarchy: 'a heterarchical system is one in which each element is either unranked relative to other elements, or possesses the potential for being ranked in a number of different ways'.[36] The existence of system does not mean the existence of *a* system. The various institutions,

---

[31] This development is associated with the work of Jacob Burckhardt, who was the first to present such a periodisation of Greek social, cultural and political history: the heroic man, the agonal man, the fifth-century man, the fourth-century man, the Hellenistic man. See Nippel 1998.

[32] See Morris 1997a.   [33] See Perlin 1985a, 1994b.

[34] For the nineteenth-century origins of functionalism and evolutionism, see Burrow 1967.

[35] See Yoffee 1979, 1988.

[36] Crumley 1987: 156; for an application of this theory to Bronze Age Cyprus, see Keswani 1996.

practices and processes do not form bounded and clear entities with machine-like functions: they are of course interlinked, but in a variety of changing configurations with different spatial and temporal extent; and they do not necessarily all follow the same rhythms, nor have the same direction.

At the same time evolutionism is equally problematic: if, instead of our entities emerging, growing and declining, and moving in a linear pattern of progress (or regression), we substitute an image of a variety of levels, in a variety of spatial configurations, and with a variety of temporal scales, conjunctures and rhythms, our approach must necessarily change.[37] The combined outcome of functionalist and evolutionist approaches is the billiard-ball effect. If societies, economies and states are unified as distinct and separate entities, then the only way to interact is as billiard balls: an external (it cannot be anything else) push creates vibrations transmitted from one ball to the other. This is the classical logic of diffusionism: the balls do not have a real space; they occupy a space only to the extent that an external push puts them into contact, which necessitates a space, but merely as substratum, external to the ball itself. They do not have a real time: a billiard ball is the same, whether in the morning or in the evening, and whether a previous player has played on the billiard table or not. From these remarks follows why both the billiard-ball effect and evolutionism are misguided. If the billiard balls do not exist as clearly bounded entities, but they change shape and configuration, then the billiard-ball image is misleading; and the compact entities needed for any evolutionary approach no longer exist.

The implication of my analysis is that we have to abandon the uniform and linear time of the national narrative based on the polis and accept the multiple temporalities and durations of historical time. The various levels of analysis that we have presented are characterised by various forms of temporalities; and quite often the temporalities of the one level might face a different direction from the temporalities of another level. All this should have been an old hat. More than half a century ago, Fernand Braudel published his revolutionary *Méditerranée*;[38] there he argued against the linear time of the traditional *histoire évènementielle*, proposing his scheme of the three durations of historical time (the event, *conjoncture*, *longue durée*, or alternatively *histoire évènementielle*, social history, geohistory).[39]

Unfortunately, ancient historians have remained indifferent to Braudel's discovery.[40] They have preferred to stick with a linear time of events and

[37] See Yoffee 1993.   [38] Braudel 1972, originally published in 1949.   [39] See also Braudel 1980: 25–54.
[40] Though Greek archaeologists, as opposed to historians, have shown interest: see the two conferences on *Annales* and archaeology in Bintliff 1991a; Knapp 1992.

periods following neatly one after the other; and the only levels of temporal analysis is still either an undifferentiated period (the archaic, the classical, the Hellenistic), or an undifferentiated century (e.g. fifth-century Athens). Furthermore, most works in ancient history still maintain a belief that the periodisation of social, political and economic history is essentially the same: there is seldom any effort to explore whether a periodisation that is based on political history (e.g. the classical period) makes equal sense for social history, or whether some processes follow their own, even opposing, temporalities. Ancient historians were surprised to find that political periodisation did not coincide with the periodisation of the landscape settlement and exploitation, as revealed by intensive archaeological surveys. Instead of the political periodisation (archaic, classical, Hellenistic), the intensive surveys found a different periodisation (archaic/early classical, late classical/Hellenistic); moreover, it is clear that, overall similarities apart, different areas followed their own path.[41] And yet, despite all these findings, little has changed in the way ancient historians periodise and study Greek history.[42]

My argument is not that a return to Braudel *per se* will solve our problems. There has been a lot of criticism of Braudel's work, which is quite justified.[43] Braudel tended to emphasise the *longue durée*, giving much less attention to the middle and short term, which he famously characterised as dust.[44] Moreover, the three levels of Braudel's analysis remain three separate levels: he failed to show how the three levels interacted and interpenetrated with each other, and how specific historical conjunctures dictated or influenced historical developments in specific rather than other ways. Having said that, the value of Braudel's discovery of the multiple durations of historical time remains enormous. The only way to improve on his work and succeed in interlinking the various durations of time, along with the importance of historical conjunctures and spatial configurations, is by specific analysis of concrete historical circumstances. I cannot provide anything more helpful on the abstract and general level of analysis that has been employed in this study.

Therefore, we have to relativise our periodisations. We should accept that there is no necessary reason for which political, economic, social, and cultural history should follow the same periodisation; that different period-isations might suit different issues at hand; and that the interlinking between the periodisations of different aspects, processes and institutions

[41] See Alcock 1993: 217–20, 1994; Bintliff 1997.
[42] See recently Osborne 2000; Hornblower 2002; Rhodes 2006. [43] See e.g. Kinser 1981.
[44] Braudel 1973: 20–1, 901–3.

is historically contingent, and cannot be established *a priori*. Moreover, the conjunctural nature of the interlinking between different time scales implies that time is not qualitatively homogeneous. This is the quality of time that Greeks expressed with the word *kairos*: it implies that events that take place at specific moments acquire excessive importance, because of the nature of the conjuncture.[45] An example from changes in scientific theory is apt:

Chaos theory in other words, does not imply that every bit of history is equally chaotic. The action of two gas particles might had have tremendous implications at a certain point in our solar system's development; but once the present order of sun and planets was emerging, the movement of trillion of particles would have counted for naught.[46]

Conjunctures, such as the emergence of Athenian supremacy, or the overthrow of the Persian empire, have rarely been studied as such in Greek history: they are either taken as natural outcomes, or as matters of chance or fortune. Instead, we need studies that will take into account the interplay between a variety of long- and short-term processes and the qualitative role of the conjunctures and events.

A TEMPORALITY OF THE POLIS?

Finally, the periodisations presented above are based on a conception of the polis as a stage of Greek history. There are a number of severe problems with this periodisation; some have been already pointed out; others will be so shortly. The first problem is one of exclusions: effectively, the scheme of Greek history based on the polis excludes both the Minoan/Mycenaean periods of Greek history, which are thought to be dominated by redistributive monarchies, and have been surrendered as a field of study to Linear B philologists and prehistoric archaeologists; and the later Hellenistic and Roman periods. In the Hellenistic and Roman periods the history of the Greek communities ceases to be an independent field of study; it is now subsumed under different entities, the Hellenistic world and the Roman empire, respectively. There is no history of Hellenistic Greece, or a history of Greece in the Hellenistic era, to give an example.

These exclusions are based on a major premise: the conceptualisation of the polis as an autonomous polity, comprising a city and its territory, and governed by its community of citizens. On this premise, the Mycenaean

---

[45] See the comments of Wallerstein 1988: 146–8.   [46] Birken 1999: 21–2; see also Perlin 1985a: 220–2.

polities can be excluded as territorial monarchies controlling whole regions; while the Hellenistic poleis can be subsumed under different entities, since they lacked political autonomy, and were dominated by the large Hellenistic monarchies and the Roman empire. Unfortunately, the premise is severely misleading. We have explored extensively the enormous variety of Greek polities of the archaic and classical periods. While many communities comprised just a city and its territory, many others comprised whole regions or attempted to control regions by a variety of forms of political incorporation. It was also always the case that the big powers of the archaic and classical Greek world always comprised much more than a city and its territory: Sparta controlled two-fifths of the Peloponnese; Athens the whole region of Attica; Argos the whole Argolic plain; Thebes, every time she was powerful, controlled most of Boiotia; and this is not to mention poleis such as Syracuse, or Cyrene.[47] These last two examples introduce the second qualification: Greek poleis were usually governed by their communities of citizens: but it was often the case that Greek polities were ruled by kings, tyrants or came under the control of outside powers, whether Greek or foreign.

Finally, if we take political autonomy as a criterion, then we will find extremely few Greek poleis that were in any meaningful sense autonomous, from the time we first have a political narrative in the aftermath of the Persian wars in 480 BCE to the battle of Chaironeia in 338 BCE. Already from 545 BCE the cities of Ionia, the birthplace of philosophy and the Ionic temple, were always subject to Persian, Athenian, Spartan and Hecatomnid rule.[48] From the late sixth century onwards many, or at times most, of the Sicilian and south Italian cities, the other birthplace of philosophy and science, were under the rule of Geloan and Syracusan tyrants,[49] the Phoenicians and the various Italian peoples.[50] In mainland Greece, most of the poleis were under the successive or co-existing rule of Sparta, Athens and Thebes, and, later in the fourth century, Macedonia. Still, one has to take into account the numerous dependent poleis of Sparta, Elis, Arcadia and Crete, and the equally numerous poleis that participated in *koina*, whether under the rule of a hegemonic polis, or on equal terms. As it will have become clear, if we take political autonomy as the defining characteristic of the archaic and classical polis, then by definition we will have to

---

[47] Hansen and Nielsen 2004: 70–4.   [48] Cook 1962.

[49] I am not referring to the domination of Gela from Gelan and Syracuse by Syracusan tyrants, which is a matter of internal politics but to the domination of other Sicilian cities by the Gelan and Syracusan tyrants.

[50] Lomas 2000.

exclude the vast majority of Greek poleis and restrict ourselves to a handful of prominent and atypical exceptions.[51] Therefore, the periodisation of Greek history on the development of the autonomous Greek polis, comprising only a single city and its territory, and governed by its citizens, can hardly cover more than a few archaic and classical Greek poleis. For the vast majority, these criteria do not make sense.

Once we realise this, it becomes easier to challenge the exclusions. It is not here the place to review the evidence about the nature and form of Mycenaean polities. The present author holds the view that the orthodox account of Mycenaean polities is extremely problematic and needs radical reconstruction. But limits of space and coherence necessitate that we leave this issue for future treatment.[52] For the time being, what needs to be stressed is the enormous variability of the Mycenaean political world. Some regions were controlled by a single 'palatial' centre (Messenia,[53] Attica); others were divided between more centres (Argolid: Mycenae, Tiryns, Midea; Boiotia: Thebes, Orchomenos); while in many regions sharing Mycenaean culture political organisation is even more fragmented and no overall centre seems to emerge (Achaia, Corinthia, Laconia).[54]

The Mycenaean Argolid was divided between three centres (Mycenae, Tiryns, Midea); but the classical Argolid was dominated by a single centre, Argos.[55] In which case should we speak of a city-state? Does it make sense to talk of territorial kingdoms in the Mycenaean period, and of a city-state in the classical? Boiotia seems to be divided between Thebes and Orchomenos, struggling to control the whole region, in both the Mycenaean and the classical periods. Is this apparent similarity to be so easily discarded?

It is highly unfortunate that Mycenologists have accepted a uniform and, in its essence, ahistorical model of *the* Mycenaean society,[56] disregarding the reasons and the processes behind the strong regional differences, and the spatial and temporal context and conjuncture. This uneasiness is still lamentably visible in efforts, for example, to explain away the fragmentation of political control in the Argolid, by appointing Tiryns as the summer resort of the king of Mycenae.[57] In both the Mycenaean and the later periods of Aegean history, the most essential characteristic is that the area is never unified under a single power, but is always fragmented into a multiplicity of political communities of varying forms.[58]

---

[51] Hansen 1994: 17.
[52] For revisionist views, see Galaty and Parkinson 1999; Driessen 2001; Sherrat 2001.   [53] Bennet 1995.
[54] Shelmerdine 1999.   [55] Pierart 1997.   [56] Chadwick 1976; Halstead 1988; Wright 1995.
[57] Maran 2000.   [58] See also the comments of Haggis 1999; Manning 1999.

Moreover, if we remember that Greek poleis were often governed by monarchs (kings, tyrants) or extreme oligarchies,[59] and that our traditional view about the government of Mycenaean societies is extremely problematic,[60] then it becomes easier to claim that we should look at the political communities of the Aegean in their *longue durée*. The plurality of forms of political communities in every period of Greek history, the regional variations, the continuities and the transformations can be grasped only by adopting a different framework.

On the other hand, we should abandon the belief that the battle of Chaironeia and the conquests of Alexander create a fundamental dividing line in Greek history, between the autonomous classical city-state and the Hellenistic poleis dominated by Hellenistic superpowers.[61] The autonomous classical city-state is a fiction: most poleis were not independent and it makes no fundamental difference whether a polis was dominated by another polis or by a monarch.[62] The fifth-century Thasians would not find their situation much different from third-century Chalcidians. Second, the aftermath of Chaironeia did not mean the annexation of Greek poleis by Macedonia. The Macedonians never succeeded in subjecting, consolidating and unifying the Greek peninsula permanently: they controlled more poleis in one region and fewer in others, more poleis in one decade and less in another, but overall they had to face other autonomous poleis (Sparta, Athens, Rhodes), alliances of poleis and federations of poleis.[63] The political scenery was equally fragmented and unstable as it was in the fifth, or even more in the fourth centuries.

Furthermore, the Hellenistic *koina* were not a subversion of classical polis autonomy, since in many ways autonomy never really existed as a viable option for most classical communities.[64] Moreover, we have already pointed that autonomy was not a precondition for polis-ness and that participation in a *koinon* or a league was the experience of very many classical poleis. In fact, one can look at the problem the other way round: when Themistocles insisted that his adversary from obscure Seriphos would not be Themistocles, if he was an Athenian, he nevertheless took it for it granted that even he would not be Themistocles, if he was from

---

[59] Barcelo 1993.
[60] See the lonely voice of Hooker 1979, 1987, 1988; also Darcque 1987. On the missing evidence for rulers in prehistoric Greece see the articles in Rehak 1995.
[61] A similar point in Gruen 1993; Camp 2000.
[62] Actually, many poleis in the Hellenistic world did benefit from being controlled by a monarchy, instead of being controlled by other poleis, as in the classical period. See Gauthier 1987/9.
[63] Compare with the picture of Asia Minor poleis in Ma 1999: 150–74.   [64] Beck 1997.

Seriphos.[65] His words display wonderfully the limitations and realities of the citizens of the vast majority of poleis. But in the Hellenistic period, a citizen of the small polis of Sicyon could become general of a huge federate army and decide on the policies of the whole Peloponnese. He was still a citizen of Sicyon, nevertheless.[66]

Moreover, the intervention or even domination of foreign powers and the interrelationship with the Eastern and Western Mediterranean was nothing new in the Hellenistic period: in the West, the expedition of Pyrrhus and the intervention of the Romans have their classical counterparts in the Athenian intervention,[67] the expedition of Timoleon[68] and the expedition of Alexander, the Molossian king.[69] In the East, one has to remember the Persian invasion and the continuous Persian role in the Peloponnesian war, the King's Peace, etc.;[70] the continuous Athenian and Spartan intervention, and even invasion, in Asia Minor and Egypt;[71] and the presence of thousands of Greeks in the East from Alcaeus' brother to the point where there were more Greeks fighting in the Persian army than in Alexander's.[72] Finally, the alleged extinction of democracy and popular participation in the Hellenistic period should be no longer argued.[73]

There has also been a growing recognition of the fact that the interaction and interpenetration between the Greek world and the Near East, which used to be the defining point of the Hellenistic age, needs to be traced back to at least the fourth century. Simon Hornblower had early on argued that Mausolus, the dynast of Caria, could be seen as a proto-Hellenistic ruler, anticipating many of the techniques and achievements of the succeeding rulers in the Hellenistic period.[74] Josette Elayi has studied the growing Greek interaction with Phoenicia during the fourth century BCE in features such as the adoption of coinage and the creation of new artistic forms.[75] Thurstan Robinson has pointed out the growing Greek interaction with Lycia, evident in coinage, new forms of political expression and new artistic forms.[76] The interaction was not one-sided; as a matter of fact, one of the most liberating features of recent scholarship is the recognition that conceiving this process as Hellenisation is deeply misleading. I have already mentioned the study of Hagemajer Allen, showing how the Greeks during the late fifth and fourth centuries came to adopt a new form of funerary monument deriving from the cultures of the Near East, in order to express new needs within their society.[77]

---

[65] Plato, *Politeia*, 329E – 330 A.   [66] Walbank 1933.   [67] Wentker 1956.   [68] Talbert 1974.
[69] Hammond 1967: 534; Manni 1962.   [70] Lewis 1977.   [71] Cartledge 1987: 314–30.
[72] Hofstetter 1978.   [73] Habicht 1997; Rhodes and Lewis 1997.   [74] Hornblower 1982: 352–3.
[75] Elayi 1988.   [76] Robinson 1999.   [77] Hagemajer Allen 2003.

It is also the case that the old image of a radical transformation of the Near East in the aftermath of the conquest of Alexander and the takeover of the new Greco-Macedonian ruling classes has come under severe attack. On the one hand there has been a growing awareness of the variety of cultures, economies and societies of the ancient Near East:

Sondages in this material confirm what an attentive reading of Herodotus would already have revealed, that the Achaemenid Empire showed a stupefying range of economic and fiscal patterns and systems. It embraced the temple-focused economies of Judah or parts of Egypt or Asia Minor, the sophisticated and age-old irrigation agriculture of Egypt, southern Mesopotamia, or Central Asia, the complex private or parastatal businesses of banking and contracting which are visible in the Murašu and other archives of fifth-century Babylonia, and the polis-economies of Phoenicia and western Asia Minor.[78]

Some of these societies, cultures and communities had marked similarities with certain societies, economies and cultures of the Greek world (which is no more of a unified world than the Near East), in part because of interaction and interpenetration, as we noted above.[79] On the other hand, the evidence for continuity in practices and processes even after the Greco-Macedonian takeover has become increasingly strong.[80] This is not to negate the real changes that took place;[81] but there should be a reconsideration of changes within the wider Eastern Mediterranean world, which should adopt a larger temporal framework; the fourth century would acquire a new importance in this novel perspective.[82] The point is not merely to make the fourth century into a 'proto-Hellenistic period', which is just begging the question; it is rather the case that we should seriously question the larger metahistorical categories that lie behind our periodisation schemes.

Therefore, the old account, juxtaposing the Greek polis with Near Eastern monarchies during the archaic-classical periods, to be followed by the new Hellenistic monarchies and the *koina* in the Hellenistic period, seems largely redundant. It creates a periodisation which is deeply problematic and misses the large changes taking place already in the fourth century, if not beyond; and the juxtaposition between the Greek polis and the Near Eastern world is deeply misleading for both. The image of the autonomous polis cannot serve as a satisfying criterion for a periodisation of Greek history, since it excludes the vast majority of Greek poleis of the

---

[78] Davies 2001: 13.   [79] Debord 1999; Briant 2002.
[80] Kuhrt and Sherwin-White 1987; Sherwin-White and Kuhrt 1993.
[81] For a balanced perspective on continuity, change and exceptionalism in the case of Egypt, see Rathbone 1989; see also McClellan 1997 on Syria.
[82] See Carlier 1994.

archaic and classical periods; and the variable realities of the political world of the archaic and classical periods show remarkable resemblances to the excluded Mycenaean and Hellenistic periods.

But the present periodisation of Greek history suffers also from its evolutionist underpinnings. The polis is presented as a stage in the evolution of Greek history, a stage with beginning, acme and end. This perception agglomerates a number of processes with obviously different, or even contrasting, temporalities, rhythms and directions. To reify these processes and represent them as a single ontological entity is both unhelpful and misleading. Furthermore, if put in this way, it is impossible to comprehend change and variation. What makes the Sicilian poleis consolidate into a territorial state under a tyrant, while the Ionian poleis, facing similar problems, do not? What makes the hundred poleis of archaic Crete be replaced by poleis with large territories and dependent poleis in the Hellenistic period?[83] What makes Achaean Pellene part of an *ethnos*, but nearby Sicyon a polis?[84]

To illustrate my point further, I will consider the problem of when the polis declined. The answer to this question has been a perennial problem for ancient historians.[85] It used to be thought once that the polis declined with the battle of Chaironeia.[86] Most historians now would not favour this answer, but the problem persists.[87] The reason is that you will get a different answer according to which criterion you choose. If one chooses to define the city-state with the criterion of autonomy, then the city-state should decline in the aftermath of the Persian wars in the mainland and even earlier in Asia Minor: the creation of the Athenian, Spartan, Theban, Macedonian and other hegemonies went hand in hand with the absence of independence of the smaller poleis. If one chooses the criterion of urbanism and restricts oneself to the Aegean world, then either the polis never even rose in the majority of cases, or it went on even after the late empire.[88] If one chooses the criterion of local self-government, then one should opt for late antiquity.[89] If one chooses the criterion of popular participation, then the city-state declined in the late Hellenistic period or even later.[90]

One should not speak then about the emergence or the decline of the polis. This needs still to be emphasised. Although speaking about the

---

[83] See e.g. Viviers 1994.   [84] See Hansen and Nielsen 2004: nos. 228, 240.

[85] See Hansen and Nielsen 2004: 19–20.   [86] See e.g. Thomas 1981: 39–43; Runciman 1990.

[87] See Gauthier 1993; Shipley 2000: 33–6, 105–6.

[88] For populations and urbanisation of Greek poleis, see Hansen 1997a, 2004a, 2004b; Ruschenbusch 1983, 1984a, 1984b, 1985.

[89] For the continuity of self-government in Hellenistic and Roman times, see Jones 1940; Dmitriev 2005.

[90] See Rhodes and Lewis 1997: 502–49 on popular participation in Hellenistic poleis.

decline of the polis has become increasingly unpopular and irrelevant, with most scholars arguing that one should look to different functions and processes of the polis in different periods, the same does not hold true about the emergence of the polis, which is still a popular subject. But it seems contradictory to retain the concept of the emergence of the polis, if the twin concept of decline has been abandoned.[91] As John Davies had already put it thirty years ago,

to speak of the polis as 'le cadre essentiel de la civilisation grecque' conceals a fundamental confusion between the polis as (a) an administrative unit, (b) as cultural unit, and (c) as power unit. Aspect (a) shows no breakdown in the fourth century or for many centuries thereafter, continuing with extraordinary vitality into the Roman period; aspect (b) shows little decline till much earlier, with the emergence of royal courts as alternative focuses for patronage, and of newer cults, which city governments did not bother to naturalise; while aspect (c) had given way long since, in area after area – Ionia, Sicily, S. Italy, Peloponnese, the Aegean –, to personal *archai*, or to Leagues and hegemonies (secularised Amphiktyonies, if one will), or to foreign domination. The breakdown of the city as power-unit is a sixth-century phenomenon, complete by 480.[92]

How can we avoid the problems created by the current periodisation? One way is to deconstruct the current use of the polis as the organising principle of the writing of Greek history. Previous chapters have tried to provide an alternative framework to the ethnocentric and internalist conceptualisation of the polis as the sole unit of analysis for Greek history. I have presented a variety of units of analysis, ranging from below the level of the polis (*koinôniai, merê*) to processes linking a variety of communities and polities into political, economic and cultural *systèmes-mondes*.[93] I have also presented the variety of forms of Greek polities and a number of analytical tools that can allow us to study their multiple interactions.[94] Finally, I have argued for the primary importance of space in the study of Greek communities, and have explored a number of levels of spatial analysis, both below and beyond the polis (poleis and their territories, poleis and regions, poleis and the *système-monde*).[95] But there is something to be added in the last chapter.

[91] See the comments of Polignac 1995: 7–9.	[92] Davies 1975: 97–8.
[93] See chapters 3 and 6.	[94] Chapter 8.	[95] Chapter 7.

CHAPTER 10

Towards new master narratives of Greek history?

This final chapter will serve as an answer to the question that many readers might wish to ask. This book has tried to show how we came to study Greek history in a Eurocentric manner; it has also tried to show why this way of studying Greek history is misleading and problematic; it has finally attempted to provide a scaffolding of what concepts we need in order to construct such an alternative history. The question now is: how do you envisage writing such a history? It is all very well arguing that we need to avoid an account centred on the polis, which usually turns out to be Athenocentric history; but given our type of evidence, what else can we do? It is all very well arguing that we need to go beyond Hellenocentric accounts; but, given the evidence surviving, how can we introduce, for example, the Phoenicians in our accounts, since none of their records has survived? It is all very well arguing that we need a story with many levels and many durations of historical time, instead of teleological and unidimensional accounts; but how is it actually possible to write such a narrative? It is all very well showing the fallacies of Eurocentric master narratives; but can we construct any other kind of master narrative, or should we simply be content with a non-Eurocentric 'histoire en miettes'?

Many more questions could be added to those above, and I will not pretend that I have a definite answer to any of them. What I will try to do here is to give indications of the ways in which I seek the solutions. The task ahead, for those who believe that we do need such an alternative history, is indeed enormous. The above questions raise two main issues: evidence and narrative. I have tried earlier to show that in our attempt to construct alternative methodological tools Aristotle is indeed of immense value. And I have tried to rehabilitate (in part at least) his view of the Greek polis. What I want to do now is to show that many of the answers to our problems can be provided by a thorough study of the ancient Greek historians.

EVIDENCE

An alternative account of Greek history, which will bring together the
different areas and regions of Greek communities and their relationships
and interactions with the wider world, must start from common denomi-
nators. This means primary reliance on a form of evidence which is available
for both early and late periods, for both the core and the periphery, for both
Greece and the wider Mediterranean, for both city and countryside, for both
elite and subaltern. This is of course archaeological evidence. Our textual
sources were written by the elite; they focus on Athens and some other large
Greek communities, telling us very little about the rest of the Greek
communities; and they tend to ignore the countryside. Since we lack written
sources for other Mediterranean peoples, we get a very distorted and
Hellenocentric image of Mediterranean history. By comparison, the poten-
tiality of archaeological evidence to give voice to the forgotten and the
speechless is indeed impressive.[1] But let us not oversimplify. It would be
naïve to believe that even archaeological evidence, notwithstanding its
egalitarian potential, would be equally telling and revealing for all things
and all types of people: even in terms of archaeological evidence, the elite is
more visible than the subaltern, the city is more visible than the countryside,
the richer and more powerful communities tend to leave more recoverable
evidence than the poor and powerless.[2]

But still this is a problem common to all periods of history and in all
forms of evidence. Despite the limitations, the possibilities opened by a
historical account based on archaeological evidence, which allows comparison and contrast, and much wider inclusion, are impressive. This is even
more the case given the expansion of archaeological research in the last few
decades. The archaeology of settlement and landscape, to give an example,
has changed our understanding of Greek history: it has challenged conventional historical periodisations;[3] it has allowed diachronic perspectives;[4] it
has shown the utility and necessity of comparative history and has drawn
archaeologists to look beyond antiquity to other periods of Greek history;[5]
it has penetrated the peripheral areas for which written sources are completely silent;[6] it has allowed us to study a subject rendered almost invisible
from the perspective of our urban-based and urban-focused sources.[7] One
could multiply examples: the archaeology of domestic space;[8] the

---

[1] Snodgrass 1987; Morris 1992, 2000.   [2] See e.g. Foxhall 1990.   [3] Alcock 1993: 217–20.
[4] Bintliff 1991b.   [5] Davies 1991; Sutton 2000.   [6] Jameson *et al.* 1994; Mee and Forbes 1997.
[7] Snodgrass 1990.   [8] D'Andria and Manino 1996; Nevett 1999; Cahill 2002.

archaeology of death ritual and social identity;[9] the archaeology of exploitation and power;[10] the archaeology of memory and the past;[11] the archaeology of exchange.[12]

These results show conclusively how much we can gain by the employment of archaeological evidence. What we lack is synthesis: incorporating the results of archaeological evidence into our narrative accounts of Greek history.[13] This has not been achieved so far, for reasons that are not difficult to grasp: the straitjacket of the polis, the linear temporalities and the functionalist and evolutionist methodologies that we have delineated.

An example of where we should go is the attempt of Michel Gras to study the archaic Mediterranean in its totality, bringing together the Greeks, the Etruscans, the Phoenicians and the Carthaginians.[14] Historians and archaeologists have been content with this approach, when it deals with 'pre'- or 'proto-historic' periods, when the absence of useful written evidence allows these wider approaches and comparisons.[15] But when we come down to the 'historical' periods, text-driven accounts, the dominance of Athens and secondarily Sparta in our written sources, and the absence of written sources from the non-Greek communities and cultures, lead to the by now well-known pattern of Greek history writing: text-centred, Athenocentric, elite-oriented, Hellenocentric. We have a comprehensive account of forms of settlement in archaic Greece;[16] nothing similar in breadth and extent is available for the classical period. What we need to do is to extend attempts like that of Gras to study the archaic Mediterranean to the 'historical' periods.[17] Ian Morris' attempt to trace through long-term changes in funeral practices wider trends towards egalitarianism through the Greek world of the polis and even beyond[18] is a very positive step in this direction, no matter whether one agrees entirely with his interpretation of the evidence.[19] Hansen's edited volume on city-state cultures is equally important in giving a Mediterranean-wide and even larger perspective, though its thematic setting does not allow for explorations of interaction.[20]

---

[9] Morris 1987, 1992, 2000; Whitley 1991.
[10] Luraghi and Alcock 2003; see also the special issue of *WA*, 33:1, 2001; Osborne 1999; Morris and Papadopoulos 2005.
[11] Alcock 2002; van Dyke and Alcock 2003.   [12] Garlan 2000a.   [13] A first step: Whitley 2001.
[14] Gras 1995b; also 1985, 1993.
[15] See Andersen *et al.* 1997, a work looking at urbanisation in the Mediterranean during the archaic period; the absence of similar works for the 'historical periods' is telling.
[16] Lang 1996.   [17] A rare case of bringing down these entrenched divisions: Dentzer 1982.
[18] Morris 1992: 145–9.   [19] I have expressed my mixed reaction in detail in Vlassopoulos 2000.
[20] Hansen 2000c; Niemeyer 2000; Torelli 2000.

The next step in terms of forms of evidence is indeed numismatics. Unfortunately, historians of antiquity until very recently have not made much use of the evidence of coins, even when it comes down to economic history.[21] But in the last few years the situation has changed enormously: scholars have dealt with coins from a variety of different perspectives, looking at social, economic, cultural and political aspects of their production, use and dissemination.[22] After archaeological evidence, coins are the form of evidence available for most Greek communities; they too allow us to overcome the bias of the written sources, centred on the big and powerful communities. Moreover, coinage provides one of the most fascinating links of the interconnectedness of the Mediterranean world. Invented by the Lydians, adopted by the Greeks, expanded through the wider Greek world in the Mediterranean and the Black Sea, adopted by Persia, Phoenicia and the other highly developed Near Eastern societies, introduced by the Greeks to the native populations of Scythia and Thrace, coinage provides tantalising hints about writing such a story.[23]

Fair enough, some critics might argue; this can be a feasible and even profitable enterprise. But there is no denying that archaeological and numismatic evidence have their limits and that there are a large number of issues in which it is only written evidence, literary and epigraphic, that can give us answers: think of politics, slavery, ideas, literature. This form of evidence, though, is available in only a very few cases: it is only Athens, and to a much lesser extent Sparta, for which we have enough evidence to write a meaningful and in-depth political, social, economic and cultural history from all of the communities of the Mediterranean in the classical period.[24] Are we not therefore forced to become Athenocentric by the very nature of our evidence, once we wish to write narrative or ask certain kinds of questions? For the rest of Greek and Mediterranean communities we have only fragments and glimpses, sometimes more illuminating, sometimes less. In the circumstances, is it not the most meaningful decision to do exactly what has been criticised in this book: a main Athenocentric account, and separate accounts for the rest of the Greeks and barbarians?

This criticism is valid; though, I hope to show, not inescapable. But before trying to answer this criticism, let me try to emphasise how much we can gain in our study of Athens itself by applying the methodological

[21] See the complaints of Lombardo 1997.
[22] Figueira 1998; Kurke 1999; Meadows and Shipton 2001; Schaps 2004; Seaford 2004.
[23] See briefly Kraay 1976.
[24] Moses Finley has been a key exponent of this view: Finley 1983: 103–5, 1985d: 61–6.

approach espoused in this study. We need to situate Athens within a complex and multifaceted world. The traditional approach to Athenian history has been to treat the Athenian polis as an exclusive club of adult male citizens. In reality, what is most fascinating about classical Athens is the variegated picture of multiple social groups, cultural backgrounds, life experiences, locales and interconnections. The picture has focused too much on the elite male Athenians, who are the authors of classical texts and play the key roles in them. There has been no attempt to study the Athenian *demos*, the cobblers, smiths, sailors and shopkeepers that formed the basis of Athenian democracy. It is equally important to study women and slaves not as separate objects from the main group of male citizens, but as parts of a complex interaction, ranging from subordination to collaboration and solidarity.[25]

Furthermore, Athens was a cosmopolitan society. The clear majority of its population consisted of foreigners, Greek and non-Greek, free and slave. Yet, there have been few attempts until very recently to take seriously into account all these foreign people that lived in Athens and the inter- action between Athenians and foreigners.[26] Even more, Athens had a high level of political, economic and cultural interaction with the contemporary Mediterranean world. Yet, there has been little attempt to see Athens as a centre of Mediterranean networks of connectivity, moving goods, people and ideas;[27] or to see Athens from the angle of its relationships with the Eastern Mediterranean, the Aegean and the Black Sea. Equally fascinating is the fact that Athens comprised the most variegated locales, giving life to the most variable experiences:[28] living in the multicultural commercial and maritime port of Piraeus was very different from living in a large agricul- tural deme, or in an isolated farmstead.[29] It is important to attempt to portray all these different settings and experiences; but it is even more important to understand the co-existence and interaction between them.[30]

Moreover, portraying Athens, for example, in the fifth and fourth centuries BCE as a monolithic 'classical Athens' is equally problematic. There is a need to understand how different time scales might point to different directions, might co-exist and interrelate. One can study how the long-term patterns of settlement and land-use co-exist with short-term fluctuations; how discourses on politics or society are reproduced, modi- fied and transformed by their use in specific conjunctures;[31] how different

---

[25] See e.g. Katz 1999.   [26] But see now Bäbler 1998; Adak 2003.
[27] But see now Tchernia and Viviers 2000.   [28] Osborne 1985.   [29] Von Reden 1995; Roy 1998.
[30] Osborne 1985; Cohen 2000; Jones 2004 is unfortunately not achieving its aim.
[31] See the comments of Wolpert 2002: xvii–xviii.

forms of material culture follow different time scales and the complexity of practices that emerge out of this.

Finally, there have been few attempts to study Athens from a comparative perspective.[32] How would Athenian politics look if we compare it with American democratic politics in the nineteenth century?[33] Athens was a cosmopolitan centre; yet there has been no attempt to understand it in the light of other cosmopolitan centres, like Venice or Amsterdam.[34] Athens was a Mediterranean commercial centre; how does it fare in comparison with Ottoman Smyrna or Marseilles?[35] I hope that the preceding comments show clearly how much it is possible to accomplish in the study of Athens by changing our perspective.

Let me now resume the main question: given the kind of evidence we have available, can we be anything else than Athenocentric? How can we insert the bits and pieces that we know about the rest of the Greek world and the wider Mediterranean into a new kind of history? This raises the issue of the form of the historical text and the form of the historical narrative. It is of course a huge issue, much debated in our days. I do not wish to burden further an already heavily burdened book with a detailed analysis of where I stand, and how I see the future. I wish only to devote the last few pages to the problem that this book has been trying to bring to our notice: the abandonment of Eurocentric, ethnocentric, functionalist and evolutionist perspectives leads to fragmentation of subject and method. One way out of this impasse is the construction of alternative methodological tools, as I have tried to do in the third part of this book. Another, and even more demanding task, is reconsidering the form of historical narrative. What narrative should we write, which will not be Eurocentric, ethnocentric, functionalist, evolutionist?

NARRATIVE

What kind of history? A history of koinai praxeis

What is the subject of history about which we want to write? An easy answer is usually given: it is the history of Greece, or of the Greeks. There are important differences, as we have seen, depending on whether one conceives such a history as a history of a geographical area (Greece, however

---

[32] An exception, but on very different terms from those proposed here, is Finley 1973a.
[33] See now Wilentz 2005. But see Rosivach 1993.   [34] Burke 1974; see e.g. Braudel 1984: 184–8.
[35] On Ottoman Smyrna, see Frangakis-Syrett 1992.

one defines it), of an imaginary entity (as when we talk of Greece and Rome) or of a people (the Greeks). Enough has been said of Eurocentrism and ethnocentrism in other contexts to make it unnecessary for me to repeat the problems arising from their core assumptions.[36]

Perhaps one might think that a history of a geographical area is a more 'objective' strategy and therefore more worth pursuing. And yet, the problems with such a conception are paramount. How is one to define a geographical area? Natural limits are hardly objective or straightforward; by now, we have come to realise that even islands, once thought of as ideal cases of clearly defined areas, are hardly that.[37] If intensity or importance of interactions is the limiting factor, then the history of Athens, for example, would have more to do with the Black Sea than with Aetolia; accordingly, a history of a geographical area defined by natural geography, and not by actual historical relations and configurations, has little to recommend it. This is even more the case when the cultural characteristics that might help us define the unity of a specific geographical area are actually dispersed over the whole Mediterranean, as in the case of the Greeks. Therefore, there can be no history, for example, of the Aegean: in the ninth century such a history would not encompass much beyond the Aegean; but in the fifth century there can be no history of the Aegean, which is not at the same time a history of the Black Sea; one cannot see the one without the other. Therefore one may write only a history *from* the Aegean (from the per- spective of the Aegean).[38]

Maybe we should seek our solution in universal history? This is equally problematic. A universal history is supposed to cover the whole world; no matter what the real technical problems of doing that may be, history is by necessity a selection of the whole of the past, based on certain criteria (in the same way that a map is a selection of what to depict, and not an actual representation of everything that exists; in which case it is not a map, but a replica of the object to be depicted).[39] And what would be the criterion for writing a history of the whole of humanity (or rather of humanity in antiquity)? It is here that the teleological assumptions of Eurocentrism and the philosophies of history enter to distort the account in ways that we should by now agree are misguided and problematic. Benedetto Croce was

---

[36] See Kyrtatas 2002: 91–131.
[37] See Horden and Purcell 2000: 224–30, 381–3; Broodbank 2002: 16–35.
[38] For the distinction between history in and history of, see Horden and Purcell 2000: 1–5; also the articles in Harris 2005.
[39] See Carr 1961: 1–24.

right that no universal history worthy of its name could ever exist: a universal history is always a history from a single perspective.

Universal histories, in so far as they are histories, or in that part of them in which they are histories, resolve themselves into nothing else but 'particular histories' – that is to say, they are due to a particular interest centred in a particular problem, and comprehend only those facts that form part of that interest and afford an answer to that particular problem.[40]

This does not mean that one cannot write a history covering the whole world from a single perspective (e.g. from the perspective of the Mediterranean and its relationship with the rest of the world, or of the development of warfare, or of the emergence of nationalism, or of the spread of monotheism, etc.). But the essential point, as pointed out by Croce, is that this is universal history only in title; universal history in the real meaning of the word is impossible; and unless one makes this point clear and explicit, one risks passing off a partial and focus-dependent history as the history of the world. We have seen far too many Eurocentric histories passing as universal histories;[41] and the dangers of this approach should by now be clear enough.

What is then the solution to our problem, if one does exist? I believe that the Greeks have given us one answer themselves. Many Greek historians attempted to write what they called *historia tôn koinôn praxeôn*, a history of common acts of Greeks and barbarians.[42] The difference between the Thucydidean strategy and that of common history is made clear by ancient authors:

He [Herodotus] chose not to record the history of a single city, or of a single nation, but to gather together accounts of many different events, which occurred in Europe and Asia, and assemble them in a simple comprehensive work. He made the Lydian empire his starting point and brought his account down to the Persian war, including in a single narrative all the important acts of Greeks and barbarians during this period of 220 years ... Thucydides came after these historians, but he did not wish to confine his history to a single locality, as Hellanicus and his imitators had done, nor to follow Herodotus and bring together in a single history the deeds accomplished by Greeks and barbarians all over the world (*ex apasês chôras*).[43]

---

[40] Croce 1921: 57.
[41] See the criticisms of Eurocentric universal history by Indian historians: Chakrabarty 2000; Guha 2002 and the articles in Stuchtey and Fuchs 2003.
[42] See e.g. Dionysius of Halicarnassus: 'He [Herodotus] has produced a common history of Greek and barbarian acts'; *Letter to Pompeius*, 3. For ancient universal history, see Burde 1974; Alonso-Nuñez 1990; Mortley 1996; Clarke 1999.
[43] Dionysius of Halicarnassus, *On Thucydides*, 5–6.

Why not attempt then to write, instead of a self-sufficient history of Greece, a history of the common acts of Greeks and barbarians (or whichever term we choose to replace this negative, yet all-inclusive term)?[44] This project would have a double advantage. On the one hand, it retains the essential point that history is always an account from a specific perspective: it is not a purported, but impossible, universal account, but an account from the perspective of the Greeks and their common acts with other peoples. In the same way, one could write about the common acts of the Persians and the barbarians (in which the Greeks would then be included) and so on. On the other hand, it argues against a self-sufficient Greek history and in favour of an inclusive strategy. In their historical works, many Greeks included barbarian history, ethnography and geography; it is something that we have deliberately omitted from our own accounts of Greek history, all for the worse.[45] My first proposal: a history of *koinai praxeis* should replace our histories of Greece or of the Greeks; and Greek historians have a lot to tell us about how to do it.

If we accept this first proposal, the next question is how we are going to organise our material. This has a double implication. On the one hand, we need to arrange our material in such a way that it tells a story, i.e. to emplot them; on the other hand we need to find a way of arranging material that will be as inclusive as possible; that will make sense and incorporate the bits and pieces of our non-Athenian knowledge. The final two sections will deal with these two questions.

History from above: emplotments and metanarratives

Since Hayden White's *Metahistory*,[46] historians have become increasingly aware of the literary aspects of their work, and the metahistorical categories and tropes on which they base their research and narrative. Although there are a growing number of studies that, following White, have attempted to study the metahistorical and narratological foundations of modern historical literature,[47] historians of antiquity are as always lagging behind. There has yet to be any study of the metahistorical and narratological foundations

---

[44] I take barbarian in the sense noted by Herodotus, when he discovered that Egyptians call the rest of the world in the same way the Greeks do, and found that perfectly plausible; Herodotus, II, 158.

[45] An account of the progressive separation of Greek history from its Near Eastern background is offered in Bernal 1987.

[46] White 1973.

[47] See Gossman 1990 on the poetics of Romantic historiography; Carrard 1992 on the poetics of *Annales* historiography.

of the works of modern historians of antiquity. It is therefore very important to pay attention to the stories that our Greek histories narrate and the plots that we construct. I will say a few words on the modes of emplotment used by historians of antiquity, before moving on to see whether ancient Greek historians have anything to contribute towards a reconceptualisation of ancient history.

It is well known that the nineteenth century was the century of nations and nationalisms; it is equally true that from the French Revolution to the Russian, Europe was dominated by titanic social struggles, turning the whole world upside down. And of course modern works on ancient history would not abstain from reflecting such tensions. Greek history was emplotted in such a way as to tell a story of national and racial destiny.[48] Some read Greek history as the story of an unsuccessful struggle for national unification that resulted in national subjugation; others saw in Macedonia the *deus ex machina* that managed to overcome national divisions and lead to national unity and triumph.[49] Of course, the struggle between Athens and Macedonia, Demosthenes and Philip, was presented as resembling the one between France and Germany.[50] On the other hand, the great social struggles of this period of European history, where land and property were key issues, had a direct reflection on the presentation of a story of ancient history: struggles about agrarian laws, the protection or overthrow of private property and so on.[51]

The post-war period, or rather the period of the Cold War, has seen two important phenomena: the cessation of national struggles and movements in Europe (though exactly the opposite in the rest of the world), where the national boundaries established either in the treaty of Versailles, or in that of Potsdam, seemed final and unassailable. The crimes of Nazism did much to drive racial issues out of the field of the academically acceptable.[52] On the other hand, under the stability of terror and the economic reconstruction of Europe, revolutions and great social struggles of a nineteenth-century scale

---

[48] For the study of Greek history through the lens of the national state, see Funke 1996. On racialism in Greek history, see Ampolo 1997: 140–9.

[49] See Beloch 1925; Glotz 1928, 1936. For German historical production on ancient Greece, see Christ 1999: chs. 3–5; for the French case, see Simon 1988.

[50] In the beginning of the nineteenth century, Macedonia resembled the expansionist France of the Napoleonic wars; later in the century, when national unification and the opposition of German authoritarianism vs. French Third Republic came to the fore, the identifications were reversed. See Funke 1996: 89–91, 99–105.

[51] See Ampolo 1997: 79–106.

[52] For racial issues in Greek history, see characteristically K. O. Müller, *Die Dorier*, Breslau, 1824; Myres 1930. The post-war elimination of such issues that form the historian's *problématique* is signalled by Will 1956.

have been largely absent from the (Western) European scene (though hardly
at all in the rest of the world).[53] Is it a mistake to look at these phenomena for
the telling absence of any large-scale or influential narratives of Greek history
in the post-war period? In contrast to the nineteenth century and the first
half of the twentieth,[54] no great scholar of the post-war period turned his
labours towards constructing a narrative of Greek history.[55]

In the absence of the previous concerns, the emplotment of Greek history
proved a difficult issue; this is probably one of the strong reasons that the
great minds of the post-war era kept away from it. It is characteristic that the
only inspiring and novel narratives that we have from the post-war period
concern archaic Greece, where the relative absence of ancient historical
narratives gives modern scholars space for originality; here, new evidence,
new forms of evidence and new approaches have led to new narratives.[56] The
difference from classical or Hellenistic history could not be greater.

We need then to rethink our emplotments and our narratives. Let us
approach the same question again: what have the Greek historians to
contribute to such a search? Can we learn from their emplotments? Can
we utilise their modes of emplotment for our own aims?

The great Greek historians emplotted their historical narratives in a
variety of ways. According to a recent ingenious interpretation by Pascal
Payen,[57] Herodotus was not the historian of the wars between Greeks and
Persians, as most of modern scholarship would like him to be. Instead, his
subject is a narrative of conquest and resistance. Herodotus has taken as his
model the *Lives* of Great Monarchs; the structure of his narrative follows
the succession of five of them (Croesus, Cyrus, Cambyses, Dareius, Xerxes)
and their conquests. But the great innovation of Herodotus is the introduction into historical discourse of the peoples that resist them; what
modern historians have described as 'ethnographic parts' of Herodotus'
work, because they do not fit their conception of the *Historiê* as the history
of the Persian Wars, are in fact (among other things, to be fair)[58]

---

[53] Hobsbawm 1994.
[54] A simple mention of the names of Niebuhr, Droysen, Grote, Meyer, Beloch, Rostovtzeff and de
Sanctis would suffice.
[55] The obvious exception is the Marxist de Ste Croix 1981; and yet it is not exactly an exception, since he
is not attempting to write a total narrative of Greek history; he is rather trying to establish that
Marxist class analysis can make sense of ancient history and in the process of doing so, he covers the
whole of Greek and Roman history. It is probably not accidental that one of the few large-scale and
innovating narrative histories of classical Greece in the post-war period comes from one of his
students; Cartledge 1987.
[56] See consecutively, Finley 1970; Murray 1980; Osborne 1996c.   [57] Payen 1997.
[58] See the points of Drews 1973: 84–96.

Herodotus' description and explanation of how the peoples manage to resist conquest. Their *ethê kai nomima* on the one hand, the spaces they occupy and utilise on the other (in the words of Payen their *altérité* and their *insularité*), are the means by which they manage to resist. Besides, notwithstanding the distinction between Greeks and barbarians, there is a more fundamental distinction in Herodotus' work, which cuts across the Greek–barbarian opposition: the opposition of conquerors and peoples who resist. Herodotus' decision to finish his account with the battle of Mycale, instead of going down to describe the glorious Greek victories against the Persians up to the battle of Eurymedon and even further on, is one indication that the Athenians have themselves become the conquerors.

This is a most inspiring interpretation of Herodotus' work. Herodotus' method allows us to overcome entrenched oppositions (Greeks/barbarians, history/anthropology, description/narrative); moreover, the subject of conquest/resistance allows us to look simultaneously at the perspective of the great powers and those that resist them; finally, given our present world situation, it is a most intriguing subject to pursue. How would Mediterranean history of the archaic and classical periods look if we narrated it from the Herodotean perspective of conquest/resistance (that is, if we extended backwards Polybius' approach)?

Thucydides wrote of course a grand narrative of *kinêsis*, with the Peloponnesian war functioning as the greatest culmination until his time of this process. The central issue of his work is the process of *dynamis* and *archê*, the process by which the material preconditions for the building of *archê* and the exercise of *dynamis* are created, the process by which other communities are dominated and the dangers and doom of *archê*.[59]

One can multiply examples. Greek history, as we saw, from the nineteenth century till the Second World War was based on a metanarrative of national unification, social struggles and the emergence of the West. Unfortunately, the emplotments and metanarratives of Greek historians have been often discarded in modern narratives of Greek history.[60]

The point, of course, is not to single out one form of emplotment, or one metanarrative used by the ancient historians, and pursue it in our accounts. If we agree that history is not the past, but our perception and textual presentation of the available remains of the past, then it should be clear that there is no single perspective from which we can read the past, nor a single plot that we have to follow. This does not mean that everything is permissible, equally right or equally important. Hayden White has

[59] Hunter 1982.   [60] Though see for example Malkin 1994b.

observed a quadri-partite form of emplotment in his analysis of nine-teenth-century historiography: romance, tragedy, comedy and satire.[61] I see no reason why a historian has to adopt a single form of emplotment in his narrative. After all, history has many faces: it is romance for some people, comedy for others, tragedy for many and satire for those lucky enough to be able to observe. Often, the comedy of the one is the tragedy of the other. There is no reason not to adopt a multiplicity of perspectives and a multiplicity of plots, and to weave them together, instead of adhering blindly to a single perspective and a single master narrative. How to do it, I believe, cannot be established beforehand.

History from below: how to fit in the pieces

We have examined what kind of emplotments we will need in order to make a story (or indeed multiple stories) out of our materials; but how can we be inclusive, how can we incorporate our bits and pieces into our accounts? I believe that, once we recognise the multiplicity of perspectives, levels, and temporalities and the fragmentary Athenocentric nature of our sources, our best solution is a recourse to large-scale narrative.

Let us have a closer look at our sources. Athenian law-court speeches are one of the best sources for social history that we could have.[62] They become Athenocentric, only because we treat them as sources from which the historian mines his information for Athenian society. On the contrary, if we treat them as *narratives*, they immediately open windows to the wider world. Consider the case of Apollodorus the son of Pasion.[63] Apollodorus has been appointed trierarch;[64] he wants to spend lavishly on his liturgy (§§ 7–10); accordingly he dismisses the Athenian drafted sailors, who were not of much value, and hires his own sailors (§§ 7–8), many of which must have been metics, or even foreigners. In the course of his extended trier-archy he sails around the whole Aegean (*passim*); he participates in some of the local wars and conflicts in the north Aegean and Thrace (§§ 20–3); he sees many of his sailors abandoning him to seek employment in the navies of northern Greece (§§ 16–17); he finds himself in the market place of Thasos, exchanging threats with his Athenian opponent (§§ 29–30); he borrows money from the network of friends of his father in Asia Minor (§§ 17–18, 56); he has to deal with the complaints of his sailors and their need to provide subsistence for their families (§§ 11–3).

---

[61] White 1973: 7–11. [62] Hunter 1994. [63] The conventional approach: Trevett 1992.
[64] Demosthenes, *Against Polycles*; see Balin 1978.

It is only our decision to treat this speech as a source of Athenian history that creates an Athenocentric account; if we treat it as a narrative, converting Apollodorus' law-court speech into a story of his trierarchic mission, we open a big window into the life of the subaltern classes; the networks of trade and credit among the wealthy; the regional history of the north Aegean; the history of the island of Thasos; and the connected history of the wider Aegean world. One could bring together in telling such a story the study of naval power in the Mediterranean history; the study of networks of mobility; the study of the history and archaeology of Thasos; the study of regional systems of interaction; the study of imperial intervention.

We can see here how the alternative concepts that we have tried to delineate could fit in with an alternative way of writing ancient history. And how many more windows, how many more concentric circles would not the narration of such a story open! Imagine Apollodorus in the agora of Thasos: would he not encounter all these famous Thasian amphoras of wine?[65] Would this not give the narrator an opportunity to tell their story and significance? Need I remind you that we know a great ancient Greek historian who excels in constructing exactly this kind of narrative links?[66] Need I argue that there must be a link between Herodotus' narrative technique and his non-Hellenocentric and non-Athenocentric history?

The old-style narratives were concerned with great men, the elite and *histoire évènementielle*. The enlargement of the field of history to include social, economic and cultural history led to the abandonment of narrative in favour of analysis and structural, synchronic exposition.[67] This has been of course a great advantage; but it allowed the survival of old-style *histoire évènementielle* by default; and it created the problems of static, unidimensional, functionalist and evolutionist approaches that we have been dealing with. If we are to combine the advantages of a new analytical framework, like the one I have presented in this book, with the possibilities offered by Apollodorus' story we clearly need a new kind of narrative. Old-style narrative history did not have space for such stories; social and economic history dismembered them into static structural analysis; how can we proceed nowadays?

I do not have a simple answer, and I do not think there should be a single answer. What I certainly think is that we need to populate our histories with real people and their different and divergent experiences. This is the surest and most fascinating way of conveying the multiplicity of perspectives, temporalities, levels and processes: for sure, attention to multiple

---

[65] Garlan 1988. [66] See de Jong 2002. [67] See Stone 1979; Carrard 1992.

temporalities, levels, processes and perspectives changes not only the content of the story, but also the nature of story-telling.[68]

Let me finish with two suggestions of what kind of narrative I envisage. Both my suggestions look back to forms of narrative that were very common in the past, but have been discarded since the historicist revolution of the nineteenth century; one more case of how the history of historiography can throw light on how to solve current problems of studying history.

The one is travel narrative. One of the most fascinating ways of writing history in the early modern period was using a fictional travel narrative in order to present to the audience the history, the institutions and the cultural interaction of the people in the past.[69] The *Voyage du jeune Anacharsis en Grèce, vers le milieu du quatrième siècle avant l'ère vulgaire*[70] by J. J. Barthélemy was the most popular work of Greek history for decades. Barthélemy was one of the most distinguished scholars of his time;[71] the travels of Anacharsis brought together the wider Mediterranean world in the classical period; and the work was supplemented by volumes showing the literary and iconographical sources behind the account.[72] Could one imagine a better history of the archaic Mediterranean and the Near East than the *Travels of Democedes*, the doctor from southern Italy, who worked for Aegina, Athens and Polycrates, the tyrant of Samos, found himself at the Persian court and managed to return to Italy again?[73]

My second suggestion refers to the need to overcome the constraints of the functionalist and structuralist methodologies employed by the majority of ancient historians. In terms of methodology, I have tried to show why the Aristotelian concepts of *koinôniai* and *merê* provide a better way of approaching social, economic and cultural history than the structuralist polarities and functionalist models usually employed.[74] But how are we to give narrative form to such a kind of analysis?

Let me give an example of what I have in mind: people write a lot about Greek perceptions of the Other, Greek racism and the Greek contempt of

---

[68] See Klein 1995.

[69] See e.g. J. Terrasson, *Séthos, histoire, ou Vie tirée des monumens anecdotes de l'ancienne Egypte, traduite d'un manuscrit grec*, Paris, 1731; W. A. Becker, *Charicles. Bilder altgriechischer Sitte zur genaueren Kenntnis des griechischen Privatlebens, I–II*, Leipzig, 1840.

[70] 7 vols., Paris, 1788–9.

[71] He deciphered Phoenician; and wrote a large number of essays, mainly of antiquarian character: see Badolle 1927.

[72] J. J. Barthélemy, *Recueil de cartes géographiques, plans, vues et médailles de l'ancienne Grèce: relatifs au Voyage du jeune Anacharsis, précédé d'une analyse critique des cartes*, Paris, 1788; P. J. B. Chaussard, *Fêtes et courtisanes de la Grèce: supplément aux voyages d'Anacharsis et d'Anténor, I–IV*, Paris, 1801.

[73] Herodotus, III, 125–38.   [74] Chapter 3.

barbarians;[75] and of course there is a lot in these accounts that is true. But it seems to me, partly because we are so used to the kind of sources we have,[76] partly because most students of ancient history did not have a training as historians,[77] so as to familiarise themselves with the kind of evidence other historians use, and the conclusions they reach, we seldom think about these issues with real people in mind; we seldom think of the sort of questions that historians familiar with more comprehensive forms of evidence ask. But even more, our non-narrative form of presenting these issues creates a static and unidimensional image.

Imagine a Greek and a Phoenician drinking a cup of wine after work in Piraeus. How would the Greek articulate his discourse about the barbarian Other? Let us say he is Athenian and he will formulate a discourse on the superiority of Athenian democracy over Oriental despotism; what would the Phoenician reply? Would the Greek speak to the Phoenician in the same way that he would speak, if he were talking only with other Greeks? How would actual, real-life contact with the Phoenician influence his perception? In Piraeus, Greeks and Phoenicians lived in the same neighbourhood, worked in the same streets, their children played in the same street and they buried their dead in the same graveyards. How did this actual, lived *experience* influence and formulate people's perception?[78]

We do not have the direct evidence to answer these questions; no records of the actual encounters and discussions have actually survived; though we do have bits and pieces of evidence that might give us an image of a possible answer, if we do ask questions in these terms. For example, we have an official Athenian inscription, which we have already met, honouring the king of Phoenician Sidon, but granting rights to 'those who have political rights (*politeuousi*) at Sidon and live there', i.e. in other words, the citizens of Sidon.[79] So the Phoenician might argue that the Athenians themselves recognised that the concept of Oriental despotism was far from the actual reality. How did the Athenians know that some Sidonians had political rights in Sidon? Surely, the Greek discourses on Oriental despotism that we find in Greek texts did not provide them with the material to raise such a possibility. Is not this inscription a result of these actual encounters that I am postulating?

---

[75] See e.g. Hartog 1988a; Hall 1989. Cartledge 2002: 51–77, offers a well-articulated presentation of such arguments.
[76] Finley 1985c.   [77] See the comments of Finley 1963a: 71–3; Reed 2003: 1–2.
[78] For the fundamental importance of actual experience for any historical account and supposition, see the classic Thompson 1978.
[79] Tod 1948: no. 139.

We have Herodotus' dialogue of the Persians on the constitution; and his insistence that such a dialogue had indeed taken place, despite the disbelief of some of his readers (hearers);[80] so we see at least one Greek who thought that the barbarians were capable of thinking and acting on their own, and not simply obeying orders. How did he come to believe this? Was it through his experience in his travels, or in his native Carian Halicarnassus, or in multi-ethnic Athens?

We have a grave inscription dating from the third quarter of the fifth century. It is an epigram in Homeric hexameter, and it reads like this: 'This is the beautiful tomb of Manes, the son of Orymaios, the best of Phrygians there ever were in wide Athens. And by Zeus, I never saw any woodcutter better than me. He died in war.'[81] We have here the epigram of a foreigner, a Phrygian, who is a manual worker and clearly proud of his craft and his manual skills. What is more, it is a reasonable supposition that he died fighting for Athens during the Peloponnesian war, or equally possibly in some other previous engagement. Thousands of metics fought alongside Athenians, every time Athens was in war.[82] How would our Phrygian converse with his Athenian mates, while serving in his Athenian regiment? What would a low-class Athenian think when reading this epigram, while passing by going to work in his workshop?

There are many questions like these that have seldom been asked; one can think of discussions between free and slaves on the nature of slavery; between rich and poor on equality; between working people on the status of manual labour; between males and females on female licence. And I think that the ancient historians offer us an example of a narrative form to use in order to think about, to think with and to narrate such issues.

This is of course the invented speech and its accompaniment, the dialogue. The brilliant Herodotean conception of including direct speech in the historical narrative,[83] in imitation once more of the epic, has been abandoned far too easily and without real reflection by modern historians.[84] Its abandonment was a result of the nineteenth-century *Historismus*.[85] After the post-

[80] Herodotus, III, 80, VI, 43.3.
[81] *Inscriptiones Graecae*, I³ 1361. Of course, predictably the interest of the few ancient historians who have dealt with this inscription has focused on dating, topography and the language and oral features of the epigram. No wonder the political and social implications of this document have never been seriously addressed. But see now the commentary in Bäbler 1998: 159–63.
[82] Adak 2003: 67–72.   [83] See the comments of Fornara 1983: 171–3.
[84] For the debate about invented speeches in early modern historiography, see Hicks 1996.
[85] Let me refrain from repeating once more the much-abused phrase of Ranke: the development has anyway more to do with late nineteenth-century conceptions of historiography, with Langlois and Seignobos, than with the Rankean generation; see Iggers 1968; Carbonnel 1976; Novick 1988.

modernist attack on historiography, we have turned our attention to the metahistorical and narratological conventions behind historical writing; since I belong to those who believe that we have to retain both the objectivity of the past, and the subjectivity of our way of studying it, the ancient form of the invented speech has much to offer in this regard.[86] As Keith Hopkins observed,

We read ancient sources with modern minds. And if we report what we do know in quasiobjective, analytical terms, then inevitably our whole language of understanding and interpretation is deeply influenced by the modern world, and who we are in it. We cannot reproduce antiquity. And religious history is necessarily subjective. We know from experience that other writers, and readers, are very likely and fully entitled to disagree. So why, then, don't we incorporate this empathetic wonder, knowledge, pseudo-scientific analysis, ignorance, competing assumptions, and disagreements into the text of the book?[87]

The invented speech or dialogue gives us a chance to narrativise such questions and transform our bits and fragments through interpretation into avenues to further reflection.[88] But we need a democratisation of the speech form: we want to include in our narratives those left out of Thucydidean-style history; to give a voice to those who have been denied one.

One may argue: is this not a subversion of the distinction between history and fiction? I think not. On the one hand, we are talking about situations, where we do have evidence, though heavily fragmented, about what happened and how people viewed it; we are not talking about how Neolithic farmers thought about war.[89] On the other hand, all historiographical work is based on procedures such as these: asking questions based on certain suppositions and concerns; selecting the evidence based on certain accepted procedures; and narrating the findings in certain ways that presuppose certain assumptions.[90] The Lydian touchstone of the validity of using the invented dialogue in historical prose is contradiction: what is in the invented part should not be contradicted by what we do have

---

[86] Munz 1997; Lorenz 1998.

[87] Hopkins 1999: 2. This is an inspiring book full of new narrative forms for studying ancient history.

[88] For such an approach to the history of Crete, see Chaniotis 2000. In this collection, every essay deals with a particular period of Cretan history and combines a fictional narrative and an accompanying commentary that establishes the sources behind the fictional narrative. If only we saw more efforts like this in ancient history!

[89] This is not to imply that we cannot learn anything about how Neolithic farmers thought about war. But the ways of learning where we can base ourselves solely on material evidence, and in time scales of hundreds of years, which do not make any sense in actual human experience, are totally different from those pertaining when we have a combination of material and uttered evidence and in time scales (e.g. fifty-year periods) that do make sense in actual human experience.

[90] See Berkhofer 1995.

as evidence (e.g. that Greeks believed in Allah); although it is perfectly fine, if it is contradicted by some sources and supported by others (which is precisely the purpose of employing such a method: giving speech to the speechless). I am happy to note that Nicholas Purcell has argued for a similar procedure:

> Where the evidence is particularly patchy this may be combined with a counter-factual enquiry in asking questions to which the answers will never be forthcoming, but which make us sensitive to the anatomy of the problem. So, we may imagine a kind of cultural homogeneity, allowing a calculation of the first kind to be made along the lines of 'what is the minimum average number of annual sailings between one city and another to promote similar religious architecture in both?'; and 'what density of traffic can be postulated to account for the spread of more or less canonical temple design across the whole Greek Mediterranean?'. The fact that such an index is an impossibility does not deprive it of usefulness in building models ... Such questions have real answers, although they are unverifiable. A spectrum of possibilities can be imagined and we can say at what end we would expect the answer to lie, and why.[91]

The sole difference between that and what I am arguing for is that, given the difference of the kind of questions I want to ask, which are not statistical but experiential, we could attempt to give a narrative form to the answer to our questions.

One can of course argue that history is not about probability or verisimilitude, but about what actually happened.[92] Which is of course true; but the purpose of the invented parts should not be to prove or to convince, but to suggest. This difference is nicely captured in Italian by the verbs *dimostrare* (demonstrate) and *mostrare* (show).[93] And in fact, I find it much more honest to our readers to contain our suggestions and assumptions in clearly fictional parts, which intend to suggest and inspire, than to bring them through the back door into our 'objective' presentation. The invented speech, by emphasising the distinction between 'objective' historical presentation of 'facts' and 'subjective' historical reconstruction and interpretation can actually be fairer to the reader than the usual historical method. This is the solution I would give to the problem of evidence: how to connect our bits and pieces into a single inclusive account; how to introduce the subaltern, the peripheral and the non-Greek; how to weave the variety of perspectives into a single account.

What I have tried to do in this chapter, and in a way in this book as a whole, is to argue that along with employing modern methodologies and

---

[91] Purcell 1990: 37.   [92] Though see Hawthorn 1991.   [93] See Ginzburg 1982.

techniques of writing history, we should turn and study seriously the methodologies, genres and techniques developed by the Greeks themselves in order to analyse and narrate their history. This is not so much because the Greeks invented everything, or because they knew their society better than we do; rather it is the case that the study of historiography teaches us that there is no natural way to do things, and that in the process of development and change many valuable things get lost or forgotten. The Aristotelian political philosophy, the Herodotean emplotment, the history of the common acts, the travel narrative and the invented dialogue are all examples of forms of narrative and analysis that could still prove of enormous value for modern historical research.

Instead of elaborating further, I am happy to note how Quentin Skinner has recently made a similar plea.[94] He has shown how Renaissance humanists rediscovered ancient rhetoric, which argued that in moral and political issues, as opposed to the sciences of mathematics and the natural world, one can always and one should always argue *in utramquem partem*. The dialogue can present both sides without smoothing away ambiguities and contradictions, and uses the techniques of eloquence to argue its case; this is why the humanists argued that it is the best expressive form of moral and political theory, as opposed to the expository form of the sciences. Skinner argues that ancient rhetoricians and Renaissance humanists were conscious of something very important, and modern theorists have abandoned too easily something that they should try to recapture. I hope that my arguments will open a similar discussion.

I have not attempted to rewrite Greek history from a different perspective in this study; I have merely tried to show that the current perspective is deeply problematic, and that an alternative perspective is both feasible and illuminating. But as the English say, the proof of the pudding is in the eating. At the end of this study, I hope that the least favourable reader will grant me that much: *Hic Rhodus, hic saltus.*

[94] Skinner 1996.

Albrow M 1996 The Global Age +
Society beyond Modernity. Cambridge
Amit M. Athens + Sea: Power A Study
in Athenian Sea Power. Brussels
+Berchem

References

Abulafia, D. (2005) 'Mediterraneans' in Harris (2005), 64–93.

Abu-Lughod, J. L. (1989) *Before European Hegemony. The World-System AD 1250–1350*. New York and Oxford.

Adak, M. (2003) *Metöken als Wohltäter Athens: Untersuchungen zum sozialen Austausch zwischen ortsansässigen Fremden und der Burgergemeinde in klassischer und hellenistischer Zeit (ca. 500–150 v. Chr.)*. Munich.

Adshead, K. (1986) *Politics of the Archaic Peloponnese. The Transition from Archaic to Classical Politics*. Aldershot.

Aigner-Foresti, L., Barzano, A., Bearzot, C., Prandi, L. and Zecchini, G. (eds.) (1994) *Federazioni e federalismo nell'Europa antica*. Milan.

Albrow, M. (1996) *The Global Age. State and Society beyond Modernity*. Cambridge.

Alcock, S. E. (1993) *Graecia Capta: The Landscapes of Roman Greece*. Cambridge.
  (1994) 'Breaking up the Hellenistic world: survey and society' in *Classical Greece: Ancient Histories and Modern Archaeologies*, ed. I. Morris. Cambridge: 171–90.
  (2002) *Archaeologies of the Greek Past: Landscape, Monuments and Memories*. Cambridge.

Ali, T. (2002) *The Clash of Fundamentalisms. Crusades, Jihads and Modernity*. London and New York.

Alonso-Nuñez, J. M. (1990) 'The emergence of universal history from the fourth to the second centuries BC' in *Purposes of History. Studies in Greek Historiography from the Fourth to the Second Centuries BC (Studia Hellenistica 30)*, ed. H. Verdin, G. Schepens and E. de Keyser. Louvain: 173–92.

Ambler, W. H. (1985) 'Aristotle's understanding of the naturalness of the City', *Review of Politics* 47: 163–85.

Amit, M. (1965) *Athens and the Sea: A Study in Athenian Sea-Power*. Brussels and Berchem.
  (1973) *Great and Small Poleis: A Study in the Relations between the Great Powers and the Small Cities in Ancient Greece*. Brussels.

Amouretti, M.-C. (1994) 'L'agriculture de la Grèce antique: bilan des recherches de la dernière décennie', *Topoi* 4: 69–93.

Amouretti, M.-C. and Brun, J.-P. (eds.) (1993) *La production du vin et de l'huile en Méditerranée / Oil and Wine Production in the Mediterranean Area (BCH Supplément XXVI)*. Athens.

A̶p̶p̶a̶d̶u̶r̶a̶i̶(̶e̶d̶)̶ ̶2̶0̶0̶1̶ ̶G̶l̶o̶b̶a̶l̶i̶z̶a̶t̶i̶o̶n̶ ̶-̶ ̶D̶u̶r̶h̶a̶m̶ ̶+̶ ̶L̶o̶n̶d̶o̶n̶
A̶r̶r̶i̶g̶h̶i̶ ̶G̶ ̶1̶9̶9̶4̶ ̶t̶h̶e̶ ̶L̶o̶n̶g̶ ̶t̶w̶e̶n̶t̶y̶ ̶c̶e̶n̶t̶u̶r̶y̶?̶
M̶o̶n̶e̶y̶ ̶P̶o̶w̶e̶r̶ ̶+̶ ̶t̶h̶e̶ ̶*References* ̶O̶r̶i̶g̶i̶n̶ ̶o̶f̶ ̶o̶u̶r̶ ̶T̶i̶m̶e̶
L̶o̶n̶d̶o̶n̶

Ampolo, C. (1997) *Storie greche. La formazione della moderna storiografia sugli antichi Greci.* Turin.

Andersen, H. D., Horsnaes, H. W., Houby Nielsen, S. and Rathje, A. (eds.) (1997) *Urbanization in the Mediterranean in the Ninth to Sixth Centuries BC (Acta Hyperborea 7).* Copenhagen.

Anderson, B. (1991) *Imagined Communities. Reflections on the Origin and Spread of Nationalism.* 2nd edn. London.

Andreau, J., Briant, P. and Descat, R. (eds.) (1994) *Economie antique: les échanges dans l'Antiquité: le rôle de l'Etat.* Saint-Bertrand-de-Comminges.

(eds.)(1997) *Economie antique: prix et formation des prix dans les économies antiques.* Saint-Bertrand-de-Comminges.

Angelis, F. de (1994) 'The foundation of Selinous: overpopulation and opportunities?' in Tsetskhladze and De Angelis (1994), 87–110.

(2000) 'Estimating the agricultural base of Greek Sicily', *Proceedings of the British School at Rome* 68: 111–48.

(2002) 'Trade and agriculture at Megara Hyblaia', *OJA* 21: 299–310.

Antonaccio, C. (2003) 'Hybridity and the cultures within Greek culture' in Dougherty and Kurke (2003a), 57–74.

Appadurai, A. (ed.) (2001) *Globalization.* Durham and London.

Archibald, Z. H. (1998) *The Odrysian Kingdom of Thrace: Orpheus Unmasked.* Oxford.

(2000) 'Space, hierarchy and community in archaic and classical Macedonia, Thessaly and Thrace' in Brock and Hodkinson (2000), 212–33.

(2002) 'The shape of the New Commonwealth: aspects of the Pontic and Eastern Mediterranean regions in the Hellenistic age' in Tsetskhladze and Snodgrass (2002), 49–72.

Archibald, Z. H., Davies, J., Gabrielsen, V. and Oliver, G. J. (eds.) (2001) *Hellenistic Economies.* London and New York.

Arrighi, G. (1994) *The Long Twentieth Century: Money, Power and the Origins of our Time.* London.

Asad, T. (1993) *Genealogies of Religion. Discipline and Reasons of Power in Christianity and Islam.* Baltimore and London.

Asdrachas, S. I. (ed.) (2003) *Ellênikê oikonomikê istoria, XV–XIX aiônes, I–II.* Athens.

Aston, T. H. and Philpin, C. H. E. (eds.) (1985) *The Brenner Debate: Agrarian Class Structure and Economic Development in Pre-industrial Europe.* Cambridge.

Austin, M. M. and Vidal-Naquet, P. (1972) *Economies et sociétés en Grèce ancienne.* Paris.

Avlami, Ch. (ed.) (2000a) *L'antiquité grecque au XIXe siècle: un exemplum contesté?* Paris.

(2000b) 'La Grèce ancienne dans l'imaginaire libéral ou, comment se débarrasser de la Terreur' in Avlami (2000a), 71–111.

(2001) 'Libertà liberale contro libertà antica' in Settis (2001), 1311–50.

Aymard, M. (1982) 'From feudalism to capitalism in Italy: the case that does not fit', *Review* 6: 131–208.

Bayly. C. A 1991
ver: ed A. G Hopkins globalization
in World History
Ver Bairoch

Bäbler, B. (1998) *Fleißige Thrakerinnen und wehrhafte Skythen: Nichtgriechen im klassischen Athen und ihre archäologische Hinterlassenschaft*. Stuttgart.

Badal'janc, J. S. (1999) 'La Rhodes hellénistique et le Nord de la Mer Noire' in Garlan (1999a), 247–53.

Badolle, M. (1927) *L'Abbé Jean-Jacques Barthélemy (1716–1795) et l'hellénisme en France dans la seconde moitie du XVIIIe siècle*. Paris.

Bagnall, R. S. (1976) *The Administration of the Ptolemaic Possessions Outside Egypt*. Leiden.

Bairoch, P. (1988) *Cities and Economic Development. From the Dawn of History to the Present*. Trans. C. Braider. London.

Baker, K. M. (2001) 'Enlightenment and the institution of society: notes for a conceptual history' in Kaviraj and Khilnani (2001), 84–104.

Balcer, J. M. (1984) *Sparda by the Bitter Sea: Imperial Interaction in Western Anatolia*. Chico, CA.

Balin, N. T. (1978) *A Commentary on (Demosthenes) 50, 'Against Polykles'*. Washington, DC.

Barcelo, P. (1993) *Basileia, Monarchia, Tyrannis. Untersuchungen zu Entwicklung und Beurteilung von Alleinherrschaft im vorhellenistischen Griechenland*. Stuttgart.

Barel, Y. (1977) *La ville médiévale: système social, système urbain*. Grenoble.

Barletta, B. A. (1983) *Ionic Influence in Archaic Sicily: The Monumental Art*. Gothenburg.

Bartlett, R. (1993) *The Making of Europe. Conquest, Colonisation, and Cultural Change, 950–1350*. London.

Baslez, M.-F. (1986) 'Cultes et dévotions des Phéniciens en Grèce. Les divinités marines' in *Studia Phoenicia, IV: Religio Phoenicia*, ed. C. Bonnet, E. Lipinski and P. Marchetti. Namur: 289–305.

(1987) 'Le rôle et la place des Phéniciens dans la vie économique des ports de l'Egée', in *Studia Phoenicia, V: Phoenicia and the East Mediterranean in the First Millennium B. C.*, ed. E. Lipinski. Leuven: 267–85.

(1988) 'Les communautés d'Orientaux dans la cité grecque. Formes de sociabilité et modèles associatifs' in Lonis (1988), 139–58.

(1996) 'Les immigrés orientaux en Grèce', *Cahiers du Centre Glotz* 7: 39–50.

Bastide, R. (1978) *The African Religions of Brazil: Toward a Sociology of the Interpenetration of Civilizations*. Trans. H. Sebba. Baltimore and London.

Bauer, S. (2001) *Polisbild und Demokratieverständnis in Jacob Burckhardts 'Griechischer Kulturgeschichte'*. Basle.

Bayly, C. A. (1991) *Rulers, Townsmen and Bazaars. North Indian Society in the Age of British Expansion, 1770–1870*. 2nd edn. Delhi.

(2002) '"Archaic" and "modern" globalisation in the Eurasian and African arena, c. 1750–1850' in *Globalisation in World History*, ed. A. G. Hopkins. London: 47–73.

Beck, H. (1997) *Polis und Koinon. Untersuchungen zur Geschichte und Struktur der Griechischen Bundesstaaten im 4. Jahrhundert v. Chr.* Stuttgart.

Becker-Schaum, C. (1993) *Arnold Herman Ludwig Heeren. Ein Beitrag zur Geschichte der Geschichtswissenschaft zwischen Aufklärung und Historismus*. Frankfurt am Main.

Bastide Brazil
Bayly C. A - ve

Berg M. Important

Beloch, K. J. (1913) *Griechische Geschichte*. Volume I, 2nd edn. Berlin and Leipzig.
(1925) *Griechische Geschichte*. Volume IV: 1, 2nd edn. Berlin and Leipzig.
Bender, T. (1986) 'Wholes and parts: the need for synthesis in American history', *Journal of American History* 73: 120–36.
(ed.) (2002a) *Rethinking American History in a Global Age*. Berkeley, Los Angeles and London.
(2002b) 'Introduction. Historians, the nation and the plenitude of narratives' in Bender (2002a), 1–21.
Bengtson, H. (1950) *Griechische Geschichte: von den Anfängen bis in die römische Kaiserzeit*. Munich.
Bennet, J. (1995) 'Space through time: diachronic perspectives on the spatial organization of the Pylian state' in Laffineur and Niemeier (1995), 587–601.
Berard, C. (ed.) (1984) *La cité des images: religion et société en Grèce antique*. Paris.
Berengo, M. (1999) *L'Europa delle città: il volto della società urbana europea tra Medioevo ed Età moderna*. Turin.
Berg, M. (1985) *The Age of Manufactures. Industry, Innovation and Work in Britain, 1700–1820*. London.
Berges, D. (1994) 'Alt-Knidos und Neu-Knidos', *Mitteilungen des Deutschen Archäologischen Instituts (Istanbul)* 44: 5–16.
Berkhofer, R. F. (1995) *Beyond the Great Story: History as Text and Discourse*. Cambridge, MA, and London.
Berlin, Ir. (1980) 'Time, space and the evolution of Afro-American society on British Mainland North America', *AHR* 85: 44–78.
Berlin, Is. (1977) *Vico and Herder: Two Studies in the History of Ideas*. New York.
(1979) 'The Counter Enlightenment' in Is. Berlin, *Against the Current. Studies in the History of Ideas*. Oxford: 1–24.
Berlinerblau, J. (1999) *Heresy in the University: The Black Athena Controversy and the Responsibilities of American Intellectuals*. New Brunswick, NJ.
Bernal, M. (1987) *Black Athena. The Afroasiatic Roots of Classical Civilization. I: The Fabrication of Ancient Greece, 1785–1985*. London.
Berve, H. (1937) *Miltiades: Studien zur Geschichte des Mannes und seiner Zeit*. Berlin.
(1967) *Die Tyrannis bei den Griechen, I–II*. Munich.
Betancourt, P. P., Karageorghis, V., Laffineur, R. and Niemeier, W. D. (eds.) (1999) *Meletemata: Studies in Aegean Archaeology Presented to Malcolm H. Wiener as he Enters his Sixty-fifth Year (Aegaeum 20)*. Liege and Austin, TX.
Bichler, R. (1983) *'Hellenismus'. Geschichte und Problematik eines Epochen-Begriffs*. Darmstadt.
Bilde, P., Engberg-Pedersen, T., Hannestad, L., Zahle, J. and Randsborg, K. (eds.) (1993) *Centre and Periphery in the Hellenistic World*. Aarhus.
Bintliff, J. (ed.) (1991a) *The Annales School and Archaeology*. Leicester.
(1991b) 'Die Polis-Landschaften Griechenlands: Probleme und Aussichten der Bevölkerungsgeschichte' in Olshausen and Sonnabend (1991), 149–202.
(1997) 'Regional survey, demography and the rise of complex societies in the Aegean', *JFA* 24: 1–38.

Birken, L. (1999) 'Chaos theory and "Western civilisation"', *Review* 22: 17–30.

Blakeway, A. (1932/3) 'Prolegomena to the study of Greek commerce with Italy, Sicily and France in the eighth and seventh centuries BC', *BSA* 33: 170–208.

Blanke, H. W. (1983) 'Verfassungen die nicht rechtlich aber wirklich sind. A. H. L. Heeren und das Ende der Aufklärungshistorie', *Berichte zur Wissenschaftsgeschichte* 6: 143–64.

Blaut, J. M. (1993) *The Coloniser's Model of the World: Geographical Diffusionism and Eurocentric History*. New York.

Blok, J. (1996) 'Proof and persuasion in Black Athena: the case of K. O. Müller', *JHI* 57: 705–24.

Blum, I., Darmezin, L., Delcourt, J.-Cl. and Helly, B. (eds.) (1992) *Topographie antique et géographie historique en pays grec*. Paris.

Boardman J. and Vaphopoulou-Richardson, C. E. (eds.) (1986) *Chios. A Conference at the Homereion in Chios 1984*. Oxford.

Bödeker, H. E., Iggers, G. G., Knudsen, J. B. and Reill, P. H. (eds.) (1986) *Aufklärung und Geschichte. Studien zur deutschen Geschichtswissenschaft im 18. Jahrhundert*. Göttingen.

Bondí, S. F. (2001) 'Interferenza fra culture nel Mediterraneo antico: Fenici, Punici, Greci' in Settis (2001), 369–400.

Bonias, Z., Brunet, M. and Sintes, G. (1990) 'Organisation des espaces et cheminements antiques à Thasos' in *Archéologie et espaces: Xe rencontres d'archéologie et d'histoire Antibes, 19–21 octobre 1989*. Juan les Pins: 71–86.

Bourriot, F. (1976) *Recherches sur la nature du génos, I–II*. Paris.

Bouzek, J. (1989) 'Athènes et la Mer Noire', *BCH* 113: 249–59.

Bowersock, G. W. (1984) 'Review of K. Christ, *Römische Geschichte und deutsche Geschichtswissenschaft*, Munich, 1982', *H&T* 23: 370–8.

Braudel, F. (1972) *The Mediterranean and the Mediterranean World in the Age of Philip II, I–II*. 2nd edn. Trans. S. Reynolds. London.

(1980) *On History*. Trans. S. Matthews. Chicago.

(1981) *Civilisation and Capitalism. I: The Structures of Everyday Life: The Limits of the Possible*. Trans. S. Reynolds. London.

(1982) *Civilisation and Capitalism. II: The Wheels of Commerce*. Trans. S. Reynolds. London.

(1984) *Civilisation and Capitalism. III: The Perspective of the World*. Trans. S. Reynolds. London.

Bravo, B. (1968) *Philologie, histoire, philosophie de l'histoire: étude sur J. G. Droysen, historien de l'antiquité*. Breslau and Warsaw.

Brenner, R. (1977) 'The origins of capitalist development: a critique of Neo-Smithian Marxism', *New Left Review* 104: 25–92.

(1982) 'The agrarian roots of European capitalism' reprinted in Aston and Philpin (1985), 213–328.

Bresson, A. (1983) 'La dynamique des cités de Lesbos' republished in Bresson (2000b), 101–8.

(1987) 'Aristote et le commerce extérieur', *REA* 89: 217–38.

(1993) 'Les cités grecques et leurs emporia' in Bresson and Rouillard (1993), 163–226.

(2000a) 'Les cités grecques, la marché et les prix' in Bresson (2000b), 263–307.

(2000b) *La cité marchande*. Bordeaux.

(2005) 'Ecology and beyond: the Mediterranean paradigm' in Harris (2005), 94–114.

Bresson, A. and Rouillard, P. (eds.) (1993) *L'Emporion*. Paris.

Briant, P. (2002) *From Cyrus to Alexander: A History of the Persian Empire*. 2nd edn. Trans. P. T. Daniels. Winona Lake, IN.

Brinkman, J. A. (1979) 'Babylonia under the Assyrian empire, 745–627 BC' in *Power and Propaganda. A Symposium on Ancient Empires*, ed. M. T. Larsen. Copenhagen: 223–50.

(1984) *Prelude to Empire: Babylonian Society and Politics, 747–626 BC*. Philadelphia.

Brock, R. and Hodkinson, S. (eds.) (2000) *Alternatives to Athens. Varieties of Political Organisation and Community in Ancient Greece*. Oxford.

Broodbank, C. (2002) *An Island Archaeology of the Early Cyclades*. Cambridge.

Brook, T. and Blue, G. (eds.) (1999) *China and Historical Capitalism: Genealogies of Sinological Knowledge*. Cambridge.

Bruhns, H. (1985) 'De Werner Sombart à Max Weber et Moses Finley. La typologie de la ville antique et la question de la ville de consommation' in Leveau (1985), 255–73.

Bruhns, H. and Nippel, W. (eds.) (2000) *Max Weber und die Stadt im Kulturvergleich*. Göttingen.

Bruit Zaidman, L. and Schmitt Pantel, P. (1992) *Religion in the Ancient Greek City*. Trans. P. Cartledge. Cambridge.

Brun, P. (1996) *Les archipels égéens dans l'antiquité grecque (V^e–IIe siècles avant notre ère)*. Paris.

Bruneau, P. (1987) 'Peparethia', *BCH* III: 471–93.

Brunet, M. (1997) 'Thasos et son Empire à la fin du Ve s. avant Jésus Christ' in *Esclavage, guerre, économie en Grèce ancienne. Hommages à Yvon Garlan*, ed. P. Brule and J. Oulhen. Rennes: 229–42.

(ed.) (1999) *Territoires des cités grecques (BCH Supplément XXXIV)*. Athens.

Burde, P. (1974) *Untersuchungen zur antiker Universalgeschichtsschreibung*. Munich.

Burford, A. (1969) *The Greek Temple Builders at Epidauros: A Social and Economic Study of Building in the Asklepian Sanctuary, during the Fourth and Early Third Centuries BC*. Liverpool.

Burke, P. (1969) *The Renaissance Sense of the Past*. London.

(1974) *Venice and Amsterdam: A Study of Seventeenth-Century Elites*. London.

(1990) 'Ranke the reactionary' in Iggers and Powell (1990), 36–44.

Burkert, W. (1992) *The Orientalising Revolution. Near Eastern Influence on Greek Culture in the Early Archaic Age*. Trans. W. Burkert and M. E. Pinder. Cambridge, MA.

Burrow, J. W. (1967) *Evolution and Society: A Study in Victorian Social Theory*. Cambridge.

Butler, E. M. (1935) *The Tyranny of Greece over Germany. A Study of the Influence Exercised by Greek Art and Poetry over the Great German Writers of the Eighteenth, Nineteenth and Twentieth Centuries.* Cambridge.

Butterfield, H. (1955) *Man on his Past. The Study of the History of Historical Scholarship.* Cambridge.

Buzan, B. and Little, R. (eds.) (2000) *International Systems in World History: Remaking the Study of International Relations.* Oxford.

Cabanes, P. (1976) *L'Epire de la mort de Pyrrhos à la conquête romaine, 272–167 av. J. C.* Paris.

  (1983) 'Les états fédéraux de Grèce du nord-ouest: pouvoirs locaux, pouvoir fédéral' in *Symposion 1979: Vorträge zur griechischen und hellenistischen Rechtsgeschichte*, ed. P. Dimakis. Cologne and Vienna: 99–111.

Cahill, N. (2002) *Household and City Organisation at Olynthus.* New Haven and London.

Calder, W. M. III and Demandt (eds.) (1990) *Edward Meyer: Leben und Leistung eines Universalhistorikers.* Leiden.

Calder, W. M. III and Schlesier, R. (eds.) (1998) *Zwischen Rationalismus und Romantik. Karl Otfried Müller und die antike Kultur.* Hildesheim.

Cambiano, G. (1984a) 'L'Atene dorica di Karl Otfried Müller', *ASNP* 14: 1045–67.

  (1984b) 'La Grecia antica era molto popolata? Un dibattito nel XVIII secolo', *Quaderni di Storia* 20: 3–42.

Camp, J. McK. (2000) 'Walls and the polis' in Flensted-Jensen *et al.* (2000), 41–57.

Canfora, L. (1987) *Ellenismo.* Rome and Bari.

  (1989) *Le vie del classicismo.* Rome and Bari.

Capogrossi Colognesi, L. (1984) 'Ed. Meyer e le teorie sull'origine dello stato', *Quaderni fiorentini per la storia del pensiero giuridico* 13: 451–69.

  (1990) *Economie antiche e capitalismo moderno. La sfida di Max Weber.* Rome and Bari.

Carbonell, C. O. (1976) *Histoire et historiens: une mutation idéologique des historiens français, 1865–1885.* Toulouse.

Cargill, J. (1995) *Athenian Settlements of the Fourth Century BC.* Leiden.

Carlier, P. (ed.) (1996) *Le IVe siècle av. J. C. Approches historiographiques.* Paris.

Carr, E. H. (1961) *What Is history?* London.

Carrard, P. (1992) *Poetics of the New History: French Historical Discourse from Braudel to Chartier.* Baltimore.

Carter, J. C. (1990) 'Metapontum – land, wealth and population' in Descœudres (1990), 405–41.

Cartledge, P. (1987) *Agesilaos and the Crisis of Sparta.* London.

  (1998) 'The economy (economies) of ancient Greece', *Dialogos* 5: 4–24.

  (2002) *The Greeks. A Portrait of Self and Others.* 2nd edn. Oxford.

Cassola, F. (1996) 'Chi erano i Greci?' in Settis (1996), 5–23.

Chadwick, J. (1976) *The Mycenaean World.* Cambridge.

Chakrabarty, D. (2000) *Provincialising Europe: Postcolonial Thought and Historical Difference.* Princeton, NJ.

Chandavarkar, R. (1998) *Imperial Power and Popular Politics. Class, Resistance and the State in India, c. 1850–1950.* Cambridge.

Chaniotis, A. (1996) *Die Verträge zwischen kretischen Poleis in der hellenistischen Zeit.* Stuttgart.

(ed.) (2000) *Erga kai êmeres stên Krêtê: apo tên proistoria ston Mesopolemo.* Herakleion.

Charpin, D. and Joannès, F. (eds.) (1992) *La circulation des biens, des personnes et des idées dans le proche orient ancien: actes de la XXXVIIIe rencontre Assyriologique internationale.* Paris.

Chase-Dunn, C. and Hall, T. (1993) 'Comparing world-systems: concepts and working hypotheses', *Social Forces* 71: 851–86.

Chaturvedi, V. (ed.) (2000) *Mapping Subaltern Studies and the Postcolonial.* London and New York.

Cherry, J. F., Davis, J. L. and Mantzourani, E. (1991) *Landscape Archaeology as Long-Term History: Northern Keos in the Cycladic Islands.* Los Angeles.

Christ, K. (1972) *Von Gibbon zu Rostovtzeff. Leben und Werk führenden Althistoriker der Neuzeit.* Darmstadt.

(1981) 'N. D. Fustel de Coulanges und die antike Gesellschaft' republished in Christ (1996b), 114–22.

(1988) 'E. Curtius und J. Burckhardt. Zur deutschen Rezeption der griechischen Geschichte im 19. Jahrhundert' republished in Christ (1996b), 123–43.

(1990) *Neue Profile zur alten Geschichte.* Darmstadt.

(1996a) 'Griechische Geschichte zwischen Adolf Holm und Ettore Lepore' in Christ (1996b), 144–56.

(1996b) *Griechische Geschichte und Wissenschaftsgeschichte.* Stuttgart.

(1999) *Hellas: griechische Geschichte und deutsche Geschichts-Wissenschaft.* Munich.

Christ, K. and Momigliano, A. (eds.) (1988) *L'Antichità nell'Ottocento in Italia e Germania / Die Antike im 19. Jahrhundert in Italien und Deutschland.* Bologne and Berlin.

Chtcheglov, A. (1992) *Polis et chora. Cité et territoire dans le Pont-Euxin.* Trans. J. and Y. Garlan. Besançon.

Ciccotti, E. (1897) *Il tramonto della schiavitú nel mondo antico: un saggio.* Turin.

Clarke, K. (1999) *Between Geography and History. Hellenistic Constructions of the Roman World.* Oxford.

Clifford, J. (1994) 'Diasporas', *CA* 9: 302–38.

Cline, E. H. (1995) 'Tinker, tailor, soldier, sailor: Minoans and Mycenaeans abroad' in Laffineur and Niemeier (1995), 265–87.

Cohen, E. (1992) *Athenian Economy and Society: A Banking Perspective.* Princeton, NJ.

(2000) *The Athenian Nation.* Princeton, NJ.

Cohn, B. S. (1987) *The Anthropologist among the Historians and Other Essays.* Delhi.

Collini, S., Winch, D. and Burrow, J. (1983) *That Noble Science of Politics. A Study in Nineteenth-Century Intellectual History.* Cambridge.

Comninel, G. C. (1987) *Rethinking the French Revolution: Marxism and the Revisionist Challenge.* London.

Cook, J. M. (1962) *The Greeks in Ionia and the East*. London.

Cook, R. M. and Dupont, J. (1998) *East Greek Pottery*. London.

Cornell, T. J. and Lomas, K. (eds.) (1995) *Urban Society in Roman Italy*. London.

Cracco, G. (1991) 'Social structure and conflict in the medieval city' in Molho *et al.* (1991), 309–29.

Croce, B. (1921) *Theory and History of Historiography*. Trans. D. Ainslie. London.

Crone, P. (1986) 'The tribe and the state' in Hall (1986), 48–77.

Crossley, C. (1993) *French Historians and Romanticism: Thierry, Guizot, the Saint-Simonians, Quinet, Michelet*. London.

Crumley, C. L. (1987) 'A dialectical critique of hierarchy' in *Power Relations and State Formation*, ed. T. C. Patterson and C. W. Gailey. Washington, DC: 155–9.

Curtin, P. D. (1984) *Cross-Cultural Trade in World History*. Cambridge.

Dandamayev, M. A. (1974) 'Social stratification in Babylonia (7th – 4th centuries BC)', *Acta Antiqua Academiae Scientiarum Hungaricae* 22: 433–44.

  (1977) 'State and temple in Babylonia in the first millennium BC' in *State and Temple in the Ancient Near East*, ed. E. Lipinski. Louvain: 586–9.

  (1981) 'The Neo-Babylonian citizens', *Klio* 63: 45–9.

  (1984) *Slavery in Babylonia: From Nabopolassar to Alexander the Great (626–331 BC)*. Trans. V. A. Powell. De Kalb, IL.

  (1987) 'Free hired labor in Babylonia during the sixth through fourth centuries BC' in *Labor in the Ancient Near East*, ed. M. Powell. New Haven, CT: 271–9.

D'Andria, F. and Mannino, K. (eds.) (1996) *Ricerche sulla casa in Magna Grecia e in Sicilia*. Galatina.

Darcque, P. (1987) 'Les tholoi et l'organisation socio-politique du monde mycénien' in *Thanatos. Les coutumes funéraires en Egée à l'age du Bronze*, ed. R. Laffineur. Liege: 184–205.

Davies, J. K. (1975) 'Review of Austin and Vidal-Naquet (1972)', *Phoenix* 29: 93–102.

  (1978) *Democracy and Classical Greece*. London.

  (1995) 'The fourth century crisis: what crisis?' in Eder (1995), 29–39.

  (1997a) 'Sparta e l'area peloponnesiaca. Atene e il dominio di mare' in Settis (1997), 109–61.

  (1997b) 'The origins of the Greek polis: where should we be looking?' in Mitchell and Rhodes (1997), 24–38.

  (1998) 'Ancient economies: models and muddles' in Parkins and Smith (1998), 225–56.

  (2000) 'A wholly non-Aristotelian universe: the Molossians as ethnos, state and monarchy' in Brock and Hodkinson (2000), 234–58.

  (2001) 'Hellenistic economies in the post-Finley era' in Archibald *et al.* (2001), 11–62.

  (2002) 'Greek history: a discipline in transformation' in *Classics in Progress. Essays on Ancient Greece and Rome*, ed. T. P. Wiseman. Oxford: 225–46.

Davies, J. L. (1991) 'Contributions to a Mediterranean rural archaeology: historical case studies from the Ottoman Cyclades', *JMA* 4.2: 131–216.

Debord, P. (1999) *L'Asie mineure au IVe siècle (412–323 a.C.). Pouvoirs et jeux politiques.* Bordeaux.

Delcourt, J.-Cl. (1990) *La vallée de l'Enipeus en Thessalie. Etudes de topographie et de géographie antique (BCH Supplément XXI).* Athens.

Demand, N. (1996) 'Poleis on Cyprus and Oriental despotism' in Hansen and Raaflaub (1996), 7–15.

(1997) 'The origins of polis: the view from Cyprus' in *Res Maritimae. Cyprus and the Eastern Mediterranean from Prehistory to Late Antiquity*, ed. S. Swiny, R. L. Hohlfelder and H. Wylde-Swiny. Atlanta, GA: 99–105.

Dentzer, J. M. (1982) *Le motif du banquet couché dans le Proche-Orient et le monde grec du VIIe au IVe siècle avant J.-C.* Rome.

Descat, R. (1987) 'L'économie d'une cité grecque au IV s. av. J.-C.: l'exemple athénien', *REA* 89: 239–54.

(1995) 'L'économie antique et la cité grecque. Un modèle en question', *Annales (Histoire et Sciences Sociales)* 50: 961–89.

(2000) 'Der Historiker, die griechische Polis und Webers "Stadt"' in Bruhns and Nippel (2000), 77–91.

Descœudres, J. P. (ed.) (1990) *Greek Colonists and Native Populations.* Canberra and Oxford.

Detienne, M. (2000) *Comparer l'incomparable.* Paris.

(2005) *Les Grecs et nous: une anthropologie comparée de la Grèce ancienne.* Paris.

Dillery, J. (1995) *Xenophon and the History of his Times.* London.

Dillon, J. (2004) *Salt and Olives: Morality and Custom in Ancient Greece.* Edinburgh.

Dmitriev, S. (2005) *City Government in Hellenistic and Roman Asia Minor.* Oxford.

Docter, R. F. and Niemeyer, H. G. (1995) 'Pithekoussai: the Carthaginian connection. On the archaeological evidence of Euboeo-Phoenician partnership in the 8th and 7th centuries B.C.', *ASNP* n.s. 1: 101–15.

Donato, R. di (1990) *Per un'antropologia storica del mondo antico.* Florence.

Dosse, F. (1994) *New History in France: The Triumph of the Annales.* Trans. P. V. Conroy Jr. Urbana, IL.

Dougherty, C. and Kurke, L. (eds.) (2003a) *The Cultures within Ancient Greek Culture: Contact, Conflict, Collaboration.* Cambridge.

(2003b) 'Introduction: the cultures within Greek culture' in Dougherty and Kurke (2003a), 1–19.

Doukellis, P. N. and Mendoni, L. G. (eds.) (1994) *Structures rurales et sociétés antiques.* Paris.

Doulgéri-Intzessiloglou A. and Garlan, Y. (1990) 'Vin et amphores de Péparéthos et d'Ikos', *BCH* 114: 361–89.

Dover, K. J. (ed.) (1992) *Perceptions of the Ancient Greeks.* Oxford.

Drews, R. (1973) *The Greek Accounts of Eastern History.* Washington, DC.

Driel, G. van (1987) 'Continuity or decay in the late Achaemenid period: evidence from southern Babylonia', in *Achaemenid History, I: Sources, Structures and Synthesis*, ed. H. Sancisi-Weerdenburg. Leiden: 159–81.

(1989) 'The Murašhus in context', *JESHO* 32: 203–29.

Driessen, J. (2001) 'Centre and periphery: some observations on the administration of the kingdom of Knossos' in Voutsaki and Killen (2001), 96–112.

Duara, P. (1995) *Rescuing History from the Nation: Questioning Narratives of Modern China*. Chicago and London.

Dubois, L. (2004) *A Colony of Citizens: Revolution and Slave Emancipation in the French Caribbean, 1787–1804*. Chapel Hill, NC.

Dunbabin, T. J. (1948) *The Western Greeks*. Oxford.

Durey, M. (1997) *Transatlantic Radicals and the Early American Republic*. Lawrence, KA.

Dyke, R. M. van and Alcock, S. E. (eds.) (2003) *Archaeologies of Memory*. Malden, MA.

Easterling, P. (2005) 'The image of the polis in Greek tragedy' in Hansen (2005), 49–72.

Eder, W. (ed.) (1995) *Die athenische Demokratie im 4. Jahrhundert v. Chr. Vollendung oder Verfall einer Verfassungsform?* Stuttgart.

Effenterre, H. van and Ruzé, F. (1994) *Nomima I. Recueil d'inscriptions politiques et juridiques de l'Archaïsme grec*. Rome.

Ehrenberg, V. (1937) 'When did the polis rise?' reprinted in *Polis und Imperium. Beiträgen zur alten Geschichte*. Zürich and Stuttgart, 1965, 83–97.

  (1960) *The Greek State*. Trans. H. Mattingly and V. Ehrenberg. Oxford.

Ehrhardt, N. (1983) *Milet und seinen Kolonien. Vergleichende Untersuchungen der kultischen und politischen Einrichtungen*. Frankfurt am Main, Berne and New York.

Elayi, J. (1987) *Recherches sur les cités phéniciennes à l'époque perse*. Naples.

  (1988) *Pénétration grecque en Phénicie sous l'Empire perse*. Nancy.

Empereur, J. Y. and Garlan, Y. (eds.) (1986) *Recherches sur les amphores grecques (BCH Supplément XIII)*. Paris.

Empereur, J. Y., Hesse, A. and Tuna, N. (1999) 'Les ateliers d'amphores de Datça, péninsule de Cnide' in Garlan (1999a), 105–15.

Empereur, J. Y. and Picon, M. (1986) 'Des ateliers d'amphores à Paros et à Naxos', *BCH* 110: 495–511.

Engberg-Pedersen, T. (1993) 'The relationship between cultural and political centres in the Hellenistic world' in Bilde *et al.* (1993), 285–315.

Ericson, B. (2005) 'Archaeology of empire: Athens and Crete in the fifth century BC', *AJA* 109: 619–63.

Etienne, R. (1985) 'Le capital immobilier dans les Cyclades à l'époque hellénistique' in Leveau (1985), 55–67.

  (1990) *Tenos II: Tenos et les Cyclades du milieu du IV s. av. J. C. au milieu du III s. ap. J. C.* Rome.

Fabbrini, F. (1983) *Translatio imperii. L'impero universale da Ciro ad Augusto*. Rome.

Fantasia, U. (1993) 'Grano siciliano in Grecia nel V e IV secolo', *ASNP* 23: 9–31.

Fears, J. R. (1990): 'M. Rostovtzeff' in *Classical Scholarship: A Biographical Encyclopedia*, ed. W. W. Briggs and W. M. Calder III. New York.

Fedi, L. (2000) 'La contestation du miracle grec chez Auguste Comte' in Avlami (2000a), 157–92.

Finley M. I. (Moses)

252   *References*

Figueira, T. (1981) *Aegina. Society and Politics*. New York.
   (1998) *The Power of Money: Coinage and Politics in the Athenian Empire*. Philadelphia.
Finet, A. (ed.) (1975) *La voix de l'opposition en Mésopotamie*. Brussels.
   (ed.) (1982) *Les pouvoirs locaux en Mésopotamie et dans les régions adjacentes*. Brussels.
Finley, M. I. (1957/8) 'Mycenaean palace archives and economic history' republished in Finley (1981a), 213–32.
   (1963a) 'Generalizations in ancient history' reprinted in Finley (1986a), 60–74.
   (1963b) *The Ancient Greeks*. London.
   (1970) *Early Greece: The Bronze and Archaic Ages*. London.
   (1973a) *Democracy Ancient and Modern*. New Brunswick.
   (1973b) *The Ancient Economy*. Berkeley and Los Angeles.
   (1977) 'The ancient city: from Fustel de Coulanges to Max Weber and beyond' republished in Finley (1981a), 3–23.
   (1979) *Ancient Sicily*. 2nd edn. London.
   (1981a) *Economy and Society in Ancient Greece*. London.
   (ed.) (1981b) 'Politics and political theory' in *The Legacy of Greece: A New Appraisal*, ed. M. I. Finley. Oxford: 22–64.
   (1982) 'Documents' reprinted in Finley (1985d), 27–46.
   (1983) *Politics in the Ancient World*. London.
   (1985a) 'Max Weber and the Greek city-state' in Finley (1985d), 88–103.
   (1985b) *The Ancient Economy*. 2nd edn. Berkeley and Los Angeles.
   (1985c) 'The ancient historian and his sources' in Finley (1985d), 7–26.
   (1985d) *Ancient History: Evidence and Models*. London.
   (1986a) *The Use and Abuse of History*. 2nd edn. London.
   (1986b) 'Anthropology and the classics' in Finley (1986a), 102–19.
Fisher, N. and Wees, H. van (eds.) (1998) *Archaic Greece: New Approaches and New Evidence*. London.
Flemming, D. E. (2004) *Democracy's Ancient Ancestors: Mari and Early Collective Governance*. Cambridge.
Flensted-Jensen, P. (ed.) (2000a) *Further Studies in the Ancient Greek Polis*. Copenhagen.
   (2000b) 'The Chalkidic peninsula and its regions' in Flensted-Jensen (2000a), 121–31.
Flensted-Jensen, P., Nielsen, T. H. and Rubinstein, L. (eds.) (2000) *Polis and Politics. Studies in Ancient Greek History Presented to Mogens Herman Hansen on his Sixtieth Birthday*. Copenhagen.
Fletcher, R. (1992) 'Time perspectivism, *Annales* and the potential of archaeology' in Knapp (1992), 35–49.
Fontana, J. (1995) *The Distorted Past. A Reinterpretation of Europe*. Trans. C. Smith. Oxford.
Forbes, D. (1952) *The Liberal Anglican Idea of History*. Cambridge.
Forment, C. A. (2003) *Democracy in Latin America, 1760–1900. I: Civic Selfhood and Public Life in Mexico and Peru*. Chicago and London.

Fontana

Fornara, C. W. (1983) *The Nature of History in Ancient Greece and Rome*. Berkeley, Los Angeles and London.

Fornis, C. (1997) 'La polis como metrópolis: Tucídides y el imperio colonial corintio' in Plácido *et al.* (1997), 63–87.

Foster, B. (1981) 'A new look at the Sumerian temple state', *JESHO* 24: 225–41.

Foxhall, L. (1990) 'The dependent tenant: land leasing and labour in Italy and Greece', *Journal of Roman Studies* 80: 97–114.

(1992) 'The control of the Attic landscape' in Wells (1992), 155–9.

(1998) 'Cargoes of the heart's desire: the character of trade in the archaic Mediterranean world' in Fisher and van Wees (1998), 295–309.

Frangakis-Syrett, E. (1992) *The Commerce of Smyrna in the Eighteenth Century (1700–1820)*. Athens.

Freitag, K. (2000) *Der Golf von Korinth. Historisch-topographische Untersuchungen von der Archaik bis in das 1. Jh. v. Chr.* Munich.

Fritz, K. von (1940) *Pythagorean Politics in Southern Italy: An Analysis of the Sources*. New York.

(1954) *The Theory of the Mixed Constitution in Antiquity. A Critical Analysis of Polybius' Political Ideas*. New York.

(1956) 'Die Bedeutung des Aristoteles für die Geschichtsschreibung' in *Histoire et historiens dans l'antiquité, Entretiens Hardt IV*. Geneva: 83–128.

Fuhrmann, M. (1979) 'Die "Querelle des anciens et des modernes", der Nationalismus und die deutsche Klassik' in *Classical Influences on Western Thought, A.D. 1650–1870*, ed. R. R. Bolgar. Cambridge: 107–29.

Fuks, A. (1984) 'Redistribution of land and houses in Syracuse in 356 B.C. and its ideological aspects' republished in A. Fuks, *Social Conflict in Ancient Greece*. Leiden: 213–29.

Funke, P. (1991) 'Zur Ausbildung städtischer Siedlungszentren in Aitolien' in Olshausen and Sonnabend (1991), 313–35.

(1996) 'Ē Arxaia Ellada: ena apotychêmeno ethnos? Zêtêmata proslêpsês kai ermêneias tês archaias ellênikês istorias stên germanikê istoriographia tou 19ou aiôna' in *Enas neos kosmos gennietai. Ē eikona tou ellênikou politismou stê germanikê epistêmê kata ton 19o aiôna*, ed. E. Chrysos. Athens: 83–105.

(1997) 'Polisgenese und Urbanisierung in Aitolien im 5. und 4. Jh. v. Chr.' in Hansen (1997d), 145–88.

(1999) 'Peraia: Einige Überlegungen zum Festlandbesitz griechischer Inselstaaten' in *Hellenistic Rhodes: Politics, Culture and Society*, ed. V. Gabrielsen, P. Bilde, T. Engberg-Pedersen, L. Hannestad and J. Zahle. Aarhus: 55–75.

Furet, F. (1984) 'From narrative history to problem-oriented history' reprinted in *In the Workshop of History*. Trans. J. Mendelbaum. Chicago and London: 54–67.

Gabrielsen, V. (1994) *Financing the Athenian Fleet. Public Taxation and Social Relations*. Baltimore.

(1997) *The Naval Aristocracy of Hellenistic Rhodes*. Aarhus.

(2001a) 'Naval warfare: its economic and social impact on ancient Greek cities' in *War as a Cultural and Social Force. Essays on Warfare in Antiquity*, ed. T. Bekker-Nielsen and L. Hannestad. Copenhagen: 72–89.

(2001b) 'The Rhodian associations and economic activity' in Archibald *et al.* (2001), 215–44.

Galaty, M. L. and Parkinson, W. A. (eds.) (1999) *Rethinking Mycenaean Palaces. New Interpretations of an Old Idea.* Los Angeles.

Gale, N. H. (1991) 'Copper oxhide ingots: their origin and their place in the Bronze Age metals trade in the Mediterranean' in *Bronze Age Trade in the Mediterranean*, ed. N. H. Gale. Jonsered: 197–239.

Garlan, Y. (1974) *Recherches de poliorcétique grecque.* Athens.

(1988) *Vin et amphores de Thasos.* Athens.

(ed.) (1999a) *Production et commerce des amphores anciennes en Mer Noire.* Aix-en-Provence.

(1999b) 'Production et commerce des amphores: contribution à l'étude du territoire des cités grecques' in Brunet (1999), 371–85.

(2000a) *Amphores et timbres amphoriques grecs: entre érudition et idéologie.* Paris.

(2000b) 'La démocratie grecque vue par Condorcet' in Avlami (2000a), 55–69.

Garland, R. (1987) *The Piraeus: From the Fifth to the First Century BC.* London.

Garnsey, P. (1988) *Famine and Food Supply in the Graeco-Roman World: Responses to Risk and Crisis.* Cambridge.

Garnsey, P., Hopkins, K. and Whittaker, C. R. (eds.) (1983) *Trade in the Ancient Economy.* London.

Gauthier, P. (1973) 'A propos des clérouques athéniennes au Ve siècle' in *Problèmes de la terre en Grèce ancienne*, ed. M. I. Finley. Paris: 163–86.

(1980) 'Etudes sur des inscriptions d'Amorgos', *BCH* 104: 197–220.

(1982) 'Les villes athéniennes et un décret pour un commerçant (*Inscriptiones Graecae*, II², 903)', *REG* 95: 275–96.

(1985) *Les cités grecques et leurs bienfaiteurs.* Paris.

(1987/9) 'Grandes et petites cités: hégémonie et autarcie', *Opus* 6–8: 187–202.

(1988) 'Poleis hellénistiques: deux notes', *EMC* 32: 329–52.

(1993) 'Les cités hellénistiques' in Hansen (1993), 211–31.

Gawantka, W. (1985) *Die sogenannte Polis: Entstehung, Geschichte und Kritik der modernen althistorischen Grundbegriffe der griechische Staat, die griechische Staatsidee, die Polis.* Stuttgart.

(1990) '"Die Monumente reden". Realien, reales Leben, Wirklichkeit in der deutschen Alten Geschichte und Altertumskunde des neunzehnten Jahrhunderts' in *Heinrich Schliemann nach hundert Jahren*, ed. W. M. Calder III and J. Cobet. Frankfurt: 56–117.

Gehrke, H.-J. (1986) *Jenseits von Athen und Sparta. Das dritte Griechenland und seine Staatenwelt.* Munich.

(1991) 'Karl Otfried Müller und das Land der Griechen', *Athenische Mitteilungen* 106: 9–35.

Gellner, E. (1983) *Nations and Nationalism.* Oxford.

Genovese, E. and Hochberg, L. (eds.) (1989) *Geographic Perspectives in History.* Oxford.

Geuss, R. (2001) *History and Illusion in Politics.* Cambridge.

Giangiulio, M. (1996) 'Avventurieri, mercanti, coloni, merecenari. Mobilità umana e circolazione di risorse nel Mediterraneo arcaico' in Settis (1996), 497–525.

Giardina, A. and Schiavone, A. (eds.) (1981) *Società romana e produzione schiavistica, I–III*. Rome.

Gilpin, R. (1981) *War and Change in World Politics*. Cambridge.

Gilroy, P. (1993) *The Black Atlantic: Modernity and Double Consciousness*. London.

Ginzburg, C. (1980) *The Cheese and the Worms: The Cosmos of a Sixteenth-Century Miller*. Trans. J. and A. Tedeschi. London.

(1982) 'Mostrare e dimostrare: Risposta a Pinelli e altri critici', *Quaderni Storici* 50: 703–10.

Giovannini, A. (1971) *Untersuchungen über die Natur und die Anfänge der bundesstaatlichen Sympolitie in Griechenland*. Göttingen.

Gledhill, J. and Larsen, M. (1982) 'The Polanyi paradigm and a dynamic analysis of archaic states' in *Theory and Explanation in Archaeology*, ed. C. Renfrew, M. J. Rowlands and B. A. Segraves. New York and London: 197–229.

Glotz, G. (1928) *La cité grecque*. Paris.

(1936) *Histoire grecque, III*. Paris.

Goitein, S. D. (1967–93) *A Mediterranean Society: The Jewish Communities of the Arab World as Portrayed in the Documents of the Cairo Geniza, I–VI*. Berkeley.

Goldsmith, M. M. (1987) 'Liberty, luxury and the pursuit of happiness' in Pagden (1987), 225–51.

Gomme, A. W. (1937) 'Traders and manufacturers in Greece' in A. W. Gomme, *Essays in Greek History and Literature*. New York: 42–66.

Gooch, G. P. (1913) *History and Historians in the Nineteenth Century*. London.

Gossman, L. (1983) *Orpheus Philologus. Bachofen versus Mommsen on the Study of Antiquity*. Philadelphia.

(1990) *Between History and Literature*. Cambridge, MA, and London.

(2000) *Basel in the Age of Burckhardt. A Study in Unreasonable Ideas*. Chicago.

Graf F. (1985) *Nordionische Kulte. Religionsgeschichtliche und epigraphische Untersuchungen zu den Kulten von Chios, Erythrai, Klazomenai und Phokaia*. Rome.

Grafton, A. (1981) 'Prolegomena to Friedrich August Wolf' republished in Grafton (1991), 214–43.

(1987) 'Portrait of Justus Lipsius' republished in Grafton (2001), 227–43.

(1991) *Defenders of the Text: The Traditions of Scholarship in an Age of Science, 1450–1800*. Cambridge, MA.

(1992) 'Germany and the West, 1830–1900' in Dover (1992), 225–45.

(1999) 'An introduction to the *New Science* of Giambattista Vico' republished in Grafton (2001), 259–78.

(2001) *Bring out your Dead. The Past as Revelation*. Cambridge, MA, and London.

Graham, A. J. (1983) *Colony and Mother City in Ancient Greece*. 2nd edn. Chicago.

Gras, M. (1985) *Trafics tyrrhéniens archaïques*. Rome.

(1991) 'Occidentalia. Le concept d'émigration ionienne', *Archeologia Classica* 43: 269–78.

(1993) 'Pour une Méditerranée des emporia' in Bresson and Rouillard (1993), 103–11.

(1995a) 'La Méditerranée occidentale, milieu d'échanges: un regard historio-graphique', in *Les Grecs et l'Occident, actes du colloque de la Villa 'Kérylos'*. Paris: 109–21.

(1995b) *La Méditerranée archaïque*. Paris.

(1997) 'L'Occidente e i suoi conflitti' in Settis (1997), 61–85.

Gras, M., Rouillard, P. and Teixidor, J. (1989) *L'univers phénicien*. Paris.

Greco, E. and Torelli, M. (1983) *Storia dell'urbanistica: il mondo greco*. Rome.

Greengus, S. (1995) 'Legal and social institutions of Ancient Mesopotamia' in *Civilizations of the Ancient Near East, I*, ed. J. Sasson. New York: 469–84.

Grell, C. (1993) *L'histoire entre érudition et philosophie: étude sur la connaissance historique à l'âge des Lumières*. Paris.

(1995) *Le dix-huitième siècle et l'antiquité en France 1680–1789, I–II*. Oxford.

Griffeth, R. and Thomas, C. G. (eds.) (1981) *The City-State in Five Cultures*. Santa Barbara, CA.

Griffiths, G. (1981) 'The Italian city-state' in Griffeth and Thomas (1981), 71–108.

Gruen, E. S. (1993) 'The polis in the Hellenistic world' in *Nomodeiktes. Greek Studies in Honour of Martin Ostwald*, ed. R. M. Rosen and J. Farrell. Ann Arbor, MI: 339–54.

Gschnitzer, F. (1958) *Abhängige Orte im griechischen Altertum*. Munich.

(1991) 'Zum Verhältnis von Siedlung, Gemeinde und Staat in der Griechischen Welt' in Olshausen and Sonnabend (1991), 429–42.

Guerci, L. (1979) *Liberta degli Antichi e liberta dei moderni. Sparta, Atene e i 'philosophes' nella Francia del 700*. Naples.

Guha, R. (2002) *History at the Limit of World-History*. New York.

Habicht, C. (1997) *Athens from Alexander to Anthony*. Trans. D. L. Schneider. Cambridge, MA, and London.

Hadjidaki, E. (1996) 'Underwater excavations of a late fifth-century merchant ship at Alonnesos, Greece: the 1991–1993 seasons', *BCH* 120: 561–93.

Hagemajer Allen, K. (2003) 'Becoming the "Other": attitudes and practices at the Attic cemeteries' in Dougherty and Kurke (2003a), 207–36.

Haggis, D. C. (1999) 'Some problems in defining Dark Age society in the Aegean' in Betancourt *et al.* (1999), 303–8.

Hall, E. (1989) *Inventing the Barbarian: Greek Self-Definition through Tragedy*. Oxford.

Hall, J. A. (ed.) (1986) *States in History*. Oxford.

Hall, J. M. (1997) *Ethnic Identity in Greek Antiquity*. Cambridge.

(2000) 'Sparta, Lakedaimon and the nature of perioikic dependency' in Flensted-Jensen (2000a), 73–89.

(2002) *Hellenicity. Between Ethnicity and Culture*. Chicago and London.

Hallo, W. W. (1983) 'The first Purim', *Biblical Archaeologist* 46: 19–26.

Halstead, P. (1988) 'On redistribution and the origins of Minoan–Mycenaean palatial economies' in *Problems in Greek Prehistory*, ed. E. B. French and K. A. Wardle. Bristol: 519–30.

Hansen.M. H

(1994) 'The north–south divide: regional paths to complexity in prehistoric Greece' in *Development and Decline in the Mediterranean Bronze Age*, ed. C. Mathers and S. Stoddart. Sheffield: 195–219.

Hammer, D. (2002) *The Iliad as Politics. The Performance of Political Thought*. Norman, OK.

(2004) 'Ideology, the symposium and archaic politics', *AJPh* 125: 479–512.

Hammond, N. G. L. (1959) *A History of Greece to 322 BC*. Oxford.

(1967) *Epirus: The Geography, the Ancient Remains, the History and the Topography of Epirus and Adjacent Areas*. Oxford.

Hansen, M. H. (1991) *The Athenian Democracy in the Age of Demosthenes. Structure, Principles and Ideology*. Oxford.

(ed.) (1993) *The Ancient Greek City-State*. Copenhagen.

(1994) 'Poleis and city-states, 600–323 B.C. A comprehensive research programme' in *From Political Architecture to Stephanus Byzantius. Sources for the Ancient Greek Polis*, ed. D. Whitehead. Stuttgart: 9–17.

(1995a) 'Kome. A study in how the Greeks designated classified settlements which were not poleis' in Hansen and Raaflaub (1995), 45–81.

(1995b) 'The autonomous city-state. Ancient fact or modern fiction?' in Hansen and Raaflaub (1995), 21–43.

(ed.) (1995c) *Sources for the Ancient Greek City-State*. Copenhagen.

(1995d) 'Boiotian poleis. A test case' in Hansen (1995c), 13–63.

(1996a) 'An inventory of Boiotian poleis in the archaic and classical periods' in Hansen (1996c), 73–116.

(1996b) 'Aristotle's two complementary views of the Greek polis' in *Transitions to Empire. Essays in Greco-Roman History, 360–146 BC, in Honour of E. Badian*, ed. R. W. Wallace and E. M. Harris. Norman, OK, and London: 195–210.

(ed.) (1996c) *Introduction to an Inventory of Poleis*. Copenhagen.

(1997a) 'The polis as an urban centre. The literary and epigraphical evidence' in Hansen (1997d), 9–86.

(1997b) 'A typology of dependent poleis' in Nielsen (1997), 29–37.

(1997c) 'Were the Boiotian *Poleis* deprived of their *Autonomia*?' in Nielsen (1997), 127–36.

(ed.) (1997d) *The Polis as an Urban Centre and as a Political Community*. Copenhagen.

(1997e) 'Emporion. A study of the use and meaning of the term in the archaic and classical periods' in Nielsen (1997), 83–105.

(1998) *Polis and City-State. An Ancient Concept and its Modern Equivalent*. Copenhagen.

(2000a) 'Introduction. The concepts of city-state and city-state culture' in Hansen (2000c), 11–34.

(2000b) 'The Hellenic polis' in Hansen (2000c), 141–87.

(ed.) (2000c) *A Comparative Study of Thirty City-State Cultures*. Copenhagen.

(2002) 'Was the polis a state or a stateless society?' in Nielsen (2002b), 17–47.

(2003) 'Ninety-five theses about the Greek polis in the archaic and classical periods. A report on the results obtained by the Copenhagen Polis Centre in the period 1993–2003', *Historia* 52: 257–82.

(2004a) 'The concept of the consumption city applied to the Greek polis' in Nielsen (2004), 9–47.

(2004b) 'Was every polis centred on a polis town?' in Nielsen (2004), 131–47.

(2004c) 'The perioikic poleis of Lakedaimon' in Nielsen (2004), 149–64.

(ed.) (2005) *The Imaginary Polis*. Copenhagen.

Hansen, M. H. and Nielsen, T. H. (eds.) (2004) *An Inventory of Archaic and Classical Poleis*. Oxford and New York.

Hansen, M. H. and Raaflaub, K. (eds.) (1995) *Studies in the Ancient Greek Polis*. Stuttgart.

(eds.) (1996) *More Studies in the Ancient Greek Polis*. Copenhagen.

Hanson, V. D. (2002) *Why the West Has Won: Carnage and Culture from Salamis to Vietnam*. London.

(2004) *Between War and Peace: Lessons from Afghanistan to Iraq*. New York.

Hanson, V. D. and Heath, J. (1998) *Who Killed Homer? The Demise of Classical Education and the Recovery of Greek Wisdom*. New York.

Harris, R. (1975) *Ancient Sippar. A Demographic Study of an Old Babylonian City (1894–1595 BC)*. Istanbul.

Harris, W. V. (ed.) (2005) *Rethinking the Mediterranean*. Oxford.

Hartog, F. (1986) 'Les Grecs égyptologues', *Annales. Economies, Sociétés, Civilisations* 41: 953–67.

(1988a) *The Mirror of Herodotus: The Representation of the Other in the Writing of History*. Trans. J. Lloyd. Berkeley.

(1988b) *Le XIXe siècle et l'histoire. Le cas Fustel de Coulanges*. Paris.

(2000) 'La Révolution française et l'Antiquité. Avenir d'une illusion ou cheminement d'un quiproquo?' in Avlami (2000a), 7–46.

Harvey, F. D. (1965/6) 'Two kinds of equality', *Classica et Mediaevalia* 26/7: 101–46.

Hasebroek, J. (1933) *Trade and Politics in Ancient Greece*. Trans. L. M. Fraser and D. C. Macgregor. London.

Haskell, F. (1991) 'Winckelmann et son influence sur les historiens' in *Winckelmann: la naissance de l'histoire de l'art à l'époque des Lumières*, ed. E. Pommier. Paris: 85–99.

Haubold, J. (2005) 'The Homeric polis' in Hansen (2005), 25–48.

Hawthorn, G. (1991) *Plausible Worlds. Possibility and Understanding in History and the Social Sciences*. Cambridge.

Hedrick, C. W. Jr (1994) 'The zero degree of society: Aristotle and the Athenian citizen' in *Athenian Political Thought and the Reconstruction of American Democracy*, ed. J. P. Euben, J. R. Wallach and J. Ober. Ithaca, NY, and London: 289–318.

Heilbron, J. (1995) *The Rise of Social Theory*. Trans. S. Gogol. Cambridge.

Held, D. (1995) *Democracy and the Global Order. From the Modern State to Cosmopolitan Governance*. Cambridge.

Henshall, N. (1992) *The Myth of Absolutism. Change and Continuity in Early Modern European Monarchy.* London.

Herman, G. (1987) *Ritualised Friendship and the Greek City.* Cambridge.

Herring, E. (1991) 'Socio-political change in the south Italian Iron Age and classical periods: an application of the peer polity interaction model', *Accordia Research Papers* 2: 31–54.

Heskel, J. (1997) *The North Aegean Wars, 371–360 BC.* Stuttgart.

Heuss, A. (1989) 'Institutionalisierung der Alten Geschichte' reprinted in *Gesammelte Schriften in 3 Bänden.* Stuttgart, 1995, 1938–70.

Hicks, P. S. (1996) *Neo-Classical History and English Culture: From Clarendon to Hume.* New York.

Hobden, S. (1998) *International Relations and Historical Sociology: Breaking down Boundaries.* London.

Hobden, S. and Hobson, J. M. (eds.) (2001) *Historical Sociology of International Relations.* Cambridge.

Hobsbawm, E. (1962) *The Age of Revolution: Europe, 1789–1848.* London.

(1994) *Age of Extremes: The Short Twentieth Century, 1914–1991.* London.

(1997) 'Barbarism: a user's guide' in E. Hobsbawm, *On History.* London: 334–50.

Hodkinson, S. and Hodkinson, H. (1981) 'Mantineia and the Mantinike: settlement and society in a Greek polis', *BSA* 76: 239–96.

Hoffman, G. L. (1997) *Imports and Immigrants: Near Eastern Contacts with Iron Age Crete.* Ann Arbor, MI.

Hofstetter, J. (1978) *Die Griechen in Persien. Prosopographie der Griechen im persischen Reich vor Alexander.* Berlin.

Hont, I. and Ignatieff, M. (eds.) (1983) *Wealth and Virtue: The Shaping of Political Economy in the Scottish Enlightenment.* Cambridge.

Hooker, J. T. (1979) 'The wanax in Linear B texts', *Kadmos* 18: 100–11.

(1987) 'Minoan and Mycenaean administrations: a comparison of the Knossos and Pylos archives' in *The Function of the Minoan Palaces,* ed. R. Hägg and N. Marinatos. Stockholm: 313–15.

(1988) 'Titles and functions in the Pylian state', *Minos* 20–2: 257–67.

Hopkins, K. (1978) *Conquerors and Slaves.* Cambridge.

(1983) 'Introduction' in Garnsey *et al.* (1983), ix–xxv.

(1999) *A World Full of Gods: Pagans, Jews and Christians in the Roman Empire.* London.

Horden, P. and Purcell, N. (2000) *The Corrupting Sea. A Study of Mediterranean History.* Oxford.

Hornblower, S. (1982) *Mausolus.* Oxford.

(1983) *The Greek World, 479–323 BC.* London.

(2002) *The Greek World, 479–323 BC.* 3rd edn. London.

Hudson, M. and Levine, B. A. (eds.) (1996) *Privatization in the Ancient Near East and the Classical World.* Cambridge, MA.

Huffman, C. A. (2005) *Archytas of Tarentum: Pythagorean, Philosopher and Mathematician King.* Cambridge.

Humphreys, S. C. (1978) *Anthropology and the Greeks*. London.

Hunter, V. (1982) *Past and Process in Herodotus and Thucydides*. Princeton, NJ.

(1994) *Policing Athens. Social Control in the Attic Lawsuits, 420–320 BC*. Princeton, NJ.

Huntington, S. P. (1998) *The Clash of Civilisations and the Remaking of World Order*. London.

Huppert, G. (1970) *The Idea of Perfect History. Historical Erudition and Historical Philosophy in Renaissance France*. Urbana, IL.

Huxley, G. L. (1972) 'On Aristotle's historical methods', *GRBS* 13: 157–69.

(1973) 'Aristotle as antiquary', *GRBS* 14: 271–86.

Iggers, G. G. (1968) *The German Conception of History: The National Tradition of Historical Thought from Herder to the Present*. Middletown, CT.

(1984) *New Directions in European Historiography*. 2nd edn. London.

Iggers, G. G. and Powell, J. M. (eds.) (1990) *Leopold von Ranke and the Shaping of the Historical Discipline*. Syracuse, NY.

Inden, R. (1990) *Imagining India*. Oxford.

Isaac, B. (1986) *The Greek Settlements in Thrace until the Macedonian Conquest*. Leiden.

Isager, S. and Skydsgaard, J. E. (1992) *Ancient Greek Agriculture. An Introduction*. London.

Jacoby, D. (1994) 'The migration of merchants and craftsmen: a Mediterranean perspective (12th – 15th century)' in *Le migrazioni in Europa, secc. XIII–XVIII*, ed. S. Cavaciocchi. Florence: 533–60.

Jameson, M., Runnels, C. N. and Andel, T. H. van (eds.) (1994) *A Greek Countryside: The Southern Argolid from Prehistory to the Present Day*. Stanford, CA.

Janni, P. (1968) 'Romanticismo e unità della Doricità: K. O. Müller', *Studi Germanici* 6.3: 13–43.

Janssen, E. M. (1979) *J. Burckhardt und die Griechen*. Assen.

Jones, A. H. M. (1940) *The Greek City from Alexander to Justinian*. Oxford.

Jones, N. F. (1999) *The Associations of Classical Athens. The Response to Democracy*. New York and Oxford.

(2004) *Rural Athens under the Democracy*. Philadelphia.

Jones, P. (1997) *The Italian City-State: From Commune to Signoria*. Oxford.

Jong, I. J. F. de (2002) 'Narrative unity and units' in *Brill's Companion to Herodotus*, ed. E. J. Bakker, I. J. F. de Jong and H. van Wees. Leiden, Boston, MA, and Cologne: 245–66.

Jongman, W. (1988) *The Economy and Society of Pompeii*. Amsterdam.

Jost, M. (1986) 'Villages de l'Arcadie antique', *Ktèma* 11: 145–58.

(1999) 'Les schémas de peuplement de l'Arcadie aux époques archaïque et classique' in Nielsen and Roy (1999), 192–247.

Kahrstedt, U. (1934) *Staatsgebiet und Staatsangehörige in Athen. Studien zum öffentlichen Recht Athens, Teil I*. Stuttgart and Berlin.

Karadima-Matsa, Ch. (1994) 'Ergastêrio paragôgês amphoreôn stê Samothrakê' in *III Epistemonikê synantêsê gia tên ellênistikê keramikê*. Salonica: 355–62.

Kardasis, V. (2001) *Diaspora Merchants in the Black Sea: The Greeks in Southern Russia, 1775–1861*. Lanham, MD.

Katz, M. (1999) 'Women and democracy in ancient Greece' in *Contextualising Classics: Ideology, Performance, Dialogue. Essays in Honour of John J. Peradotto*, ed. T. M. Falkner, N. Felson and D. Konstan. Lanham, MD: 41–68.

Kaviraj, S. and Khilnani, S. (eds.) (2001) *Civil Society: History and Possibilities*. Cambridge.

Kaye, H. J. (1984) *The British Marxist Historians. An Introductory Analysis*. London.

Keen, A. G. (2002) 'The *poleis* of the southern Anatolian coast (Lycia, Pamphylia, Pisidia) and their civic identity: the "interface" between the Hellenic and the barbarian *Polis*' in Tsetskhladze and Snodgrass (2002), 27–40.

Kelley, D. R. (1970) *Foundations of Modern Historical Scholarship. Language, Law and History in the French Renaissance*. New York and London.

Kelley, R. D. G. (2002) 'How the West was one. The African diaspora and the re-mapping of U.S. history' in Bender (2002a), 123–47.

Keswani, P. S. (1996) 'Hierarchies, heterarchies and urbanization processes: the view from Bronze Age Cyprus', *JMA* 9.2: 211–50.

Kiechle, F. K. (1979) 'Korkyra und der Handelsweg durch das adriatische Meer im 5. Jhr. v. Chr.', *Historia* 28: 173–91.

Kingsley, P. (1995) *Ancient Philosophy, Mystery and Magic. Empedocles and the Pythagorean Tradition*. Oxford.

Kinser, S. (1981) 'Annaliste Paradigm? The geohistorical structuralism of Fernand Braudel', *AHR* 86: 63–105.

Kirsten, E. (1956) *Die griechische Polis als historisch-geographisches Problem des Mittelmeerraumes*. Bonn.

Klein, K. L. (1995) 'In search of narrative mastery: postmodernism and the people without history', *H&T* 34: 275–98.

Klempt, A. (1960) *Die Säkularisierung der universalhistorischen Auffaschung. Zum Wandel des Geschichtsdenkens im 16. und 17. Jahrhundert*. Göttingen, Berlin and Frankfurt am Main.

Knapp, A. B. (ed.) (1992) *Archaeology, Annales and Ethnohistory*. Cambridge.

(1993) 'Thalassocracies in Bronze Age Eastern Mediterranean trade: making and breaking a myth', *WA* 24: 332–47.

Koebner, R. (1951) 'Despot and despotism: vicissitudes of a term', *Journal of the Warburg and Courtauld Institute* 14: 275–302.

Koerner, R. (1993) *Inschriftliche Gesetzestexte der frühen griechischen Polis*. Cologne.

Koselleck, R. (1972) 'Einleitung' in *Geschichtliche Grundbegriffe. Historisches Lexikon zur politisch-sozialen Sprache in Deutschland, I*, ed. O. Brunner, W. Conze and R. Koselleck. Stuttgart: xiii–xxiii.

(1985) *Futures Past. On the Semantics of Historical Time*. Trans. K. Tribe. Cambridge, MA, and London.

Kraay, C. M. (1976) *Archaic and Classical Greek Coins*. London.

Kriedte, P. (1983) *Peasants, Landlords and Merchant Capitalists. Europe and the World Economy, 1500–1800*. Trans. V. R. Berghahn. Leamington Spa.

Kriedte, P., Medick, H. and Schlumbohm, J. (1981) *Industrialisation before Industrialisation: Rural Industry in the Genesis of Capitalism*. Trans. B. Schempp. Cambridge.

Krieger, L. (1989) *Time's Reasons: Philosophies of History Old and New*. Chicago and London.

Kryjickij, S. D. (1999) 'Les particularités de la colonisation grecque dans le territoire d'Olbia pontique' in Brunet (1999), 259–71.

Kuhrt, A. (1998) 'The Old Assyrian merchants' in Parkins and Smith (1998), 16–30.

Kuhrt A. and Sherwin-White, S. (eds.) (1987) *Hellenism and the East*. London.

Kullmann, W. (1992) *Il pensiero politico di Aristotele*. Milan.

Kurke, L. (1999) *Coins, Bodies, Games, and Gold: The Politics of Meaning in Archaic Greece*. Princeton, NJ.

Kuznetsov, V. D. (2001) 'Archaeological investigations in the Taman peninsula' in Tsetskhladze (2001), 319–44.

Kyrtatas, D. I. (2002) *Kataktôntas tên archaiotêta: istoriografikes diadromes*. Athens.

Lachmann, R. (2000) *Capitalists in Spite of Themselves: Elite Conflict and Economic Transitions in Early Modern Europe*. Oxford and New York.

Laffineur, R. and Niemeier, W. D. (eds.) (1995) *Politeia: Society and State in the Aegean Bronze Age (Aegaeum 12)*. Liege and Austin, TX.

Lambert, S. D. (1994) *Rationes Centesimarum. Sales of Public Land in Lykourgan Athens*. Amsterdam.

Lang, F. (1996) *Archaische Siedlungen in Griechenland: Struktur und Entwicklung*. Berlin.

Laronde, A. (1996) 'L'exploitation de la *chora* cyrénéenne à l'époque classique et hellénistique', *Comptes Rendus de l'Académie des Inscriptions*: 503–27.

Larsen, J. A. O. (1936) 'Perioeci in Crete', *CPh* 31: 11–22.

(1968) *Greek Federal States: Their Institutions and History*. Oxford.

Larsen, M. T. (1976) *The Old Assyrian City-State and its Colonies*. Copenhagen.

(1989) 'Orientalism and Near Eastern archaeology' in *Domination and Resistance*, ed. D. Miller, M. J. Rowlands and C. Tilley. London: 229–39.

(2000a) 'The city-states of the early Neo-Babylonian period' in Hansen (2000c), 117–27.

(2000b) 'The Old Assyrian city-state' in Hansen (2000c), 77–87.

Lavelle, B. M. (1992) 'The Pisistratids and the mines of Thrace', *GRBS* 33: 5–23.

Lefons, C. (1984) 'Jacob Burckhardt: della civilta comme cittadinanza', *ASNP* 14: 1337–84.

Lehmann, G. A. (2000) *Ansätze zu einer Theorie des Griechischen Bundesstaates bei Aristoteles und Polybios*. Göttingen.

Lekas, P. (1988) *Marx on Classical Antiquity. Problems of Historical Methodology*. Sussex and New York.

Lepore, E. (1968) 'Per una fenomenologia storica del rapporto citta-territorio in Magna Grecia' in *La citta e il suo territorio: atti del settimo convegno di studi sulla Magna Grecia*, ed. P. Romanelli. Naples: 29–66.

(1970) 'Strutture della colonizzazione focea in Occidente', *Parola del Passato* 25: 19–54.

Le Roy Ladurie, E. (1978) *Montaillou: Cathars and Catholics in a French Village 1294–1324.* Trans. B. Bray. London.

(1980) *Carnival in Romans. A People's Uprising at Romans, 1579–1580.* Trans. M. Feeney. Harmondsworth.

Leveau, P. (1984) 'La question de territoire et les sciences de l'Antiquité: la géographie historique, son évolution de la topographie à l'analyse de l'espace', *REA* 86: 5–115.

(ed.) (1985) *L'origine des richesses dépensées dans la ville antique.* Aix-en-Provence.

Lévêque, P. and Vidal-Naquet, P. (1996) *Cleisthenes the Athenian: An Essay on the Representation of Space and Time in Greek Political Thought from the End of the Sixth Century to the Death of Plato.* Trans. D. A. Curtis. Atlantic Highlands, NJ.

Levine, J. M. (1991) *The Battle of the Books: History and Literature in the Augustan Age.* Ithaca, NY.

Lévy, E. (1990) 'La cité grecque: invention moderne ou réalité antique?', *Cahiers du Centre G. Glotz* 1: 53–67.

Lewis, D. M. (1977) *Sparta and Persia.* Leiden.

(1997) 'Democratic institutions and their diffusion' republished in D. M. Lewis, *Selected Papers in Greek and Near Eastern History.* Cambridge and New York: 51–9.

Lewis, M. W. and Wigen, K. E. (1997) *The Myth of Continents. A Critique of Metageography.* Berkeley, Los Angeles and London.

Ligt, L. de (1991) 'Demand, supply, distribution: the Roman peasantry between town and countryside II: supply, distribution and a comparative perspective', *Münstersche Beiträge zur Antike Handelsgeschichte* 10: 33–77.

Linebaugh, P. and Rediker, M. (2000) *The Many Headed Hydra. Sailors, Slaves, Commoners and the Hidden History of the Revolutionary Atlantic.* Boston, MA.

Liverani, M. (1993) 'Nelle pieghe del despotismo: organismi rappresentivi nell' antico oriente', *Studi Storici* 34: 7–33.

(1997) 'The ancient Near Eastern city and modern ideologies' in *Die Orientalische Stadt: Kontinuität, Wandel, Bruch,* ed. G. Wilhelm. Saarbrücken: 85–107.

Livesey, J. (2001) *Making Democracy in the French Revolution.* Cambridge, MA, and London.

Lock, P. and Sanders, G. D. R. (eds.) (1996) *The Archaeology of Medieval Greece.* Oxford.

Lohmann, H. (1992) 'Agricultural and country life in classical Attica' in Wells (1992), 29–60.

(1993) *Atene: Forschungen zu Siedlungs- und Wirtschaftsstruktur der klassischen Attika.* Cologne.

(1995) 'Die Chora Athens im 4. Jahrhundert v. Chr.: Festungswesen, Bergbau und Siedlungen' in Eder (1995), 515–48.

Lomas, K. (2000) 'The polis in Italy: ethnicity, colonization and citizenship in the Western Mediterranean' in Brock and Hodkinson (2000), 167–85.

Lombardo, M. (1997) 'Circolazione monetaria e attività commerciali tra VI e IV secolo' in Settis (1997), 681–706.

(2000) 'Profughi e coloni dall'Asia Minore in Magna Grecia (VII–V sec A.C.)' in *Magna Grecia*, 189–224.

Lonis, R. (ed.) (1988) *L'étranger dans le monde grec*. Nancy.

Loomis, W. T. (1998) *Wages, Welfare Costs and Inflation in Classical Athens*. Ann Arbor, MI.

Loraux, N. (1991) 'Reflections of the Greek city on unity and division' in Molho *et al.* (1991), 33–51.

(2002) *The Divided City: On Memory and Forgetting in Ancient Athens*. Trans. C. Pache and J. Fort, New York.

Lordkipanidzé, O. and Lévêque, P. (eds.) (1990) *Le Pont-Euxin vu par les Grecs: sources écrites et archéologie*. Paris.

Lorenz, C. (1998) 'Can histories be true? Narrativism, positivism and the "metaphorical turn"', *H&T* 37: 309–29.

Losemann, V. (1998) 'Die Dorier im Deutschland der dreißiger und vierziger Jahre' in Calder and Schlesier (1998), 313–48.

Loukopoulou, L. D. (1989) *Contribution à l'histoire de la Thrace Propontique durant la période archaïque*. Athens.

Lucassen, J. (1995) 'Labour and early modern economic development' in *A Miracle Mirrored. The Dutch Republic in European Perspective*, ed. K. Davids and J. Lucassen. Cambridge: 367–409.

(2001) 'Mobilization of labour in early modern Europe' in Prak (2001a), 161–74.

Ludden, D. (ed.) (2002) *Reading Subaltern Studies. Critical History, Contested Meaning and the Globalisation of South Asia*. London.

Luraghi, N. and Alcock, S. E. (eds.) (2003) *Helots and their Masters in Laconia and Messenia: Histories, Ideologies, Structures*. Washington, DC.

Ma, J. (1999) *Antiochos III and the Cities of Western Asia Minor*. Oxford.

(2003) 'Peer–polity interaction in the Hellenistic age', *P&P* 180: 9–39.

McClellan, M. C. (1997) 'The economy of Hellenistic Egypt and Syria: an archaeological perspective' in *Ancient Economic Thought, I*, ed. B. B. Price. London and New York: 172–87.

MacDonald, B. R. (1981) 'The emigration of potters from Athens in the late fifth century B.C. and its effect on the Attic pottery industry', *AJA* 85: 159–68.

McInerney, J. (2000) *Under the Folds of Parnassos: Land and Ethnicity in Ancient Phokis*. Austin, TX.

McKechnie, P. (1989) *Outsiders in the Greek Cities in the Fourth Century BC*. London and New York.

Mackil, E. (2004) 'Wandering cities: alternatives to catastrophe in the Greek polis', *AJA* 108: 493–516.

Malkin, I. (1994a) 'Inside and outside: colonisation and the formation of the mother city' in *Apoikia: scritti in onore di Giorgio Buchner*, ed. B. d'Agostino and D. Ridgway. Naples: 1–9.

(1994b) *Myth and Territory in the Spartan Mediterranean*. Cambridge.

(ed.) (2001) *Ancient Perceptions of Greek Ethnicity*. Washington, DC.

(2002) 'Exploring the concept of "foundation": a visit to Megara Hyblaia' in *Oikistes. Studies in Constitutions, Colonies and Military Power in the Ancient*

World Offered in Honour of A. J. Graham, ed. V. B. Gorman and E. W. Robinson. Leiden: 195–225.

Mandelbaum, M. (1971) *History, Man and Reason. A Study in Nineteenth-Century Thought*. Baltimore and London.

Manni, E. (1962) 'Alessandro il Molosso e la sua spedizione in Italia', *Studi Salentine* 14: 344–52.

Manning, S. W. (1999) 'Knossos and the limits of settlement growth' in Betancourt *et al.* (1999), 469–80.

Manuel, F. E. (1959) *The Eighteenth Century Confronts the Gods*. Cambridge, MA.

Maran, J. (2000) 'Tiryns-Mauern und Paläste für namenlose Herrscher' in *Archäologische Entdeckungen. Die Forschungen des Deutschen Archäologischen Instituts im 20. Jahrhundert, I*, ed. K. Rheidt, A. Schöne-Denkinger and A. Nünnerich-Asmus. Mainz am Rhein: 118–23.

Marchand, S. L. (1996) *Down from Olympus. Archaeology and Philhellenism in Germany, 1750–1970*. Princeton, NJ.

Marinovic, L. P. (1988) *Le mercenariat grec au IVe siècle avant notre ère et la crise de la polis*. Trans. J. and Y. Garlan. Paris.

Martin, T. R. (1985) *Sovereignty and Coinage in Classical Greece*. Princeton, NJ.

Maslennikov, A. A. (2001) 'Some questions concerning the early history of the Bosporan state in the light of recent archaeological investigations in the eastern Crimea' in Tsetskhladze (2001), 247–60.

Mathieu, G. (1925) *Les idées politiques d'Isocrate*. Paris.

Mattingly, D. J. and Salmon, J. (eds.) (2001): *Economies beyond Agriculture in the Classical World*. London and New York.

Mattingly, D. J., Stone, D., Stirling, L. and Lazreg, N. B. (2001) 'Leptiminus (Tunisia): a "producer city"?' in Mattingly and Salmon (2001), 66–89.

Mayhew, R. (1997) *Aristotle's Criticism of Plato's Republic*. Oxford.

Mazarakis-Ainian, A. (1993) 'Epiphaneiakes ereynes stên nêso Kythno. To teichos tês archaias Kythnou', *AE*: 217–53.

(1998) 'Oropos in the early Iron Age' in *Euboica: l'Eubea e la presenza euboica in Calcidica e in Occidente*, ed. M. Bats and B. D'Agostino. Naples: 179–215.

Mbembe, A. (2001) 'At the edge of the world: boundaries, territoriality and sovereignty in Africa' in Appadurai (2001), 22–51.

Meadows, A. and Shipton, K. (eds.) (2001) *Money and its Uses in the Ancient Greek World*. Oxford and New York.

Mee, C. and Forbes, H. (eds.) (1997) *A Rough and Rocky Place: The Landscape and Settlement History of the Methana Peninsula, Greece*. Liverpool.

Meek, R. L. (1976) *Social Science and the Ignoble Savage*. Cambridge.

Meier, C. (1990) *The Greek Discovery of Politics*. Trans. D. McLintock. Cambridge, MA, and London.

(2005) *From Athens to Auschwitz: The Uses of History*. Trans. D. L. Schneider. Cambridge, MA.

Meier, C. and Rüsen, J. (eds.) (1988) *Historische Methode*. Munich.

Meiggs, R. (1972) *The Athenian Empire*. Oxford.

(1982) *Trees and Timber in the Ancient Mediterranean World*. Oxford.

Meiggs, R. and Lewis, D. (1969) *A Selection of Greek Historical Inscriptions to the End of the Fifth Century BC.* Oxford.

Meikle, S. (1995) *Aristotle's Economic Thought.* Oxford.

Meinecke, F. (1957) *Machiavellism: The Doctrine of 'Raison d'état' and its Place in Modern History.* Trans. D. Scott. London.

(1972) *Historism: The Rise of a New Historical Outlook.* Trans. J. E. Anderson. London.

Mele A. (1982) 'La Megale Hellas pitagorica; aspetti politici, economici e sociali' in *Megale Hellas: nomme e imagine. Atti del XXI Convegno di studi sulla Magna Grecia.* Taranto: 33–80.

Merrington, J. (1976) 'Town and country in the transition to capitalism' in *The Transition from Feudalism to Capitalism,* ed. R. Hilton. London: 170–95.

Meyer, E. (1907) *Geschichte des Altertums, I.* 2nd edn. Stuttgart and Berlin.

(1910) 'Zur Theorie und Methodik der Geschichte' in E. Meyer, *Kleine Schriften zur Geschichtstheorie und zur wirtschaftlichen und politischen Geschichte des Altertums.* Halle: 1–78.

Meyer, H.-C. and Moreno, A. (2004) 'A Greek metrological *koine*: a lead weight from the western Black Sea region in the Ashmolean Museum, Oxford', *OJA* 23: 209–16.

Meyer-Zwiffelhoffer, E. (1995) 'Alte Geschichte in der Universalgeschichtsschreibung der Frühen Neuzeit', *Saeculum* 46: 249–73.

Middleton, D. F. (1982) 'Thrasybulus' Thracian support', *CQ* 32: 298–303.

Mieroop, M. van de (1997a) 'Why did they write on clay?', *Klio* 79: 7–18.

(1997b) *The Ancient Mesopotamian City.* Oxford.

(1999a) *Cuneiform Texts and the Writing of History.* London.

(1999b) 'The government of an ancient Mesopotamian city: what we know and why we know so little' in *Priests and Officials in the Ancient Near East,* ed. K. Watanabe. Heidelberg: 139–61.

Miliori, M. (2000) 'Archaios Ellênismos kai Philellênismos stê Bretanikê istoriographia tou 19ou aiôna. Oi politikes kai êthikes diastaseis tou "ethnikou" kai oi eyryteres sêmasiodotêseis tês ellênikês istorias', *Mnêmôn* 20: 69–104.

Miller, M. C. (1997) *Athens and Persia in the Fifth Century BC: A Study in Cultural Receptivity.* Cambridge.

Millett, P. C. (n.d.) 'Alfred Zimmern's *Athenian Commonwealth* revisited'. Unpublished paper.

Mintz, S. W. (1985) *Sweetness and Power. The Place of Sugar in Modern History.* New York.

Mitchell, B. (2000) 'Cyrene: typical or atypical?' in Brock and Hodkinson (2000), 82–102.

Mitchell, L. G. and Rhodes, P. J. (eds.) (1997) *The Development of the Polis in Archaic Greece.* London.

Molho, A., Raaflaub, K. and Emlen, J. (eds.) (1991) *City States in Classical Antiquity and Medieval Italy.* Stuttgart.

Möller, A. (2000) *Naukratis: Trade in Archaic Greece.* Oxford and New York.

Momigliano, A. (1950) 'Ancient history and the antiquarian' reprinted in Momigliano (1966b), 1–39.

(1952) 'George Grote and the study of Greek history' reprinted in Momigliano (1966b), 56–74.

(1954) 'M. I. Rostovtzeff' reprinted in Momigliano (1966b), 91–104.

(1955) 'Introduction to the Griechische Kulturgeschichte by Jacob Burckhardt' reprinted in Momigliano (1977c), 295–303.

(1958) 'The place of Herodotus in the history of historiography' reprinted in Momigliano (1966b), 127–42.

(1966a) 'Giulio Beloch' trans. in Momigliano (1994), 97–120.

(1966b) *Studies in Historiography*. London.

(1970) 'La città antica di Fustel de Coulanges' trans. in Momigliano (1977c), 325–43.

(1975) 'The use of the Greeks' reprinted in Momigliano (1977c), 9–23.

(1977a) 'Max Weber and Eduard Meyer: apropos of city and country in antiquity' reprinted in Momigliano (1980b), 285–93.

(1977b) 'Eighteenth-century prelude to Mr. Gibbon' reprinted in Momigliano (1980b), 249–63.

(1977c) *Essays in Ancient and Modern Historiography*. Oxford.

(1980a) 'The place of ancient historiography in modern historiography' reprinted in Momigliano (1984c), 13–36.

(1980b) *Sesto contributo alla storia degli studi classici e del mondo antico*. Rome.

(1981) 'Premesse per una discussione su Eduard Meyer' trans. in Momigliano (1994), 209–22.

(1982a) 'The origins of universal history' reprinted in Momigliano (1984c), 77–103.

(1982b) 'New paths of classicism in the nineteenth century' reprinted in Momigliano (1994), 223–85.

(1984a) 'The rediscovery of Greek history in the eighteenth century: the case of Sicily' reprinted in Momigliano (1984c), 133–53.

(1984b) 'Premesse per una discussione su K. O. Müller', *ASNP* 14: 895–909.

(1984c) *Settimo contributo alla storia degli studi classici e del mondo antico*. Rome.

(1985) 'Un "Ritorno" alla etruscheria settecentesca: K. O. Müller' trans. in Momigliano (1994), 302–14.

(1990) *The Classical Foundations of Modern Historiography*. Berkeley and Los Angeles.

(1994) *Studies on Modern Scholarship*, ed. G. W. Bowersock and T. J. Cornell. Trans. T. J. Cornell. Berkeley and Los Angeles.

Mommsen, W. and Osterhammel, J. (eds.) (1989) *Max Weber and his Contemporaries*. London.

Monheit, M. L. (1997) 'Guillaume Bude, Andrea Alciato, Pierre de l'Estoile: Renaissance interpreters of Roman law', *JHI* 58: 21–40.

Montiglio, S. (2005) *Wandering in Ancient Greek Culture*. Chicago.

Moran, W. L. (1992) *The Amarna Letters*. Baltimore and London.

Morel, J.-P. (1966) 'Les Phocéens en Occident: certitudes et hypothèses', *Parola del Passato* 21: 378–420.

(1975) 'L'expansion phocéenne en Occident: dix années de recherches (1966–1975)', *BCH* 99: 853–96.
(1982) 'Les Phocéens d'Occident. Nouvelles données, nouvelles approches', *Parola del Passato* 38: 479–96.
(1983) 'Les relations économiques dans l'Occident grec' in *Modes et processus de transformation dans les sociétés antiques.* Pisa and Rome: 549–76.
(1985) 'La manufacture, moyen d'enrichissement dans l'Italie romaine?' in Leveau (1985), 87–111.
Moreland, J. F. (1992) 'Restoring the dialectic: settlement patterns and documents in medieval central Italy' in Knapp (1992), 112–29.
Morgan, C. (1990) *Athletes and Oracles: The Transformation of Olympia and Delphi in the Eighth Century BC.* Cambridge.
(1991) 'Ethnicity and early Greek states: historical and material perspectives', *PCPhS* 37: 131–63.
(2000) 'Politics without the polis: cities and the Achaean ethnos c. 800–500 BC' in Brock and Hodkinson (2000), 189–211.
(2001) 'Ethne, ethnicity and early Greek states, ca. 1200–480 BC: an archaeological perspective' in Malkin (2001), 75–112.
(2003) *Early Greek States beyond the Polis.* London and New York.
Morgan, C. and Coulton, J. J. (1997) 'The polis as a physical entity' in Hansen (1997d), 87–144.
Morgan, C. and Hall, J. (1996) 'Achaian poleis and Achaian colonization' in Hansen (1996c), 164–232.
Morley, N. (1996) *Metropolis and Hinterland. The City of Rome and the Italian Economy, 200 BC – AD 200.* Cambridge.
Morris, I. (1987) *Burial and Ancient Society: The Rise of the Greek City-State.* Cambridge.
(1991) 'The early polis as city and state' in Rich and Wallace-Hadrill (1991), 25–57.
(1992) *Death Ritual and Social Structure.* Cambridge.
(1994) 'Village society and the rise of the Greek state' in Doukellis and Mendoni (1994), 49–53.
(1997a) 'Periodisation and the heroes: inventing a Dark Age' in *Inventing Ancient Culture*, ed. M. Golden and P. Toohey. London: 96–131.
(1997b) 'An archaeology of equalities? The Greek city-states' in Nichols and Charlton (1997), 91–105.
(1998a) 'Remaining invisible. The archaeology of the excluded in classical Athens' in *Women and Slaves in Greco-Roman Culture: Differential Equations*, ed. S. Murnaghan and S. Joshel. New York: 193–220.
(1998b) 'Archaeology and archaic Greek history' in Fisher and van Wees (1998), 1–91.
(2000) *Archaeology as Cultural History. Words and Things in Iron Age Greece.* Oxford.
Morris, I. and Raaflaub, K. (eds.) (1997) *Democracy 2500?* Dubuque, IA.
Morris, S. P. and Papadopoulos, J. K. (2005) 'Greek towers and slaves: an archaeology of exploitation', *AJA* 109: 155–225.

Mortley, R. (1996) *The Idea of Universal History from Hellenistic Philosophy to Early Christian Historiography*. Lampeter.

Mossé, C. (1962) *La fin de la démocratie athénienne: aspects sociaux et politiques du déclin de la cité grecque au IVe siècle avant J.C.* Paris.

(1979) 'Citoyens actifs et citoyens "passifs" dans les cités grecques: une approche théorique du problème', *REA* 81: 141–9.

Most, G. W. (ed.) (2001) *Historicization – Historisierung*. Göttingen.

Muhlack, U. (1988) 'Von der philologischen zur historischen Methode' in Meier and Rüsen (1988), 154–80.

(1991) *Geschichtswissenschaft im Humanismus und in der Aufklärung. Die Vorgeschichte des Historismus*. Munich.

Muhlberger, S. and Paine, P. (1993) 'Democracy's place in world history', *Journal of World History* 4: 23–45.

Munz, P. (1997) 'The historical narrative' in *Companion to Historiography*, ed. M. Bentley. London and New York: 851–72.

Murray, O. (1980) *Early Greece*. London.

(1993) '*Polis* and *Politeia* in Aristotle' in Hansen (1993), 197–210.

(2000) 'What is Greek about the polis?' in Flensted-Jensen *et al.* (2000), 231–44.

(2005) 'Zeno and the art of polis maintenance' in Hansen (2005), 202–21.

Murray, O. and Price, S. (eds.) (1990) *The Greek City-State from Homer to Alexander*. Oxford.

Myres, J. L. (1927) *The Political Ideas of the Greeks, with Special Reference to Early Notions about Law, Authority, and Natural Order in Relation to Human Ordinance*. New York.

(1930) *Who Were the Greeks?* Berkeley.

(1953a) *Herodotus: Father of History*. Oxford.

(1953b) *Geographical History in Greek Lands*. Oxford.

Nafissi, M. (2005) *Ancient Athens and Modern Ideology. Value, Theory and Evidence in Historical Sciences: Max Weber, Karl Polanyi and Moses Finley*. London.

Nelson, E. (2004) *The Greek Tradition in Republican Thought*. Cambridge.

Nenci, G. (1993) 'Agrigento e la Sicilia nel quadro dei rifornimenti granari del mondo greco', *ASNP* 23: 1–7.

Nevett, L. C. (1999) *House and Society in the Ancient Greek World*. Cambridge.

Nichols, D. L. and Charlton, T. H. (eds.) (1997) *The Archaeology of City-States: Cross-Cultural Approaches*. Washington, DC, and London.

Nicolet, C. (ed.) (2000) *Mégapoles méditerranéennes. Géographie urbaine rétrospective*. Rome.

Nielsen, T. H. (1996a) 'Arkadia. City-ethnics and tribalism' in Hansen (1996c), 117–63.

(1996b) 'A survey of dependent poleis in classical Arcadia' in Hansen and Raaflaub (1996), 63–105.

(ed.) (1997) *Yet More Studies in the Ancient Greek Polis*. Stuttgart.

(2000) 'Epiknemidian, Hypoknemidian and Opountian Lokrians. Reflections on the political organisation of East Lokris in the classical period' in Flensted-Jensen (2000a), 91–120.

(2002a) *Arcadia and its Poleis in the Archaic and Classical Periods.* Göttingen.

(ed.) (2002b) *Even More Studies in the Ancient Greek Polis.* Stuttgart.

(ed.) (2004) *Once Again: Studies in the Ancient Greek Polis.* Stuttgart.

Nielsen, T. H. and Roy, J. (eds.) (1999) *Defining Ancient Arcadia.* Stuttgart.

Niemeyer, H.-G. (2000) 'The early Phoenician city-states on the Mediterranean. Archaeological elements for their description' in Hansen (2000c), 89–115.

Nippel, W. (1980) *Mischverfassungstheorie und Verfassungsrealität in Antike und früher Neuzeit.* Stuttgart.

(1990a) 'Prolegomena zu Eduard Meyers Anthropologie' in Calder and Demandt (1990), 311–28.

(1990b) *Griechen, Barbaren und 'Wilde'. Alte Geschichte und Sozialanthropologie.* Frankfurt am Main.

(1998) 'Von den "Altertümern" zur Kulturgeschichte', *Ktèma* 23: 17–24.

Nisbet, R. A. (1969) *Social Change and History: Aspects of the Western Theory of Development.* New York.

Nitz, H.-J. (ed.) (1993) *The Early Modern World-System in Geographical Perspective.* Stuttgart.

Nixon, L. and Price, S. (1990) 'The size and resources of the Greek cities' in Murray and Price (1990), 137–70.

Novick, P. (1988) *That Noble Dream: The 'Objectivity Question' and the American Historical Profession.* Cambridge.

Ober, J. (1989) *Mass and Elite in Democratic Athens. Rhetoric, Ideology and the Power of the People.* Princeton, NJ.

(1993) 'The polis as a society: Aristotle, John Rawls and the Athenian social contract' in Hansen (1993), 129–60.

Ogden, D. (ed.) (2002) *The Hellenistic World. New Perspectives.* London.

Olender, M. (1992) *The Languages of Paradise: Race, Religion, and Philology in the Nineteenth Century.* Trans. A. Goldhammer. Cambridge, MA.

Olshausen, E. and Sonnabend, H. (eds.) (1991) *Stuttgarter Kolloquium zur Historischen Geographie des Altertums, 2, 1984 und 3, 1987.* Bonn.

Oppenheim, A. L. (1964) *Ancient Mesopotamia. Portrait of a Dead Civilization.* Chicago and London.

(1967) 'A new look at the structure of Mesopotamian society', *JESHO* 10: 1–26.

(1969) 'Mesopotamia – land of many cities' in *Middle Eastern Cities*, ed. I. M. Lapidus. Berkeley and Los Angeles: 3–18.

Osanna, M. (1992) *Chorai coloniali da Taranto a Locri: documentazione archeologica e ricostruzione storica.* Rome.

Osborne, M. J. and Byrne, S. G. (1996) *The Foreign Residents of Athens. An Annex to the Lexicon of Greek Personal Names: Attica.* Louvain.

Osborne, R. (1985) *Demos: The Discovery of Classical Attika.* Cambridge.

(1987) *Classical Landscape with Figures. The Ancient Greek City and its Countryside.* London.

(1988) 'Social and economic implications of the leasing of land and property in classical and Hellenistic Greece', *Chiron* 18: 279–323.

Perlin F.

(1991a) 'Pride and prejudice, sense and subsistence: exchange and society in the Greek city' in Rich and Wallace-Hadrill (1991), 119–45.

(1991b) 'The potential mobility of human populations', *OJA* 10: 231–52.

(1996a) '*Classical Landscape* revisited', *Topoi* 6: 49–64.

(1996b) *Greece in the Making, 1200–479 BC.* London.

(1996c) 'Pots, trade and the archaic Greek economy', *Antiquity* 70: 31–44.

(1998) 'Early Greek colonisation? The nature of Greek settlement in the West' in Fisher and van Wees (1998), 251–70.

(1999) 'Archaeology and the Athenian empire', *TAPhA* 129: 319–32.

(ed.) (2000) *Classical Greece: 500–323 BC.* Oxford.

Ostwald, M. (2000) *Oligarchia: The Development of a Constitutional Form in Ancient Greece.* Stuttgart.

Ostwald, M. and Lynch, J. P. (1994) 'The growth of schools and the advance of knowledge' in *Cambridge Ancient History, VI: The Fourth Century BC.* 2nd edn. Cambridge: 592–633.

Pagden, A. (ed.) (1987) *The Languages of Political Theory in Early-Modern Europe.* Cambridge.

Papadopoulos, J. K. (1997a) 'Phantom Euboians', *JMA* 10: 191–219.

(1997b) 'Innovations, imitations and ceramic style: modes of production and modes of dissemination' in *Techne: Craftsmen, Craftswomen and Craftsmanship in the Aegean Bronze Age (Aegaeum 16)*, ed. R. Laffineur and P. P. Betancourt. Liege and Austin, TX: 449–62.

Papadopoulos, J. K. and Paspalas, S. A. (1999) 'Mendaian as Chalkidian wine', *Hesperia* 68: 161–88.

Parker, R. (1996) *Athenian Religion: A History.* Oxford.

Parkins, H. and Smith, C. (eds.) (1998) *Trade, Traders and the Ancient City.* London and New York.

Parthasarathi, P. (1998) 'Rethinking wages and competitiveness in the eighteenth century: Britain and South India', *P&P* 158: 79–109.

Payen, P. (1997) *Les îles nomades: conquérir et résister dans l'Enquête d'Hérodote.* Paris.

Perlin, F. (1985a) 'Space and order looked at critically: non-comparability and procedural substantivism in history and the social sciences' republished in Perlin (1994a), 215–51.

(1985b) 'State formation reconsidered' republished in F. Perlin, *The Invisible City. Monetary, Administrative and Popular Infrastructures in Asia and Europe, 1500–1900.* Aldershot, 1993, 15–90.

(1994a) *Unbroken Landscape: Commodity, Category, Sign and Identity: Their Production as Myth and Knowledge from 1500.* Aldershot.

(1994b) 'Interpreted time and interpreter's time: mechanicism, organicism and entropy' in Perlin (1994a), 276–96.

Perlman, P. (1996) 'Polis hypêkoos: the dependent polis and Crete' in Hansen (1996c), 233–87.

Pfeiffer, R. H. (1935) *State Letters of Assyria.* New Haven, CT.

Philippson, A. (1904) *Das Mittelmeergebiet: seine geographische und kulturelle Eigenart.* Leipzig.

Phillips, M. S. (2000) *Society and Sentiment. Genres of Historical Writing in Britain, 1740–1820.* Princeton, NJ.

Picon, M. and Garlan, Y. (1986) 'Recherches sur l'implantation des ateliers amphoriques à Thasos et analyse de la pâte des amphores thasiennes' in Empereur and Garlan (1986), 287–309.

Pierart, M. (1997) 'L'attitude d'Argos à l'égard des autres cités d'Argolide' in Hansen (1997d), 321–51.

Pirenne, H. (1927) *Les villes du Moyen Age: essai d'histoire économique et sociale.* Brussels.

Plácido, D., Alvar, J., Casillas, J. M. and Fornis, C. (eds.) (1997) *Imágenes de la Polis.* Madrid.

Pleket, H. W. (1993) 'Agriculture in the Roman empire in comparative perspective' in *De Agricultura: In Memoriam Pieter Willem de Neeve,* ed. H. Sancisi-Weerdenburg *et al.* Amsterdam: 317–42.

Pocock, J. G. A. (1975a) 'Early modern capitalism: the Augustan perception' in *Feudalism, Capitalism and Beyond,* ed. E. Kamenka and R. S. Neale. London: 62–83.

(1975b) 'British history: a plea for a new subject', *Journal of Modern History* 47: 601–21.

(1975c) *The Machiavellian Moment. Florentine Political Thought and the Atlantic Republican Tradition.* Princeton, NJ.

(1985) 'The mobility of property and the rise of eighteenth-century sociology' in J. G. A. Pocock, *Virtue, Commerce and History. Essays on Political Thought and History, Chiefly in the Eighteenth Century.* Cambridge: 103–23.

(1999) *Barbarism and Religion. II: Narratives of Civil Government.* Cambridge.

(2005) *Barbarism and Religion. IV: Barbarians, Savages and Empires.* Cambridge.

Polanyi, K., Arensberg, C. M. and Pearson, H. W. (eds.) (1957) *Trade and Market in the Early Empires: Economies in History and Theory.* Glencoe.

Poliakov, L. (1974) *The Aryan Myth: A History of Racist and Nationalist Ideas in Europe.* Trans. E. Howard. London.

Polignac, F. de (1984) *La naissance de la cité grecque. Cultes, espace et société, VIIIe–VIIe siècles avant J.-C.* Paris.

(1995) 'Repenser la "cité"? Rituels et société en Grèce archaïque' in Hansen and Raaflaub (1995), 7–19.

Polverini, L. (1979) 'Bibliografia degli scritti di Giulio Beloch', *ASNP* 8: 1429–62.

(1988) 'Il carteggio Beloch-Meyer' in Christ and Momigliano (1988), 199–219.

(ed.) (1990) *Aspetti della storiografia di Giulio Beloch.* Naples.

Pomeranz, K. (2000) *The Great Divergence: Europe, China and the Making of the Modern World Economy.* Princeton, NJ.

Pope, M. (1988) 'Thucydides and democracy', *Historia* 37: 276–96.

Postan, M. M. (1975) *The Medieval Economy and Society.* Harmondsworth.

Postgate, J. N. (1992) *Early Mesopotamia: Society and Economy in the Dawn of History.* London.

Potts, A. (1994) *Flesh and the Ideal: Winckelmann and the Origins of Art History.* New Haven, CT.

Powell, M. (1977) 'Sumerian merchants and the problem of profit', *Iraq* 39: 23–9.

Prak, M. (ed.) (2001a) *Early Modern Capitalism. Economic and Social Change in Europe, 1400–1800*. London and New York.

(2001b) 'Early modern capitalism. An introduction' in Prak (2001a), 1–21.

Prakash, G. (1990) 'Writing post-Orientalist histories of the Third World: perspectives from Indian historiography', *CSSH* 32: 383–408.

Pritchett, W. K. (1974) *The Greek State at War, II*. Berkeley, Los Angeles and London.

Purcell, N. (1990) 'Mobility and the polis' in Murray and Price (1990), 29–58.

Raaflaub, K. (1993a) 'Homer to Solon. The rise of the *Polis*. The written sources' in Hansen (1993), 41–105.

(ed.) (1993b) *Anfänge politischen Denkens in der Antike: Die nahöstlichen Kulturen und die Griechen*. Munich.

(1997) 'Politics and interstate relations in the world of early Greek poleis: Homer and beyond', *Antichthon* 31: 1–27.

(2004) *The Discovery of Freedom in Ancient Greece*. Chicago and London.

Rancière, J. (1999) *Disagreement: Politics and Philosophy*. Trans. J. Rose. Minneapolis and London.

Rathbone, D. (1989) 'The ancient economy and Graeco-Roman Egypt' in *Egitto e storia antica dell'Ellenismo all'età Araba*, ed. L. Criscuolo and G. Gerasi. Bologna: 159–76.

Rauh, N. K. (1993) *The Sacred Bonds of Commerce: Religion, Economy and Trade Society at Hellenistic – Roman Delos, 166–87 BC*. Amsterdam.

(2003) *Merchants, Sailors and Pirates in the Roman World*. Brimscombe Port and Charleston.

Rawson, E. (1969) *The Spartan Tradition in European Thought*. Oxford.

Reden, S. von (1995) 'The Piraeus – a world apart', *G&R* 42: 24–37.

Redfield, J. M. (2003) *The Locrian Maidens: Love and Death in Greek Italy*. Princeton, NJ.

Reed, C. M. (2003) *Maritime Traders in the Ancient Greek World*. Cambridge.

Reger, G. (1994) *Regionalism and Change in the Economy of Independent Delos, 314–167 BC*. Berkeley and Los Angeles.

Rehak, P. (ed.) (1995) *The Role of the Ruler in the Prehistoric Aegean (Aegaeum 11)*. Liege and Austin, TX.

Rehm, W. (1936) *Griechentum und Goethezeit. Geschichte eines Glaubens*. Leipzig.

Reill, P. H. (1975) *The German Enlightenment and the Rise of Historicism*. Berkeley, Los Angeles and London.

Renfrew, A. C. (1972) *The Emergence of Civilisation: The Cyclades and the Aegean in the Third Millennium BC*. London.

Renfrew, A. C. and Cherry, J. F. (eds.) (1986) *Peer Polity Interaction and Socio-Political Change*. Cambridge.

Reviv, H. (1969) 'On urban representative institutions and self-government in Syria–Palestine in the second half of the second millennium BC', *JESHO* 12: 283–97.

(1988) '*Kidinnu*: observations on privileges of Mesopotamian cities', *JESHO* 31: 286–98.

Rostovtzeff. M. I

Rhodes, P. J. (2006) *A History of the Classical Greek World 478–323 BC*. Oxford.

Rhodes, P. J. and Lewis, D. M. (1997) *The Decrees of the Greek States*. Oxford.

Rhodes, P. J. and Osborne, R. (2003) *Greek Historical Inscriptions, 404–323 BC*. Oxford.

Rich, J. and Wallace-Hadrill, A. (eds.) (1991) *City and Country in the Ancient World*. London and New York.

Rihll, T. E. (2001) 'Making money in classical Athens' in Mattingly and Salmon (2001), 115–42.

Rihll, T. and Wilson, A. G. (1991) 'Modelling settlement structures in ancient Greece: new approaches to the polis' in Rich and Wallace-Hadrill (1991), 59–95.

Roberts, T. J. (1994) *Athens on Trial. The Antidemocratic Tradition in Western Thought*. Princeton, NJ.

Robertson, R. (1992) *Globalization. Social Theory and Global Culture*. London, Newbury Park and Delhi.

  (2003) *The Three Waves of Globalization. A History of a Developing Global Consciousness*. New York.

Robinson, E. W. (1997) *The First Democracies. Early Popular Government outside Athens*. Stuttgart.

Robinson, T. (1999) 'Erbinna, the "Nereid Monument" and Xanthus' in Tsetskhladze (1999), 361–77.

Roseberry, W. (1989) *Anthropologies and Histories. Essays in Culture, History and Political Economy*. New Brunswick and London.

Rosivach, V. J. (1993) 'Agricultural slavery in the northern colonies and in classical Athens', *CSSH* 35: 551–67.

Rossetti, L. and Furiani, P. L. (1993) 'Rodi' in *Lo spazio letterario della Grecia antica. Volume I: La produzione e la circolazione del testo, Tomo II: L'ellenismo*, ed. G. Cambiano, L. Canfora and D. Lanza. Rome: 657–715.

Rossi, P. (1984) *The Dark Abyss of Time: The History of the Earth and the History of Nations from Hooke to Vico*. Trans. L. G. Cochrane. Chicago.

Rostovtzeff, M. I. (1922) *Iranians and Greeks in South Russia*. Oxford.

  (1926) *A History of the Ancient World, I*. Oxford.

  (1932) *Caravan Cities*. Trans. D. and T. Talbot Rice. Oxford.

  (1941) *The Social and Economic History of the Hellenistic World, I–III*. Oxford.

Rougemont, G. (1990) 'Géographie historique des Cyclades. L'homme et le milieu dans l'Archipel', *JS*: 199–220.

  (1992) 'Delphes et les cités grecques d'Italie du sud et de Sicile' in *La Magna Grecia e i grandi santuari della madrepatria: atti del trentunesimo convegno di studi sulla Magna Grecia*. Taranto: 157–91.

Roussel, D. (1976) *Tribu et cité: études sur les groupes sociaux dans les cités grecques aux époques archaïque et classique*. Paris.

Rousset, D. (1999) 'Centre urbain, frontière et espace rural dans les cités de Grèce centrale' in Brunet (1999), 35–77.

Roy, J. (1967) 'The mercenaries of Cyrus', *Historia* 16: 287–323.

  (1997) 'The perioikoi of Elis' in Hansen (1997d), 282–320.

(1998) 'The threat from the Piraeus', in *Kosmos: Essays in Order, Conflict and Community in Classical Athens*, ed. P. Cartledge, P. Millett and S. von Reden. New York and Cambridge: 191–202.

(1999) 'The economies of Arcadia' in Nielsen and Roy (1999), 320–81.

(2000) 'Problems of democracy in the Arcadian confederacy' in Brock and Hodkinson (2000), 308–26.

Runciman, W. G. (1990) 'Doomed to extinction: the polis as an evolutionary dead-end' in Murray and Price (1990), 347–67.

Ruschenbusch, E. (1983) 'Zur Wirtschafts- und Sozialstruktur der Normalpolis' *ASNP* 13: 171–94.

(1984a) 'Modell Amorgos' in *Aux origines de l'hellénisme: la Crète et la Grèce. Hommage à Henri van Effenterre*. Paris: 265–71.

(1984b) 'Die Bevölkerungszahl Griechenlands im 5. und 4. Jh. v. Chr.', *ZPE* 56: 55–7.

(1985) 'Die Zahl der griechischen Staaten und Arealgrösse und Bürgerzahl der "Normalpolis"', *ZPE* 59: 253–63.

Sahlins, M. (1976) *Culture and Practical Reason*. Chicago.

(2004): *Apologies to Thucydides. Understanding History as Culture and Vice Versa*. Chicago and London.

Said, E. (1978) *Orientalism*. New York and London.

Sakellariou, M. B. (1989) *The Polis-State: Definition and Origin*. Athens.

Salmon, J. B. (1984) *Wealthy Corinth. A History of the City to 338 BC*. Oxford.

(1999) 'The economic role of the Greek city', *G&R* 46: 147–67

Samman, K. (2001) 'The limits of the classical comparative method', *Review* 24: 533–73.

Sampson, R. V. (1956) *Progress in the Age of Reason. The Seventeenth Century to the Present Day*. London.

Sanchez, P. (2001) *L'Amphictionie des Pyles et de Delphes: recherches sur son rôle historique, des origines au IIe siècle de notre ère*. Stuttgart.

Sanders, G. D. R. (1996) 'Two *castra* on Melos and their relationship in the Archipelago' in Lock and Sanders (1996), 147–77.

Sarikakis T. C. (1986) 'Commercial relations between Chios and other Greek cities in antiquity' in Boardman and Vaphopoulou-Richardson (1986), 121–31.

Saxonhouse, A. (1992) *Fear of Diversity. The Birth of Political Science in Ancient Greek Thought*. Chicago.

Ščeglov (Chtcheglov), A. (1990) 'Le commerce du blé dans le Pont septentrional (seconde moitié du VIIe – Ve siècle)' in Lordkipanidzé and Lévêque (1990), 141–59.

Schachter, A. (1981–94) *The Cults of Boiotia, I–IV*. London.

Schaps, D. M. (2004) *The Invention of Coinage and the Monetization of Ancient Greece*. Ann Arbor, MI.

Schaumkell, E. (1905) *Geschichte der deutschen Kulturgeschichtsschreibung von der Mitte des 18. Jahrhunderts bis zur Romantik*. Leipzig.

Scheidel, W. (1996) *Measuring Sex, Age and Death in the Roman Empire: Explorations in Ancient Demography*. Ann Arbor, MI.

Schneider, H. (1988) 'Schottische Aufklärung und antike Gesellschaft' in *Alte Geschichte und Wissenschaftsgeschichte. Festschrift für Karl Christ zum 65. Geburtstag*, ed. P. Kneissl and V. Losemann. Darmstadt: 431–64.

(1990) 'Die Bücher–Meyer Kontroverse' in Calder and Demandt (1990), 417–45.

Schofield, M. (1991) *The Stoic Idea of the City*. Cambridge.

(1993) 'Plato on the economy' in Hansen (1993), 183–96.

Scholten, J. B. (2000) *The Politics of Plunder. Aitolians and their Koinon in the Early Hellenistic Era, 279–21 BC*. Berkeley, Los Angeles and London.

Schubert, C. and Brodersen, K. (eds.) (1995) *Rom und der griechische Osten. Festschrift für Hatto H. Schmitt zum 65. Geburtstag*. Stuttgart.

Schuller, W. (1979) 'Zur Entstehung der griechischen Demokratie außerhalb Athens' in *Auf den Weg gebracht: Idee und Wirklichkeit der Gründung der Universität Konstanz*, ed. H. Sund and M. Timmermann. Konstanz: 433–47.

Seaford, R. (1994) *Reciprocity and Ritual: Homer and Tragedy in the Developing City-State*. Oxford.

(2004) *Money and the Early Greek Mind: Homer, Philosophy, Tragedy*. Cambridge.

Seibert, J. (1979) *Die politischen Flüchtlinge und Verbannten in der griechischen Geschichte: Von den Anfängen bis zur Unterwerfung durch die Römer*. Darmstadt.

Settis, S. (ed.) (1996) *I Greci. Storia, cultura, arte, societa. II: Una storia greca. I. Formazione*. Turin.

(ed.) (1997) *I Greci. Storia, cultura, arte, societa. II: Una storia greca. II. Definizione*. Turin.

(ed.) (2001) *I Greci. Storia, cultura, arte, societa. III: I Greci oltre la Grecia*. Turin.

Shapiro, H. A. (1996) 'Tradizioni regionali, botteghe e stili d'arte' in Settis (1996), 1181–207.

Shaw, B. (1993) 'The early development of M. I. Finley's thought: the Heichelheim dossier', *Athenaeum* 81: 177–99.

Shaw, J. W. (1989) 'Phoenicians in Southern Crete', *AJA* 93: 165–83.

Shelmerdine, C. W. (1999) 'A comparative look at Mycenaean administration(s)' in *Floreant studia Mycenaea*, ed. S. Deger Jalkotzy, S. Hiller and O. Panagl. Vienna: 555–76.

Sherratt, S. (2001) 'Potemkin palaces and route-based economies' in Voutsaki and Killen (2001), 214–38.

Sherratt, E. S. and Sherratt, A. (1993) 'The growth of the Mediterranean economy in the early first millennium BC', *WA* 24.3: 361–78.

Sherwin-White, S. M. (1978) *Ancient Cos. An Historical Study from the Dorian Settlement to the Imperial Period*. Göttingen.

Sherwin-White, S. and Kuhrt, A. (1993) *From Samarkhand to Sardis: A New Approach to the Seleucid Empire*. London.

Shionoya, Y. (ed.) (2001) *The German Historical School. The Historical and Ethical Approach to Economics*. London and New York.

Shipley, G. (1987) *A History of Samos, 800–188 BC*. Oxford.

(1993) 'Distance, development, decline? World-systems analysis and the 'Hellenistic' world' in Bilde *et al.* (1993), 271–84.

(1997) '"The other Lakedaimonians": the dependent perioikic poleis of Laconia and Messenia' in Hansen (1997d), 189–281.

(2000) *The Greek World after Alexander, 323–30 BC*. London.

Shulsky, A. N. (1991) 'The "infrastructure" of Aristotle's *Politics*: Aristotle on economics and politics' in *Essays on the Foundation of Aristotelian Political Science*, ed. C. Lord and D. K. O'Connor. Berkeley and Los Angeles: 74–III.

Simon, C. (1988) 'Alte Geschichte in der Dritten Republik 1871–1914', *Storia della storiografia* 13: 29–66.

Simonsuuri, K. (1979) *Homer's Original Genius. Eighteenth-Century Notions of the Early Greek Epic (1688–1798)*. Cambridge.

Skinner, Q. (1996) *Reason and Rhetoric in the Philosophy of Hobbes*. Cambridge.

(2002) 'From the state of princes to the person of the state' in Q. Skinner, *Visions of Politics. II: Renaissance Virtues*. Cambridge: 368–413.

Slot, B. J. (1982) *Archipelagus turbatus: les Cyclades entre colonisation latine et occupation ottomane c. 1500–1718*. Istanbul.

Smith, A. (1976) *An Inquiry into the Nature and Causes of the Wealth of Nations, I–II*. Oxford.

Snell, D. C. (2001) *Flight and Freedom in the Ancient Near East*. Leiden.

Snodgrass, A. (1980) *Archaic Greece: The Age of Experiment*. Berkeley and Los Angeles.

(1986) 'Interaction by design: the Greek city-state' in Renfrew and Cherry (1986), 47–58.

(1987) *An Archaeology of Greece: The Present State and Future Scope of a Discipline*. Berkeley and Los Angeles.

(1990) 'Survey archaeology and the rural landscape of the Greek city' in Murray and Price (1990), 113–36.

(1993) 'The rise of the polis. The archaeological evidence' in Hansen (1993), 30–40.

Sobel, M. (1987) *The World they Made Together: Black and White Values in Eighteenth-Century Virginia*. Princeton, NJ.

Sordi, M. (ed.) (1994) *Emigrazione e immigrazione nel mondo antico*. Milan.

Spek, R. J. van der (1987) 'The Babylonian city' in Kuhrt and Sherwin-White (1987), 57–74.

Springborg, P. (1992) *Western Republicanism and the Oriental Prince*. Cambridge.

Spruyt, H. (1994) *The Sovereign State and its Competitors: An Analysis of System Change*. Princeton, NJ.

Stanford, W. B. and McDowell, R. B. (1971) *Mahaffy: A Biography of an Anglo-Irishman*. London.

Starr, C. G. (1977) *The Economic and Social Growth of Early Greece 800–500 BC*. New York.

Ste Croix, G. E. M. de (1972) *The Origins of the Peloponnesian War*. London.

(1981) *The Class Struggle in the Ancient Greek World*. London.

Stein, G. J. (1999) *Rethinking World-Systems. Diasporas, Colonies and Interaction in Uruk Mesopotamia*. Tucson, AZ.

Stocking, G. W. Jr (1987) *Victorian Anthropology*. New York.

Stone, E. (1997) 'City-states and their centres: the Mesopotamian example' in Nichols and Charlton (1997), 15–26.

Stone, L. (1979) 'The revival of the narrative', *P&P* 85: 3–24.

Strasburger, H. (1990) 'Umblick im Trümmerfeld der griechischen Geschichts-Schreibung', in *Studien zur Alten Geschichte, III*. Hildesheim and New York: 167–218.

Stroud, R. S. (1998) *The Athenian Grain-Tax Law of 374/3 BC (Hesperia Supplement 29)*. Princeton, NJ.

Stuchtey, B. and Fuchs, E. (eds.) (2003) *Writing World History, 1800–2000*. Oxford.

Subrahmanyam, S. (1997) 'Connected histories: notes towards a reconfiguration of early modern Eurasia', *MAS* 31: 735–62.

Sutton, S. B. (ed.) (2000) *Contingent Countryside: Settlement, Economy and Land Use in the Southern Argolid since 1700*. Stanford.

Tagliamonte, G. (1994) *I figli di Marte: mobilità, mercenari e mercenariato italici in Magna Grecia e Sicilia*. Rome.

Talbert, R. J. A. (1974) *Timoleon and the Revival of Greek Sicily 344–317 BC*. Cambridge.

Tarrant, H. (1990) 'The distribution of early Greek thinkers and the question of "alien influences"', in Descœudres (1990), 621–8.

Tchernia, A. and Viviers, D. (2000) 'Athènes, Rome et leurs avant-ports: "mégapoles" antiques et trafics méditerranéens' in Nicolet (2000), 761–801.

Te Brake, W. (1998) *Shaping History. Ordinary People in European Politics, 1500–1700*. Berkeley, Los Angeles and London.

Thiesse, A.-M. (1999) *La création des identités nationales: Europe XVIIIe–XXe siècle*. Paris.

Thom, M. (1995) *Republics, Nations and Tribes*. London and New York.

Thomas, C. G. (1981) 'The Greek polis' in Griffeth and Thomas (1981), 31–69.

Thomas, R. (2000) *Herodotus in Context: Ethnography, Science and the Art of Persuasion*. Cambridge and New York.

Thompson, E. P. (1967) 'Time, work-discipline and industrial capitalism' republished in Thompson (1993b), 352–403.

—— (1978) *The Poverty of Theory and Other Essays*. London.

—— (1980) *The Making of the English Working Class*. 2nd edn. Harmondsworth.

—— (1985) *Double Exposure*. London.

—— (1993a) 'The patricians and the plebs' in Thompson (1993b), 16–96.

—— (1993b) *Customs in Common. Studies in Traditional Popular Culture*. New York.

Tilly, C. (1983) 'Flows of capital and forms of industry in Europe, 1500–1900', *Theory & Society* 12: 123–42.

—— (1984) *Big Structures, Large Processes, Huge Comparisons*. New York.

—— (1989) 'The geography of European statemaking and capitalism since 1500' in Genovese and Hochberg (1989), 158–81.

Tise, L. E. (1998) *American Counterrevolution. A Retreat from Liberty, 1783–1800*. Mechanicsburg, PA.

Tod, M. N. (1948) *A Selection of Greek Historical Inscriptions, II: From 403 to 323 BC*. Oxford.
Torelli, M. (2000) 'The Etruscan city-state' in Hansen (2000c), 189–208.
Tortorelli-Ghidini, M., Storchi-Marino, A. and Visconti, A. (eds.) (2000) *Tra Orfeo e Pitagora. Origini e incontri di culture nell' antichità*. Naples.
Treister, M. Y. (1996) *The Role of Metals in Ancient Greek History*. Leiden.
Trevelyan, H. (1934) *The Popular Background to Goethe's Hellenism*. London.
Trevett, J. (1992) *Apollodoros, the Son of Pasion*. Oxford.
Tribe, K. (1978) *Land, Labour and Economic Discourse*. London.
Tritsch, F. (1929) 'Die Stadtbildung des Altertums und die Griechische Polis', *Klio* 22:1–83.
Trouillot, M.-R. (1995) *Silencing the Past: Power and the Production of History*. Boston, MA.
Tsetskhladze, G. R. (1998a) 'Greek colonisation of the Black Sea area: stages, models and native population' in Tsetskhladze (1998c), 9–68.
  (1998b) Who built the Scythian and Thracian royal and elite tombs?, *OJA* 17: 55–92.
  (ed.) (1998c) *The Greek Colonisation of the Black Sea Area. Historical Interpretation of Archaeology*. Stuttgart.
  (ed.) (1999) *Ancient Greeks West and East*. Leiden, Boston, MA, and Cologne.
  (ed.) (2001) *North Pontic Archaeology. Recent Discoveries and Studies*. Leiden.
Tsetskhladze, G. R. and De Angelis, F. (eds.) (1994) *The Archaeology of Greek Colonisation. Essays Dedicated to Sir John Boardman*. Oxford.
Tsetskhladze, G. R. and Snodgrass, A. M. (eds.) (2002) *Greek Settlements in the Eastern Mediterranean and the Black Sea*. Oxford.
Tsotsoros, S. N. (1986) *Oikonomikoi kai koinônikoi mêchanismoi ston oreino chôro: Gortynia, 1715–1828*. Athens.
Tsoukalas, K. (1977) *Exartêsê kai anaparagôgê. O koinônikos rolos tôn ekpaideytikôn mêchanismôn stên Ellada (1830–1922)*. Athens.
Tuck, R. (1999) *The Rights of War and Peace: Political Thought and the International Order from Grotius to Kant*. Oxford.
Tuplin, C. (1987) 'The administration of the Achaemenid empire' in *Coinage and Administration in the Athenian and Persian Empires*, ed. I. Carradice. Oxford: 109–67.
Turner, F. M. (1981) *The Greek Heritage in Victorian Britain*. New Haven, CT, and London.
  (1989) 'Why the Greeks and not the Romans in Victorian Britain?' in *Rediscovering Hellenism. The Hellenic Inheritance and the English Imagination*, ed. G. W. Clarke. Cambridge: 61–81.
Unwin, T. (1991) *Wine and the Vine. A Historical Geography of Viticulture and the Wine Trade*. London and New York.
Vacalopoulos, A. E. (1976) *The Greek Nation, 1453–1669. The Cultural and Economic Background of Modern Greek Society*. Trans. I. and P. Moles. New Brunswick.
Vallet, G. (1963) 'Les routes maritimes de la Grande Grèce' republished in Vallet (1996), 309–21.

Vernant J. P (1962) Les origines de la pensée grecque. Paris

280   *References*

(1996) *Le monde grec colonial d'Italie du Sud et de Sicile*, Rome.

Vallet, G. and Villard, F. (1963) 'Céramique grecque et histoire économique' republished in Vallet (1996), 253–69.

Vandermersch, C. (1994) *Vins et amphores de Grande Grèce et de Sicile IVe–IIIe s. avant J.C.*, Naples.

Veenhof, K. R. (1977) 'Some social effects of Old Assyrian trade', *Iraq* 39: 109–18.

(1997) '"Modern" features in Old Assyrian trade', *JESHO* 40: 337–66.

Vegetti, M. (1995) 'The Greeks and their gods' in *The Greeks*, ed. J. P. Vernant. Trans. C. Lambert and T. L. Fagan. Chicago: 285–98.

Velissaropoulos, J. (1980) *Les naucleres grecs: recherches sur les institutions maritimes en Grèce et dans l'Orient hellénise*. Geneva and Paris.

Venturi, F. (1963) 'Oriental despotism', *JHI* 24: 133–42.

(1989) *The End of the Old Regime in Europe, 1768–1776: The First Crisis*. Trans. R. Burr Litchfield. Princeton, NJ.

(1991) *The End of the Old Regime in Europe, 1776–1789, I–II*. Trans. R. Burr Litchfield. Princeton, NJ.

Vernant, J. P. (1962) *Les origines de la pensée grecque*. Paris.

Vidal-Naquet, P. (1964) 'Notes de Karl Wittfogel et la notion de mode de production asiatique' reprinted in Vidal-Naquet (1990b), 277–317.

(1979) 'La formation des Athènes bourgeoises' (with N. Loraux) trans. in Vidal-Naquet (1995), 82–140.

(1990a) 'La place de la Grèce dans l'imaginaire des hommes de la Révolution' trans. in Vidal-Naquet (1995), 141–69.

(1990b) *La démocratie grecque vue d'ailleurs: essais d'historiographie ancienne et moderne*. Paris.

(1995) *Politics Ancient and Modern*. Trans. J. Lloyd. Cambridge.

Vilatte, S. (1991) *L'insularité dans la pensée grecque*, Paris and Besançon.

(1995) *Espace et temps: la cité aristotélicienne de la politique*. Besançon.

Vinogradov, J. G. (1980) 'Die historische Entwicklung der Poleis des nördlichen Schwarzmeersgebietes im 5. Jahrhundert v. Chr.' republished in Vinogradov (1997), 100–32.

(1987) 'Der Pontos Euxeinos als politische, ökonomische und kulturelle Einheit und die Epigraphik' republished in Vinogradov (1997), 1–73.

(1997) *Pontische Studien: kleine Schriften zur Geschichte und Epigraphik des Schwarzmeerraumes*. Mainz.

Viviers, D. (1994) 'La cité de Dattala et l'expansion territoriale de Lyktos en Crète centrale', *BCH* 118: 229–59.

Vlassopoulos, K. (2000) 'Archaiologikes martyries kai istorika porismata: problêmata methodou kai ermêneias', *Ta Historika* 33: 379–402.

(2003) '*Persikon de karta dôron o stratos*: Ê diaplokê Ellênôn misthophorôn kai Persikou kosmou me basê tên Kyrou Anabasê tou Xenophônta', *Ariadnê* 9: 31–58.

(forthcoming) 'Imperial encounters: discourses on empire and the uses of ancient history during the eighteenth century' in *Hegemony and Cornucopia. Classical Scholarship and the Ideology of Imperialism*, ed. M. Bradley and E. Reisz.

(n.d.) 'The frogs and the pond: Modern Greek lessons for ancient historians', unpublished paper.

Voutsaki, S. and Killen, J. (eds.) (2001) *Economy and Politics in the Mycenaean Palace States (PCPhS Supplement 27)*. Cambridge.

Vries, J. de (1976) *The Economy of Europe in an Age of Crisis*. Cambridge.

(1984) *European Urbanisation 1500–1800*. London.

(1994) 'The Industrial Revolution and the Industrious Revolution', *Journal of Economic History* 54: 249–70.

(1999) 'Great expectations: early modern history and the social sciences', *Review* 22: 121–49.

Wagner, C. (1991) *Die Entwicklung Johann Gustav Droysens als Althistoriker*. Bonn.

Walbank, F. W. (1933) *Aratos of Sicyon*. Cambridge.

Wallace-Hadrill, A. (1991) 'Elites and trade in the Roman town' in Rich and Wallace-Hadrill (1991), 241–72.

Wallerstein, I. (1974) *The Modern World-system. I: Capitalist Agriculture and the Origins of the European World Economy in the Sixteenth Century*. New York.

(1988) 'The invention of timespace realities: towards an understanding of our historical system' republished in Wallerstein (1991), 135–48.

(1991) *Unthinking Social Science: The Limits of Nineteenth-Century Paradigms*. Oxford.

Wallinga, H. T. (1993) *Ships and Sea-Power before the Great Persian War: The Ancestry of the Ancient Trireme*. Leiden.

Walter, U. (1993) *An der Polis teilhaben. Bürgerstaat und Zugehörigkeit im archaischen Griechenland*. Stuttgart.

Walther, G. (2001) 'Theodor Mommsen und die Erforschung der römischen Geschichte' in Most (2001), 241–58.

Washbrook, D. (1988) 'Progress and problems: South Asian economic and social history, c. 1720–1860', *MAS* 22: 57–96.

(1990) 'South Asia, the world-system and world capitalism', *Journal of Asian Studies* 49: 479–508.

Wasowicz, A. (1999) 'Modèles d'aménagement des colonies grecques: ville et territoire' in Brunet (1999), 245–58.

Waterman, L. (1930) *Royal Correspondence of the Assyrian Empire, I–III*. Ann Arbor, MI.

Weber, M. (1958) *The City*. Trans. D. Martindale and G. Neuwirth. New York and London.

(1976) *The Agrarian Sociology of Ancient Civilisations*. Trans. R. I. Frank. London.

Wees, H. van (1995) 'Politics and the battlefield: ideology in Greek warfare' in *The Greek World*, ed. A. Powell. London: 153–78.

Weil, R. (1964) 'Philosophie et histoire. La vision de l'histoire chez Aristote' in *La 'Politique' d'Aristote, Entretiens Hardt XI*. Geneva: 159–89.

Wells, B. (ed.) (1992) *Agriculture in Ancient Greece*. Stockholm.

Welskopf, E. C. (ed.) (1974) *Hellenische Poleis. Krise, Wandlung, Wirkung, I–IV*. Berlin.

Wentker, H. (1956) *Sizilien und Athen: die Begegnung der attischen Macht mit den West-Griechen.* Heidelberg.

Werner, R. (1995) 'Untersuchungen zur Geschichte und Struktur des Italiotenbunds' in Schubert and Brodersen (1995), 287–96.

West, M. L. (1997) *The East Face of Helicon: West Asiatic Elements in Early Poetry and Myth.* Oxford.

White, H. (1973) *Metahistory: The Historical Imagination in Nineteenth-Century Europe.* Baltimore.

Whitehead, D. (1977) *The Ideology of the Athenian Metic (PCPhS Supplement 2).* Cambridge.

(2000) *Hypereides: The Forensic Speeches.* Oxford.

Whitley, J. (1991) *Style and Society in Dark Age Greece.* Cambridge.

(2001) *The Archaeology of Ancient Greece.* Cambridge.

Whittaker, C. R. (1995) 'Do theories of the ancient city matter?' in Cornell and Lomas (1995), 9–26.

Wilentz, S. (2005) *The Rise of American Democracy: Jefferson to Lincoln.* New York and London.

Will, E. (1956) *Doriens et Ioniens: essai sur la valeur du critère ethnique appliqué à l'étude de l'histoire et de la civilisation grecque.* Paris.

Will, E., Mossé, C. and Goukowsky, P. (eds.) (1975) *Le monde grec et l'Orient, Tome II: Le IVe siècle et l'époque hellénistique.* Paris.

Winterling, A. (1995) 'Polisübergreifende Politik bei Aristoteles' in Schubert and Brodersen (1995), 313–28.

Wittenburg, A. (1984) 'I Dori di K. O. Müller', *ASNP* 14: 1031–44.

Wohlleben, J. (1992) 'Germany, 1750–1830' in Dover (1992), 170–202.

Wokler, R. (1987) 'Saint-Simon and the passage from political to social science' in Pagden (1987), 325–38.

Wolf, E. R. (1982) *Europe and the People without History.* Berkeley and Los Angeles.

Wolpert, A. (2002) *Remembering Defeat: Civil War and Civic Memory in Ancient Athens.* Baltimore and London.

Wong, R. B. (1997) *China Transformed. Historical Change and the Limits of European Experience.* Ithaca, NY, and London.

Wood, A. (2002) *Riot, Rebellion and Popular Politics in Early Modern England.* London.

Wood, E. M. (1988) *Peasant-Citizen and Slave: The Foundations of Athenian Democracy.* London.

Woolf, S. J. (1968) 'Venice and the Terraferma: problems of the change from commercial to landed activities' republished in *Crisis and Change in the Venetian Economy in the Sixteenth and Seventeenth Centuries,* ed. B. Pullan. London: 175–203.

Wright, J. C. (1995) 'From chief to king in Mycenaean Greece' in Rehak (1995), 63–80.

Wright, J. K. (1997) *A Classical Republican in Eighteenth-Century France: The Political Thought of Mably.* Stanford.

Wrigley, E. A. (1967) 'A simple model of London's importance in changing English society and economy 1650–1750', *P&P* 36: 44–70.

Yack, B. (1986) *The Longing for Total Revolution: Philosophic Sources of Social Discontent From Rousseau to Marx and Nietzsche.* Princeton, NJ.

  (1993) *The Problems of a Political Animal. Community, Justice and Conflict in Aristotelian Political Thought.* Berkeley, Los Angeles and London.

  (1997) *The Fetishism of Modernities. Epochal Self-Consciousness in Contemporary Social and Political Thought.* Notre Dame, IN.

Yalouris E. (1986) 'Notes on the topography of Chios' in Boardman and Vaphopoulou-Richardson (1986), 141–68.

Yavetz, Z. (1976) 'Why Rome? Zeitgeist and ancient historians in early 19th century Germany', *AJPh* 97: 276–96.

Yoffee, N. (1979) 'The decline and rise of Mesopotamian civilization: an ethno-archaeological perspective on the evolution of social complexity', *AmAnt* 44: 5–35.

  (1988) 'Orienting collapse' in *The Collapse of Ancient States and Civilizations*, ed. N. Yoffee and G. Cowgill. Tucson, AZ: 1–19.

  (1993) 'Too many chiefs? (or safe texts for the 90s)' in *Archaeological Theory: Who Sets the Agenda?*, ed. N. Yoffee and A. Sherratt. Cambridge: 60–78.

  (2000) 'Law courts and the mediation of social conflict in ancient Mesopotamia' in *Order, Legitimacy and Wealth in Ancient States*, ed. J. Richards and M. van Buren. Cambridge: 46–63.

Zahrnt, H. (1971) *Olynth und die Chalkidier: Untersuchungen zur Staatenbildung auf der Chalkidischen Halbinsel im 5. und 4. Jahrhundert v. Chr.* Munich.

Index

Jeffrey Kopstein + Sven Steinmo eds.

Growing Apart? America + Europe in the Twenty-first Century

C Cambridge: Cambridge University Press, 2008

Curtius, E. 45
Cyclades 163, 167
Cyprus 153, 210
Cyrene 153, 160, 188, 214
Cythnos 163
Cyzicus 185

Davies, J. K. 155, 199, 208, 220
Delos 184
Delphi 181
Democedes 235
democracy
  conceived as an entity 119–20
  from a Near Eastern perspective 116–17
  origins 119–20
  and the world system 89–90, 94–5
demography 48, 128–30
Demosthenes 138
Detienne, M. 61, 66
Dinarchus 180
Diodorus 16, 40
Dion 181
Dionysius I of Syracuse 152, 179
Dorians 38, 43
Dougherty, C. 187
Dunbabin, T. J. 54
Durkheim, E. 47
Droysen, J. G. 34

economy
  conceptions of 36, 89
  manufacture 130, 137–8, 139–40, 160
  services 160
Egypt 83, 102, 177
Ehrenberg, V. 44, 53
Elayi, J. 217
Elis 51, 154, 161, 191, 201
Emmius, U. 21
emporion 174, 181, 184
Ephesus 196
Epirus 201, 209
ethnos 57, 60, 78, 80, 192, 193–5
Etruria 170
Euboia 59
Eurocentrism 3, 123, 126–7, 203–6
evolutionism 33–4, 46–7, 49–50, 190, 201, 209, 211, 219
exchange 48, 130–3
  in agricultural products 133, 138–9, 158–9
  amphoras 132, 159, 172, 173, 183, 234
  avant-port 164, 170
  Bronze Age 132
  demand 133
  in metals 132
  redistribution 160

regional specialisation 138
use of territories for exchange 158–9

Finley, M. I. 35, 39, 48, 50, 53, 56, 58, 59, 62, 62–3, 104, 114, 119–20, 123, 124, 125, 130, 133, 136, 188, 200
French Revolution 28–9, 36, 39, 123
functionalism 46–7, 210
Fustel de Coulanges, N. D. 35, 44, 45–7, 48, 49

Gabrielsen, V. 198
Gatterer, J. C. 26
Gawantka, W. 37
geography, historical 49, 55, 161–2
Gernet, L. 47
Gillies, J. 39
Gilpin, R. 199
globalisation 8–9
Glotz, G. 47
Graham, A. J. 151
Gras, M. 223
Gravisca 185
Greek history
  Athenocentric approach 186, 233–4
  British approach 39, 41, 61
  French approach 47, 53, 66–7
  German approach 45, 49, 62
  Hellenocentric approach 186
  Italian approach 66–7
  as history of an area 227
  as *koinai praxeis* 226–9
  and local history 16, 58, 65
  and modern approaches 61–2
  as narrative 53, 58, 206, 226–40
  as national history 3–4, 21–2, 36–8, 40–2, 48–9, 58, 206
  and Near East 26, 33–4, 53–4, 56, 59
  and Occidentalism 2–4
  as part of Mediterranean history 48
  and politicisation 38–9, 44, 207, 230–1
  and Rome 42
  and the two currents 44, 52
Grote, G. 39, 40, 48
Gschnitzer, F. 193
guilds 131

Hagemajer Allen, K. 217
Hammond, N. G. L. 53
Hansen, M. H. 64–5, 223
Heeren, A. H. L. 21, 27–8, 49, 59
Held, D. 120
Hellênika 16, 40, 52, 58
Heracleia Pontica 161, 172
Herodotus 16, 83, 102, 180, 228, 231–2, 234, 237

Plato 180

Made in the USA
Lexington, KY
06 June 2013